Political Identity

Political Identity

Thinking Through Marx

Robert Meister

Basil Blackwell

First published 1990
First published in USA 1991

Basil Blackwell, Inc.
3 Cambridge Center
Cambridge, Massachusetts 02142, USA

Basil Blackwell Ltd
108 Cowley Road, Oxford, OX4 1JF, UK

Library of Congress Cataloging in Publication Data

Meister, Robert, 1947–
Political Identity: Thinking Through Marx
Includes bibliographical references
1. Marx, Karl. 1818–1883.   2. Historical materialism.   I. Title
HX39.5.M423   1991   335.4′1–dc20   90–273
ISBN 0–631–17417–6
ISBN 0–631–17746–9 (pbk.)

British Library Cataloguing in Publication Data
A CIP catalogue record for this book is available from the British Library.

Typeset in 10 on 12 pt Sabon
by Setrite Typesetters Ltd, H.K.
Printed in Great Britain by Billing and Sons Ltd, Worcester

For Andrew and Thomas

Contents

Acknowledgements

This book would not have been conceived without extraordinary teachers. I was first introduced to Marxian thought at Princeton by Michael Walzer and Stuart Hampshire, and pursued my ideas under the exacting and selfless supervision of Gregory Vlastos whose continuing faith in my work has sustained me over the years. At Oxford I benefitted greatly from the supervision and support of Isaiah Berlin and Patrick Gardiner as I carried my study of Marxism in unexpected directions. At Harvard I had the pleasure of continuing discussion with Michael Walzer whose thought and friendship have influenced me in ways that are only partially acknowledged in the text that follows.

Much of the form this work has taken is due to the encouragement of several generations of extraordinary students at the University of California, Santa Cruz − especially those in Politics 106, "Marxism as a Method," and History of Consciousness 209, "Studies in Marx and Hegel." Over the years the ideas presented in this book have benefitted from the close critical response of graduate students including the late Gary Reed, Bill Pietz, Barry Kātz, Stuart Burns, Robert Marotto, Richard Anderson, John Hunter, Rick Zinman, Paul Edwards, John Ely, Mark Reinhardt, Bill Robinson, Chris Kern, and Jeremy Elkins. I am also grateful for the dedication of a series of research assistants including Eric Berg, Sarah Bernstein, Martin Yabroff, Brinda Rao, Douglas Reed, Melody Butler, Grace Lee, and Nabil Zumout. Special mention is due to Connie Alvarez who was extraordinarily helpful at a time when the manuscript was undergoing major revision.

This book would not have been completed without the help of the friends and colleagues who have commented on parts of the manuscript in one or more of its many versions. These include Jim O'Connor, Hélène Moglen, Richard Musgrave, Fred Jameson, Alok Rai, Susan Willis, Stuart Hampshire, Richard Wasserstrom, Grant McConnell, Gregory Vlastos, Harry Harootunian, David Hoy, John Schaar, and Wamba dia Wamba. Jerry Neu has generously read each version of this manuscript, and Mahmood Mamdani has at crucial points talked through most of the major ideas with me. My greatest debt, however, is to Norman O. Brown with whom I have discussed every aspect of this project in all of its many versions, and whose tireless criticism, stimulation, and encouragement have kept my work alive. With friends and colleagues such as these one can always count on disagreement: although those mentioned above are no doubt responsible for many of the virtues of this book, its errors and inadequacies remain my own.

My family alone can fully appreciate the ways in which this project gives new meaning to the Marxian expression "congealed labor." My wife Ritu has had to live with this book from the beginning, and for her many acts of indulgence, forbearance, and faith I will always be indebted. My young sons Andrew and Thomas came into this project relatively late, and have taught me more than they now understand. As a wager on the future, this book is for them.

Research on this project has been generously supported by grants from the Academic Senate of the University of California at Santa Cruz. I am grateful to my publisher at Blackwell's, Stephan Chambers, to Kirstie Morrison who edited my manuscript, and to two anonymous readers for their thoughful comments. Betsy Wootten, Susan Nishiyama, John Ely and Janice Meister graciously assisted in the task of proofreading.

R.M.

Introduction

Why Marx?

Why do we need yet another interpretation of Marx at a moment when the doctrines of Marxism are being rejected almost everywhere – even in countries that have undergone Marxist revolutions? To ask and answer such a question we must know who "we" are. This book is written in the conviction that Marx himself provides the only rigorous and viable way of addressing the issue of political identity from within institutions that are, broadly speaking, both liberal and capitalist.

That conviction, and this book, have been long in gestation – or so it has seemed to me, my friends, and family. The first version of this manuscript was completed shortly before May, 1968; the present version in the aftermath of Tienanmen Square and at a moment of vast transformation in the political and economic regimes of Eastern Europe. Between 1968 and 1989 the manuscript has been taken up and abandoned many times; and, although I think the main lines of my interpretation of Marx have remained fairly constant as the world has changed, looking back on intermediate versions I can sense the distortions in phrasing that resulted from my effort to express my solidarity with the hopes of various social movements both in the United States and in the Third World. The present moment has largely freed me from the temptation to provide such expressions, and has thus enabled me to offer a more astringent interpretation of a Marx who can show us how to start over again in the emerging world market economy.

I must stress that this book is not (or not merely) an exercise in philosophical 'afterthought'[1] – a reconsideration of Marx after the party's over. The period over which I have worked on Marx has been marked by the continuing emergence of new social movements and antagonisms, many of which are understood by their participants through analogies

---

[1] Cf. *Hegel's Philosophy of Right* (tr. Knox), pp. 12–13.

with Marx's interpretation of the role of the working class under capitalism. With the reemergence of organized civil society in the states of Eastern Europe[2] these apparently "post-Marxist" forms of collective action have not diminished — they have spread. As the politics of identity becomes increasingly salient throughout the world, I believe that Marx's own theorizing — the underlying basis of his commitment to the working class — remains our only comprehensive model for understanding political identity under modern conditions.[3] This book is an effort to use that model as a basis for new thought about political identity by recognizing Marx's own conclusions about the working class as a special, and important, application of a more general method.

My perception that the broader theme of political identity has *superseded* Marx's discussion on class is largely consistent with much recent literature,[4] but my claim that a concern with political identity also *underlies* Marx's discussion of class is, I think, unusual. This book presents Marx as an intellectual, engaged in the issues of his time, whose method of social analysis is also a technique of self-analysis. The chapters that follow embody the premise that Marx's own political identification with the working class was largely a product of such analysis, and that throughout his life he used his analytical method to interrogate his political instincts, and those of the movements with which he identified.

I believe that the unique virtue of Karl Marx as an object of study is not that he provides us with a creed or vision that might be called communism, but that he teaches us how to test the relation between commitment and analysis in forming our political identity. There are other, more inspiring, socialist visionaries who can be read in our utopian moods, or as a break from hard analysis. Marxian analysis, as I see it, is a way of starting from where we are — an antidote to the politics of wishing we were somewhere, or someone, else. At a time when conventional distinctions between "left" and "right" are everywhere in flux, and when all claims to be the agent of the progressive forces of history are open to legitimate doubt, there is a greater need than ever to rethink the issues that underlie the politics of identity.

My purpose in the text that follows is both to provide a defensible interpretation of Marx's own project and to begin again where he left off.

---

[2] Recent history has outrun any hope of giving meaningful references. For useful theoretical discussions of this topic see Keane (ed.), *Civil Society and the State*, part 3, and Bobbio, "Gramsci and the Conception of Civil Society" and "Civil Society."

[3] Cf. the views of Laclau and Mouffe in *Hegemony and Socialist Strategy*.

[4] See, e.g., Offe, "The New Social Movements."

Academically, this book addresses those who are not yet ready to consign the study of Marx to nineteenth-century intellectual history; politically, it speaks for "we" who, having felt the world move under our feet, are once again looking for a place to stand. I believe, however, that my academic and political objectives are not wholly distinct. Any plausible defense of the continuing relevance of Marx's method must directly confront the relation between the texts that he produced and texts that we must endeavor to write today. It is in this confrontation that I see my challenge and my opportunity: to give a reading of Marx that will also demonstrate how to write *through* Marx about politics as we know it.

Reading Marx

Reading Marx presents a problem that sets him apart from other great political thinkers. Although the masterworks of Plato, Aristotle, Hobbes, and Rousseau may be aimed, consciously or unconsciously, at the views of past authorities, their form as self-contained arguments reflects a struggle to break free of such influences.[5] Marx, however, chose to piggyback his views on those of other writers, explicitly using their terms of discourse to build his analysis, instead of arguing from first principles. This preoccupation with critical exposition — often of entire fields of literature — is reflected in the titles or subtitles of Marx's major writings, including *Capital: A Critique of Political Economy*.

To modern readers the targets of Marx's criticism will seem to vary greatly in importance. Sometimes he attacked the giants of an earlier generation, such as the philosopher Hegel and the economists Smith and Ricardo; sometimes Marx's targets were lesser contemporaries or movements that would now be largely forgotten but for him. Yet, even in addressing these he generally followed his practice of close textual analysis. As readers of Marx, we cannot avoid reading the sources that are preserved in his critique, whether we are aware of doing so or not.[6]

The heavy presence of other writers in Marx's texts suggests that the importance of his writings today might be considered to depend upon the

[5] Cf. Harold Bloom, *The Anxiety of Influence*.
[6] If so, modern readers face a double danger. Those who seek a fresh understanding of Marx's arguments without confronting his sources run the risk of attributing to him some of the views that he opposed. Yet those who seek a new appreciation of the intellectual influences on Marx are in danger of minimizing the extent to which he differed with the views of his opponents. In either case Marx's own claims are taken to reflect those that he criticized, whether implicitly or explicitly.

continuing prestige of the works that he criticized. If this were so, his detractors would have an easy task. They could argue that Marx shared the limitations of his timebound sources, or assert that, outside the context of those sources, his arguments could not stand on their own. In responding, Marx's defenders have two strategic options: either they must give his views new support, independent of his own writings, or they must somehow restate the theories of the writers that he criticized in a way that has relevance today. Corresponding to these strategies are two broad approaches to a sympathetic reading of Marx. I shall call them "Marxism as a doctrine" and "Marxism as a method."

Marxism as a doctrine

The first approach, an attempt to restate Marxism as a doctrine, regards Marx's reliance on critique as a misfortune for subsequent readers. The ideal result of this approach would be to produce a version of Marx that could be used even by those who do not read his works or rely on his arguments − a surrogate for the primary work of political and social thought that Marx never wrote.

In the 1960s and 1970s many interpreters tried to extract from Marx's writings his own substantive positions on specific subjects.[7] By attempting to disentangle Marx's thought from its function as critique, these interpretations treated Marx as the definitive authority on the terms of the discourse in which he participated: Marxism, in such interpretations, would then consist of using terms such as "alienation" or "value" as Marx might have defined them in a work beginning from first principles. In principle such sympathetic restatements of Marx were meant to offer readers the choice of accepting or rejecting him as a thinker in his own right. In practice, however, proponents of "Marxism as a doctrine" often failed to support the views they ascribed to Marx with the independent arguments required of a first-order theory.

This weakness has been addressed in the 1980s by a literature that attempts to restate and defend Marx's main conclusions using the frame-

[7] The enterprise of developing "Marxism as a doctrine" may be inferred from titles such as the following: *The Social and Political Thought of Karl Marx* (Avineri); *Marxism and Ethics* (Kamenka); *Marxist Economic Theory* (Mandel); *Marx's Theory of Alienation* (Mészáros); *Alienation: Marx's Conception of Man in Capitalist Society* (Ollman); *Marx's Theory of Ideology* (Parekh); *The Concept of Nature in Marx* (Schmidt); *Estrangement, Alienation, and Exploitation* (Torrance); *Philosophy and Myth in Karl Marx* (Tucker); *Human Nature: The Marxian View* (Venable).

works of methodological individualism and analytic philosophy. Writers committed to the project of "analytical Marxism" have already gleaned from Marx's work a body of intelligible doctrines about society and history that must be taken seriously, even by those who dismiss his method.[8] In general "analytical Marxism" avoids transposing the errors and terminological confusions of Marx's sources into modern reconstructions of his views; but it does not avoid the risk — endemic to "Marxism as a doctrine" — of understating the degree to which Marx's own positions were specific responses to the views that he criticized. Moreover, in directly translating Marx into the mainstream methodologies of today, the new analytical Marxists assume the scientific validity of these approaches, thereby denying to their version of Marx the power to criticize our dominant discourses as he did those of his own time.[9]

Marxism as a method

Despite the advances of "analytical Marxism," this book pursues a second approach to reading Marx — an approach that makes a virtue of the fact

---

[8] See, e.g., Gerald A. Cohen, *Karl Marx's Theory of History: A Defence*; Elster, *Making Sense of Marx*; Przeworski, *Capitalism and Social Democracy*; Roemer, *A General Theory of Exploitation and Class*; Wolff, *Understanding Marx*; and Wright, *Classes*. Some important examples of this approach are collected in Roemer (ed.), *Analytical Marxism*.

[9] Elster and Roemer rely on methodological individualism because they accept it as scientifically valid. In addition, they argue that the best of Marx's own arguments made implicit use of this method rather than the dialectical method derived from Hegel.

But even if Marx can be considered a precursor of the methodological individualism now favored by mainstream economists, he may be no less a precursor of other models of explanation that may come to supersede it. Among these are the dynamical systems models now favored by many natural scientists. (See, e.g., Thom, *Structural Stability and Morphogenesis*.) Such models as applied to the social sciences would give structural explanations of structural change without relying on either methodological individualism or methodological collectivism. Who is to say that similar methods might not take over mainstream economics, providing a better scientific basis for testing Marxian hypotheses than we now have? If Marxism should not be limited by the prevailing methodologies of his day, why should it now presuppose the validity of our own dominant models of social explanation?

In contrast to the analytical Marxists my justification for translating Marx into our contemporary debates does not necessarily assume that these debates are scientifically superior to those he addressed.

that Marx wrote mostly critical works, and that regards his way of arguing from and against other texts as often more important than his specific
conclusions. Instead of trying to extract what Marx *said* so as to restate it
more exactly and directly, "Marxism as a method" attempts to identify
what Marx *did* with the theoretical material available to him, the philosophy and social science of his day. This approach assumes that the
essential core of Marx's teaching lies in the way he used the literatures he
criticized: that learning how to read *from* Marx, and learning how to *read*
Marx, present the same intellectual challenge; and that a living Marxism
should bear much the same relation to our mainstream and dissenting
thinkers that Marx bore to their counterparts in his day.

In this respect "Marxism as a method" is one way of attempting to
modernize Marx – sharing with "analytical Marxism" the goal of bringing
Marx back into contact with mainstream discourse, even if this means
rejecting some of his substantive conclusions.[10] Yet "Marxism as a
method" differs from "analytical Marxism" in its view of how Marx can
best be restated today. Rather than abstracting his particular views from
their intellectual and political context, my approach sees Marx's articulated
relation to his context as perhaps his most important general contribution
to political thought. My argument is not, however, that the apparently
general force of Marx's claims must be relativized to their specific intellectual context – although I believe that this is a sound hermeneutical
premise from which to start. I propose, rather, to defend the relevance of
Marx outside of his context by extending the relevance of his context to
our own. Where possible I shall, therefore, attempt to interpret Marx's
sources by transposing them into the structure of debates that engage us
today. By arguing for the continuing relevance of Marx's sources to our
own concerns, I hope to establish the value of Marx's insights in his time
and the continuing power of his method to illuminate current issues.

Marx, our contemporary

My interest in recovering Marx's own method of critique bears little
relation to what is commonly called Marxist *methodology* – a "scientific"
language for discussing politics and history based on the terminology of

---

[10] Although I share the reluctance of analytical Marxists to imitate the way Marx
wrote, I shall argue throughout this book that we should continue to emulate the
way he read.

Marx, Lenin and their professed followers.[11] Indeed, the chapters that follow stand largely apart from efforts to write in a received tradition of Marxist ideas, taking Marx's own project as their model rather than the work of his successors.

Marx's intellectual example should encourage us to build on largely non-Marxist sources for purposes of developing a Marxian social analysis today.[12] Marx himself did not (of course) rely on sources that were distinctively Marxist, and instead built his arguments on the critique of writings that came from the intellectual establishment and from the counterculture, from the political Right as well as the political Left. By analyzing these sources Marx learned important truths, not merely about the deficiencies and blindspots of particular authors, but also about the overall structure and limitations of the social thought of his day.

To fulfill my ambition of providing both a study of Marx and a continuation of his work, the book should in principle follow three bodies of literature at once: Marx's writings, Marx's sources, and debates about parallel issues today. Rather than developing my argument in a kind of bibliographical lockstep, however, I have chosen as a practical matter to use these bodies of literature somewhat differently in addressing different topics. There are three reasons for this choice: the first is that my desire for thematic unity, and a continuous line of argument, has prevented me from following too closely the path of Marx's own intellectual biography; the second is that the problems of theoretical exposition differ as one moves across academic disciplines; the third is that finding recent parallels to Marx's sources poses different challenges in some fields than in others.

In the chapters that follow I shall claim that some of Marx's sources, such as Hegel, have not been surpassed by modern scholarship, even when they would seem to have been forgotten. On particular subjects I believe that we can find Hegel's counterparts everywhere in the contemporary academy – sometimes in a single thinker, such as Samuel Huntington,

---

[11] For a largely fruitless effort to define the "scientific" status of Marxist-Leninist thought see Althusser, *Lenin and Philosophy*, and Althusser and Balibar, *Reading Capital*.

[12] The reader will probably note, however, that my critique of mainstream social thought is also a critique of much of academic Marxism. In the current academic environment, Marxism has been partially incorporated in many disciplines as either a specialized subfield or an alternative methodology with its own distinctive terms of discourse. In contrast I believe that Marx's own method – the approach he followed in his writings – provides a way of reading and confronting those disciplines in their entirety, including their left-wing variants.

sometimes in the structure of an entire debate or academic field. In dealing with matters addressed by Hegel — such as the state, freedom, and political participation — I have therefore found it possible to apply Marx's method directly to both his sources and our own.

I have been less direct in my treatment of Marx's critique of the Left-Hegelian liberation theorists — Bauer, Feuerbach, and Stirner. Their works, often focusing on religion, have been largely forgotten by modern writers outside the field of Marx scholarship;[13] yet their basic ideas are continually being reinvented in new guises by the cultural Left today. Rather than focus on the specific issues addressed by the Left-Hegelians of the 1840s, I have tried to raise parallel issues by looking at recent forms of conscious-ness-raising. Although many examples of countercultural theory would have served my purpose,[14] I have chosen for the sake of continuity to focus throughout this book on recent feminism as my main contemporary representative of the cultural Left.

The classical political economists, Smith and Ricardo, have yet a differ-ent current status than either Hegel or the Left-Hegelians. They are widely recognized as seminal thinkers to whom contemporary debates return at critical points; yet it is difficult to argue that their thought encapsulates the current state of economics as a whole. To find direct parallels to classical political economy we must look to specific literatures in political economy that are at an equivalent stage of development. One such literature is the recent debate between supply- and demand-side versions of Keynesian economic policy; a second is the effort by theorists such as Samuelson to reconcile the claims of micro- and macroeconomics; a third is the recent theoretical discussion of whether the *world* economy is simply a matter of trade (a market), or also a division of labor (a mode of production). Referring to these literatures, however superficially, has allowed me to reconstruct the achievement of Smith and Ricardo at the moment Marx encountered it, and to translate important parts of the Marxian critique of classical political economy into current issues.

As I transpose Marxian arguments into the various literatures described above, I shall not necessarily take Marx's own left-wing political commit-ments as the key to understanding the political implications of his method

---

[13] See McLellan, *The Young Hegelians and Karl Marx*. For an overview see Kolakowski, *Main Currents of Marxism*, vol. 1, chs 1—9. For further references see chapter 3, or 8, below.
[14] Some of the best examples are accounts of various cultures of resistance in New-Left historiography of the 1960s and 1970s. See, e.g., Edward P. Thompson, "The Moral Economy of the English Crowd in the Eighteenth Century" and *The Making of the English Working Class*.

today.[15] Writing for a radical audience, Marx sometimes felt the need to defend the relevance of some establishment thinkers by distinguishing their work from that of vulgar apologists for the status quo, and at times I shall do likewise. Throughout this book, moreover, I give great weight to Marx's lifelong attack on the politics of subjectivity in all its manifestations, including both establishment liberalism and the social movements of the counterculture. The Marx described in these pages will thus sometimes appear to be equally critical of views typically associated with both the Right and the Left.[16]

This formulation presupposes that we already know who the Left is, and how people come to identify with it. Today, however, the agendas that have defined both Left and Right since the French Revolution are everywhere open to question. Lacking traditional benchmarks of political self-definition, we need a return to the kind of rigor Marx brought to his analysis of the conventional distinctions between Right and Left.

Materialism and critique

I shall argue in the succeeding chapters that beginning again with Marx would require us to abandon the various forms of idealism that characterize

---

[15] Cf. Gilbert, *Marx's Politics.*

[16] This opens me, I suppose, to the charge that my animus is directed mainly against the Left. In defending myself against such a charge, I feel that I must also defend Marx, who, although undoubtedly a figure of the Left, devoted much of his writing to the critique of avowedly socialist movements and thinkers. Even though Marx did not blame the Left for the evils of capitalism, his criticisms of radical politics and thought sometimes seem harsher, and less generous, than those directed against the pillars of bourgeois theory — a fact that may seem surprising to some readers and reprehensible to others who think that Marx should have suppressed his criticisms of the Left in order to make a common cause against the real enemy.

There are at least two plausible ways of justifying Marx's apparent severity toward the Left in a way that is consistent with his political commitments. A political justification is that his criticisms were directed *to* the Left, and not against it. According to this argument we should not read Marx's political writing as an expression of radical politics as he found it, but rather as an effort to make that politics more effective, coherent, and disciplined. A more theoretical justification is that the critique of capitalist democracy requires a continuing critique of the role of the Left within it — especially a Left that is in constant danger of becoming merely a sub-culture. Marx, according to this justification, was attempting to bring the cultural Left back into serious political confrontation with mainstream thought and institutions. Both of these arguments might apply today, insofar as the distinction between Right and Left remains meaningful in our political culture.

most recent approaches to political identity — the stress on the optionality of subjective identification, the projection of false hopes — in favor of a materialist understanding of the structure of institutional contradictions. The theme of Marx's materialism will figure into the conclusions of parts I and II, and form the basis of part III.[17] There I shall argue that Marx's use of materialism as a heuristic presumption in his critique of ideology enabled him to reach substantive conclusions about society through the critique of textual materials.

By interpreting Marx's materialism as a central part of his approach to textual analysis I distinguish this work from most recent efforts to discuss the role of materialism in Marx's thought. Interpretations of Marx that are based on rational choice theory tend to treat his materialism as an expression of the view that political action is an expression of economic self-interest, a view that Marx is said to hold in common with neo-classical economics and much of liberal theory.[18] Other approaches attempt to develop a "scientific" vocabulary of Marxism by reifying such distinctions as "base and superstructure."[19] My view of Marx's materialism interprets it as functioning heuristically in the critique of the multiple and competing institutional frameworks through which we come to understand our world. As these frameworks come to be increasingly differentiated, I argue that materialism requires us to proceed for purposes of Marxian critique *as if* they all nevertheless tell the same story.

I shall suggest in chapter 10 that Marx's heuristic use of materialism in the critique of social science resembles Kant's heuristic use of various metaphysical ideas in the critique of epistemology. Marx engaged in close analysis of the theories through which different institutions account for their impact on each other in order to arrive at a critical analysis of the forces that must be at work in a single social 'world' that could be so described from within. At a much more general level Kant used a critical analysis of what it means to have a particular viewpoint on the world in order to discover something of what the world must be like to be so understood.

If materialism is a central part of Marx's "method" as described above, then my proposed return to Marx is not merely a defense of the political

---

[17] See esp. chapter 10, below.

[18] See, e.g., Elster, *Making Sense of Marx*, ch. 1; and Przeworski, "The Ethical Materialism of John Roemer," and "The Material Bases of Consent." I do not wish to deny that at various points in his analysis of capitalist societies Marx expressed such a view, and I doubt that either Przeworski or Elster would wish to assert that explanations of behavior based on rational self-interest exhaust the enterprise of Marxian ideological critique.

[19] See, e.g., Althusser, "Ideology and Ideological State Apparatuses," and Althusser and Balibar, *Reading Capital*.

importance of producing more secondary literature — more theories about theories. I believe that Marx's ultimate purpose in engaging in critique was to arrive at a politics, and that this should be our purpose as well. My argument for returning to Marxism as a method is thus a prefatory step toward the restoration of a viable Marxian political project under modern conditions.

This book is a present-day continuation of the underlying project that sustained Marx's own commitment to the working class — a materialist analysis of the politics of identity in more or less democratic capitalist states. Part I, "The Politics of Subjectivity," addresses various forms of cultural politics by using Marx's joint critique of Hegel and the Left-Hegelians to criticize recent views of institutional freedom and of 'liberation as consciousness-raising' that have been reflected in both philosophy and radical social history. Part II, "The Critical Theory of Democracy," shows how Marx's differences with his sources and contemporaries (the Jacobin socialists, Tocqueville, and once again Hegel) can illuminate recent debates among social scientists about whether political participation through pre-existing group identities is a form of co-optation or a form of empowerment. Part III, "Political Materialism," recasts Marx's critique of classical political economy as an argument about the relationship between commodity prices and political demography, introducing a "critical theory of accounting" to complement the "critical theory of democracy" developed in part II.

Although this book comes to completion at a moment when twentieth-century Marxism has all but ceased to function as an ideological alternative to capitalism, the Marxism presented here does not presuppose the continuing existence of external pressures on capitalism, such as those arising out of competition with world communism to control the economic development of the Third World. Following Marx's own example, I stress rather the internal problems arising out of the 'normal' development of capitalist democracies and, like Marx, I focus on the differentiation of state and civil society in an integrated world market. The Marx presented here will, I believe, be more faithful to his own enterprise than much of twentieth-century Marxism. Nevertheless, I too shall feel free to reinterpret Marx and to deviate from his own emphases and concerns whenever this is necessary in order to articulate a way of thinking politically that has continuing relevance in the world as we now find it on the threshold of the twenty-first century.[20] In the chapters that follow I shall argue that the Marx who emerges from this reinterpretation can

[20] Perhaps my most significant departure from the historical Marx lies in my effort to purge Marxian analysis of what I call the "revolutionary mystique" — the Jacobin tradition that links Rousseau to Lenin, and beyond. (See chapter 5, below. Cf. Colletti, *From Rousseau to Lenin*.) In chapter 11 I reject part of Marx's formulation of the labor theory of value, and in chapters 4 and 10 I explicitly de-emphasize some of Marx's statements on ideology and materialism.

make substantial contributions to diverse fields such as philosophy, democratic theory, economics, social history, political sociology, and cultural theory, and that his political materialism provides a model (perhaps our only model) of the unity of social thought under present conditions.

Part I
The Politics of Subjectivity

1   Identity and Ideology

History and class consciousness

The intellectual development of Western Marxism is largely a response to the apparent failure of two competing views of historical progress. The first is the *liberal/apologetic* view that Marx himself attacked in the nineteenth century. In this view the institutions of democratic capitalism allow for the progressive realization of both liberty and equality, which in turn promotes the progressive development of those institutions. At least since the end of World War II, however, Western Marxists have also had to contend with the apparent failure of a second view, the *Marxist/determinist* view of history. According to this view, democratic capitalism leads to the inexorable polarization of classes and the ultimate breakdown of the capitalist system in revolutionary class struggle.

Both views have proven, thus far, to be patently untrue. If liberal apologists underestimated the degree of oppression that would persist under democratic capitalism, orthodox Marxists have underestimated the effectiveness of liberal political culture and democratic institutions in co-opting the working classes. In reality, Western institutions have continued to reproduce social inequality, using repression when necessary. Yet these institutions have also been sustained by a value system that appears to gain increasing support from a deradicalized working class.

It is impossible to overestimate the effect on Western Marxists of their disappointment in the working class. Marx had argued that, just as liberal capitalism was historically necessary, so was its revolutionary overthrow, and predicted that all the elements of working class formation would inevitably flow together to create the blend of theory and practice needed to carry out a successful revolution. In contrast, the distinctive history of Western Marxism originates in the failure of the working class to fulfill this historical mission.[1] Western Marxists recognize that class consciousness

---

[1] In this respect Western Marxism and Bolshevism have a common origin. It is not

does not necessarily develop along with the capacity of a class[2] to wage effective struggle, nor does class struggle necessarily spring from class-based oppression. Lacking faith that a proletarian revolution is inevitable, many reject the notion of historical inevitability itself, especially as applied to liberal capitalism.[3] Their Marxism has become an argument for the ultimate contingency of the status quo: if existing institutions are not "historically necessary," Marxists can believe that revolution is still possible − even if it is not inevitable.

To preserve their belief in the possibility of revolution Western Marxists have increasingly emphasized the subjective and contingent aspects of politics. For many years, Marxist intellectuals in the West felt free to argue that in continuing to support liberal regimes industrial workers misunderstood their material interests under capitalism. Those workers who were not self-consciously revolutionary were then considered to be victims, not only of exploitation, but of "false consciousness" as well.[4] So long as Marxist intellectuals continued to assume that objective interests under capitalism are immutable, they could proceed on the faith that the material liberation of workers would inevitably follow from their cultural liberation.[5]

---

surprising that, despite their vast differences, both can plausibly claim to originate as interpretations of the thought of Lenin. For differing versions of this claim see, e.g., Althusser, *Lenin and Philosophy*, and Colletti, *From Rousseau to Lenin*.

[2] For a discussion of "class capacity" see Therborn, "Why Some Classes are More Successful than Others."

[3] A partial exception is Gerald A. Cohen, who defends the intelligibility of a determinist theory of history while making it clear that he is not necessarily committed to the truth of that theory. (N.B., the theory he states is based on the autonomy of technological development and not on class struggle *per se*.) See Cohen, *Karl Marx's Theory of History: A Defence*. For further elaboration see Cohen, "Reconsidering Historical Materialism" and "Forces and Relations of Production."

[4] See esp. Perry Anderson, *Considerations on Western Marxism*. For a discussion in terms of "hegemony" see Anderson, "The Antinomies of Antonio Gramsci."

[5] According to Perry Anderson, the master-thinkers of cultural Marxism in the West have been Lukács, Gramsci, and to a lesser extent, Sartre. In Lukács's view, capitalism depends on the ability of the bourgeoisie to represent its particular class consciousness as an expression of universally valid ideas. He argued that through their uncritical acceptance of the universality of bourgeois ideas workers come to believe that their own interests are only partial and subjective, reflecting a vision of reality that cannot stand as an alternative "totality" to the bourgeois world-view. Gramsci argued along similar lines that in liberal regimes popular consent to the system is gained through cultural institutions that promote acceptance of the "hegemonic" ideas of the bourgeoisie. To make a revolution under such conditions

Behind this faith, however, lay the recognition that a crucial stage of revolutionary struggle would take place at the level of culture where the outcome was highly contingent. The initial acceptance of this view posed little theoretical problem for orthodox Communists, since Marx himself had provided independent grounds for thinking that capitalist exploitation could be rigorously defined without reference to the felt experience of individual workers.[6] Over time, however, Western Marxists would rely increasingly on cultural factors to explain why even adherence to the Party had failed to create a revolutionary working class.[7]

Eventually this focus on cultural struggle came to jeopardize the theoretical linkage between revolutionary politics and the interests of the working class.[8] In retrospect, the logical erosion of classical Marxism in the West is easy to trace as an expression of growing disaffection between socialist intellectuals and industrial workers. To begin with the argument that "false consciousness" (or its equivalent) is all that stands in the way of proletarian revolution assumes that ending collective exploitation is the *only* undistorted material interest of workers as such — that a transition to socialism would be in the objective interests of workers under capitalism. If, however, we assume that many workers have more to lose than their

----

workers, he believed, would need "counter-hegemonic" ideas produced by their own "organic intellectuals." Writing a generation later, the young Sartre took up this challenge — using the vocabulary of immanence versus transcendence to argue for the need to liberate consciousness from the "facticity" of everyday life.

Although Lukács, Gramsci, and Sartre are now considered adoptive godfathers by recent theorists of cultural politics, they originally offered their accounts of working-class consent to capitalism as a defense of the need for a Leninist vanguard party in the West. Lukács plausibly claimed to be a Leninist to the end of his long life. Gramsci saw the role of the counterculture in the democratic West as similar to the role that Lenin attributed to the hegemonic party in the East — that of providing revolutionary vision to a working class otherwise mired in narrow self-interest. Sartre did not break with the Party until 1956.

See Perry Anderson, *Considerations on Western Marxism*; Lukács, *History and Class Consciousness*; Gramsci, *Prison Notebooks*; and Sartre, *Being and Nothingness* and "Merleau-Ponty."

[6] On the need to reformulate the conceptual basis of such a position, see Roemer, "New Directions in the Marxian Theory of Exploitation and Class." For a rigorous definition of capitalist exploitation that allows for consent see Roemer, *A General Theory of Exploitation and Class*, ch. 7.

[7] On these developments see, generally, Anderson, *Considerations on Western Marxism*.

[8] At the level of practice, political ideology had always been somewhat dissociated from grassroots organizing among workers.

chains, we must entertain the possibility that the immediate end to capitalist exploitation would not always be to their material advantage.[9] Unless we then concede that socialism is morally wrong whenever it imposes real sacrifices on workers, the link between socialism and working class interests would lose its special significance.

If we acknowledge, however, that socialism could sometimes legitimately call upon workers to transcend their material interests, the arguments for it would have to be based on moral grounds (such as the critique of alienation) that might be equally compelling to other social groups, including even the bourgeoisie. From here it is a short step to recognizing that the circumstances in which socialism would require self-sacrifice from workers have not been exceptional in the twentieth century. Recent historical studies show that under many circumstances the democratic state has made capitalism serve the material interests of most workers better than available alternatives, due largely to the dependence of workers on high growth rates and the success of organized labor in influencing economic policy. If these studies prove to be correct, the continuing political radicalism of the New Left would amount to the moral repudiation of its historical conclusions.[10]

Today, the stance of many "post-Marxists," including the German Greens, is that progressives must ultimately choose between the interests of the working class and a socialism that is viewed as a transcendent vision of human potential.[11] They argue that, if the transition to socialism depends on mobilization around non-material (or even anti-materialist) interests,

[9] Using rational-choice theory John Roemer has recently attempted to define the special conditions under which the end to capitalist exploitation would be in the material interests of workers. Interestingly, his criterion is the point at which it would be rational for workers to secede from capitalism, disregarding any benefits they might receive from expropriating the wealth of capitalists as well as any costs of revolution. See Roemer, A General Theory of Exploitation and Class, chs 7 and 9.

[10] This seems to be the general position of both Adam Przeworski and Claus Offe: see Przeworski, Capitalism and Social Democracy; Offe, Disorganized Capitalism, Contradictions of the Welfare State, and esp. "Challenging the Boundaries of Institutional Politics: Social Movements Since the 1960s." (Cf. Hibbs, "On the Political Economy of Long-run Trends in Strike Activity.") Charles Sabel has explored the connections between the moral and the material basis of workers' solidarity and segmentation in Work and Politics.

[11] For an explicit theoretical defense of this position see Offe, "The New Social Movements," and a subsequent version of the same essay, "Challenging the Boundaries of Institutional Politics."

there is no reason to believe that the working class is more likely to lead in this movement than many other elements of society, and considerable reason to believe the contrary. Divorced from their commitment to promote working class interests, many on the Left now feel free bitterly to attack working class culture as an unfertile ground for revolutionary consciousness.

The politics of culture

Following its disillusionment with the working class, the Left in the West has turned increasingly to the politics of culture as a substitute for the politics of class interest. In orthodox Marxist terms this means considering the influence of the "superstructure" on the "base," or in the terminology of Lukács, the "totalizing" effect of a world view on underlying practices.

The cultural turn in Marxism intersects with a broader critique of logical positivism in the social sciences that calls into question many Marxist assumptions about the meaning of historical change.[12] This critique, evolving out of the 1960s, focused on the impossibility of defining a causal relationship between ideas and social practices. If ideas are, rather, constitutive of practices, and inseparable from them, then the 'brute facts' about a form of life can only be described by reference to the theories and values that make it meaningful to participants. A social practice, then, is essentially a form of life with its own internal moral logic: at its core there is no gap to be filled between cultural meanings and material relations. When everything can be included in the interpretation (or 'thick description') of the whole, there is little justification for isolating any part and calling it "the explanation." For fundamental social change, the unit of analysis becomes the whole of the social formation.

This view suggests that the only real changes are "total" changes, and that these are not by their nature subject to causal explanation. If the part itself must be explained in terms of its function in the whole, the whole cannot then be explained by the autonomous development of that part. Indeed, the whole cannot be explained at all in a causal sense. The logic of causal explanation and prediction is limited to changes at the margins where meanings remain constant; in transformations of the social whole 'meanings' inevitably change as much as 'reality.' New possibilities do not emerge in society unless the grounds of perceived necessity also change.

[12] For an expression of the post-Marxist attack on positivism and "instrumental reason" see, e.g., Habermas, *Theory and Practice*.

These changes are "paradigm shifts" – radical breaks between discontinuous and incommensurable 'worlds.'[13]

Such paradigm shifts can be called "revolutions," but this is only a descriptive term, referring to an irreversible change in the constitutive ideas of a social reality.[14] The post-modern idea of "revolution" follows from the interpenetration of human reality and human understanding and assumes that a radical contingency lies at the core of human history. According to this view, revolutions themselves cannot be explained or predicted, much less justified, since there is no historically privileged standpoint from which they can be. Revolutions, thus conceived, are neither necessary nor inevitable, but they are always possible.

To many academic Marxists these intellectual currents could be used to separate what is living and dead in Marx's theory of historical materialism. Dead is the idea of historical inevitability, and with it the hope of explaining and predicting revolutions as a necessary outcome of class struggle. Class would now be a "relation," and capital a "process" within the totality of a "social formation." To culturalists the living Marxism then becomes an interpretation of capitalism as a total system that would enable us to see how everything that happens within the framework of capitalism invariably strengthens the system, foreclosing the possibilities for fundamental change. The political problem would then be to identify those forms of consciousness that lie outside of the dominant cultural system called capitalism. Through interpreting capitalism as an all-encompassing cultural system, Western "post-Marxism" can hold forth the continuing *possibility* of revolution by suggesting that anything *not* supportive of the total system would be intrinsically revolutionary – a part of the *alternative*.

This new perspective on Marxism rules out *ab initio* any faith that the industrial working class, as an integral part of the capitalist totality, could cause a revolutionary change.[15] Rather than focusing on mainstream workers, "post-Marxism" tends to concentrate on marginal or transitional groups whose interests have not been incorporated by the system, and whose values have not yet been co-opted. In the cultural resistance of such groups it sees an alternative vision of the whole which the dominant

[13] For a midstream attempt to synthesize these tendencies see Bernstein, *The Restructuring of Social and Political Theory*.

[14] For an important source of many of these ideas see Kuhn, *The Structure of Scientific Revolutions*.

[15] Many Western Marxists assume that without such "revolutionary consciousness" those seizing power will not achieve true revolution, and that this basic truth has been sadly demonstrated by the history of the "actually existing" workers' states. The latter phrase is Rudolf Bahro's. (See Bahro, *The Alternative in Eastern Europe*.)

system has thus far failed to comprehend. According to the "post-Marxist" view the evils of capitalism are much like those of imperialism – each has a tendency on the one hand to assimilate and homogenize diverse cultural values, and on the other to divide in order to rule. Capitalism then appears as a specific but pervasive form of cultural domination in which market society succeeds in imposing its system of meanings on alien forms of life that continue alongside it. In "post-Marxist" thought the hegemony of capitalist discourse precedes the articulation of material interests and constitutes the fundamental injustice of capitalism.

As soon as the paradigm of language supplants the model of production, exploitation appears as merely another way of being misunderstood. What remains for Marxism is, then, to articulate the connections between the various discourses of resistance without translating them into a single dominant language that would replicate the evils of capitalism itself.[16] But since capitalism is also marked by its very tendency to absorb group diversity, debates on the Left will focus on distinguishing those forms of cultural expression that transcend the capitalist totality from those that can be easily incorporated within it.

In the debates over the radical potential of different cultural expressions there is always a dialectic of expectation and disillusionment, resistance and co-optation, righteousness and despair. During the rise of a radical movement the cultural Left sees a transcendent critique in the expression of every apparently immanent value, such as the demand for liberty or equality. In the decline of such a movement the cultural Left can demonstrate that even apparently transcendent demands, such as universal love, perform an immanent function in legitimating reality.

Within the framework of "post-Marxist" thought we have come to expect that the loci of resistance will be many, even as the forms of domination are everywhere the same.[17] The high tradition of Western Marxism has thus apparently ended with the acknowledgement that capitalism produces, not socialism, but pluralism. To this phenomenon, however, the attitude of post-Marxist scholars is ambivalent: where capitalism seems to divide and

---

[16] See, e.g., Laclau and Mouffe, *Hegemony and Socialist Strategy*. For an attempt to restate Marxism using the paradigm of language see Coward and Ellis, *Language and Materialism*.

[17] Many now argue that this generalization applies to socialist experiments in democratic centralism as well as to avowedly capitalist regimes. (Thus, Afghanistan was called the "Soviet Vietnam.") Holders of this view often claim, however, that the historical stability of capitalism depended upon its ability to manipulate and absorb group differences, while the historical stability of Leninist regimes depended on imposing a repressive unity.

rule, they call for popular unity; but where capitalism threatens to crush group differences, they often insist that these are unassimilable expressions of the struggle for autonomy. As an alternative to liberal capitalism, post-Marxist revolutionary consciousness now claims to be a transcendent form of unity that respects group differences by recognizing their common psychological root in the struggle against oppression.[18]

From this perspective a generation of leftist scholars has rewritten the history of failed social movements to show revolutionary potential outside the working class. In many of these studies the existence of a material interest in revolutionary change is either assumed or ignored, while a given movement's failure is ascribed to the absence or weakness of a revolutionary counterculture. Politically, much of this scholarship aims to build a new culture of resistance out of the memory of past defeat – thereby creating the basis of a revolutionary tradition for popular movements of the future.[19]

After a series of real analytical advances, the academic Left in the West is now coming full circle to recommending the utopian socialism and subjectivist politics that Marx began his career by rejecting in such writers as Bauer, Hess, Feuerbach, Ruge, and Stirner.[20] Insofar as this is so, the best critic of "post-Marxist" thought may yet be Marx himself.

Class, culture, and political identity

A critique of recent versions of the politics of culture can allow us to recover much of the intellectual and political impetus behind Marx's own thought. The Karl Marx described in the following chapters began his work as an alienated leftist student in a political culture something like that of the 1960s and early 1970s. Traditional authority was bankrupt, yet the evils of modernity were widely denounced and the traditions it displaced extolled. There was cultural ferment in many areas – feminism, new nationalism, innovation in the arts and crafts. Alongside the decay of established religion was a growth in popular cults and communitarian movements. Government had many clients but few supporters. Revolutionary passions were themselves becoming traditions to which citizens throughout society paid lip service. Some believed that they were living in

[18] See, e.g., Laclau and Mouffe, *Hegemony and Socialist Strategy.*
[19] These issues are discussed further in chapters 3, 5 and 6, below. See also Perry Anderson, *In the Tracks of Historical Materialism.*
[20] For a discussion of Marx's critique of some of these writers see chapters 3 and 7, below. For a sampling of some of their writings see Stepelevich (ed.), *The Young Hegelians: An Anthology.*

a post-revolutionary age, others felt they were in a pre-revolutionary age. Many, including Marx, believed that they lived between revolutions: because the culture was revolutionary and the regime was not, they thought that the present order could not last, and that the counterculture carried the seeds of the new order that would replace it.[21] The events of 1848 disappointed Marx's hopes and led him to revise his revolutionary expectations. In this respect, too, he was similar to others on the Left before and since.

Within his context, however, Marx came to a unique perspective on the relation between theory and practice in capitalist societies. He recognized that under capitalism we cannot comfortably take up an individual point of view without first envisioning society as a whole — that, while all cultures provide implicit interpretations of themselves,[22] capitalist cultures do so explicitly through a steady dose of theory. Through theory we can claim to stand outside our society at the very moment we seek to understand it from within. To Marx it followed that we are most within our culture when we try to stand apart from it. Living in a society that was attempting to comprehend itself as a totality from within, he found it illuminating to read a social theory as though it were part of the social order that it seeks to encompass.[23] In doing so he was able to ask what role comprehensibility (or its absence) plays in maintaining a social form: is a proposed understanding compatible with the continuing existence of the social form thus understood? or does comprehension bear the same relation to a given form of life that knowing that you are asleep does to waking up?[24] In posing such questions Marx thought that the intrinsic problems in formulating the best available theories must also be problems about the role of theory itself in completing the social reality it depicts. These problems would in turn reveal the points at which changes in the social order resist comprehension from within.

Marx believed that a radical politics would require us to identify ourselves at the sites at which the social order cannot be comprehended without being transformed, forcing us to take a political standpoint toward the agents of social transformation — for or against — a standpoint that could ultimately have implications for almost everything we do. Over the course of a lifetime, Marx used this insight as the basis for a politics that

---

[21] Cf. Bell, *The Cultural Contradictions of Capitalism*.

[22] See Geertz, *The Interpretation of Cultures*.

[23] The self-definition of a society is especially evident in the theories it generates to distinguish itself from societies that it regards as 'early' or 'other'. See chapter 7, below.

[24] See chapter 2, below.

was disciplined as well as radical. He identified himself as a socialist among others, but, unlike the others, he knew that a politics is not merely a set of transcendent ideals or goals. Having a politics also means articulating the relationship between one's views about the world and one's position within it. Marx's approach to political analysis committed him to the view that one's politics is a matter of identity that is not wholly given, and not wholly chosen.

Of course Marx's own application of this method led him to identify politically with the interests of the industrial proletariat – a conclusion that had implications for almost everything he did. In the course of his writings Marx argued that the identity of the proletariat was uniquely significant in four respects: (1) *epistemologically*, it provided a perspective within society that could comprehend the emergent whole; (2) *politically*, it located a large and growing number of people who could wield increasing power in a democratic age; (3) *socially*, the proletariat performed functions that gave it great structural leverage within the capitalist mode of production; (4) *historically*, the proletariat's material interests would become increasingly difficult to contain (or satisfy) within political forms that operate under the constraints of the capitalist mode of production. Marx's conclusion, based on these four points, was that even an avowedly democratic state must ultimately turn against its dissatisfied proletarian constituents. He believed that, once this illegitimate act occurred, the proletariat would have both the vision and strength to overthrow the state as a necessary step in transforming the mode of production itself.[25]

It is important to stress, however, that Marx's political identification with the interests of the proletariat was a conclusion, and not an assumption. This makes his analytical framework especially relevant to those who may doubt his conclusion, but for whom the question of political identity remains important. Never has Marx's conclusion about the significance of the proletariat been more widely doubted on the Left than it is today, and never has his framework of analysis been imitated more widely, or less fruitfully.

The search for "new social movements," begun by the New Left, remains an effort to find an identity that might replace the industrial proletariat as a theoretically privileged agent of historical change.[26] For each potential candidate to play this role, claims have been made that parallel at least

[25] For an early expression of this view see Marx, "A Contribution to the Critique of Hegel's *Philosophy of Right*: Introduction" (tr. Livingstone and Benton), pp. 252–7.
[26] Among the candidates proposed for this role have been women, non-whites, gays, and even potential victims of environmental pollution or thermonuclear destruction – a category that would, potentially, include everyone. Some, such as

some of the claims Marx made for the political identity of the proletariat. The implicit point of such claims is that self-conscious movements based on the "new" identities can have at least some of the qualities of vision, strength, or historical destiny that traditional Marxists have ascribed to class-conscious proletarian parties.[27] Usually, however, the analogy with Marxism is equally illuminating for what is left out. Thus far, each of the "new social movements" conspicuously lacks either an epistemological vision, a political majority, structural leverage, or a historical trajectory — and often it lacks one or another combination of these. Such gaps in the analogy to Marx's view of the working class are usually filled with moral exhortation or cynical despair — a style reminiscent of an earlier Marxism in decline.

The post-Marxist literature on political identity has had its effect. The rhetoric of political mobilization surrounds us today, now trivialized to describe our selective investment of ego in particular social positions that are given to us. Even within our mainstream culture the slogans of dead revolutionary movements survive as metaphors of personal involvement, allowing advertisers to rely on the same techniques in promoting 'product identification' that political activists use in promoting causes.[28]

Our ability to identify with a variable subset of our pre-defined social positions suggests a degree of choice that does not amount to self-definition: although our identities are subject to change, they feel like stable stand-points from which we make other decisions; although our identities are products of conscious deliberation, their formation can be influenced by factors subject to external control. As we continue to occupy a multiplicity of roles, our inner and our outer lives are each filled with social content, and yet they remain partly different. Even our most fundamental identities

---

Isaac Balbus, seem to suggest that a new left can be based on *all* such movements at once. (See Balbus, *Marxism and Domination*.) Others, building more directly on Marx, pin their hopes on a group called variously "the new middle class," "the professional-managerial class," or simply "decommodified labor." (See Offe, "The New Social Movements.") Still others believe that the fundamental task is to articulate the parallels between the specific oppressions of various groups that might be joined together as a popular front around progressive issues. (See Laclau and Mouffe, *Hegemony and Socialist Strategy*.)

[27] Cf. Gerald A. Cohen, "The Workers and the Word: Why Marx Had the Right to Think He Was Right," and Haraway, "Situated Knowledges: The Science Question in Feminism and the Privilege of Partial Perspective."

[28] Recently, some drinkers of Coca Cola mobilized around that identity to success-fully demand that the original flavoring be returned to the market. Was this an effective protest movement, or a successful marketing device?

can now appear to be contingent, like our preferences, and yet given, like our loyalties.

In place of the traditional Marxist analysis of class interest and class consciousness our contemporary situation now confronts us with the problem of political identity in its most general form: To what extent is political identity governed by social circumstances? To what extent is it a matter of belief and conscious choice? At this general level political identity becomes a problem because we hold, at once, two different views of politics. The first is that our politics is something that we *think*. According to this view, politics has to do with our ability to stick up for our beliefs — to embrace our ideals sincerely and single-mindedly. But in the second view, our politics is something that we *have* no matter what we think. According to this view, being who one *is* in a political situation structures and controls the objective significance of thinking what one thinks, such that articulating a political identity often amounts to better understanding one's specific situation.[29] If political identity spans the variable relation between our social position and our subjective feelings, there must be a kernel of truth in the politics of culture: even material goods have symbolic significance, and our attachments to them presuppose a complex system of meanings that are local, given, and highly contingent on circumstance.[30]

[29] These two sides of political identity lie just below the surface of recent social thought. Many theories of welfare and distributive justice, for example, assume a domain of possible social positions to which unequal values are to be attached. But although these theories frequently appear to take the range of relevant identities as given, the debates between them often hinge on how the relative value of these social positions is constituted. Is it determined entirely by the contingent preferences of individuals? If so, justice can be described as the solution to a bargaining game in which only utilities matter. Or is there, rather, a scale of representative social positions that precede, and give meaning to, the formation of contingent preferences? If so, an adequate account of justice partly depends on the given cultural meaning of certain specific goods ("primary goods") for the bearers of preexisting identities.

This latter point has long been recognized by those who study the dynamics of social change. In considering the reasons that certain longstanding misfortunes become outrageous to their victims only at a specific historical moment, scholars argue that a "sense of injustice" is a precondition of political mobilization, and also a product of given identities formed in past political struggle.

On welfare and justice, see Rawls, *A Theory of Justice*; Dworkin, "What is Equality," Parts I and II; and Roemer, "The Mismarriage of Bargaining Theory and Distributive Justice." See also Sen, "Utilitarianism and Welfarism," and Posner, *The Economics of Justice*, part I. For reflections on the moral dynamics of social change see, e.g., Moore, *Injustice*, part I, "The Sense of Injustice."

[30] See Walzer, *Spheres of Justice*.

Whatever the value of this insight, however, the politics of culture does not exhaust the problem of political identity with which Marx wrestled. That problem arises within a culture at moments of conflict and stress. Its symptom is the appearance of more or less articulated theories that allow us to differentiate among a range of social goods between those that are ideals and those that are mere interests, and then to decide which to internalize and which to regard as part of our environment. As Marx understood it, the emergence of political identity is the epistemological process within a culture through which a conflict of goods also takes the form of a conflict of rights.

Such a transformation is reflected in many of the familiar problems facing populist social movements in a democracy. In their initial appeal populists identify their demands as democratic, suggesting that democracy itself is what they want as opposed to other goods that have come to dominate the political realm.[31] Yet these same populists also make claims for the political significance of how they must identify themselves in making those demands, often arguing that their victory would reconstitute the political majority around a new social identity. Have they, perhaps unknowingly, attempted to change the meaning of democracy for the political culture? If so, only later historians will be able to judge whether the populists succeeded in doing something that might have been literally unintelligible for them to attempt at the outset. Or are the populists rather struggling with the relation between their politics as something that they think and as something that they have? If so, their problem is how to identify themselves when acting politically within a given culture − how to grasp the relation between their ideals and their interests.

Marx's view of ideology was not simply an effort to reduce ideals to interests, but was rather part of a broader conception of how identity is formed. Within discussions of political identity the concept of ideology allowed Marx to talk about the ways in which collective actors themselves distinguish between their ideals and their interests. He often argued that a collective social actor may become more or less effective in promoting its interests because of what it takes to be its ideals − claiming that the bourgeoisie, for example, is often most effective in promoting its material interests when it espouses the ideal democracy. Marx also argued that a collective social actor's ability to promote its ideals will depend upon how well it conceptualizes its interests − claiming that the working class, for example, would be more effective in promoting the ideal of socialism if it had a clear understanding of its material interests.

[31] Examples might be security or privacy.

Once we understand that Marx's view of ideology is not a cynical debunking of ideals as interests, we can appreciate the sophistication that he brought to the problem of political identity. Throughout his work he recognized that what appears to observers as a conflict between ideals and interests is often experienced by the actor as a tension between objectivity and subjectivity: what is the significance of thinking what one thinks, given who one is? what is the significance of being who one is, given what one thinks? how can we articulate the relationship between what we regard as the necessity of our position and what we regard as our personal point of view toward it, especially if when acting on the one we must somehow bracket the other?[32] Marx believed that the process of forming a self-conscious identity is the inner dimension of the way in which society individuates us, enabling us over the course of a lifetime to internalize some of our social positions and to externalize others.[33]

In parts II and III we shall take up Marx's mature view of the problem of identity in political and economic life, but first we must explore his understanding of the problem at the abstract level of social epistemology. To do so, we shall focus on his early critique of both Hegel and the Left-Hegelians − a joint critique that laid the methodological groundwork for Marx's lifelong analysis of concrete institutions.

[32] If we act on our personal point of view, we may have to bracket our understanding of the necessity of our position; if we steel ourselves to act on necessity, we may have to bracket our personal point of view. (See chapters 2 and 3, below.)
[33] See, e.g., Erikson, Identity and the Life Cycle.

2 Freedom of Mind

Desire and expectation

For Hegel, the paramount philosophical problem of modern social thought is to understand the relation between what we want and what we get. He saw that theoretical descriptions of modern society often begin with an apparent tension between two points of view: viewed externally, modern society seems to subject the individual to intense social control; viewed internally, it leaves him prey to ungoverned desire. This suggests the abstract possibility that modern institutions will generate great dissatisfaction with the forms of life they provide. Yet, in fact, many individuals in modern society seem to do what is expected of them while believing that their actions are largely a reflection of their desires. Hegel believed that, lacking a coherent culture, modern societies must generate *theories* to explain this paradoxical relation between what people want and what they get. The mechanisms at work in such theories today vary from the economist's invisible hand to the psychologist's model of conditioning, the sociologist's model of conformity and deviance, and the internalized domination described by Foucault. Yet behind these differences lies a common effort to relate the apparent opacity of institutional outcomes to the ultimate subjectivity of individual desire. Hegel made this point explicit in his endeavor to generalize about the function of social theory within the forms of life that call for it. For him, the philosophical impetus behind all social theory is the need to grasp the problematic role of subjective freedom in the organization of modern life.

Hegel believed that our experience of freedom as a problem is rooted in our memories of the children we were. When we are children, our desires sometimes have a perverse relation to our expectations of fulfillment: we are capable of no longer wanting something once we know we can get it, and of wanting it all the more because we know we cannot have it.[1] In

[1] For a recent anti-Hegelian effort to address the perverse interactions between our desires and our beliefs, see Elster, *Sour Grapes.*

Hegel's reconstruction this capacity to form desires that do not adapt us to our circumstances is the primal source of our experience of freedom. He claims that we first experience freedom as a demand that is not exhausted by the satisfaction of any particular desire. We thereby come to understand the meaning of our freedom through recognizing the lack of it. In the fearful transition to modern adulthood this lack of freedom can become an all-consuming problem: when we see fewer connections between our desires and our expectations, both our will and our fate can seem increasingly arbitrary. We then come to experience our freedom as an unavoidable tension between bondage to inner caprice and enslavement to outer necessity.[2] Childish freedom, the willful denial of this tension, becomes an ideal that is intrinsically unrealizable.

Maturity for Hegel begins with the demand for a form of freedom that can be realized in the lives that are given to us. If childhood ends with the recognition that both our inner and our outer lives can be arbitrary and capricious, our mature desire for freedom then becomes a self-conscious need for control, both of ourselves and of the world. By achieving self-control we would cease to be slaves to our desires, adjusting them, rather, to our possibilities. Our desires, suitably adjusted, would become fulfillable as part of our experience of greater control over the world. But, if both what we want and what we get are, to begin with, arbitrary and contingent, why do we continue to regard the connection between them as a matter of freedom? The answer, according to Hegel, lies in our need to think of ourselves as complete *individuals*, living lives that have a shape and integrity over time, and that become acceptable to us through being understandable to others. Mature freedom is the potential for comprehending one's life over time within the framework of a historically given set of institutions. Hegel believed that extending this potential to everyone is the promise of the modern world — a promise that is fulfilled by a philosophical interpretation of the role of social science in legitimating the institutions it purports to explain.[3]

At its most general level Hegel's own philosophy was an attempt to address the overarching problem of modernity — understanding yourself

[2] Which of these do we then regard as our true selves — the inner arbitrariness of our will, or the outer arbitrariness of our fate? Do we regard ourselves as the slaves of passion, of inner desires, of emotional and physical needs? (Spinoza described this inner condition as a form of "human bondage.") Or do we rather regard ourselves as having potentially compatible desires that could be jointly gratified if the world were not so recalcitrant?

[3] The foregoing is an interpretive summary of the introduction to the *Philosophy of Right* in the light of some of the main arguments of the *Phenomenology of Spirit*.

as free while living out one particular life among others. To perform this task, Hegel devised, at different times, two philosophical methods. These he called the "phenomenological" and the "logical."[4] The *phenomenological method* is concerned with overcoming the arbitrariness of subjective experience that becomes apparent when we discover that we exist as objects for others whose order of experience is not the same as our own. The problem this poses is overcome in the phenomenological method when we can fully acknowledge the point of view of the other as part of our own. The parallel problem addressed by the *logical method* is that general desires give particular objects their meaning, and yet no particular object can satisfy our general desires. This is overcome according to the logical method when a fully realized individual understands *the universal significance of being who he is in particular.*

Unlike most approaches to philosophy, neither of Hegel's methods begins with simple definitions of the concepts we use when we think about our lives in modern institutions. The phenomenological method begins at one remove from this. Put crudely, it describes what it feels like to think the way we do.[5] The logical method takes us one remove further from our ordinary concepts: it describes what it looks like to feel and think the way we do.[6]

[4] The logical method is used in such works as the *Philosophy of Right*, the *Encyclopedia*, and of course the *Logic*. The phenomenological method is used, obviously, in the *Phenomenology of Spirit*, as well as in some of Hegel's earlier writings. The best recent overview of Hegel's thought can be found in Charles Taylor, *Hegel*.

[5] In analyzing a problem in political philosophy such as punishment, Hegel's phenomenological method would be concerned, not with giving a definition of punishment, but with describing how each party in a punishing relationship self-consciously interacts with the other. In this social practice both parties must have an understanding of how the other understands what each is doing. Each is aware simultaneously of being an object for the other, and also a subject whose feelings about the reasons for punishing are a necessary part of the struggle for recognition that is the real experience of punishment. The question is not whether as a matter of definition "punishment is not punishment unless it is deserved" (cf. Bradley, *Ethical Studies*). Punishment is an interactive practice that is also highly institutionalized. In being punished one undergoes suffering intentionally inflicted by someone who acts as though one deserves it.

[6] Returning to our example of punishment (n. 5, above), the focus of Hegel's logical method would be to explain why a justified punishment must actually be inflicted. Such an explanation would proceed by treating the experience of punishment as an embodiment of the thoughts that constitute it. The universal side of the experience of punishment would be the sense of being treated as a citizen. (As citizens we are *all* subject to punishment.) The particular side of the experience of

Subject and object

Hegel's phenomenological method deals with thought as experience. In traditional philosophy the word "phenomenon" refers to any experience, but Hegel's phenomenology treats all thought as an outgrowth of a single dominant and overarching experience — the experience of being an embodied mind.[7] As he described it, this is an experience of being simultaneously both a *subject* and an *object*; a someone and a something; an "I" and a "me." The phenomenological method is an effort to understand these two aspects of our experience as mutually necessary to our development.

Greatly simplified, Hegel's fundamental argument in the *Phenomenology* is an account of how psychological independence is rooted in material and

---

punishment would be the sense of being treated as an enemy. (Punishment isolates us from our fellow citizens.) In distinguishing between these two sides of our experience of punishment Hegel argues that they are mutually necessary, and that the realization that comes through the actual infliction of punishment by a penal institution is the experience of being someone who is both citizen and enemy — both universal and particular. Using these terms, Hegel's logical method would enable us to describe punishment as the experience a prisoner has of being treated as an individual. Thus, for a Hegelian the concrete task of the criminal justice system is to both actualize and legitimate punishment by according the public enemy individuated treatment from the moment of arrest.

The foregoing account of punishment would reveal the problem that states have in attempting to institutionalize the punishment of political movements: collective punishment is often indistinguishable from political repression, creating enemies where once there were citizens.

[7] Hegel believed that we experience our own incarnation as a problem because the objects of our desires are at once general and particular. By grasping the universal significance of our particular commitments (e.g. to projects and persons), Hegel argued, we are able to realize our freedom in and through the living of fully embodied lives.

Like Luther, Hegel believed that Embodied Mind (the Incarnation) was the original idea that entered world history when Christianity superseded and encompassed Greek thought. Theologically, Hegel's view is a continuation of the characteristically Augustinian problem of relating *Eros* and *Agape*: does God love the world only for its good qualities, or is His love an investment of grace in our particular being, with all its deficiencies? (See Luther, "The Freedom of a Christian," and Hegel, *Early Theological Writings* and *The Philosophy of History*, part 4. Cf. Nygren, *Agape and Eros*, Kung, *The Incarnation of God*, and Tillich, *The Protestant Era*.)

social dependency.[8] According to Hegel, social relations between conscious subjects are mediated by the need of each for material things. This means that others can control us by controlling the external objects we need and value. It also suggests that our awareness of material needs has a social dimension, even to begin with: we need things partly because they are recognized as valuable by others as a means of social control; the satisfaction of our needs is in part, therefore, a way of gaining recognition from others for the autonomy of our desires. For this reason Hegel insisted that the relative value of things is inherently intersubjective: the things we need will define the nature of our dependency, autonomy, and power in relation to others.[9]

Not surprisingly, the abstract account of social reality given by market economics provides a good example of Hegel's view of the self-conscious mind carving out its sense of independence by distinguishing between its material and social dependency. Markets would not exist if we did not need material objects in order to survive. Yet possessions have value in the marketplace only insofar as they are socially recognized as valuable by others. In a system of exchange, ownership is a form of social power allowing us to fulfill our needs by satisfying the needs of others.[10] We become a legitimate subject of desire in the market only at those moments when we are also conscious of being an object of desire for another who needs us to need him. By internalizing his point of view we can seek to satisfy our needs through satisfying his. The economist's notion of "effective demand"[11] means that the more we have that is of value, the more our needs will be recognized. Yet it also suggests that the market recognizes only those desires on which it depends – desires that are mediated by the knowledge that fulfilling them satisfies the needs of others. Thus, in an important sense our only real economic need is a need to be needed.[12] Yet, by distinguishing between our material and social needs economic theory allows us to believe that we are free.

[8] See appendix 1, below.

[9] In more recent parlance Hegel believed that we cannot have a theory of rights (relations among persons) without an implicit theory of goods (relative values of things), and vice versa.

[10] For later discussions of the sociology of exchange see Blau, *Exchange and Power in Social Life* and Simmel, *The Philosophy of Money*.

[11] In economics this notion is not a measure of unmediated desire, and presupposes the market as a barrier to the direct satisfaction of needs. For Marx's view of the phenomenology of "effective demand" see appendix 3, below.

[12] Marx gives a negative interpretation of this aspect of the phenomenology of markets in his early writings. See, e.g., Marx, "Excerpts from James Mill's *Elements of Political Economy*," and appendix 3, below.

Much of Hegel's *Phenomenology* describes the dynamic relation between the material objects we are able to externalize as needs, and the social other we must internalize in order to conceive the outside world as we do. He describes how we distinguish ourselves as subjects from a material world of things at the same time that we become aware of ourselves as objects in a social world of others. He then describes how a self that is originally constituted by the *difference* between social and material relations must struggle to recognize the *connections* between them – the ways in which the material world is socially constituted and the social world is materially grounded.[13]

From the foregoing type of analysis Hegel concluded that we identify objects as part of an external world by internalizing the standpoint of others toward the contents of our own minds. The opening arguments of the *Phenomenology* suggest that at the very moment when we self-consciously recognize our needs as desires, we also become socialized – that in learning to see ourselves from another's point of view, we become as another to ourselves.[14] Indeed, the basic philosophical insight throughout the *Phenomenology* is that self-consciousness *necessarily* consists of taking the standpoint of another toward the contents of our own minds. He referred to this standpoint as "alienation," which he defined generally as any experience we may have of the relation between consciousness and self-consciousness.[15] Hegel saw alienation in this general sense as the root of all progress.[16] He believed that enlightenment would come from the continuing struggle to analyze and confront the nature of the other that we internalize as the self.[17]

Hegel's *Phenomenology* drew out the implications of this argument. Since each desire is simultaneously social and material, it organizes our experience along two dimensions: as we have seen, the desire differentiates us as subjects from the objects we lack, and it defines a social self through

[13] Lucio Colletti points out that Hegel could have properly called himself a dialectical materialist. (See Colletti, *Marxism and Hegel*.)

[14] Hegel proposed the same solution to the philosophical problems of skepticism (knowledge of the external world) and solipsism (knowledge of other minds). In essence the solution to both problems lies in the experience of being an object of another's needs. This allows one to incorporate the perspective of the other into oneself, and to understand subjectivity as the consciousness of the other. (See Charles Taylor, "On the Opening Arguments of the *Phenomenology*," and Kojève, *Introduction to the Reading of Hegel*, ch. 1.) [15] See appendix 1, below.

[16] "The equilibrium of the whole is not the unity which remains with itself, nor the contentment that comes from having returned into itself, but rests on the alienation of opposites." (Hegel, *The Phenomenology of Spirit*, p. 295.)

[17] As a Lutheran, Hegel believed that in serving God the Christian freely alienates

which we can be recognized as objects by others. Because our desires have these two dimensions, however, Hegel saw that the very process of forming them places us under a double risk: by self-consciously desiring material objects we reify the external world and unconsciously repress our social dependence on others; yet, by self-consciously desiring social recognition we reify our conflicts with others, and unconsciously repress our own material needs. Hegel concluded that in order to fully understand ourselves as embodied subjects we must learn to self-consciously take the point of view of others toward our own needs. In this way our desires would become fully socialized, just as the material world becomes fully civilized. From the standpoint of Hegel's philosophy, economic theory attempts to perform this function within its limited domain, showing how the market socializes our needs while transforming our material environment.[18]

Yet behind the optimistic conclusion of Hegel's *Phenomenology* lies the fundamental insight that the attainment of self-knowledge is inseparable from social struggle. By showing that desire is inherently intersubjective, Hegel delineates a connection between our social and material needs that

---

himself, accepting his alienation as the appropriate relation between his consciousness and his self-consciousness. The Christian's individual relationship with a loving God allows him to acknowledge the necessary disjunction between his inner life and the external world. Poised between a transcendent God and an alien world, the Christian's faith stands for his freedom.

We should note that the word "alienation" is in origin a theological term that describes man's relationship to God. In the Christian view the sinner is saved when he becomes alienated from himself so that he can live for the sake of God. By renouncing the power and the glory of this world, and accepting the power and the glory that are God's, the Christian liberates himself from earthly bondage. In this sense God becomes the Christian's true lord and master (note the terms). In *On Christian Doctrine* Augustine defines the sinner as essentially "unalienated" – a person who takes joy in himself, glorying in his power over others and in the satisfaction of his desires. The Christian saint, having undergone a process of "self-alienation," takes joy only in the joy that God takes in him. (In Augustine's view the Christian temporarily resolves the problem of serving two masters by publicly promising to "render unto Caesar that which is Caesar's," while believing that in the end there shall be only the kingdom of the Lord in which "the meek shall inherit the Earth." Cf. the passage in Milton's *Paradise Lost* where Lucifer says, "Better to reign in hell than serve in heaven.")

[18] Correspondingly, a Left-Hegelian critique of the market would argue that it dissolves social relations while destroying the physical environment. In his earliest reflections on economics Marx offered just such a phenomenological critique of the market. (See Marx, *Early Writings*, pp. 259–400.) His arguments along these lines are discussed further in appendix 3, below.

is necessary rather than contingent: we do not merely demand recognition as a means of fulfilling our desires for material objects; we also become conscious of our need of material objects as a way of demanding recognition as desiring subjects. This gives almost all our desires a social significance that is ultimately inseparable from their satisfaction. We want our desires satisfied as such, that is, because they are desires; whatever we get will not satisfy us, unless we also believe that we got it *because* we wanted it.[19] Getting what we want, therefore, inevitably reflects upon an underlying struggle for social domination.[20]

In a pivotal argument, Hegel used the metaphor of the master and the slave to describe how the struggle for domination is part of the development of self-conscious freedom.[21] The master and slave each experience only one side of freedom. The master knows that what he does is up to him, but does not know why he does it. The slave knows what he does and why, but knows that it is not up to him. The idea of fully realized freedom that emerges out of slavery is freedom as *self*-mastery. But Hegel saw that self-mastery is not possible within the relationship of slavery. There is nothing in the master's side that would lead to it. (Even if, unconsciously, he is already a slave to passion, becoming consciously a slave to reason would have little intrinsic appeal.) The slave, on the other hand, could comprehend what freedom is only by imagining what it would be like to be his own master. He would thereby cease to be a slave in his own mind, while imagining a self-conscious freedom that his master does not actually possess. Just as one cannot understand what it means to be asleep without first

[19] Ultimately, Hegel's analysis takes us to the point where our desires are purely self-reflexive — abstracted from any particular content they become desires for recognition as such. At this point *all* that we desire is the desire of another to satisfy us. Our self-conception then becomes distinct from any of the particular desires we experience.

In this regard Hegel noted that humans are sometimes capable of risking their lives to gain recognition for their desires, even though they assume that death would preclude any possibility of satisfaction. Such a risk is conceivable because humans are capable of thinking of their lives as wholes, the recognition of which has a meaning beyond their fear of death. (Only when we are capable of thinking of ourselves as living a life can we ask what kind of life is worth living.)

[20] We are all familiar with the point at which the struggle for recognition begins in the life of a young child: "He doesn't want milk; he just wants attention." (Freud repeatedly suggests that the struggle for recognition and identity, even to the death, is an important part of the fantasy life of young children.)

[21] See, Kojève, *Introduction to the Reading of Hegel*; Hyppolite, *Genesis and Structure of Hegel's 'Phenomenology of Spirit,'* ch. 3; and Hegel, *The Phenomenology of Spirit*, ch. 4.

awakening, so one cannot understand what it means to be a slave without hoping for and demanding freedom. The one-time slave who has become his own master is the paradigm of modern freedom.

Hegel believed that this paradigm of freedom transcends the struggle that produced it, allowing liberated slaves to achieve a higher form of consciousness than their former masters. For the slave, liberation becomes possible only when he recognizes that he has collaborated in his own subjugation — that the master has done nothing to him that the slave has not also done to himself. If slavery consists of unconsciously internalizing the master, the slave who recognizes this turns the means of his past repression into the basis of his future strength: by overcoming the internal master who prevented him from living for himself, the liberated slave realizes that he is capable of becoming for himself the free man that he has always been. Such full liberation, however, would require confrontation rather than escape; mere escape would leave the slave masterless without ever fully freeing him from his need for the master's approval. For this reason, Hegel, like later liberation theorists, argued that to be freed the slave must know that he is psychologically capable of killing the master.[22] But because this master inhabits the slave's own mind, the struggle for liberation is metaphorical as well as real, and for modern man it is never-ending.[23]

[22] In *The Wretched of the Earth* Frantz Fanon takes wars of national liberation as a paradigm of class struggle, arguing that self-identity can be created only through a willingness to identify and annihilate the internalized "other." The paradigm of Third World liberation movements as articulated by Fanon had a major influence on the Marxism of Western thinkers such as Sartre and Jameson.

[23] According to Hegel, Christian religion is the spiritual self-mastery of slaves who become free. The faithful, recognizing that they could not have been enslaved to others if they were not also slaves to their own earthly needs, convert to the belief that their true lord and master is not on earth but in heaven. In relation to God, the Christian is then both free and mastered since he is bound by an act of faith that is freely given. The Master who truly rules him is now the One who recognizes his freedom. In this respect Hegel accepted the Lutheran argument that Christians are free in the mind of God, even if all earthly rulers believe otherwise. (In the *Phenomenology of Spirit*, ch. 4.B, Hegel argued that Christianity, like Stoicism, teaches that if God is your true master, you are free even when you seem to be in chains.)

Thus conceived, the advent of Christianity introduced a radically new principle into world history: where the ancient Greek world had been concerned with an objective ethical order, Christianity let loose the problem of subjectivity. This forever changed the agenda of philosophy from a concern with Good alone to a concern with Freedom — i.e. with reconciling the objective ethical order and the

According to Hegel, the guilty struggle to become one's own master lies at the root of the modern politics of equality and self-respect. His phenomenology teaches that self-mastery is conceivable only for those who know what it means to be mastered by someone other than themselves — who incorporate the viewpoint of the other into their own. If so, the self-respect that such persons gain from liberation is threatened whenever the autonomy of their own point of view is not respected by others. When accepting another's authority or love feels like a form of subjugation, self-respect becomes an issue for which the subordinate in the relationship may be willing to struggle, and even to die. The resulting demand for equality, whether political or social, is always a form of "abolitionism"[24] that negates a particular hierarchy of ruler and ruled. As an expression of self-respect, egalitarianism rejects one or another basis of social domination by insisting on the irreducibility of one's own point of view as a total perspective on the others that threaten to subsume it.

---

recognition of subjective desires. But in Christianity this reconciliation is only transcendent. The Christian accepts his alienation in this world, and puts his faith in the world to come.

For Hegel, secularizing the Christian conception of spiritual freedom is the philosophical challenge of the modern world. In his political philosophy he sought to demonstrate how under modern conditions individual freedom can be recognized in this world, and not only by an other-worldly God. Modern institutions, as Hegel conceived them, embody freedom of mind by allowing us to believe that what we do is ultimately up to us, even as they shape the way we come to know our own minds. According to Hegel, this achievement of modern institutions incorporates the notion of subjective freedom into the self-understanding of the world, thus incarnating the way in which God understands Himself. In the Hegelian state the transcendent Christian conception of freedom of mind becomes actual for more than the chosen few. As a modern citizen, the secular Christian is reconciled to the necessity that follows from the public recognition of free choice. (See Luther, "The Freedom of a Christian" and *Hegel's Philosophy of Right* (tr. Knox) preface and paras 341–60, *The Phenomenology of Spirit*, chs 4.B, 6.B.b, and 7.C, *Lectures on the History of Philosophy* vol. 3, pp. 1–25 and 146–155, and vol. 1, pp. 384–448, *The Philosophy of History*, pp. 318–457, and part II.

Nietzsche countered this view by insisting that Christianity was not a form of spiritual liberation, but only a "slave-morality." In essence he believed that the Roman Empire converted to Christianity when faced with slave revolts for the same reason that rebellious children are sent off to Sunday school — that Spartacus and Oedipality are the same, phenomenologically speaking. (See Nietzsche, "The Genealogy of Morals" and *Beyond Good and Evil*, para. 260.)

[24] Cf. Walzer, *Spheres of Justice*, p. xii.

The limits of phenomenology

Phenomenological analysis is a penetrating way of talking about mediated social relationships and of dealing with individual pathologies and problems. The nature of the phenomenological method is to focus on what each needs the other to be, and what each needs the other to need of him or her. Relationships are easy to dissect, describe, and diagnose in this way.[25] A phenomenological analysis of romantic love and marriage, like Hegel's discussion of the master and the slave, would be the story of a struggle for recognition based on mutual need. If the intrinsic progression from love to marriage required male domination, then the liberation of women would consist of overcoming their vulnerability to the male point of view. If not, women's liberation might consist of a fully mutual recognition of needs. Here, each of the lovers would be intensely needed by the other to be what each most needs to be — and each would acknowledge this about both self and other.[26]

But whereas phenomenology is good for tracing the evolution of any social relationship (doctor/patient, buyer/seller, etc.), it is much less useful in analyzing the underlying structure of such relationships. The reason for this is simple. The distinction between subject and object, between inner and outer, between self and other — and, ultimately, between what we identify as our action and what we identify as our fate — is just a description, after the fact, of our own mental state. The central relation between consciousness and self-consciousness is a relationship between self and other that has already been internalized in the way in which we alternately subjectify and objectify our own experience. Both the strength and weakness of phenomenology lie in the fact that these basic dichotomies are easily reversible with respect to any given content.

[25] Consider, for example, romantic love. Hegel would account for romantic love as an expression of the need to be recognized as being for another the kind of subject that one wishes to be for oneself. When a man and woman are looking for love each desires the free gift of the other's commitment or desire. Yet loving, and being loved, are also sources of power. Phenomenology captures this in terms of the simultaneous need for both recognition and liberation — the tension between wanting to be loved on the one hand, and wanting to be in love on the other. Romantic love in particular is felt as an intense need to be desired by an object that you desire, and, ultimately, to have your desire itself desired by your object. The lover internalizes the relationship between self and other as a relationship *within* the self. If alienation is the Hegelian name for the general relation of consciousness and self-consciousness, then love is the willing embrace of alienation.

[26] Although such full mutuality might make the lovers *compatible*, it would not necessarily make them *equal*.

Consider the familiar love triangle. Phenomenological analysis can give a vivid and accurate description of whatever happens over time, but it cannot explain why the opposite of these events did not happen. The unfaithful husband, for instance, can feel that his marriage to his wife is simply an alienated institutional form, and regard his libido as his real self. (This may be what he tells his mistress.) Or he may feel that his relationship with his wife is his real self, and that his libido is like an allergy which he will be able to control over time. (This may be what he tells his wife.) In the former case he objectifies his marriage and subjectifies his desire for his mistress. In the latter case he subjectifies his marriage and objectifies his desire for his mistress. While both accounts may be factually consistent with his behavior, in each account the husband takes the opposite elements to constitute himself and his world.

This descriptive flexibility makes phenomenology a poor technique for *explaining* the structure of institutions and relationships. If the unfaithful husband's marriage breaks up, phenomenology will be sensitive to his experience of libido as self and marriage as other. Yet, if his marriage does not break up, its preservation can be described with equal sensitivity as just the opposite experience. In either case the function of phenomenology is merely diacritical: it marks the changing distinction between self and other in the individual's experience, but does not account for how his life develops at the intersection of multiple institutional frameworks. In describing the vicissitudes of love and marriage, phenomenology can reveal the contradictory experiences of domination, freedom, and equality in each relationship. Yet it can give no account of what free love would look like, or of how freedom might be realized in the institutional recognition of equality.

Our evaluation of Hegel's phenomenological method must thus be mixed. In any developing social relationship, phenomenology allows us to ask pertinent questions about each person's situation: which of his feelings is he externalizing, and what part of the social world is he internalizing? how does he understand himself, and how does he expect to be understood? what are the respective roles of objectification and subjectification in his self-understanding? We must conclude, however, that the phenomenological method itself is no guide to answering such questions – it simply provides the slots into which the answers can be inserted.

Despite the limitations of the phenomenological method, its descriptive power makes the entire Hegelian enterprise plausible. Our account of Hegel's phenomenology thus far yields the following insights: that the personal is political; that politics is about conflict and struggle; that self-liberation is a never-ending process; that equality is not a presupposition, but a struggle for recognition under concrete forms of domination; and that individual freedom is not given, but won in a struggle to become one's own master — to become, that is, both master and subject at the same time. These insights suggest radical political conclusions — debunking all established institutions — that have by now become articles of faith on the contemporary Left.

Hegel's own critique of phenomenology, however, allowed him to avoid such radical political conclusions, and to direct his attention to institutional reform. From the mature perspective of Hegel's logic the defect of the phenomenological approach to freedom is clear: there is either a one-sided focus on freedom *for* itself, or a one-sided focus on freedom *in* itself, but the two are never brought into harmony.[27]

Universal and particular

Hegel had moved beyond the limitations of the phenomenological method by the time he wrote his *Philosophy of Right*. Unlike the genetic approach of the *Phenomenology*, which takes us from infancy to adulthood, Hegel's logical method presupposes the mature world as we now know it. The *Philosophy of Right* begins by showing that we understand what it means to be an individual by realizing the relationship between two apparently contradictory experiences of having a will — the experience that what I do is up to me, and the experience of knowing what I am doing. Together, these experiences make us aware of our subjective freedom. They are, respectively, the will "in itself" and "for itself."

The key terminology of the logical method — the "in itself"/"for itself" distinction — is a transposition of certain features of the phenomenological method into a different form. Simple consciousness is an initial approximation to our experience in itself. Self-consciousness is an initial approximation to our experience for itself. Alienation is the experience of the difference between understanding our experience in and for itself — the

---

[27] "Absolute Knowledge" is Hegel's phenomenological description of understanding your freedom in itself and for itself. This is vaguely described at the end of the *Phenomenology of Spirit* in an interesting, but highly metaphorical, chapter (ch. 8). Kojève argues that Hegel's abandonment of the phenomenological method in favor of the non-genetic approach of the *Logic* was based on the claim that "the end of history" was reached at the Battle of Jena — a view that Kojève defends with characteristic brilliance. (See Kojève, *Introduction to the Reading of Hegel*, ch. 6) For another view of the relation between the phenomenological and logical methods, see Hyppolite, *Genesis and Structure of Hegel's 'Phenomenology of Spirit*,' part 7, and "On the *Logic* of Hegel."

experience of seeing our subjectivity as an object of thought, and of seeing the world as a figment of our subjective fancies. This, as we have seen, is a reversal of subjectivity and objectivity, and also a sign of the collapse of the distinction between them. If it turns out that you can either objectify consciousness and subjectify the self, or subjectify the self and objectify consciousness, then the language of subject and object will prove to be an unsatisfactory way to capture what may really be a highly fluid process of internalization and externalization of our experience – a process more accurately captured in the logical terms of the distinction between "in itself" and "for itself."[28]

As an approach to the problem of embodied mind, the logical method allowed Hegel to focus on how we come to realize that we are free by living a determinate existence. He was struck with the fact that in modern society we get just the right number of firemen, teachers, and steel workers while at the same time allowing all of them to feel that they are fulfilling their individuality. How can each one feel that he or she is making a choice, even though, collectively, they do nothing other than what would be expected of them? Hegel's general answer is given by the procedures of modern bureaucracy. These procedures recognize the needs of the individual by acknowledging his self-understanding in the process by which he is understood; yet they also induce the individual to meet the needs of society when he articulates his self-understanding in ways that incorporate how he expects to be understood.

Freedom of the individual, then, is the development of an identity through which one gains recognition for one's choices by learning how to make the reasons for them intelligible to others. The free individual realizes the relationship between acting for reasons he understands for himself, and gaining respect from others for the choice he has made in itself. When others (or the state) can treat him as though his particular situation were a matter of choice, they can also hold him responsible for it.[29] As applied to political philosophy, Hegel's logical method was an effort to derive the Idea of the free individual from the two moments of the Concept of what it means to live a life both in and for itself.[30]

Indeed, all of Hegel's arguments in the *Philosophy of Right* consist of deriving an Idea from the two moments of its Concept. The word "Idea"

[28] See appendix 1, below.
[29] N.B., the recognition of choice appears as a positive moment in the derivation of freedom from the Concept of the Individual, just as it appeared as a negative moment in the derivation of the individual from the Concept of the Will. See appendix 1, below.
[30] See appendix 1, below.

as Hegel uses it, however, is drastically different from the ordinary usage of "idea" to connote a mental construct. For Hegel, an Idea is an actuality which is realized through the process of being understood. The Idea of health, for example, is nothing other than the hospital. The hospital realizes the relation between the universal need of the patient for a cure and whatever particular medical treatment the doctors provide. In coming to understand himself as a medical patient the suffering person learns to articulate his complaints in terms of the specific requirements of medical treatment. His conception of health is defined by the removal of diseases that his doctor can treat. On their side the doctors learn to articulate the reasons for their treatment in a way that seems responsive to the patient's felt complaints. This allows the patient to realize his health in the process of undergoing the treatment the hospital provides.[31]

By parallel reasoning, Hegel argued that the realization of the Idea of freedom is the state − another institution which could not be what it is except in virtue of how it is understood. Political freedom for Hegel is not some serendipitous relationship between what we want and what we get; it is rather the way in which we come to see what we want in terms of what we get, and what we get in terms of what we want. In Hegel's view becoming free requires that the individual understand himself by grasping how he is understood in the modern state. In thus realizing our freedom, Hegel argued, we achieve an understanding of ourselves that at the same time reconciles us to the world as we find it.

Hegel concluded that by understanding our lives as they appear to the state we can each realize ourselves to be free, while still being someone in particular: to be free, then, is to be recognized as an individual by an institution that one recognizes as a state. When this occurs, we are no longer in the state because we are free, we are free because we are in the state. Thus, Hegel's theory of political freedom carries a double burden − explaining why it is necessary for individuals to live determinate lives in order to realize their freedom,[32] and why individuals must understand themselves to be free in order to find those lives acceptable.

[31] By similar reasoning, Hegel would say that the Idea of nature can only be realized through the institution of science. Nature exists for itself as theory, and in itself as facts that can disconfirm theory. Science as an institution is the self-understanding of nature, requiring that our theories be falsifiable in relation to the observational facts. Nature becomes actual in and for itself through the tension between theory and data implicit in the methods of science. (Hegel also argued that the Idea of God is realized in organized religion. Insofar as God needs our worship to become more actual, religion is the medium through which God understands Himself as existing in the world.)

[32] E.g., we must actually be firemen, professors, or students.

Interpretation and critique

There is, however, one major variation in the general application of Hegel's logical method: he recognized that, historically, some forms of life become stable institutions when they are fully comprehended from within; others, once understood from within, must cease to exist. The real political stakes in his philosophy lie in his effort to demonstrate that marriage and the state, to give two examples, are of the former type, whereas slavery and feudalism are forms of life that resist full comprehension from within. Yet Hegel gave no general account of a fundamental difference between those forms of life that are preserved, and those that are superseded, by being understood.[33] He simply used the logical method to draw at different times two quite different conclusions about the role of comprehension within historically evolving social practices.

Outside of the *Philosophy of Right*, Hegel frequently used the logical method to demonstrate that the realization of certain Concepts is incompatible with their institutionalization. We may call these realizations "awakenings," loosely following Hegel's (semi-serious) discussion of the Concept of sleep in the *Philosophy of Mind*.[34] What is sleep? (1) The universal moment of your experience of sleep is that you are not asleep. You are trying to go to sleep. Sleep is a negation of your present state. This is sleep for itself. (2) The particular moment, sleep in itself, is the way we understand the sleep of another: the other person is asleep without realizing it. (3) In Hegel's sense the realization of the Idea of sleep would consist of waking up. In awakening you realize that you were asleep, but this makes it no longer possible to be asleep. To realize that you were asleep is to be awake.[35]

The *Philosophy of Right*, however, is mainly concerned with Concepts that are compatible with their full realization, rather than those, like sleep, that must be abolished at the moment that they are realized. Hegel's substantive argument throughout is that of all political forms *only* the

---

[33] In this regard the overall optimism of the *Philosophy of Right* is somewhat belied by the gloom at the end of its preface: "When philosophy paints its grey in grey, then has a shape of life grown old ... The owl of Minerva spreads its wings only with the falling of the dusk." (*Hegel's Philosophy of Right* (tr. Knox), p. 13.)

[34] Para. 398, pp. 65ff.

[35] Elsewhere, Hegel argues that the two moments of the Concept of feudalism cannot be realized without being superseded by Enlightenment — the historical equivalent of an awakening. See *The Philosophy of History*, introduction and part 4, and *The Phenomenology of Spirit*, pp. 294–363. Cf. *Lectures on the History of Philosophy*, vol. 3, pp. 157–408.

modern state is strengthened by the degree to which it is understood from within.[36]

The logical method gave Hegel a partial solution to the problems in using the phenomenological method to analyze institutions and relationships. As we have already seen, phenomenology cannot explain why insight into a romance or marriage sometimes breaks it up and sometimes stabilizes it; phenomenology merely describes whatever happens as a form of liberation. In contrast, the logical method brings to the fore the explanatory problem that phenomenology evades by promising to tell us whether, in a given relationship, liberation must take the form of 'awakening' or 'institutionalization.'

The success of the logical method as an approach to social science will depend on how far we are persuaded by Hegel's substantive analyses. But since the object of "logical" analysis is to show the extent to which comprehending a given form of life is compatible with living it, Hegel hoped and expected that persuading us that a particular analysis is correct would also have an element of self-fulfilling prophecy. A successful Hegelian analysis of any given institution should "reconcile us to the actual." In some cases this would mean accepting the fact that our institutions or relationships have already decayed beyond hope of revival. More often, Hegel believed, we would be persuaded to accept the inescapable logic of the lives we already lead. Apparently, he assumed that the difference between radical critique and interpretive legitimation lay, not in the logical method itself, but in the objects to which it was applied.

This assumption may have prevented Hegel from noticing that the logical method itself contained an ambivalence similar to that which we found in phenomenology. We saw above that in phenomenology the reversible processes of subjectification and objectification contain the possibility of either enlightenment or self-deception. By the time Hegel repudiated phenomenology as a method, he might have argued that enlightenment consists of recognizing this reversibility, and self-deception of denying it. Such an insight might also have led Hegel to develop the logical method, which was based implicitly on distinguishing between awakenings and institutionalizations as alternative possibilities. Yet he never noticed that this distinction was not itself grounded in his philosophy, and that, at a higher

---

[36] Hegel insisted, moreover, that we cannot be free without realizing that we are. This implies that Rousseau made a philosophical mistake in claiming that primitive man was free without realizing it, and that enlightened man "woke up" to a realization of his own bondage. Cf. Rousseau, *The Social Contract*, and *Hegel's Philosophy of Right* (tr. Knox), introduction.

level, it too was reversible.[37] At their best, Hegel's logical analyses show what it would mean to live within an institution that one takes to be legitimate. Yet in such arguments there is a kind of distancing — implicit even in our word "legitimation" — that reveals the boundaries of our social forms from the inside out. Hegel's legitimations allow us to live within our institutions as though we had somehow awakened from them. To this extent his interpretation of what it means for a particular institution to be fully realized is always partially disillusioning. Similarly, his awakenings often make us nostalgic for the forms of life to which we cannot return. To this extent Hegel's logical critiques are always partially legitimating.[38]

Just as Hegel's phenomenological analysis shows us the processes of experience where philosophy and rhetoric meet, so his logical analysis occupies the common ground in thought between social science and ideology. By embedding social science within the institutions it explains, he shows how such explanations satisfy the institution's need for legitimation. This is why his arguments describing the logic of social practices and institutions shimmer between immanent critique and legitimating interpretation, and why they produce both disillusionment and reconciliation. At stake in these arguments is nothing more nor less than the continuing existence of a form of life, and this in turn depends on how successfully it allows us to distinguish between the universal and particular meaning of our experience within it. In giving his philosophical defence of the legitimacy of modern institutions Hegel also shows us how ideology works to legitimate them.[39]

[37] This point emerged in conversation with Jeremy Elkins.

[38] The argument above partially undermines Hegel's sharp distinction between awakenings and institutionalizations. One (perhaps unwanted) implication of Hegel's theory is that the ideology that legitimates the modern state also makes us nostalgic for feudalism (and that the ideology that legitimates marriage makes us nostalgic for dating).

[39] As Marx was later to see, Hegel's logic shows how social thought functions in legitimating the institutions it comprehends. In characteristically Hegelian arguments it matters little whether the institution was grounded upon the plausibility of the theory, or the theory on the needs of the institution. For this reason Marx believed that Hegel's deepest insights can be stated as critiques — they reveal the need of institutions for legitimation, and the contingency and artificiality of the conceptual constructs through which this need is met. Yet the very ambivalence of Hegel's logic also served to warn Marx that self-conscious critique can implicitly perform the same legitimating function that Hegel ascribes to more neutral interpretations of institutional life — enabling the critic to comprehend his role in the institutions that he rejects in his imagination. For this reason Marx's arguments

The deep connection between Hegelian philosophy and institutional ideology can be made apparent if we attempt a logical analysis of the familiar problems of love and marriage that we earlier described phenomenologically. According to Hegel the institution of marriage is the realization of the Idea of free love. Following his logical method there would be two moments of the Concept of love. In its universal moment love would be experienced as a need, a negation of one's present condition. As something desired, it is as changeable as one's inner life. In its particular moment, however, love is experienced as something ascribed. Here it is no more changeable than one's social position.[40] According to Hegel, the Idea of free love can be realized once we grasp that the two moments of the Concept are mutually necessary, and this occurs in the institution of marriage. After getting married because we are in love we come to realize that we are in love because we are married. We then understand our love in terms of what is good for our marriage, rather than basing our continued marriage on whether we are still in love.

In Hegel's view freedom in marriage is achieved through a simultaneous transformation in one's understanding both of oneself and of one's situation. Let us begin with an unmarried woman who is keeping house for a man. When asked to describe her daily activities she might say that she does things for him. Now let us suppose, as sometimes happens, that there is a romance between them. Despite his professions of love, she might initially experience her situation as one of unfreedom in both her work and personal life. If so, she could express this by articulating the demand that she be allowed to do things for herself in her work, and also that he begin to do things for her in their relationship. Suppose he takes what she says seriously, and in responding to her joint demands he marries her. To the observer, however, she continues in more or less the same activities as before. How can it be said that she has come to realize her freedom?

Hegel would say that, as a married woman, she could understand herself and her situation differently, even though they might appear to be unchanged but for the marriage. What she previously might have done for herself she now does for him for her; as his wife she does on her own behalf what he

---

often demonstrated the disconcerting parallelisms between the arguments of bourgeois intellecutuals and their leftist critics. (See below, e.g., chapters 3, 4, 9, and the appendices.)

[40] On one side love is a passion; on the other it is a circumstance. Yet we wish to be slaves to neither our passions nor our circumstances. Hegel believed that if love is not to be simply a form of alienation, an ideology of human bondage, it must become a way of realizing our freedom. For him this meant that it must be realized in an institution.

would want done for her sake. What she previously might have done for him she now does for her for him because, as his wife, she acts for her own sake in doing things on his behalf.[41] She would eventually describe her possible desires and interests in terms of the givenness of her marriage, rather than describing the continuing possibility of their marriage in terms of the givenness of her desires and interests. Her love would increasingly come to be based not on contingent matters of feeling but on her understanding of herself as loved. She would thus have the satisfaction of knowing that everything she does is up to her while at the same time doing only what is expected.

Before going on I should make it clear that Hegel is *not* saying that all women are free in all marriages. He is rather showing what it means to realize fully that one is married. To the extent that a woman does not understand herself in this way, she has less of a marriage. The more her desires are grounded in her marital duties, the more of a marriage she has.[42]

Hegel would intend this point to be as much about the facts of her relationship as it is about her attitude toward it. There may need to be observable changes in her husband's behavior in order for her to understand his pursuit of his career as something that he now does for her. Yet such improvements in his behavior will strengthen their marriage only to the extent that they in fact produce this attitude. While free love in Hegel's sense may require as much change in one's external reality as in one's attitude toward it, Hegel's core argument is that both sorts of development occur together.

While Hegel intends his argument to support the legal institution of marriage, a modern version of his view might recognize that the idea of marriage in his sense is especially important in defining the love of those who do not avail themselves of the legal institution. In Hegel's view, marriage gives actuality to the two moments of the concept of love: the

---

[41] Consider the traditional wife of the male politician (Pat Nixon leaps to mind). When she campaigns she gives the impression of doing it for him for her. This transforms a behavior that would otherwise be quite demeaning into an impression of what it would look like to feel free.

[42] Neither is Hegel saying that all individuals realize their freedom in all modern states. As we shall see, he is arguing that a state is more internally stable, and hence more of a state, to the extent that its policies make it possible for individuals to realize their freedom. To this end, reform may be called for. But the criterion of a successful reform of the state will be the extent to which it increases political stability. A reform will fail by this criterion to the extent that it unleashes further demands that destabilize the state. (See chapters 8 and 9, below.)

moment of loving, and of being loved. In the ideal marriage each of these moments is grounded in the other because one's feelings are also understood as duties. The continuing availability of marriage is thus especially important in the internal dynamics of non-marital conjugal relationships.[43] When such relationships become serious they raise issues of commitment that must be worked out in terms of marriage. Even if some true marriages are never legalized, the issue of marriage is inescapable, especially for those who seek to realize free love according to their own definition – that is, without benefit of the institutional form. In rejecting the hypocrisy of the conventional marriage their lives are often dominated by the Hegelian ideal.

The foregoing suggests that we can restate Hegel's view of the logic of marital love as a metaphor for his entire theory of freedom. Suitably updated, the Hegelian claim is that we do not need to remake the institution of marriage in order to allow for free love. Rather, we understand our problems in conjugal relations through the Idea of marriage, whether we are married or not. This is consistent with acknowledging that some people might be able to realize this Idea without getting married, while others who are nominally married might fail to do so. The Hegelian point is that once you have realized the Idea of marriage, your love is grounded in the institution. This is what we mean when we speak of "working on our marriage," as distinct from being in love. Hegel would have seen such an emotional transformation as a sign of maturity, suggesting that mediated reflexivity has replaced the immediacy of passion in the life of the married couple.

Freedom of mind

Taken as a whole, Hegel's concept of freedom of mind can be seen as an expansion of the argument that marriage is free love. For Hegel freedom of mind, embracing both the knower and the known, is rooted in the claim that some things cannot remain as they are when they are understood, and that other things cannot become as they are until they are understood. Freedom of mind, then, concerns historical development no less than

---

[43] Even if two lovers decide not to get married, they feel unfree if the institution of marriage is not available to them as a facility for expressing their commitment to each other. For this reason some gays now demand the right to get married even though many of the pertinent aspects of marriage can be handled through ordinary contracts.

personal psychology. This is what Hegel means when he says history is the process of mind becoming actual.[44]

In the development of freedom of mind, Hegel is describing a process of mutual transformation of the knower and the known. Both the world and the self must change in order for each to become understandable.[45] Hegel's view of historical and psychological development is powerful, but in the modern world we can no longer share Hegel's sanguine view of world history. Although some defenders of modernization still cling to a view of history that holds that political development leads inevitably to the realization of individual freedom, too many man-made catastrophes have occurred in this century for us to be confident that mankind is transforming both its nature and its world for the better. In this context Hegel's progressive view of history will appear to many as a cynical rationalization of the status quo. Instead of increasingly coming to know what we want as an anticipation of what we can get, and of coming to appreciate what we get in terms of what we want, we find ourselves continuing to make tragic choices.

Twentieth-century thinkers have, therefore, faulted Hegel for his apparent optimism about the relation between the two sides of freedom of mind. Their critique has been based on the underlying insight that there is no necessary connection between what it takes to change the knower, and what it takes to change the known. It may sometimes be the case that knowledge empowers us to change the world,[46] and some changes in the

---

[44] In *The Old Regime and the French Revolution* Tocqueville argued that the French Revolution was not really necessary, since the centralized modern state had already come into being under the monarchy. The Hegelian question is whether the revolution was necessary in order to realize the implicitly modern character of the Old Regime. Could the modern state have been fully developed without the revolutionary moment of realization that this was no longer feudalism? Even though Tocqueville probably believed the contrary, his own account implies that it was necessary for the French Revolution to take place in order for the implicit rationality of the Old Regime to become actual for the citizens of the post-revolutionary state established by Napoleon. (See chapters 5 and 6, below.)

[45] To achieve understanding, the world must be located within the self as knowledge; but the self must also be located in the world to know how it is going to be understood. We can trivialize this by saying that freedom of mind is just a matter of choosing our perspective. But of course the real problem is that we cannot simply choose our perspective. In order to know, we must see the world as a whole, and in order to know that we know, we must know that we are part of the whole that we see. Even in taking a particular point of view, we must also know that we are free.

[46] Science leads to technology.

world may promote greater self-knowledge. But better understanding of the world is not always the same as having more power to transform it, nor does a better understanding of the self necessarily require (or produce) change for the better in the world. In some cases, greater self-knowledge reveals our limitations in the world rather than expanding our opportunities for self-realization.

The effect of the twentieth-century critique is to separate the two sides of the Hegelian picture of freedom – freedom as a change in the knower, and freedom as a change in the known. Hegel believed that these were two aspects of a single concept of freedom – two sides of the same experience. His modern critics tend to think that these are two independent conceptions of freedom: in one conception, freedom is a matter of knowing what you are doing and why; in the other, freedom consists in knowing that what you do is up to you, knowing that the world gives you a choice. Hegel's critics differ about which of these conceptions should be called freedom. They agree, however, in thinking that Hegel's attempt to identify them as moments of the same concept is ideological and dangerous. The cumulative result of the critique of Hegelian idealism is that modern philosophy has moved from the effort to reconcile two moments of the Concept of freedom to the analysis of two competing concepts of freedom – positive and negative.

The twentieth-century debate between positive and negative freedom is especially well-represented in the writings of Stuart Hampshire and Isaiah Berlin.[47] Hampshire, following in the tradition of Spinoza, connects freedom with self-knowledge. His basic idea is that our reasons for acting are inevitably transformed the more we know about the constraints around us: no matter how few our options, he believes, we can always step back and ask what our reasons for acting are to be. According to Hampshire, the free individual recognizes an immediate identity between his actions and his reasons (between what he is doing and why) when he comprehends and accepts the rational necessity under which he acts. As an ideal of self-determination, freedom of mind would then consist in being able to act in the present for the sake of the future, unconflicted by the past.[48] In the

---

[47] See Hampshire, *Freedom of Mind*, *Freedom of the Individual*, and *Thought and Action*; and Berlin, *Four Essays on Liberty* and "'From Hope and Fear Set Free'."

[48] Freedom, according to Hampshire, enables us to act. In some respects achieving this kind of freedom resembles the "method" by which actors are taught to perform in the theater. "Method" acting is self-understanding as self-control. Using the "method," actors are trained to overcome confusions and divisions of mind that relate to past experiences when they were not in their role. The impediments of the past are confronted and removed so that the actor can be sincere and single-minded in his role. (In another version of the "method," more suitable to Berlin's theory of freedom, the actor "gets in touch with" some deep experience of his own

absence of a Hegelian confidence in institutions,[49] Hampshire tells us that freedom of mind will consist in an individual's knowledge that his actions, under any given set of circumstances, are determined by reasons he can embrace wholeheartedly. The free individual's goal is to be able to act with sincerity and single-mindedness, no matter what the circumstances, and this is achieved through a process of self-clarification that overcomes a divided mind.

Isaiah Berlin, following in the tradition of John Stuart Mill, argues that the meaning of freedom should be restricted to the idea that what you do is up to you. Freedom's real limitations, then, lie in the world, and not in the mind. Greater knowledge of the *world* may reveal that our options are fewer than we thought. Such knowledge may help us to choose, but it does not give us choices. Greater knowledge of the *self* may transform the desires of the knower, reconciling him to necessity. But this knowledge is not in itself liberating if the known world does not change. (Berlin insists that the truth does not make you free, unless it happens to be true that you are free.) In the absence of a Hegelian faith in the transformation of the world, the view that freedom consists in self-knowledge may be like a happy tune that slaves can whistle while they work. Real freedom, according to Berlin, consists in the range of available choices that will not be impeded as a result of the actions of others. In Berlin's view anyone who lacks such options is not free, whatever he may think: true freedom consists in correctly knowing, not why we choose, but that we could have chosen otherwise.[50]

---

so that he can play his role more *authentically*.)

The "method" in acting is directly opposed to the view that acting consists of imitating what it would look like to be in character while keeping a clear sense of oneself. Its ideal is, rather, to enable the actor to achieve the state of realizing his character in himself and for himself at the same time. This ideal is perhaps most fully achieved by dancers when they become for themselves what they look like to the audience, instead of having an internal sense of wires and pulleys. (Cf. Trilling, *Sincerity and Authenticity*, and Diderot, *The Paradox of Acting*.)

[49] And Spinoza's rationalist faith in the identity of mind and world.

[50] When Martin Luther said, "Here I stand, I can do no other," he was a free man in Hampshire's sense, but not necessarily in Berlin's. For Luther to be free in Berlin's sense it would not help that he was sincere, that he believed his action to be necessary, or that he was for himself what he was for others. It must rather be argued that he had a real choice, and that he selected the option that allowed him the greatest degree of authentic self-expression. This suggests that a free choice between options is not the arrival at a state of mind in which one is no longer ambivalent about what to do. Rather, freedom of choice requires that one have the option to express oneself authentically – that one's situation be sufficiently

Hampshire and Berlin focus on different parts of Hegel's argument that freedom is a simultaneous transformation in the knower and the known.[51] For Hampshire, greater freedom requires a transformation in the knower that allows the knower to act. For Berlin, greater freedom requires a transformation in the known that indicates real options and possibilities. Hampshire's notion of freedom stresses the experience of freedom for us, the choosers. Berlin takes the other side of the post-Hegelian coin, and focuses on our freedom as we would demand to have it recognized by others. Freedom as Berlin conceives it is not rational self-realization that overcomes divided minds, but rather the presence of options that allow for the authentic expression of our roots, our past, our quirky animal natures — however twisted and divided these may be.

Hampshire and Berlin disagree about the experiences that are most fundamental to freedom, and each implies that the other takes a one-sided point of view. In replying to Berlin, Hampshire could acknowledge that there may be real limits to our possibilities, while insisting that Berlin disregards the way in which our knowledge of our situation can change our conception of ourselves. All knowledge of the world, according to Hampshire, is also to some degree self-knowledge. In replying to Hampshire, Berlin could acknowledge that for many of us freedom has become identical with self-respect, an important value in its own right, while insisting that self-respect might be achieved in many situations in which a person is unfree. Self-respect, according to Berlin, is neither necessary nor sufficient for freedom.

---

indeterminate so that one's action can be seen as the expression of one's nature, and ultimately of oneself.

While Hampshire's view of freedom as sincerity is compatible with rational determinism, Berlin's view of freedom as authenticity is dependent upon the idea that determinism is false. (See Berlin, "Historical Inevitability.") He believes that each of us has an authentic self which can either be expressed or stifled depending on the real options available to us. From a Hegelian perspective Berlin's conception of freedom as authenticity is freedom in itself, or for others: when others regard our free choices as opaque to reason, they impute those choices to the quirks of our authentic selves. A modern social order that allows for freedom in Berlin's sense would tolerate a high level of incoherence and inefficiency if this is the price of allowing for spontaneous self-expression.

[51] Hampshire and Berlin would raise quite different issues about our model Hegelian argument that marriage is free love. For Hampshire the woman's freedom would depend upon whether she could sincerely commit herself in the way that her marriage requires. For Berlin it would depend upon whether the marriage expands or contracts her real options for authentic self-expression.

Both Hampshire and Berlin seek to bring clarity to our discussions of freedom, rescuing them from the kind of Hegelian optimism about institutions that has led to the delusions of this century. Yet, ironically, their opposing views, taken as a complementary pair, recreate the basic structure of Hegel's claim that freedom transforms both the knower and the known. In their respective positive arguments they bring out the force of Hegel's view that freedom is self-realization, and that it is also world-transformation. In their respective critical arguments they reinforce Hegel's point that either account of freedom, taken on its own, is hopelessly one-sided. The full Hegelian view can no longer be identified with that of either philosopher, but the tensions that Hegel sought to reconcile now appear as competing positions that structure the debates within the institution of academic philosophy.

Taken together, Hampshire and Berlin allow us to reconstruct what is left of Hegel's theory of freedom in the aftermath of the modern critique. As described above, their theories of freedom (the best we have) are efforts to eliminate the ideological character of Hegel's theory of freedom of mind by strictly separating the cognitive and institutional aspects of freedom that Hegel endeavored to join. Through this device these theories neatly suppress Hegel's claim that modern freedom is *whatever* makes institutions comprehensible from within. Yet they do not ever really supplant this view: Hampshire does not provide an account of the role of institutional life in his conception of the self; and Berlin does not account for the malleability of the self in his conception of institutions.

If Hegel's view of freedom remains relevant to the basic controversies that drive modern philosophy, then we may also learn something from the arguments of his nineteenth-century critics. Where Hegel had argued that modern freedom consists in freedom of mind, the Left-Hegelian response of writers such as Bauer, Feuerbach, and Stirner was that in modern institutions liberation consists in 'consciousness-raising.' We must now address this view, if we are to avoid mistaking it for Marxism. We will then be able to trace the emergence of Marx's own view from a joint critique of Hegel's tendency to celebrate existing institutions, and the Left-Hegelian wish to transcend them.

3 Liberation as Consciousness-Raising

Opacity and transparency

As we have seen, Hegel's theory of freedom of mind contains two distinct types of self-realization. The first I have described as 'awakenings,' drawing on Hegel's discussion of sleep. Here, realizing oneself to be in a given condition is incompatible with remaining in that condition. The second variant I have described as 'institutionalizations,' drawing on Hegel's discussion of the state. Here, realizing oneself to be in a given condition is necessary in order to be in that condition.

Hegel's nineteenth-century critics attacked this distinction from both the Left and the Right, while continuing to accept self-realization as the goal of freedom. Left-wing critics argued that self-realization is *always* a form of awakening, that freedom is incompatible with institutionalization, that everyday life in institutions is like being asleep. They believed that we are only free in those moments when we wake up and break out of what Blake had called our "mind-forged manacles." Right-wing critics argued just the opposite. For them, freedom is the voluntary internalization of constraint in the apparent form of reason, in which case *any* conscious acceptance of order is enough to make us free. Both sides accepted Hegel's general account of freedom of mind while rejecting his distinction between freedom as awakening and freedom as institutionalization. Each of these critiques could be the basis for objecting to the Hegelian account of marriage as free love, developed in the previous chapter: the radical objection would be that no institutionalized commitment is compatible with free love; the traditionalist objection would be that any marriage that is acceptable to its participants is ipso facto an embodiment of freedom.

These debates bring us, as they brought Marx, to the crux of Hegel's political philosophy – the attempt to account for the opacity of human institutions. Hegel represents the opacity of institutions as necessary to our attainment of self-realization – a process which in his view occurs through understanding how we are understood. As we saw in chapter 2, the characteristic Hegelian mode of argument constantly makes us aware of the difference between what it looks like to feel the way we do and what it feels like to look the way we do. According to Hegel, the demands that we make when we think we are doing what we want will acquire a different significance when we recognize that our knowledge of what we want is rooted in what we are supposed to be doing.

Hegel's need to defend the opacity of institutions implied that they had already become partially transparent. Conservative theories that decried this development were exercises in futility, attempting to close the barn door on modernity after the cow of tradition had already escaped.[1] In a post-revolutionary world, however, uncritical acceptance of traditional authority is impossible to expect, and this made the right-wing attack on Hegel increasingly difficult to sustain.

The left-wing critique was considerably more appealing to the thinkers among whom Marx came of age in the 1840s. These radical intellectuals attacked Hegel's reliance on institutional mediation as a solution to the problems of modernity, arguing that Hegelian philosophy does not really overcome the experience of alienation which motivates it. For those not uncritically immersed in a given way of life, subjectivity could continue to be a problem. It might be experientially difficult, for example, to act as a selfish egoist in the marketplace if one thought this was only justified because it produced the greatest good of all. How should one then feel about oneself when behaving as an egoist? Would the egoism one shows to others appear to oneself to be grounded in a better set of motives that are simply misunderstood *by* others?

Hegel's apparent recognition that our actions have a different significance for others[2] than they do for us suggested to the Left-Hegelians that modern institutions deny us an important source of gratification – the immediate experience of performing actions that have the same meaning for others as for ourselves. This concern with immediacy was the root of the radical criticism of Hegel in Marx's day. The critics felt that Hegel was rationalizing the actual, in the ordinary sense of making excuses for all of the defects in the way things are. His novel excuse, that the existence of these defects is a necessary moment in realizing the objectivity of the actual, could be applied to anything from flaws in the prison system to the persistence of poverty in the marketplace. To his left-wing critics Hegel seemed to be simply showing how, in the modern world, everything had to be as it was in order to be comprehensible.

---

[1] Cf. Edmund Burke, *Reflections on the Revolution in France*, for a similarly futile attempt.
[2] And in themselves.

According to Hegel's critics, the kernel of truth in his view was its emphasis on the role of subjective understanding in maintaining the status quo. Everything for Hegel hangs on the thin thread of how it is understood. "If this is the case," the Left-Hegelians seemed to ask, "why not stop rationalizing the actual? Without our subjective participation, institutions will wither away."

In place of the Hegelian ideal of opacity and mediation, these thinkers held out an ideal of transparency and immediacy. In opaque institutions our intentions are mediated by the 'invisible hand': by trying to do one thing we in fact accomplish another.[3] To become aware of such 'invisible hand' effects we need to rely on social theories about the aggregate effects of individual choice. In what we might call "transparent social relations" there would be no need for theory in this sense, because there would be no difference between what we are trying to do and what we expect to have happen to us as a consequence. In such a world we could produce the good of all by trying to be altruistic, rather than egoistic. Instead of trying to satisfy our own needs by creating needs in others, we would communicate directly − without the mediation of the market − in the hope that others would respond as fellow humans.

This philosophy of radical subjectivity was the Left-Hegelian position. In his very earliest writings Marx saw a certain amount of merit in it[4] but, as we shall see, he soon discarded it. In doing so, he fixed in his mind the discipline of objectivity he had learned from Hegel, while seeing the need to mount his own independent critique of both views.[5] Yet there remained something in Marx which regarded social transparency as an ideal.[6] While such utopian moments became rarer and rarer as his method matured, one

---

[3] For a general discussion of the general form of 'invisible hand' explanations, see Nozick, *Anarchy, State and Utopia*, pp. 18−22.
[4] See, e.g., Marx, "Excerpts from James Mill's *Elements of Political Economy*," written in 1844.
[5] See Marx and Engels, *The Holy Family*, and *The German Ideology*.
[6] "If we assume *man* to be *man*, and his relation to the world to be a human one, then love can be exchanged only for love, trust for trust, and so on. If you wish to enjoy art you must be an artistically educated person; if you wish to exercise influence on other men you must be the sort of person who has a truly stimulating and encouraging effect on others. Each one of your relations to man − and to nature − must be a *particular expression*, corresponding to the object of your will, of your *real individual* life. If you love unrequitedly, i.e. if your love does not call forth love in return, if through the *vital expression* of yourself as a loving person you fail to become a *loved person*, then your love is impotent, it is a misfortune." (Marx, "Economic and Philosophical Manuscripts," p. 379.)

finds passages throughout his works presenting communism as the ideal of a purely transparent world — a world in which not only the state, but theory itself, would wither away since nothing would have to be explained about our situation in order to complete it.[7]

Before developing Marx's own critique of both Hegel and the Left-Hegelians, it is necessary to establish the relevance of Left-Hegelianism to current concerns. This is harder to do than it was with Hegel, since their works do not have the timeless quality of great philosophy. Nevertheless, to the extent that our institutional world remains Hegelian, these thinkers take positions that are still available to us, and which have many counterparts today.[8]

Institutions and social movements

The modern counterparts of Left-Hegelianism — academic survivors of the New Left — characteristically reject the study of established institutions and focus on the genesis of social movements engaged in popular protest. They attack mainstream scholarship for writing history from the point of view of the winners, and thereby rationalizing the outcome. Instead, they write history from "the bottom up," in order to demonstrate that institutions

---

[7] Cf. the account of this in Gerald A. Cohen, "Karl Marx and the Withering Away of Social Science" reprinted in *Karl Marx's Theory of History: A Defence*, appendix I.

[8] In order to convey this, however, we must translate the debates of the 1840s to matters of more topical concern. When the Left-Hegelians wrote, the hot topic was the critique of religion — a subject Marx called in 1844 "the prerequisite of all criticism" (Marx, "A Contribution to the Critique of Hegel's Philosophy of Right" (tr. Livingstone and Benton), p. 243). German theologians had begun to study the relation of the historical Jesus *in himself*, the man who walked in Galilee, to the Christ *for us*. This lent itself to a debate within a Hegelian framework between a Christian humanism, which was a worship of man, and a Christian spiritualism, which glorified the transcendent deity. Since, as we have seen, the idea of incarnation lies at the core of Hegel's thought, the target of this debate was Hegel's thesis that the actualization of Christ was the Idea of God in Man.

For a fine anthology of Left-Hegelian writings see Stepelevich, *The Young Hegelians*. The theological issues addressed in this note are discussed in Schweitzer, *The Search for the Historical Jesus*. For presentations of Left-Hegelian thought on its own terms see the following English-language sources: Hook, *From Hegel to Marx*; Kolakowski, *Main Currents of Marxism*, vol. 1, chs 2–4; Lobkowicz, *Theory and Practice*; McLellan, *The Young Hegelians and Karl Marx* and *Marx Before Marxism*; and see also the symposium, "Feuerbach, Marx and the Left Hegelians."

which are widely accepted as necessary are merely contingent.[9] Their
political analysis begins with a presumption in favor of change, and
regards social stability as the product of a complex strategy of repression.
Since institutional stability is presumed to be illegitimate, New Left studies
of social movements generally take an ambivalent view of the forms of
consciousness that make institutions seem acceptable from within: on the
one hand, human consciousness appears as the product of the spontaneous
impulse to resist domination; on the other, it allows for social co-optation,
making the overt use of institutional coercion less necessary.

Much of the left-wing historiography of social movements today makes
implicit use of Hegel's phenomenology to attack the claims of his logic.
Even while resisting generalization, the historical studies that have emerged
from the New Left rely on the phenomenological insight that consciousness
itself is a product of struggle which requires us to internalize repression by
the other, and that 'raising consciousness' is merely a stage in this dialectic of
resistance and repression. If this is the case, then an institutionalized
liberation movement is virtually a contradiction in terms: liberation consists
of a brief moment of collective spontaneity that transcends the isolation
imposed by consciousness itself.[10]

[9] For paradigmatic studies of "history from the bottom up" see, e.g., Guha,
Elementary Aspects of Peasant Insurgency, and Edward P. Thompson, *The Making
of the English Working Class.* (See also Guha and Spivak (eds), *Selected Subaltern
Studies.*)

Among the leading recent feminist versions of "history from the bottom up" are
the following: Davis, "Women's History in Transition: The European Case";
Kelly-Gadol, "The Social Relations of the Sexes: Methodological Implications of
Women's History" and "Did Women have a Renaissance?"; and Lerner, "Placing
Women in History: Definitions and Challenges."

For an interesting typology of radical historiographies see Robert Gordon,
"Critical Legal Histories."

[10] Perhaps the most explicit statement of the epistemological foundation of New
Left historiography can be found in Ranajit Guha's recent theoretical defenses of
"subaltern studies" where he characterizes all forms of social consciousness as
specifications of the dyadic relation between "domination and resistance." (See
Guha, "Dominance without Hegemony and its Historiography.") For a more elaborate, if idiosyncratic, epistemology of resistance, see the works of Foucault.
Catherine MacKinnon provides a sophisticated theoretical argument for women's
consciousness-raising in "Feminism, Marxism, Method and the State: An Agenda
for Theory."

Francesco Alberoni has offered a sociological theory that attempts to encompass
recent scholarship on the antithesis between social movements and their institutionalization (see Alberoni, *Movement and Institution*).

The main varieties of New Left historical scholarship on social movements are broadly similar to the Left-Hegelian forms of liberation-theory that Marx encountered in the 1840s. I believe that there are essentially three major approaches to the study of liberation as consciousness-raising, and that in these three approaches we can hear the echoes of Bauer, Feuerbach, and Stirner – the main targets of *The German Ideology* and *The Holy Family.*

(1)   The first version of New Left scholarship attacks the tendency of social institutions to operate under the guise of natural necessity to thwart the fulfillment of human desires. Where the mainstream scholar invokes the necessary consequences of institutional logic, the radical scholar describes social institutions as human products in order to show that social outcomes are contingent – that man is capable of negating his fate merely by overcoming the illusions of false objectification. In this variant of left-wing theory social alienation would consist of uncritically identifying with one's particular role – such as that of a woman within the family, or a worker within the factory – and liberation would consist of mentally withdrawing from that role in order to seek recognition for one's universal identity as a person, or perhaps as a citizen.

Using this approach, workers who are alienated can be described as trapped in a "false consciousness" imposed by managers who are themselves compelled to repress universal human feeling because of their complete absorption in their social roles. In contrast, liberated workers would take an instrumental attitude toward their jobs. They would join unions for instance, not to become better workers, but in order to give priority and expression to their personal and political goals.[11]

As applied to the study of social history, this approach suggests that a protest movement remains truly radical only insofar as it asserts universal interests against the system, but that such a movement is easily incorporated when it begins to promote particular interests within the system. A typical narrative shows how leaders first acquire critical consciousness, and then lose it in attempting to achieve mass support by focusing on immediate material demands at the expense of fundamental human values. The radical social historian demonstrates how such a strategy backfires when a movement, which has tapped the popular need for a transcendent alternative to the present order, appears only to be raising limited demands. In the end, he argues, radical movements are defeated by their own pragmatic concessions. (As when workers are organized only to promote the particular interests of their union.)

[11] See, e.g., Blauner, *Alienation and Freedom.*

By reversing the process of objectification in modern institutions, this first strand of intellectual radicalism suggests that consciousness of the alienation imposed by social roles is a way of feeling free. Such an approach to history from the bottom up follows in the footsteps of Bruno Bauer's critique of Hegel by criticizing mainstream institutional history as a form of 'divide and rule' that invades human consciousness itself.[12]

(2) The second variant of intellectual radicalism attacks the tendency of modern institutions to assimilate the particularity of sensuous human experience into the form of a universal ideology. Radical scholars expose this universality as an illusion, resulting in each specific instance from incorporating the perspective of the other as one's own, while simultaneously denying the validity of one's own experience by projecting it onto the other. To these radicals, social alienation consists of role-withdrawal — the inability to identify with one's 'own' point of view — and liberation comes through role-identification.

According to this variant of liberation-theory, alienated workers, for example, might be trapped in an instrumental or an adversary mentality that prevents them from taking pride in their own accomplishments, whereas liberated workers would be able to identify with their roles — perhaps as managers already do — and hence become more "achievement oriented."[13] The radical project would then require that social roles, such as worker and mother, be wrested from alienating institutions, such as the factory and marriage, and redefined in a way that would validate the human experience of performing such roles.

As applied to radical interpretations of social history, this approach suggests that experiences that had previously been regarded as forms of co-optation can be revalidated as the felt reality of the only forms of liberation that were possible under oppressive conditions.[14] The contemporary proto-type of this approach was the rediscovery of the radical potential of

[12] For a striking expression of Bauer's view on the matters discussed in the fore-going paragraphs see Bauer, "The Trumpet of the Last Judgement over Hegel."
[13] See, e.g., McClelland, *The Achieving Society*. Cf. John Goldthorpe, et al., *The Affluent Worker in the Class Structure*, vol. 3. For discussions of female "fear of achievement" see Kundsin (ed.), *Women and Success: Anatomy of Achievement*.
[14] This historiographical impulse appears today in feminists who study sites of domesticity, such as women's sewing circles, as the social locations where women develop and express transfamilial bonds of solidarity. See, e.g., Cott, *The Bonds of Womanhood*; Smith-Rosenberg, "The Female World of Love and Ritual"; Ann Douglas, *The Feminization of American Culture*; Sklar, *Catherine Beecher: A Study in American Domesticity*; and Davis, *Society and Culture in Early Modern France*.

religious revivals and other forms of popular traditionalism.[15] The social historians who celebrate this potential typically argue that such popular movements founder in their quest for a universal appeal. In becoming assimilated to the dominant ideology these movements lose touch with the particular experiences of the people whose lives they are seeking to change.

By reversing the process of false subjectification, this second strand of intellectual radicalism within modern institutions suggests that the alienation of consciousness is a way of feeling free. This approach to history from the bottom up follows in the footsteps of Feuerbach's critique of Hegel by criticizing mainstream institutional history for projecting the homogenizing effect of bureaucratic forms onto human consciousness itself.[16]

(3) The third variety of liberation as consciousness-raising sets the first two against each other. Using the critical arguments of both views, it recognizes that modern institutions incorporate us when we assert our particular interests and assimilate us when we argue against them by invoking universal values. Given this ability of modern institutions to absorb opposition, liberation would consist of a brief moment of choice between two forms of failure. In this view it would be "bad faith" either to identify with one's role or to believe that one can ever transcend it. Liberation would here consist of keeping one's options open and adopting an ironical stance whenever one is called upon to "get involved."[17]

Historians who apply this view to the study of social protest movements tend to argue that, despite the inevitability of failure, brief eruptions of spontaneous freedom are to be respected and even cherished. The critical perspective of these historians serves to remind us that there is an ever-present tension in all social movements between asserting universal interests and serving the needs of the immediate constituency. If the movement asserts universal interests, it runs the risk of being assimilated into the hegemonic ideology of the ruling class; if it serves the needs of the immediate constituency, it risks being incorporated as a particular interest group. Because both possibilities are forms of co-optation, the history of

[15] See, e.g., Edward P. Thompson, *The Making of the English Working Class*, ch. 11, and some of the "liberation theologies" of Latin America.
[16] Where Marx saw religion as *both* the opiate of the people and the cry of the oppressed creature, 'Feuerbachian' feminism sees the social institutions of domesticity as the cry of oppressed creatures who have only to realize they are crying in order to cease to be oppressed.
[17] See Sartre, *Being and Nothingness*, part 4 and conclusion. See also Gerald A. Cohen, "Bourgeois and Proletarians" and "Beliefs and Roles."

the movement itself must be seen as an existential struggle to maintain the liberating potential of the universalist and particularist options, while denying the co-optative reality. The radical historian who follows this paradigm knows that ultimately social movements are disorganized by their failures and deradicalized by their success.[18] While the movement lasts, however, there will be moments of authentic choice and vision that can later be celebrated. In the end the experience of collective defeat results in the glorious autobiographies of individuals – *The Ego and His Own*.[19]

This is the third strand of contemporary radicalism. Against the mainstream view that we must accommodate our choices to institutions it takes the form of insisting that, ultimately, we "own" our lives – that we have only the reality that we make or interpret. Such is the politics of those for whom nothing is too good and nothing good enough; of those who want neither a job that will involve them enough to change them, nor a job in which they cannot get involved; of those for whom the consciousness of alienation is a fact of daily life. As a defense of liberation as the fully ironic consciousness of alienation, this third approach echoes important aspects of Max Stirner's critique of Hegel.

Liberation and consciousness-raising

Having developed Hegel's theory of freedom of mind using the example of marriage, we can illustrate the arguments above by translating the variants of Left-Hegelianism into three versions of the feminism of the 1970s that focused on the radical critique of the family.[20] Each of these versions would take Hegel to task for his thesis that marriage is free love by recognizing the continuing alienation of women within marriage. Each would reject Hegel's thesis with a different version of the claim that, if marriage is not free love, then liberation is consciousness-raising.

In the neo-Hegelian account of marriage put forward in chapter 2, the

[18] Cf. Piven and Cloward, *Poor People's Movements*.

[19] This is the title of Max Stirner's Left-Hegelian defense of individualism.

[20] Although I shall focus mainly on the literature of the 1970s, the phase of feminist thought that concerns me began with the publication of Betty Friedan's *The Feminine Mystique* in 1963, and has extended into the 1980s. Although I do not directly consider those recent developments in feminist theory that are less focused on the family, I suspect that much of this scholarship could be considered a further elaboration of the three basic positions described here. For a survey article on feminist literature that tends to support the broader applicability of at least my first two categories, see Snitow, "Pages from a Gender Diary: Basic Divisions in Feminism."

wife must be able to regard herself as free while being married to someone in particular. Marriage indeed made a difference to the servant woman in my hypothetical example, but that difference might have been between asking for time off so that she could get herself a birthday present, and shopping for a birthday present for herself from him − or between helping him to further his career for his sake, and doing so for her own sake as well. If entering into a neo-Hegelian marriage were sufficient to turn female subservience into an institutionalized version of free love, the only essential difference between these two conditions might be in the way the woman understood how she was understood by the man.

In response to such an account a modern feminist might ask, "Why should a woman marry if the difference between being a wife and being a servant is not in her external reality, but only in her interior point of view toward it?" If the neo-Hegelian is right in concluding that the actuality of marriage requires such a mental transformation on the part of the woman,[21] a Left-Hegelian feminist would argue that such an interpretation of marriage should be read as a critique. This critique would show how the stability of marriage is ultimately dependent upon accepting its ideology. (It might also show that the institution of marriage is patriarchal through and through − depending upon the effect of the ideology of marriage on the attitudes of the man.)

In the abstract, Hegel's logical method might have left room for such a feminist conclusion. Instead of claiming that sexual liberation is institutionalized in marriage, he could have argued that the realization of sexual liberation supersedes marriage in much the way that waking up is both a realization and a supersession of sleep. He could then have contemplated the end of marriage as a form of life. Although Hegel did not make such an argument, neither did he in fact claim that modern marriage is the institutional form in which the meaning of all other social relationships is finally realized. He thought, rather, that marriage derives its modern significance as part of the modern state and economy in which it plays a supporting institutional role.[22]

But to preserve my analogy I want to ignore Hegel's complexities, as his critics also did, and simply look at the various ways in which our three versions of Left-Hegelianism would play themselves out as criticisms of a Hegelian conception of marriage as free love. These criticisms would stress Hegel's emphasis on marriage as a transformation of the knower, rather

[21] See, e.g., Marabel Morgan, *The Total Woman.*
[22] *Hegel's Philosophy of Right* (tr. Knox), part III, esp. pp. 111−16. Cf. Landes, "Hegel's Conception of the Family," and Westphal, "Hegel's Radical Idealism: Family and State as Ethical Communities."

than the known – of the wife rather than the 'relationship' – and suggest that the decision of a woman to marry and remain married is the result of 'lowered expectations'[23] that reconcile her to the actuality of her life.

(1) In participating in our hypothetical debate about marriage, the first of our critical philosophers, Bruno Bauer, might have said that the modern family woman's real problem is role-identification: she is so caught up in her particular sex-roles that she does not see the universal significance of what she is doing. The 'Bauerite' feminist would then describe her alienated life as a series of moves from daughter to wife to mother – with sisterhood as a potentially disruptive inkling of her universal potential. In reflexively making these moves the family woman may never acquire the critical awareness that she is constantly making choices. Within the family structure she would simply be absorbed in what is expected of her without recognizing her power to reject and transcend her particular roles.[24] To the extent that her self-conception is simply what others impose upon her, the 'Bauerite' would say that the family woman suffers from the alienation of her consciousness, and that in order to be liberated she needs to embrace self-conscious alienation. If, however, she withdrew her mental identification with her female roles, she would come to believe that she is not *really* doing all the things the men in her life think she is doing.[25] By taking such a step, the "liberated woman" refuses to relate to men as fathers, husbands, and sons. For her the solution to the problem of being someone in particular, a "woman," is to become someone universal, a "person." Our feminist 'Bauer' would conclude that only by abolishing the family, and the role determination that it implies, can we abolish the particular identities that have given women a degraded sense of themselves.[26]

[23]The phrase recalls Jerry Brown's effort (when Governor of California in the 1970s) to persuade liberals to embrace the moral desirability of economic decline.
[24] The notion that woman's bonds are ultimately her own creation is a feminist parallel to Bauer's actual critique of organized religion. In religion, he argued, purely man-made forces appear as an external necessity set over against man. To say that they are man-made for Bauer was to say that man is capable of negating them; for a feminist to say that women's bonds are "man-made" has even more radical implications.
[25] These implications were developed in feminist autobiographies of the 1970s, and in fiction of that period written from a feminist autobiographical perspective. See, e.g., French, *The Women's Room*; Mary Gordon, *Final Payments*; and Piercy, *Going Down Fast*.
[26] For examples of this variant of radical feminism, see the following works: Firestone, *The Dialectic of Sex*; Atkinson, *Amazon Odyssey*; Robin Morgan (ed.), *Sisterhood is Powerful*; and, more recently, Wittig, "One is not Born a Woman" and "The Category of Sex."

(2)   The second version of the view that liberation is consciousness-raising is Ludwig Feuerbach's. As a participant in our hypothetical debate about marriage and the family,[27] he might argue today that the desirable features a woman attributes to marriage are simply projections of the feminine capacities she radiates. Indeed, his rhetoric is so close to our own that we can easily transpose it without feeling its weight. If he had been writing as a feminist, Feuerbach might well have declared, "The traditional family has become a projection of a woman's own best qualities, which are specifically female, onto others, who are generally male. It is the woman who bears the children and makes the home. She does these things while acting in her specific capacity as a mother and wife — not as an abstract 'person.' Yet her busband is seen by the outside world as the head of the household, a perspective that is ultimately shared by his self-alienated wife. When such a woman looks at her family, she is looking in a mirror while failing to see herself. As a result she denies herself the sense of self-realization that should come from the natural expression of her powers." Speaking more formally, a 'Feuerbachian' feminism would tell us that women have been deluded by the pull of the universal into denying their particular biological reality.[28] They must now repossess their own female

---

[27] Feuerbach himself was an intellectual influence on such advanced thinkers on the 'women's question' as George Eliot, his English translator, and her companion, George Henry Lewes. (See Haight, *George Eliot*.)

[28] Feuerbach might have called this her "species being," if he had not already identified the entire human species with male biology; yet modern feminists should not hold his occasional lapses into male preconceptions too much against him. The historical Feuerbach believed that we need to revalidate human experience as sensuous human history. For him the point of human liberation is not to gain greater power and control but rather to appreciate life as we experience it. Since today these two alternatives are widely regarded as "masculine" and "feminine," Feuerbach's agenda for philosophy could be described as "refeminization" by those who believe in a specifically feminist epistemology. In substance Feuerbach argued that, to be fully natural and fully human, we must become capable of intense gratification of our subjective needs without feeling dominated and controlled by others. He urged us to focus on the joy of being who we are in particular in order to overcome the evils wreaked upon us by the universal standpoint of all previous philosophy. For Feuerbach a "philosophy of the future" would be concerned essentially with validating the passive experiences of sensuous persons who are at present alienated from their own bodies. It would stress the ways in which expressions of human needs would no longer be alienating. The following passages are representative: "The new philosophy bases itself on the *truth of love*, on the *truth of*

consciousness as a genuinely human experience, not something that needs to be made comprehensible to men. Their "liberation" thus depends on becoming comfortable as women. Rather than abstracting the role of parenting from that of mothering, they must reassert the primacy of the natural mother.[29] In doing so they would refeminize the family, making it a woman's domain.[30]

(3)   The third variant of liberation as consciousness-raising is represented by Max Stirner, the author of *The Ego and His Own*. As a precursor of the modern existentialists, Stirner might have argued that today's feminist faces an impossible choice between identifying herself as a woman or as a human being.[31] For a feminist in the mode of Stirner there could never be sufficient and general grounds for making such a choice: some women would feel limited by choosing a particular role with which they must identify fully; others would feel forever thwarted if they were not emotionally absorbed in a role with which they could fully identify; a few, with full ironic awareness, would not want a role with which they have to

---

feeling ... Where there is no love there is no truth ... The new philosophy proceeds from the principle: I am a real and sensuous *being; indeed, the whole of my body is my ego, my being itself ...* [T]he new philosopher thinks *in peace and harmony with the senses ...* [T]he new philosophy *joyfully ...* recognizes the truth of sensuousness: It is *sensuous* philosophy with an *open heart*." (Feuerbach, "Principles of a Philosophy of the Future," in *The Fiery Brook: Selected Writings of Ludwig Feuerbach* (tr. Hanfi), pp. 226−7.)

·   For further developments of Feuerbach's view, see Feuerbach, "The Necessity of a Reform of Philosophy" and "Preliminary Theses on the Reform of Philosophy" in *The Fiery Brook*. For recent perspectives in feminist epistemology see Kristeva, "Women's Time," and the various views represented in Harding and Hintikka (eds), *Discovering Reality: Feminist Perspectives on Epistemology, Metaphysics, Methodology, and Philosophy of Science*, and in Belenky, Clichy, Goldberger and Tarule, *Women's Ways of Knowing*.

[29] See, e.g., Chodorow, *The Reproduction of Mothering*.

[30] There is a large feminist literature that takes this perspective. See, e.g., Daly, *Gyn/Ecology*; Echols, "The New Feminism of Yin and Yang"; Gilligan, *In a Different Voice*; Greer, *Sex and Destiny: The Politics of Human Fertility*; Rich, *Of Women Born* and *On Lies, Secrets and Silence*; Ruddick, "Maternal Thinking"; See also the works of the so-called women's "essentialists" in France: e.g., Cixous, "The Laugh of the Medusa," and Irigaray, "And the One Doesn't Stir Without the Other."

[31] For a critical reconstruction of the stages of recent feminist theory around this impossible choice see Snitow, "Pages from a Gender Diary: Basic Divisions in Feminism."

identify, and would not accept a role with which they could not identify.[32] This last position, which parallels Stirner's own, is the position of some recent feminists who cannot bear any conception of marriage that requires them to embrace their femininity, but who also cannot accept any conception of marital roles that obliges them to withdraw from their femininity.[33] They need constantly to reinterpret the meaning of their lives – indeed the meaning of their gender – because they believe that the real issue for each woman is to choose the basis of her own uniqueness. Rather than categorically embracing or fully repudiating their feminine roles, they seek to become better able to accept responsibility for the particular choices they must make in living their lives.[34]

The politics of defeat

In the previous sections we saw how Bauer, Feuerbach, and Stirner each made one of three moves available to radically minded people within the

[32] A modern-day Stirner might see the women's movement as faced with the cruel irony of perpetually oscillating between our first two variants of liberation as 'consciousness-raising:' in the workplace it must equalize between men and women; yet it must also equalize among women with regard to the choice between traditional and non-traditional roles. The irony is that often one cannot equalize between women and men and still remain neutral between homemakers and career women; yet, if one tries to equalize between traditional and non-traditional women's roles, one will often have to discriminate against working women in relation to men. In facing this irony, existential feminism must make it possible for women to choose, fully and responsibly, when to play traditional or non-traditional roles. (These dilemmas are discussed more fully in chapters 9, 10, and 12, below.)

[33] See, e.g., de Beauvoir, The Second Sex.

[34] Because Stirnerite feminists tend to oscillate between the Bauerite and Feurbachian alternatives, it is difficult to find writers, other than de Beauvoir, who can be placed in my third category without equivocation. Nevertheless, I believe that important elements of the Stirnerite position described above can be found in the following feminist works: Delphy, Close to Home: A Materialist Analysis of Women's Oppression; Dinnerstein, The Mermaid and the Minotaur; Flax, "The Political Unconscious and the Patriarchal Unconscious"; Haraway, "A Manifesto for Cyborgs" and "Situated Knowledges"; Rose, "Women's Work, Women's Knowledge," and Dorothy Smith, "Women's Perspective as a Radical Critique of Sociology." Some aspects of the rhetoric of Monique Wittig also resemble the Stirnerite position: See Wittig, "One is not Born a Woman" and "The Straight Mind." For another treatment of this category of feminist thought see Butler, "Variations on Sex and Gender: Beauvoir, Wittig, and Foucault."

type of modern institutions Hegel described: Bauer spoke for critical transcendence, Feuerbach for sincerity, and Stirner for authenticity. The dialogue among the competing voices implicit in the three-headed monster of Left-Hegelianism is reproduced across the spectrum of the Left today in the discourse between critical theory, cultural romanticism, and existent-ialism.[35] All three of these perspectives characteristically reject a Hegelian optimism that the development of modern institutions creates ever-widening possibilities for individual self-realization. The main variants of modern cultural radicalism see institutional thinking, rather, as a threat and barrier to the development of full human potential, and celebrate the struggle for liberation against an oppression that is implicitly assumed to be an artifact of a Hegelian belief in institutions.[36]

Despite the often extreme rhetoric of Left-Hegelianism, its underlying premise is not a fundamental criticism of Hegel so much as a claim that Hegel did not understand the radical implication of his own theory of freedom of mind. If Hegel's philosophy is basically correct, our institutions can exist only insofar as we believe them to be necessary. Institutional legitimacy is then revealed to be nothing holy and eternal, but rather a fetish that ceases to have power when we stop believing in it.

Left-Hegelianism, as we have seen, essentially consists of the recognition that all institutions hang on the slender thread of acquiescence by the people who are subject to them. From this recognition it follows that people can liberate themselves from the oppressive weight of modern institutions by withdrawing their psychological support from the ideological assumptions on which those institutions are based.[37] A thoroughly Left-Hegelian politics often amounts to the view that marriage, law, and the state are all like malign versions of Tinkerbell. The Left-Hegelian claim that institutions can be changed by changing people's minds is based implicitly on Hegel's view that institutions exist by virtue of how they are understood.

Despite their common Hegelian premises, each of the three paradigms of radical thought discussed in this chapter is based on its own highly general assumptions about the phenomenology of social protest — assumptions

---

[35] See appendix 1. For recent feminist counterparts see Benhabib and Cornell (eds), *Feminism as Critique*.

[36] For a defence of the potential legitimacy of institutional thinking based on some of the features for which it tends to be attacked by Left-Hegelians, see Mary Douglas, *How Institutions Think*.

[37] For example, life in marriage (or the workplace) could be changed by raising the consciousness of those who are oppressed in these relations.

that can serve to explain the collapse, as well as the rise, of social movements. Although the stated objective of many radical scholars is to contribute to the creation of a 'revolutionary' counterculture, each of the three forms of radical scholarship discussed above is also a rehearsal of the experience of defeat – nurturing a conscious acceptance of alienation that presents itself as an alternative to the delusions of mainstream social science.

(1) The Bauerite, as we have seen, attributes the eventual defeat of radical protest movements to the assertion of particular interests at the expense of universal principles. According to this scenario of failure, a movement that abandons its universal aspirations will be incorporated by the state as a special interest. Radical social history in this first version reconciles us to such an outcome by lamenting our continuing inability to affirm the transcendence of ideals under modern conditions. The Bauerite scholar can 'let go' of his revolutionary attachments by recognizing that there is something deeply alienating about a movement that requires its adherents to compromise the ideals for which they fight.

(2) The Feuerbachian attributes the ultimate collapse of a radical protest movement to the abandonment of its own particular point of view in favor of the (relatively) universal values of the dominant culture. According to this scenario of failure, the movement sells out its future potential as the basis of a counter-hegemonic culture in order to assimilate its demands into the cultural mainstream. Radical social history in this second mode reconciles us to the defeat of revolutionary hopes by lamenting our inability under modern conditions to be sustained by the immediacy of our associations. The Feuerbachian scholar can 'let go' of his revolutionary attachments by recognizing that there is something deeply alienating about a struggle built on ideas that ultimately disempower the people who wage it by negating the value of their life experience.

(3) The Stirnerite attributes the inevitable demise of radical protest movements to the long-term impossibility of avoiding both incorporation and assimilation. According to this scenario of failure, no radical social movements can ultimately succeed in maintaining an alternative universal vision of the whole that is also rooted in particular needs and interests. Social history in this third mode reconciles us to the inevitability of defeat by arguing that radical social movements will be eventually co-opted no matter what strategy of survival they choose. Yet the Stirnerite scholar need not ever 'let go' of his revolutionary attachments once he recognizes that there is something deeply alienating in regarding oneself as *bound* – either by universal ideals or through sentiments based on particular circumstance.

These are the main scenarios of protest within our radical discourse today. Each can be invoked by the protagonists of any given social movement to provide an analysis distinguishing that movement from the failures that preceded it. Movements wishing to avoid the dangers of incorporation sketched in our first scenario would claim to have regained the ability to express transcendent values; those wishing to avoid the dangers of assimilation sketched in our second scenario would claim to be based on a renewed capacity for associational solidarity. A movement self-consciously responding to the third scenario would presumably deny that it has any pretence of building lasting oppositional institutions, preferring instead to provide a short-term outlet for the expression of social frustrations and utopian hopes. Whichever of these scenarios is invoked by a particular protest movement, the alternative scenarios are available to the critical social historian attempting to describe what went wrong in a way that places new events within the mythologies of our radical past. The frequent shifting between these three scenarios as applied to any given movement reflects the political oscillation between different dialectics of hope and betrayal within the common left tradition of protest and defeat.[38]

Hegel's revenge

If the foregoing account of the politics of defeat provides a reasonably accurate description of the academic Left in recent decades, then we, like Marx, should ask what such an array of scholarship signifies about the political world it is attempting to comprehend. Of course many of the positions we have ascribed to Bauer, Feuerbach, and Stirner seem in harmony with views expressed by Marx himself in his early writings. As a young radical intellectual, Marx shared their strong sense that Hegel did not fully capture the subjective experience of living within modern institutions. Yet Marx also saw that the theories of Left-Hegelians were simply rehearsals for the next defeat. Eventually, Marx recognized the pathology of leftist thought in his time as Hegel's revenge on those who had not fully faced and exorcised the ghost of the politics of subjectivity.

[38] Some American radicals have been able to shift effortlessly between the paradigms described above in analyzing the political struggles over the welfare state. Social Security, for example, generally appears in their analysis as a political defeat for the Left, except when cutbacks are threatened, when it appears as a political victory worth preserving. See the discussion of Piven and Cloward in chapter 6, below.

In focusing on the role of subjectivity within Hegelian institutions, each of the Left-Hegelian thinkers shared Hegel's emphasis on the importance of self-realization. But instead of viewing contemporary institutions as a means of self-realization, they claimed that the very need for institutional mediation makes self-realization impossible. For the Left-Hegelians self-realization required a return to unmediated experience, and they believed that this could occur only through liberating consciousness from its dependence on institutional frameworks that promise to explain how we are free within them.[39] Marx repeatedly pointed out that such ideas could not be detached from the Hegelian framework they claimed to have transcended.[40]

In the course of criticizing the Left-Hegelians, Marx learned a further lesson from Hegel about the role of ideas within the situation that they comprehend: when we look at ideas objectively they appear as part of the subject who thinks them, even though subjectively they seem to interpolate the thinking mind into the world it conceptualizes. Put more concisely, Marx's point was that we are part of the situation we see, and that by seeing it we make the situation part of us. This argument implicitly repeated Hegel's own logical critique of the phenomenological method on which Left-Hegelianism had relied, revealing the objective futility of thinking that we can subjectively reject the institutions in which we live. In *The German Ideology* Marx exposes this futility with occasionally devastating sarcasm by repeatedly noting that the German ideologists conceive a self that wants no part of the situation of which it remains a part. Marx saw that the Left-Hegelian, in identifying only with what he thinks, denies the objective significance of his thinking it, thereby ignoring Hegel's lesson that in the modern world what we think must be regarded as part of the institutional framework through which we think it.

In response to the Left-Hegelians, Marx repeatedly insists that the politics of mental withdrawal has an objective significance that is ultimately indistinguishable from the kind of self-realization Hegel says we can find through the politics of participation: by rejecting the world in one's mind

---

[39] For a discussion of relatively recent forms of politics as therapy see Jacoby, "The Politics of Subjectivity." For an alternative interpretation of Marx's critique of Left-Hegelianism see Fleischmann, "The Role of the Individual in Pre-Revolutionary Society: Stirner, Marx, and Hegel."

[40] See Marx and Engels, *The German Ideology* (pp. 23–31) for various passages such as the following (on p. 29): "[N]ot one of these modern critics has even attempted a comprehensive criticism of the Hegelian system ... – each extracts one side of the Hegelian system and turns this against the whole system as well as against the sides extracted by the others." For further discussion, see appendix 1, below.

one becomes better able to continue living in it.[41] In the politics of withdrawal there is only a change in the knower, making him more acceptable to himself, instead of the change that Left-Hegelians hoped for in both the knower and the known.[42] Marx saw the Left-Hegelian radical as the *reductio ad absurdum* of the politics of reconciliation. As his politics goes on within him, the world goes on without him. All that he ultimately changes is his mind.

Marx's mature method abandons the politics of reconciliation that ties both Right and Left to the existing order. Instead, he sought to ground his politics in the forces through which the social world is changing itself.[43] Marx recognized, however, that he had to do so from within the world that was being transformed. He therefore rooted his political analysis in the critique of the ideologies on which the politics of reconciliation was based. We are now in a position to take up Marx's general approach to the critique of ideology.

[41] For further discussion of this point see appendix 2, below.

[42] In rejecting Hegel's tendency to glorify institutions through false objectification, Hegel's radical critics sought in effect to repudiate institutions by means of false subjectification. Cf. Lukács, *History and Class Consciousness.*

[43] As he would say in "The Eighteenth Brumaire," "Men make their own history, but not of their own free will; not under circumstances they themselves have chosen." (Marx, "The Eighteenth Brumaire," p. 146.) For discussions of Marx's political materialism see below, chapters 4, 9, and especially 10.

4   From Alienation to Ideology

Marx and Hegel

As a young intellectual, Marx was far more successful than his contemporaries on the Left[1] in building a radical politics out of the critique of Hegelian thought. In general, Marx agreed with Hegel that political wisdom begins with the distinction between forms of self-realization that reconcile us to the way things are and those that require us to abolish the present order and transform it into something altogether different. Yet Marx differed with Hegel's view of where to make this distinction, rejecting in particular Hegel's thesis that the liberal market state was the inevitable institutional realization of the different moments of the concept of freedom.

In feeling the power of Hegel's theory of the state, the young Marx increasingly directed his anger at the institutions that could make themselves understandable in the way Hegel described. Indeed, some of his most important insights came at the points where he was angry because of the truth of the theory that he was criticizing. At such points he began to move from commentary to critique, not just of the theory, but of the social institutions it describes and of the reasons its description holds true.[2] Although these insights remained crude and undeveloped during his youth, they continued to inform Marx's writing and analysis long after he had

[1] A possible exception was Arnold Ruge, whose relation to the young Marx I have not begun to address in this work. Ruge's ideas are represented in "Hegel's 'Philosophy of Right' and the Politics of our Times" and "A Self-Critique of Liberalism."

[2] Because Marx constantly tested his reactions to real problems by interrogating the theories that make these problems seem necessary, his substantive conclusions are often couched in the critique of those theories. For further elaborations and illustrations of this point see the preface and chapter 1, below (esp. n. 39), and chapters 7, 8, 10, and 11, above.

abandoned the study of Hegel.[3] In the present chapter we will try to extract the permanent lessons Marx derived from his study of Hegel, and explain their broader significance.

The philosopher and the world

For Hegel, all problems are merely instances of the general problem of *comprehensibility*. The power of a Hegelian explanation of anything whatever lies in showing that it must be as it is in order to be understandable. In giving such an explanation the Hegelian philosopher directly addresses the problems of the person who seeks to realize himself in the process of understanding the world. According to Marx, however, this person is none other than the Hegelian philosopher himself, whose fundamental problem, as a philosopher, lies in the need to better understand the necessity of the problems with which he deals.[4] In ignoring his own peculiarity, "The *philosopher*, himself an abstract form of alienated man, sets himself up as the *measure* of the alienated world."[5]

Marx here suggests that, despite its apparent generality, Hegel's philosophy focuses on a problem that is most acute for those who work mainly with ideas: the feeling of alienation that arises from the experience of being misunderstood.[6] Such a feeling of alienation can indeed diminish

---

[3] My analysis in this chapter builds on aspects of a number of alternative accounts of Hegel's influence on Marx. See, e.g., Hyppolite, "Marx and Philosophy" and "On the Structure and Philosophical Presuppositions of Marx's *Capital*", and Althusser, *For Marx*.

[4] Marx, "Critique of Hegel's Dialectic and General Philosophy" (tr. Livingstone and Benton), pp. 384–491.

[5] Marx, "Critique of Hegel's Dialectic and General Philosophy" (tr. Bottomore), p. 200.

[6] "The whole *history of alienation*, and of the retraction of alienation, is, therefore, only the *history of the production* of abstract thought ... *Estrangement*, which thus forms the real interest of this alienation and of the supersession of this alienation, is the opposition of *in itself* and *for itself*, of *consciousness* and *self-consciousness*, of *object* and *subject*, i.e. the opposition in thought itself between abstract thought and sensible reality ... All other contradictions and movements are merely the *appearance*, the *cloak*, the *exoteric* form of these two opposites which are alone important and which constitute the *significance* of the other, profane contradictions. It is not the fact that the human being *objectifies* himself *inhumanly*, in opposition to himself, but that he *objectifies* himself by *distinction* from and in *opposition* to abstract thought, which constitutes alienation as it exists and as it has to be transcended." (Ibid., pp. 200–1.)

through a Hegelian process of reconciliation to the actual. The need to overcome alienation in Hegel's sense might be felt, for example, by a bureaucrat who is passed over for promotion. Had he not applied for the promotion he might be satisfied in his present job, but now that he has not been chosen he finds his own freedom of choice oppressive. For him the appropriate resolution might be to better understand how he is perceived by the institution in which he works: the better he understands his world, the more he is reconciled to how he will be understood.[7]

Marx noticed, however, that Hegelian alienation is not the only problem of unfreedom that *some* people feel. Some people would continue to feel unfree, not because the world is incomprehensible, but because of how they understand it to be.[8] The issue for them is not to understand the world in a way that will allow for greater self-realization, but, rather, to change it.[9] Consider, for example, the difference between the ordinary bureaucrat who could be reconciled to a negative promotion decision by

---

[7] Sometimes the bureaucracy will need to reform itself in order to become more understandable, but often it is enough for it merely to improve its communications.

[8] Marx argues that although Hegel is "well ahead of his time," his "genuine criticism," especially in later works such as the *Philosophy of Right*, is marred by an "uncritical positivism and equally uncritical idealism." Because of this defect Hegel continues to portray the human reality of alienation in relation to wealth, religion, etc., as though the only difficulty consisted of the abstract relation of consciousness to self-consciousness. According to Marx, phenomenological opposition is thus a form of "criticism which has not attained self-clarity but in so far as it grasps the *estrangement* of man − even though man appears only in the form of minds − *all* the elements of criticism are concealed within it, and often *prepared* and *worked out* in a way that goes far beyond Hegel's own point of view." ("Critique of Hegel's Dialectic and General Philosophy" (tr. Livingstone and Benton), pp. 385−6.)

[9] "*Religious* suffering is at one and the same time the *expression* of real suffering and a protest against real suffering ... The abolition of religion as the *illusory* happiness of the people is the demand for their *real* happiness. To call on them to give up their illusions about their conditions is to *call on them to give up a condition that requires illusions* ... Criticism has plucked the imaginary flowers on the chain not in order that man shall continue to bear that chain without fantasy or consolation but so that he shall throw off the chain and pluck the living flower." (Marx, "A Contribution to the Critique of Hegel's *Philosophy of Right*: Introduction" (tr. Livingstone and Benton), p. 244.)

Elsewhere, Marx comments: "The philosophers have only *interpreted* the world, in various ways; the point, however, is to *change* it." (Marx, "Theses on Feuerbach," XI.)

understanding better how the bureaucracy sees him, and a minority bureaucrat who might become outraged by understanding how the bureaucracy sees him. (The latter might only be reconciled to a promotion process that had an affirmative action component.) Hegel's philosophy as a way of understanding the world does not preclude changing it, but he clearly suggests that the only philosophically respectable reasons for changing the world are to make it more understandable.

In reading and transcribing Hegel, Marx began to wonder whether there was more than Hegel thought to the difference between self-realizations that supersede a form of life, and those that institutionalize it. Might there be a fundamental difference between the *social* positions of those who need only to understand the world in order to live acceptably within it, and those who would need to change it for their concrete problems of unfreedom to be resolved?[10] In moving beyond Hegel, Marx sought to define "objective" differences between those forms of discontent that merely express a general alienation and those that are not reconcilable with the existing order.[11] He thus began his search for specific combinations of identities and issues the political expression of which would increase, rather than diminish, the level of antagonism in society. This search is the germ of Marx's *critique* of Hegel's theory of alienation − a theory that is often mistaken for Marxism by bourgeois radicals.

Marx concluded from his early study of Hegel that, even if alienation is a universal description of the human problem, overcoming alienation is not the universal solution. By the mid-1840s he had come to see that the radical attack on alienation in its Hegelian form is a political luxury, expressing the desire to be reconciled to the world in the form of a complaint.[12] In acknowledging this, however, Marx did not rule out the possibility of a disciplined radicalism that takes account of Hegel's insight into the objective significance of our political posturings. The beginning of political discipline for a bourgeois radical, according to Marx, is to dis-

---

[10] See Marx, "A Contribution to the Critique of Hegel's *Philosophy of Right*: Introduction" (tr. Livingstone and Benton), pp. 252−7. (See also Marx, "Theses on Feuerbach" and Marx and Engels, *The German Ideology*.) For a brief autobiographical description of this period in Marx's thought, see his introduction to *The Critique of Political Economy*, written in 1858.

[11] What is the difference between the causes of unhappiness that call for reconciliation and those that call for confrontation? I suggested in the introduction, above, that for radical intellectuals this question calls for both social analysis and self-analysis.

[12] See Marx and Engels, *The German Ideology*, pp. 23−30.

tinguish between those problems that fit Hegel's abstract account of alienation, and those that do not.[13]

Before continuing, we can summarize the first major tenet of Marx's method as follows:

The problem of alienation is not the only problem of unfreedom, nor are the theories necessary for overcoming alienation sufficient to reconcile everyone to life in the modern world.

Objectivity

In his critical reconstruction of Hegel, Marx stresses that Hegel is always concerned with how knowledge constitutes its object — how our cognitive need for objectivity invariably determines the nature of the object itself. Hegel's general strategy for coping with the problem of objectivity is to show that *some* particularity of content is necessary to our experience of objectification as such, even when he does not explain why objectification has this or that particular content. If things are not as we would like them, this for Hegel is simply another way of realizing their externality — that they are not mere projections of our wishes.[14]

This strategy recurs nearly everywhere in Hegel's thought, whether he uses the phenomenological or the logical method, and moving outside of his texts we can see that his general form of argument has many concrete applications. If our scientific theories prove to be false, Hegel would say that this is just another way of realizing the objectivity of the external world. (Science is not simply a projection of our own predictions.)[15] If

---

[13] Failing to achieve such reconciliation at the personal level, the radical may find himself in the position of the free love advocate whose sexual radicalism is merely a subjective orientation toward the stability of marriage as an institution. By rejecting marriage in his mind, the free spirit becomes reconciled to the continuing existence of marriage in the world, without which his own life-style would lose its significance. His 'sexual politics' will thus express his alienation, without putting him in fundamental antagonism to the way things are.

[14] For Hegel, the task of philosophy is to reconcile us to our problems by showing that their ultimate source — the experience of alienation — is also the precondition for all knowledge. As we saw in chapter 2, his philosophy works by bringing objectivity back to intersubjectivity, thereby showing that the recalcitrance of the external world to our wishes is really a way of understanding our own subjectivity as it appears to others, and that the apparent abrasion between our inner and outer lives is necessary for us to develop objective knowledge of our own subjectivity.

what happens to us in jail does not feel like punishment, this simply enables us to realize that legal punishment is not whatever we may imagine, but rather an objective fact to which we must be reconciled. If university requirements do not appear to have educational value, we must recognize that this is because education too has its objective moment.

Marx believed that this strategy of argument obscured Hegel's real insights into the specific characteristics of the objects that we experience ourselves to have in the world, and from which we distinguish ourselves in developing our particular self-consciousness. For Hegel, as we have seen, it was "not the *particular* character of the object but its *objective* character which constitutes the offence."[16] Marx in contrast was interested in the kind of subject we must act as if we were in order to deal with the specific objects we confront in the world.

> *Man* is directly a *natural being* ... [T]he *objects* of his drives exist outside him as *objects* independent of him; but these objects are objects of his *need*, essential objects, indispensable to the exercise and confirmation of his essential powers ... To *be* objective ... to have object, nature and sense outside oneself ... to be oneself object, nature and sense for a third person is one and the same thing ... A being which does not have its nature outside itself is not a natural being and plays no part in the system of nature. A being which has no object outside itself is not an objective being. A being which is not itself an object for a third being has no ... objective relationships and its existence is not objective.[17]

Whereas Hegel sees the general problem of "objectification" as loss of object, Marx sees the "objective" condition of men as a reflection of the material objects they create through their labor. While implicitly acknowledging that there may be a general philosophical problem about objectivity as such, Marx saw much of what Hegel said as a reflection of a more specific problem about the character of the objects from which individuals are alienated — a problem that can be addressed only "through the cooperation of mankind and as a result of history."[18] For Marx the real

---

[15] As suggested above, a Hegelian philosophy of science equates the objectivity of the external world with the intersubjectivity of researchers. The potential falsifiability of theory by data is then a necessary condition of having reproducible experiments performed by different members of the scientific community. (Cf. Popper, *The Logic of Scientific Discovery*.)

[16] Marx, "Critique of Hegel's Dialectic and General Philosophy" (tr. Livingstone and Benton), p. 391.

[17] Ibid., pp. 389–90.

[18] Ibid., p. 386.

problem posed by our experiences of a world of objects is not objectification in general,[19] but rather our specific relations to the objects with which we are dealing[20] – a problem that is not automatically overcome by recognizing that we must perceive them *as* objects in order to achieve greater self-knowledge.[21] For some of us, at least, the problem will lie in the kinds of objects they are – and in how we must identify ourselves in order to deal with them.[22]

Instead of bringing everything back to the philosophical contradiction between objectivity and subjectivity, the general problem of the embodied mind, Marx concluded that we should focus on the existence of both objective and subjective contradictions in our concrete experiences.[23] Is

[19] This point was first stressed, I believe, by Jean Hyppolite in "Alienation and Objectification," esp. pp. 81–6.

[20] "Hunger is the acknowledged need of my body for an *object* which exists outside itself and which is indispensable to its integration and to the expression of its essential nature." (Marx, "Critique of Hegel's Dialectic and General Philosophy" (tr. Livingstone and Benton), p. 390.)

[21] "It is entirely to be expected that a living, natural being equipped and endowed with objective ... powers should have *real* natural *objects* ... and that its self-alienation should take the form of the establishment of a *real*, objective world ... as something *external* to it, a world which does not belong to its being and which overpowers it. There is nothing incomprehensible or mysterious about that. It would only be mysterious if the contrary were true ... An objective being acts objectively, and it would not act objectively if objectivity were not an inherent part of its essential nature. It creates and establishes only objects because it is established by objects ... [I]ts *objective* product simply confirms its *objective* activity." (Ibid., pp. 388–9.)

[22] For a series of illustrations of this point see Marx's section on "Money" in the "Economic and Philosophical Manuscripts," pp. 375–9.

In a provocative article Nathan Rotenstreich suggests that Marx's critique of Hegel on alienation and objectivity secularized a mystical strand of Christianity in which the experience of "standing outside oneself" could have the redemptive implications that Augustine attached to "self-alienation." (See Rotenstreich, "On the Ecstatic Sources of the Concept of Alienation" and, more generally, *Basic Problems of Marx's Philosophy*.)

[23] Marx believed that Hegel was right in thinking that our problems are rooted in what parts of our experience we internalize and externalize, but wrong in thinking that there is a basic problem at the level of the general experience of alienation itself (which was for Marx a valuable human capacity). According to Marx, our problems arise rather at the level of the particular content of the consciousness and self-consciousness we distinguish. See appendix I, below, and Marx, "Critique of Hegel's Dialectic and General Philosophy" (tr. Livingstone and Benton), e.g. p. 386.

there an objective contradiction in being the person you are understood to be by others? Is there a subjective contradiction in your motives if you have the kinds of objects that you understand as your world? If there are both types of contradiction, what are the relations and disparities between them? Such questions were to guide Marx's lifelong reading of the political economists, whom he first approached during his period of intensive Hegelian study.[24]

We can now summarize the second major tenet of Marx's analytical method as follows:

Instead of focusing on a single contradiction between subject and object, we should analyze the specific contradictions that appear on the sides of both subjectivity and objectivity.

Alienation and ideology

Marx's third methodological conclusion sets the stage for his mature work by superseding the view of alienation shared by the theories of both Hegel and his left-wing critics.

According to Hegel, theory is necessary in order to fill the gap between how we understand ourselves and how we are understood. Theology is one example of a theory that performs such a function; economics is another insofar as it explains our relation to material things through the relation between our self-interest and the needs of others. To the extent that a partial gap remains, Hegel believed that it would be filled for some by feelings of political alienation and withdrawal, for others by a "philosophy of right" that overcomes such feelings. He argued that when our theories finally make us feel at home in a world of others, alienation would be overcome and the struggles for recognition that characterize "history" as we know it would also come to an end.[25]

---

[24] We shall see in part III that Marx's mature critique of political economy is grounded in the analysis of the subjective contradictions in what we must regard as our needs and motives in order to participate in the market, and of the objective contradictions in the ways in which we must understand ourselves to be perceived in market relations. For an admittedly preliminary approach to some of these questions see, also, Hyppolite, "On the Structure and Philosophical Presuppositions of Marx's *Capital*."

[25] As we saw in chapter 2, Hegel called this final form of theory "absolute knowledge." Absolute knowledge would consist of theories that can account for

Marx believed, as we have seen, that our real problems — those that call for theory — arise out of the specific relations between the kind of subject one is and the kinds of objects one has.[26] Although his approach incorporates the Hegelian insight that theory is often a necessary part of the social practice that it comprehends, Marx saw the self-confirming need for theory within a form of life as a symptom of a specific social pathology, indicating the ways in which that form of life is radically incomplete. Marx's new agenda was to analyze that pathology by looking directly at specific theories as they function within the reality they interpret.

Instead of studying the general problem of alienation of which *all* theories are symptoms, Marx was now free to study specific theories as symptoms of the particular problems in the world that give rise to such theories. His specific critiques of religion, politics, and economics only infrequently described theory as an effort to overcome alienation as such, and were concerned more typically with how a particular theory would account for its role as part of the world it views.

From (around) 1845 on, the direct concern with alienation played a diminishing role in Marx's thought, as he came to understand that Hegel's concept of alienation marks the space that *theory* fills within a form of life. In an implicit sense, Marx's final criticism of Hegel was reflected in his decision to replace Hegel's use of "alienation" with the term "ideology."

---

their role *within* the social practices they purport to be *about*, allowing us to see the world as a whole, while still knowing that we are part of the world we see. For a description of "absolute knowledge" as the "end" of the struggles over recognition and identity that characterize "history," see Kojève, *Introduction to the Reading of Hegel*, ch. 6.

[26] In a Marxian critique of Augustinian Christianity, the Hegelian contradiction between subjectivity and objectivity would be replaced by an analysis of the objective and subjective contradictions in the Christian's experience of God. Marx might have argued, for example, that on the subjective side Augustinian theology represses a real contradiction in how the Christian must understand himself in order to comprehend the difference between how he is perceived by man and by God. In order to identify with God's will the Christian must first become capable of accepting God's forgiveness for his sins — of recognizing that God's love is undeserved. But how can he both accept God's love and maintain his self-respect without having a contradictory perspective on his own motives as he acts in the world? "Religion is indeed the self-consciousness and self-esteem of a man who has not yet won through to himself, or who has already lost himself again ... The criticism of religion is therefore in *embryo* the *criticism of that vale of tears* of which religion is the *halo*." (Marx, "A Contribution to the Critique of Hegel's *Philosophy of Right*: Introduction" (tr. Livingstone and Benton), p. 244.)

Henceforward, he would be concerned to discover what real problems a specific theory reflects beyond overcoming the alienation of the theorist.[27]

Before further elaborating Marx's approach to ideological criticism, we can usefully summarize the third major tenet of his method:

We must drop our Hegelian concern for the alienation of the theorist, and instead focus directly on the critique of theories as ideologies that are part of the institutional framework they encompass.

Wholes and parts

What is the relation between Marx's critique of Hegel's view of alienation, and Hegel's own rejection of his early phenomenological method? As we saw in chapter 2, Hegel's phenomenology is limited to being descriptive rather than explanatory because the key distinction between subjectivity and objectivity can always be reversed. Is Marx simply arguing in his critique of ideology that Hegel's logic does not avoid the fatal flaw that infected Hegel's phenomenology? Marx's commentary on Hegel in his unpublished study notes is so rudimentary and undeveloped that it is difficult to answer for certain. At times Marx even seems to be giving a phenomenological critique of Hegel's logic, ignoring the development of Hegel's own thought.[28] But with the caveat that we have here little more than promising student notes, I think it is possible to see the embryo of Marx's mature view.

The mature Marx would acknowledge Hegel's ability to notice the subjective and objective contradictions in our experience, but would criticize Hegel on the ground that he developed the logical method to avoid facing up to this insight. For Marx, the flaw in Hegel's logical method is that it remains a way of redeeming the phenomenological enterprise of reconciling subjectivity and objectivity by transposing the problem of alienation onto institutions. Marx saw that for Hegel the philosophical significance of social institutions lies in their ability to realize themselves in the ideologies they articulate.

For Marx, the critique of institutional ideologies would replace Hegel's logic as the proper response to the defects of phenomenology. In his mature analysis of ideology Marx was not primarily concerned with the

---

[27] The foregoing discussion suggests a "break" in Marx's thought, but not of the sort that Althusser describes in *For Marx*.

[28] See, e.g., Marx, *Economic and Philosophical Manuscripts*, pp. 348–58, and "Excerpts from James Mill's *Elements of Political Economy*," pp. 259ff.

descriptive truth or falsity of social theories, but rather with their self-confirming properties as part of the institutional world they interpret.[29] According to Marx, successful ideologies legitimate institutional reality by distinguishing between what needs to be explained and what needs to be justified. In doing so they suppress the recognition of contradictions in the objects we are understood to be and in the subjective motives with which we identify. This means that the objective and subjective contradictions in our experience of the social and material world reappear in ideology as problems of explanation and justification: the objective contradictions are transposed as contradictions in what the theory takes to be an *explanation* within its domain; the subjective contradictions are transposed as contradictions in what the theory takes to be a *justification*.[30]

In the ideology of liberal capitalism, for instance, the theory of political economy *explains* behavior which may in turn be *justified* by a theory of morality, whether utilitarian or Kantian. In this sense the market ideology would appear to have two parts — economics and morality — each with its own domain. Yet these parts of liberal ideology can also separately encompass the whole domain — providing a critical perspective on each other as we come to see morality from an economic point of view and economics from a moral point of view. In a manner characteristic of ideologies, the explanatory theories of the economist contains implicit justifications and the justificatory theories of the moralist contains implicit explanations.

A concise illustration of the foregoing point occurs in a well-known passage from his early writings in which Marx describes how the spheres of economics and morality separate and converge in the experience of prostitution, seen as both a specific phenomenon and a general feature of life in markets:

> I might ask the political economist: am I obeying economic laws if I make money by prostituting my body ... His answer will be: your acts do not contravene my laws, but you should find out what Cousin Morality and Cousin Religion have to say about it ... But who should I believe, then? The morality of political economy is *gain*, labour and thrift, sobriety; — and yet

[29] In its mature form, Marx's method of ideological criticism was centrally concerned with the role that a totalizing interpretation of an institution plays within the institution it interprets. For subsequent history of the concept of totality in the Marxist tradition see Jay, *Marxism and Totality*.
[30] These points will be developed further in the discussion of recent theories of democracy in chapter 9.

political economy promises to satisfy my needs. The political economy of morality is the wealth of good conscience, of virtue, etc. But how can I be virtuous if I do not exist? And how can I have a good conscience if I am not conscious of anything. It is inherent in the very nature of estrangement [read "ideology" after 1845] that each sphere imposes upon me a different and contrary standard: one standard for morality, one for political economy, and so on. This is because each of them is ... is centred upon one particular area of estranged essential activity; each is related in an estranged way to the other.[31]

The distinction that Marx here draws between morality and economics can be replicated within both morality and economics. In the domain of morality, utilitarian ethics can represent the "economic" side — except of course when utilitarianism stands for the general good against the various private rights that operate in the market. In the domain of economics we have already seen in the previous two chapters that the theory of the "invisible hand" has a "moral" side — allowing the businessman to justify his behavior by explaining the market and to explain his behavior by justifying the market.[32]

Throughout part III we shall see that Marx uses this style of argument to constantly suggest that each of the elements that the economist tries to connect as part of a single system already reflects the others as a part of itself, and that each does so in a potentially contradictory way.[33]

We can now summarize the fourth major tenet of Marx's method as follows:

The focus on ideology shifts debate from the relations between subject and object to the relations between wholes and parts: in ideologies competing pictures of the whole characteristically appear as parts of each other.

[31] Marx, "Economic and Philosophical Manuscripts" (written in 1844), p. 362. In commenting on Chevalier's critique of Ricardian political economy from the perspective of morality, Marx continues: "The relationship of political economy to morality is either an arbitrary and contingent one ... or it is *essential* ... Moreover, the opposition between political economy and morality is only an *apparent* one. It is both an opposition and not an opposition." (Ibid., p. 363.)
[32] Cf. the treatment of this topic in *Hegel's Philosophy of Right*, (tr. Knox) esp. in the sections on "Intention and Welfare" and "The System of Needs."
[33] For further discussion of this critique of political economy see appendix 3, below.

Materialism

Although Marx learned from Hegel that how people understand their situation plays an important role in making that situation what it is, Marx also believed that theory brings a mental completion to a situation that is changing people in ways they do not fully understand. His critique of ideology thus had a double goal: on the one hand he sought to determine how our situation is being transformed by virtue of the way it is being understood; on the other hand he was concerned with what our subjective experience leads us to deny about the process of objective transformation to which we are reacting.

From the very beginning of *The German Ideology*, Marx and Engels repudiated the radical focus on alienated consciousness by asserting that man is not merely able to desire objects, but also to produce the *means* of getting what he desires. Tools are new objects that are the means of transforming other things into objects of desire. As such, tools themselves become independent objects of desire. In producing tools, man simultaneously begins to produce new needs that go beyond his biology.[34]

To Marx it followed that human history has an independent development on the objective side of Hegel's picture. This meant that the error of the German ideologists was not only that they misunderstood the significance of what they were saying as part of the situation about which they were saying it — this much is merely Hegel's revenge — but that they also failed to recognize that the objective significance of what they were saying (and thinking) is constantly in the process of being transformed. While they went ahead thinking as they liked, they and their fellow humans were behaving in ways that created new needs, and that thereby changed the objective significance of their thought. Marx believed that in the final analysis it is on the objective side of the Hegelian picture that the real transformation occurs.[35]

---

[34] In writing *The German Ideology*, however, Marx and Engels make what seems to be a slip of the pen. At one point they say that production of the means of satisfying needs is the "first historical act" — i.e., that the production of tools gives man a history. Yet in the following paragraph they say that the "first historical act" is the production of new needs that are themselves man-made, and social rather than biological in character. (See Marx and Engels, *The German Ideology*, p. 42.) While this might simply be a mistake attributable to the fact that Marx and Engels never edited and published this manuscript, I believe that for Marx the production of the means of satisfying needs, and the production of needs that are transformed in the course of being satisfied, are the same "first" historical act.

[35] For a fuller discussion of the metaphysical basis of Marx's materialism, see chapter 10, below.

We would be mistaken, then, to think that the thesis of *The German Ideology* is that our ideas are mere reactive reflexes within an historical reality that goes on at a material level. Although Marx's choice of language might sometimes suggest such an interpretation,[36] when he speaks of a material reality that is transforming itself he generally recognizes that it is doing so through our actions and as a consequence of our beliefs, but not necessarily in accordance with them. To a significant extent the objective world of which he speaks is the one we objectify in the theories by which we interpret ourselves − a social world that includes the behavior of individuals who are actively and consciously interpreting that behavior in the process of engaging in it. Essentially, *The German Ideology* is about the relationship between one's beliefs and one's participation in the objective processes by which the world is transforming itself, whether one is aware of it or not. Here, as in his later works, Marx argues that the material interrelations of family, market, and state are changing historically, and that in every cycle their reproduction is affected by this cumulative change.[37]

[36] I have in mind such unfortunate, and often-quoted, passages in *The German Ideology* as the following: "Conceiving, thinking, the mental intercourse of men, appear at this stage as the direct efflux of the material behaviour ... If in all ideology men and their circumstances appear upside-down as in a *camera obscura*, this phenomenon arises just as much from their historical life-process as the inversion of objects on the retina does from their physical life process." (Marx and Engels, *The German Ideology*, p. 36)

But cf., "[The] mode of production must not be considered simply as being the reproduction of the physical existence of individuals. Rather, it is a definite form of expressing their life, a definite *mode of life* on their part. As individuals express their life, so they are. (Ibid., p. 31)

[37] The development of *The German Ideology* went on from the analysis of basic philosophical premises in Bauer, in Feuerbach, and in Stirner, to a detailed examination of what Stirner had to say about the alienation of people in the economy. In the latter section Marx and Engels show that most of Stirner's descriptions were generalizations of the experience of a property-owning intellectual, the value of whose property depended upon specific social conditions to which he was oblivious.

In examining Stirner's view in detail, Marx and Engels were concerned with the specificity of the historical contradictions of which Stirner became conscious in the form of existential libertarianism. Marx's critique began with careful analysis of the conceptual framework Stirner used to describe the experience of being in a market, and continued with an effort to identify what was changing in the objective conditions of Germany to make Stirner's situation appear to him as it did. To the extent that Marx was successful in these arguments, he was able to reaffirm his criticism of radicals who merely adopt a posture that makes the world as it is more acceptable. For an argument that anticipates some of Marx's critique of Stirner, see Hess, "The Recent Philosophers."

Marx's fifth major methodological conclusion may be summarized as follows:

The social whole in which we live is undergoing a process of material transformation, partly as a result of how it is understood, but not necessarily in accordance with that understanding.

With the addition of the materialist thesis we can now consider how a Marxist analysis of social protest movements would differ from the Left-Hegelian paradigms we considered in the previous chapter. We shall see in part III[38] that instead of focusing on a perpetual struggle against domination (whether economic, racial, sexual, and so forth),[39] Marxian materialism asks the crucial questions of what times these are, and how one institutional structure is reflected in, and itself reflects, the development of another. In studying feminist movements, for example, Marxian materialism would critically analyze the relations between the family, state, and market as they evolve historically.[40] In doing so it would ask why each of these institutions appears to be internally repressive when it does, and in which of them the weakness or the strength of the social order lies at a given moment:[41] when, historically, has women's oppression in the family been

[38] See esp. chapters 10 and 12.

[39] Some writers, such as Foucault, see the forms of domination as highly specific. In contrast the manifestoes that announced the most recent wave of feminist consciousness-raising describe the family, the state, and capitalism as instances of the general phenomenon of "patriarchy" that is nearly universal in human history. (See, e.g., "The SCUM Manifesto," and "The Redstocking Manifesto," reprinted in Robin Morgan (ed.), *Sisterhood is Powerful*, pp. 577–83 and 598–601. Cf. Hartsock, *Money, Sex, and Power: Toward a Feminist Historical Materialism*.)

[40] Much of radical theory sees the struggle against domination always and everywhere. This represents all history as a recurrent struggle for liberation that remains constant even under changing conditions. Because this process of liberation is largely in one's mind it must be repeated by each individual on each day of each relationship. It follows that one never really needs to know where one stands historically. This is, perhaps, fortunate for feminism, since the theory of patriarchal domination offers no counterpart to the concept of accumulation in Marx's mature theory of social change. To many radical feminists the time is always now, and the struggle for liberation is everywhere the same. In the ever-present struggle against patriarchal domination the general stances of Bauer, Feuerbach, and Stirner are always relevant and mutually corrective: together, they describe the recurrent cycle of feminist politics and of feminist lives. (On the latter point cf. two works by Betty Friedan: *The Feminine Mystique* and *The Second Stage*.)

[41] Cf. Marx and Engels, *The German Ideology*, pp. 179–83, 193–7.

supported by discrimination in the work force, and when has the opposite been true? when has the state reinforced, or offset, the oppression of women in the family, or at work?[42] In raising such questions a feminist informed by Marxism would know better than to think that consciousness-raising is itself revolutionary.[43] She would demand to know whether specific tactics of subjective withdrawal and heightened disaffection would strengthen or weaken the family, the state, or capitalism, respectively.[44]

The practitioner of Marxian analysis as described in this chapter would not be satisfied with interpreting popular protest in whatever form as a response to class oppression, or to oppression simply speaking. Instead of relying on the phenomenology of liberation to explain why political protest occurs at all, Marxian materialism is directly concerned with the variable relation between the subjective forms that political action takes, and its objective social base. Marx's approach should therefore be useful in deciding which protest movements should be supported, and on which issues. Even if we continue to believe that ultimately socialism will not come about unless the working class is organized around socialist ideas, a Marxist political analysis should help in deciding the hard cases of when and whether to support progressive demands not embraced by the working class, or demands of the working class that are not yet ideologically progressive. Indeed, what makes such cases hard is that we cannot always trust our intuitions about which ideas and social forces are progressive to begin with.

In my view Marx's materialism did not allow him to claim a moral or observational standpoint for assessing historical change from outside the framework of existing institutions, but rather remained a part of his critique of ideology.[45] Marx's constant goal in ideological criticism was to produce an institutional analysis that would locate the issues and identities through which transformation was possible from within. The conclusion

---

[42] But note that some similar questions are raised (if not answered) in an essentially Left-Hegelian framework by Frances Olsen. See Olsen, "The Family and the Market: A Study in the Ideology of Legal Reform."

[43] As Marx says, "This demand to change consciousness amounts to a demand to interpret reality in another way, i.e., to recognise it by means of another interpretation." Marx and Engels, *The German Ideology*, p. 30.

[44] As a feminist, her own political position would be based largely on which of these institutional responses would be better for women, both immediately and in the long term.

[45] This claim is further elaborated in chapter 10, below.

of such an analysis is not yet another theory of history, but a political argument suited to our own place and time.[46]

By allowing us to stand squarely within politics as we find it, Marx's method is largely an attempt to understand the ways in which the values that can lead to social change are already embedded in our institutions, albeit in contradictory ways. This takes us beyond a politics that consists only of imagining how the world might look (or be) if only people thought about it differently. The Marxian analysis of ideology enables us to start always from where we are, and to see that what we already think is part of the significance of being who we are.

Marxism and relativism

It should be clear from the foregoing comments that Marxian analysis does not necessarily yield political arguments that can be universally valid at all times and places. Yet the fact that Marx stands in opposition to universalism in ethics and politics does not necessarily make him subject to the criticism most often raised against moral relativism,[47] which charges that without the requirement of universality morality becomes a matter of subjective opinion. To critics of moral relativism, admitting that the applicable standards of morality may depend on who we are commits us to the view that genuine moral argument will be impossible among those who do not already share our attitudes and values. The view that morality is a matter of subjective preference is regarded by many philosophers as a cardinal vice in contemporary moral thought. I believe, however, that Marx successfully resists the inference from relativism to subjectivism, and with it the principal objection to moral relativism.

If Marxism stands against universalism in ethics, it stands even more strongly against subjectivism. In the context of Marx's comprehensive view of ideology these two positions are complementary: Marx's argument

[46] Of course Marx had a theory of history, but it did not derive from his critique of ideology. For an illuminating discussion of this theory — contrasting it with Hegel's — see Gerald A. Cohen, *Karl Marx's Theory of History: A Defence*. For discussion of the role of historical analysis in Marxian political rhetoric see chapters 5, 6, and 12, below.

[47] The view that historically grounded moral arguments must be relativistic has been raised again by Ronald Dworkin in his critique of Michael Walzer's *Spheres of Justice*. See Dworkin, "To Each His Own" and "'Spheres of Justice': An Exchange."

against universalism in ethics shows that the moral significance of a given judgement is historically contingent on who one is in a given situation; his argument against subjectivism shows how historically valid moral judgements can be grounded in the normative contradictions that are already embedded in an institutional structure. Taken together, these arguments demonstrate that moral claims are ultimately historical, and that historical analysis can have genuine moral force.[48]

Marx's entire method of analysis is then a way of interrogating and criticizing our subjective intuitions by locating their significance within a structure of institutions. Far from suggesting that morality is whatever we happen to think it is, the Marxian critique of ideology allows us to *make* arguments about the moral significance of who we are in a given situation. To the extent that such arguments are possible, the historical relativity of morals loses its sting.[49]

Stripped of its tie to subjectivism, moral relativism is no longer objectionable *per se*. The possibility of moral argument can be preserved, even as the moral relevance of one's particular location becomes, increasingly, its focus. Marxian political analysis can, then, allow us to reopen the "who/whom" questions from which moral philosophers have taught us to abstract in the name of Kantian universalism. These are the questions of who has the standing to make what arguments, against whom, and under what historical conditions.[50]

The ethical claim we can make for Marx's method is that it differs from two forms of critique for which it is often mistaken. The first may be termed a liberal or transcendental critique and depends upon acceptance of a universal moral value or principle by which a given form of life might stand condemned. The second may be termed an Enlightenment or skeptical

---

[48] For an interesting quasi-Hegelian argument about the role of moral principles in institutional analysis see Dworkin, *Law's Empire*. See also chapters 9 and 12, below.

[49] Cf. Bernard Williams, *Ethics and the Limits of Philosophy*, and Nagel, *The View from Nowhere*.

[50] In the *German Ideology* Marx and Engels argued against the neo-Kantian impulse to ground moral argument in a presuppositionless philosophy. They insisted, rather, that we begin with a study of man as an historically grounded social being. (See Marx and Engels, *The German Ideology*, p. 31.) Drawing on the points above we can now advance their argument by focusing on the contradictions in what a historically given set of institutions represents *as* moral. Far from denying the importance of ethics in politics, this approach would provide ethical arguments with a new grounding rooted in the forces that are changing our social structure from within.

critique. Those who engage in the latter form of critique give a convincing interpretation of a form of life that could not be accepted by those who live within it, thereby calling the values of participants into question without necessarily committing the critic to alternative values.

Unfortunately, most commentators have cast Marx's critique of ideology into one of these two molds. Some argue that its moral force depends upon its demonstration that capitalism violates universal norms of justice, equality, or freedom. Without this unstated assumption, they say, Marx's arguments would be merely descriptive. Other commentators argue that Marx's critical method shows that the survival of democratic capitalism is historically contingent on factors that could not be acknowledged by those who accept the system as justified. Without this unstated assumption, they say, Marx's analysis would not provide a critical perspective on the legitimating values of capitalism itself.[51]

Neither of these interpretations properly captures the moral force that Marx intended for his method of ideological criticism. In a provocative recent book[52] the philosopher Bernard Williams examines the range of moral attitudes available to those who accept a critique of a given way of life. He entertains only two possibilities. The first is that accepting the critique will reduce one's tolerance of the form of life it condemns. Such an attitude might today be appropriate to an Afrikaner who rejects apartheid as a violation of universal human rights. The second possibility is more complicated. Here, accepting the critique may merely distance one from the form of life the critique rejects. Such an attitude might be appropriate to someone who has grown away from a family religion or from a cultural tradition which has continuing value to the people who practice it, but which fails to satisfy those who take a special pride in the coherence or universality of their beliefs.[53] While the critic may feel that a given form of life is no longer acceptable once it has been seen to rest on contingent beliefs, any appropriate anger associated with such a criticism may be only a temporary effect of the guilt of separation. Eventually the critique may lead to an enlightened tolerance of a form of life to which the critic can never return as an insider, but which he may eventually be able to visit and even enjoy. If Williams has identified the only options, then a Marxian

[51] See, e.g., the conflicting positions represented in Marshall Cohen et al. (eds), *Marx, Justice, and History*. See also Allen Buchanan, *Marx and Justice*.

[52] Bernard Williams, *Ethics and the Limits of Philosophy*, esp. ch. 9.

[53] For a challenge to the "coercive" view of philosophical argument as imposing intellectual consistency, see Nozick, *Philosophical Explanations*, introduction. For reflections on necessitarianism in social theory see Unger, *Politics*, esp. part I, *False Necessity*.

critique would justify only two possible attitudes toward capitalist democracies: we must either reject capitalism in the name of the transcendent values of socialist justice, or we must live in capitalism as resident aliens once our initial disillusionment has been replaced by tolerance. Marx would have repudiated both of these attitudes, however, and rightly so.

Marx believed that his critique of capitalist democracies would justify in workers a moral attitude of unavoidable confrontation with established institutions – a possibility Williams does not consider. By focusing directly on the question of political identity, he was centrally concerned with the moral relevance of the positions we already occupy in a social order that we cannot escape except in our imaginations. Marxian moral criticism does not rely on values outside of capitalist democracy, nor does it distance us mentally from the system in which we will continue to live. The conclusions of Marxian analysis require us, rather, to address our form of life on its own terms.

Theory and practice

Through his early critique of Hegel and the Left-Hegelians, Marx developed the rudiments of a method for assessing how arguments *about* our institutions are functioning *within* them. This method does not itself add to our existing repertoire of such ideals as equality or freedom, but rather directs our attention to the way in which these ideals already enter alternately into the justification and explanation of the impact of our different institutions on each other, and to the ways in which they already function alternately as explanatory models and moral norms in our political discourse. When a new political demand is made for equality, Marxian analysis allows us to see it, not merely as a utopian projection, but also as a dialectical reversal of what needs to be explained and what needs to be justified about the impact of two or more institutional spheres upon each other. In developing this framework of analysis Marx distinguished himself from the liberals, socialists, and conservatives of his day – and of ours.

For Marx, the characteristic illusion of liberalism is that our politics is what we think it is – indeed, that our politics is whatever we think. Marx argues, rather, that our politics is also something that we *have* – that what we *think* is part of it, but does not exhaust it. Marxism thus provides, at a personal level, a way of interrogating the role of our political beliefs within our politics and, at an institutional level, a way of interrogating the role of social science and political theory within the state: what gap or lack in our politics is filled by our political beliefs? what gap or lack in the modern state reflects the need for theory?

Marxism, as I see it, is not just another theory of socialism. Unlike most other proponents of socialism, Marx had a method of analysis that gave him insight into the ideological meaning of revolutionary politics in non-revolutionary situations, and into the meaning of being a socialist under capitalism. He recognized that political theories, no matter how radical their intent, can have a perverse practical effect on those who hold them. This effect occurs when the perspective that theories give us on our institutions, as though seen from the outside, makes us increasingly unable to learn from the complexities of how our institutions treat us from within. (We thus come to accept the fact that we are unhappy under capitalism by understanding that we are, after all, socialists.) Although Marx himself was a socialist − as were many in his day − he was not a utopian. His socialism was based on a disciplined approach to political analysis that would not allow him to abstract from the historically given situation to imagine some alternative world in which he could act more transparently to promote his convictions.

In criticizing other socialists, however, Marx did not take the cynical position − common to enlightened conservatives − that, whatever we may think, what we do will only strengthen the existing institutional order. As we have seen, he came close to such a view when he argued that the romantic Left's conscious rejection of the status quo amounts to little more than practical accommodation by means of psychological withdrawal. Nevertheless, his intent was not to give aid and comfort to the political establishment, but rather to provide a cautionary discipline to revolutionary politics. The source of this discipline was the Hegelian lesson that the persistence of modern institutions − depending, as it does, on our subjective participation − requires them to reproduce the kinds of problems that they are capable of resolving. Through his early critique of ideology, however, Marx also attacked Hegel's failure to distinguish adequately between those problems through which existing institutions strengthen themselves, and those problems through which institutions are weakened and ultimately transformed.

Marx's distinctive approach to politics consisted in an effort to find an underlying distinction between the conflicts that support a political order, and those that can threaten or transform it. By addressing the role that our political consciousness, and even our political opposition, plays in co-opting us, Marx's technique of ideological criticism attempted to identify the limits on the capacity of the political order to institutionalize conflict. Marx believed that the results of such an analysis could guide certain political movements in attempting to undermine the state by playing upon the ways in which the state attempts to undermine them. If this characterization of Marx's enterprise is correct, the conclusion of a Marxian analysis of the role of theory within politics cannot be another theory. A Marxian conclusion must rather link specific arguments to particular social identities by showing how such a linkage could transform the social order from within.[54]

In sum, Marx's analysis of ideology begins with Hegel's insight that modern politics is about the role of subjectivity within modern institutions, but it goes on to reject the forms of political subjectivism that would seem to follow from this. For Marx the focus of political analysis was on how the institutional ideologies of modern states simultaneously organize our understanding of the world and our understanding of ourselves. As we have seen, our institutions operate largely through their ability to structure from within the kinds of claims that we can make about them. They distinguish between what needs to be justified and what needs to be explained, between what counts as a justification, and what as an explanation. Marx's basic data were the ways that our multiple institutions actively define their relation to each other through a repertoire of explanatory and normative principles that allow us to view each institution simultaneously from the inside out and from the outside in.

Marx's critique of ideology directs our attention to the multiple forms in which modern politics represents our institutions, not as the embodiment of some inevitable natural plan, but as the contingent reflection of our interests and beliefs. Through ideology these institutions make our lives within them appear to be simultaneously transparent and opaque, allowing us to live in a contingent set of determinate social relations by seeing in their particularity the meaning and content of our subjective freedom to choose our point of view.

The two major ideologies that Marx studied throughout his life were democratic theory and market theory. In the course of these studies he elaborated and refined the method he sketched in his early critique of Hegel and the Left-Hegelians. The subjects of democracy and markets shall concern us in the remainder of this book. In part II we shall begin with Marx's analysis of the revolutionary potential of democratic theory in the modern state.

---

[54] This view of the relation of political analysis to political argument follows the view of the unity of theory and practice that Marx sketched in his *Theses on Feuerbach*.

Part II
The Critical Theory of Democracy

5 The Revolutionary Mystique

Marxism and democracy

Marx's attitude toward democracy has seemed to many commentators at best confusing, and at worst unprincipled. In "The Eighteenth Brumaire" he began by presenting the initial demand for wider suffrage as potentially revolutionary, and ended by showing how the subsequent extension of suffrage was instead co-optative. Throughout his extensive correspondence he suggests that socialists are made by fighting for political democracy and undone by settling for it.[1]

The world-wide controversy over Marx's legacy today turns largely on its ambiguous relation to democracy. By exposing democratic procedures as a tool of the bourgeoisie, Marx seems to lay the groundwork for abandoning democracy in the name of revolutionary goals, leading many critics to see his thought as a major threat to democratic values. Yet Marx's defenders can respond that his critique of bourgeois institutions is itself grounded in democratic theory. By invoking democratic ideas against the institutions that claim to embody them, Marx often implied that true democracy would require (or produce) a new, and revolutionary, organization of society.

This debate hinges for both sides on Marx's treatment of democracy as an ideology. Marx's critics argue that he thereby stressed the instrumental role of democracy in legitimating existing institutions. His defenders claim that rather he pointed to democracy's status as a transcendent ideal through which existing institutions can be criticized. Both sides presuppose that Marxism is to be ultimately judged by whether his critique of ideology is compatible with a commitment to democratic political values (or, perhaps,

---

[1] For an elegant treatment of subsequent developments in the relationship between socialism and democracy see Przeworski, "Social Democracy as an Historical Phenomenon."

to any political values at all). This, I believe, is a misguided approach to the relation between political values and ideological criticism.

In part II we shall see that Marx's real contribution to democratic thought is an elaboration of the more complex view of ideology developed in part I. Marx would later write that, after completing *The German Ideology*, he and Engels abandoned their study of philosophy to the "gnawing criticism of the mice"[2] to focus more directly on their underlying concern with politics and economics. In doing so, however, Marx continued to develop the insights he gained from his critique of Hegel and the Left-Hegelians, drawing on his abstract critique of the politics of subjectivity to participate in the ongoing struggle over the meaning of democracy in the modern world. Part II will show how Marx's joint critique of Jacobin and anti-Jacobin democratic thought[3] both parallels and develops the joint critique of Hegel and the Left-Hegelians discussed in part I.

* * * *

The ambivalence in Marx's view of democracy arises out of a tension between the procedural and substantive aspects of democratic theory. Procedurally, democratic theory is concerned with who decides political questions: the principle of "majority rule" determines what part of society should rule the others in the event of disagreement. The substantive aspect of democratic theory is concerned with the appropriate grounds of political decisions: the principle of "political equality" purports to be a standard for agreement about which of two competing visions of the whole is a better expression of intrinsically democratic values. The implicit tension between these two fundamentals of democracy, political equality and majority rule, has had a formative influence on the development of socialist thought, setting the conflicting terms in which both utopian socialists and social democrats have tried to use democratic institutions to promote a more egalitarian social order.

The main current of American socialist thought has been based on the principle of political equality, sometimes to the exclusion of majority rule.

---

[2] See Marx, *A Contribution to the Critique of Political Economy*, preface, p. 22.
[3] To an international audience the most familiar exponents of these two points of view are Thomas Paine and Alexis de Tocqueville. See, e.g., Paine, *The Rights of Man*, and Tocqueville, *The Old Regime and the French Revolution*. A brief and useful account of the Jacobins and Jacobinism in their proper French context has recently become available in Furet and Ozouf (eds), *A Critical Dictionary of the French Revolution*, pp. 704–14.

In the United States political history has been conventionally interpreted by liberals and socialists alike to be an effort by majorities to use state power to oppress minorities. There has thus been no great confidence that an American socialism would be compatible with majority rule. In consequence, American socialists have tended to be secessionist rather than confrontational — seeking the right to become socialists at their own expense, and as examples, rather than by expropriating the expropriators. These socialists typically assert the right to pursue their socialist vision as a distinctive political identity rooted most often in the immigrant experience, or in the personal taste for social experimentation. They thus invoke the ideas of democratic pluralism to defend their existence as an ideological community,[4] demanding political toleration, if not respect, from the majority for their implicitly utopian ideas. One answer to Sombart's query, "Why is there no socialism in America?" is that socialist utopians have been cut off from the revolutionary implications of the idea of majority rule in democratic thought.

In contrast the main current of European socialist thought has been firmly wedded to majority rule, sometimes at the expense of political equality. European political history has been conventionally interpreted by liberals and socialists alike as an effort by minorities to use their control of state power to oppress majorities. This, as we shall see, gave rise to the expectation that the political dictatorship of the majority would result in social transformation.[5] Socialist liberation could then consist of the takeover of the state by a permanent majority that would not need the illusion of official neutrality between social groups to legitimate its interests, and that might eventually dispense with the coercive uses of the state altogether.[6] Proceeding on the somewhat utopian assumption that the unequal power of groups in society was an artifact of the power of the state, European social democrats have typically argued that democracy as majority rule would supersede pluralism and the consequent need to equalize among social groups. A partial answer to more recent questions about the failure of parliamentary socialism[7] is that social democrats have been cut off from the equalizing idea of democratic pluralism.

---

[4] For a powerful theoretical defense of socialism as democratic pluralism, written outside of the American context, see Buber, *Paths in Utopia*.

[5] This argument is especially striking in Paine, *The Rights of Man*.

[6] For a discussion of these ideas see Spitz, *Majority Rule*. Cf. Offe, "Legitimation Through Majority Rule?"

[7] See, e.g., Miliband, *Parliamentary Socialism*, ch. 10, "The Sickness of Labourism" and Nairn, "The Nature of the Labor Party." For later thoughts on these subjects see Miliband, *Capitalist Democracy in Britain*, and Nairn, *The Break-Up of Britain*.

Although Marx began his career as a Jacobin socialist in the European tradition, his originality as a political thinker lay in his method for analyzing the objective role of socialist and mass democratic movements within the context of liberal pluralism. For Marx the first task of class analysis was to identify the real work of politics that goes into maintaining the relationship between the way in which society is organized for purposes of majority rule and the way in which it is organized for purposes of political equality.

Political equality and majority rule

Marx was not, however, the first to analyze the class basis of democratic values, such as majority rule and political equality. Long before Marx, Aristotle argued in general terms that the part of society that rules will inevitably dictate the ruling ideals, and that democratic values are largely an expression of the class consciousness of the ruling majority. He observed that equality often appears as the substantive value promoted by democracy because the demand for equality typically expresses the interests of the majority which rules, but acknowledged that democracy was not necessarily tied to egalitarian ideals — other values might be advanced by a majority that lived off a poor and exploited minority. Since Aristotle, many political philosophers have described the connection between the procedural and substantive values of democracy as a sometimes delicate relationship between majority rule and political equality, mediated by class interest and cultural tradition.[8]

Rousseau was the first major political theorist to identify a basic tension between these two fundamental democratic ideas in any political community that remains divided between rulers and ruled. He justified majority rule as a realization of the substantive value of political equality as a common good for the whole community;[9] yet Rousseau also saw that, as a procedure, majority rule merely determines which part of society may govern the others in its own interest. If citizens participate in democratic decisions based on their particular interests, either as individuals or as members of groups, Rousseau argued that their votes will simply reflect those interests rather than their differing perspectives on a common good. Taking men as they are, he concluded that adherence to democratic procedures would not produce substantively democratic results.[10]

[8] See *The Politics*, bks 4−6, and the apocryphal *Constitution of Athens*.
[9] See Rousseau, *The Social Contract* and *Discourse on the Origins of Inequality*. Much of what immediately follows is an exposition of *The Social Contract*.

To resolve this tension Rousseau attempted to forge a new conceptual link between the two aspects of democracy. In doing so, however, he had to reject the idea that democratic procedures must uncritically aggregate the preferences of men as we find them. For Rousseau everything depends rather on how citizens identify themselves at the moment of democratic participation. He argued that the procedures of collective self-government would produce substantively democratic results only if all those affected by a decision could participate in making it, and if each participant were solely concerned with determining what is in the common interest of all in their capacity as equal citizens. Citizens, so conceived, would be heard to disagree only in their view of what the common answer to the common question will be. In settling *such* disagreements, the procedure of using a majority vote to decide political questions would not amount to majority rule. Rather, the outcome of the vote would be convincing evidence to everyone of what the public interest, the "General Will," really is.

Rousseau concluded that to govern ourselves as democratic "citizens" we must overcome the narrower interests and identities that divide us as "men." He argued optimistically that our attachments to the bonds of self-interest and group division are not part of human nature, but rather socially conditioned responses to the threat of domination. Without such a threat, Rousseau believed that democracy could liberate us from the vice of preferring private advantage to public equality. As democratic citizens we could learn to value civility and equality as intrinsic goods. Ideally, personal autonomy and collective control could then be achieved simultaneously insofar as we would each be obeying only those laws that we had rationally given to ourselves.

The Rousseauian synthesis of collective self-government and the public interest is not only a utopian ideal but also an analytical tool for understanding politics as we find it. The method of analysis suggested by the theory of the General Will filters out the distorting effects of individualism and pluralism in public choice, thereby providing a definition of the public interest even in situations where the moral liberation of citizens has not yet been achieved.[11]

As an analytic, Rousseauian democracy allows us to put the issue of substance and procedure in its essentially modern form. Rousseau clearly

[10] Plato made a similar criticism of majority rule, but never really entertained the possibility that it might be a means of arriving at the public good. See esp. Plato, *Gorgias* and *The Republic*.

[11] See Barry, "The Public Interest."

believed that formally democratic procedures would be *sufficient* to produce substantively democratic outcomes if individuals formulated their preferences in terms of democratic values, and not otherwise. It is less clear whether he believed that formally democratic procedures are *necessary* to achieve democratic results.

There is ample basis for denying that Rousseau was committed to the intrinsic value of democratic procedures. He clearly thought that democratic procedures alone would not reveal the public interest in the absence of the necessary transformation of man's social nature which good laws themselves might bring about. The state, he argued notoriously, may therefore "force us to be free," repressing our particular wills as men in the name of our common interest as citizens so that the substantive value of democratic equality could ultimately prevail. Rousseau apparently believed that such a path may be legitimately pursued both by a "legislator" in making law and by a "magistrate" in enforcing it, provided that the law itself is something that free and equal citizens *could have* chosen as their "true" will.[12]

Yet it is equally possible to argue on solid Rousseauian grounds that adherence to democratic procedures is a necessary condition for reaching substantively democratic results. Rousseau clearly believed that neither the legislator nor the magistrate is more likely to be right about the public interest than anyone else, even assuming he is asking the right question. Assuming that no one could correctly identify the public interest without undergoing the transformative experience of democratic participation, Rousseau's theory would seem to require that formally democratic procedures be maintained so that conversion to substantive democratic values can take place, undistorted by the illegitimate effort of rulers to impose their own particular will on the people.

The ghost of Rousseau

Since the Second World War, both the detractors and the defenders of Marxism have been largely concerned with the relevance of Rousseau's attack on individualism and pluralism to the actually existing political systems in the East and the West. Critics of the "totalitarian" regimes in the East have taken them at their word to be "Marxist." The standard critique of "Marxist totalitarianism," however, focuses mainly on the Rousseauian rationale for curtailing democratic procedures in order to repress individuality and group diversity — arguing that, instead of taking

[12] Rousseau, *The Social Contract*, ch. 7.

men as they are, "totalitarian democracies" force men to be free.[13] During the same period Marxist critics of Western "democracies" have attacked the claims of those regimes to represent the public interest. In doing so they revive the Rousseauian objection to taking men as they are by representing them as individuals or as members of particular groups. Thus divided, democratic citizens are particularly susceptible to defining their political interests in ways that assume, rather than challenge, a continuing system of social control. The left-wing critics of liberal pluralism argue that collective decisions made in the common interest would allow consideration of alternatives that are democratic in substance as well as in form — and that would thus make way for a transformation in social relations.

In both of these arguments Marxism supplies a link, implicit in Rousseau, between political democracy and social revolution. "People's democracies" in the East are criticized for relying on Marxism to falsely assume that a social revolution has occurred; "liberal democracies" in the West are criticized, citing Marx, for falsely assuming that a social revolution is no longer necessary. It is therefore worth examining these proposed linkages between Rousseauian democracy and Marxist revolution in more detail.

As an official ideology in the East, Marxism allows existing states to claim that they are "democratic" because they are "revolutionary," suggesting indeed that this follows almost by definition. A truly "Marxist" government is defined, since Lenin, as a revolutionary party in power; a true revolution, as an act of direct democracy on the part of the people. By imputing a revolution to "the people" a Marxist government in power ceases to be merely a class party, and becomes the heir to Rousseau's identification of popular sovereignty and the General Will. Such a regime can then claim the paradoxical status of a "revolutionary government" in which the party continues to rule by direct democracy, and the state purports to govern by absolute decree. After the revolution, "democracy" in this sense would no longer require competitive elections, civil liberties, and respect for diversity. The task would be the creation of the "new man."

In this interpretation official Marxism can be easily condemned as a modern version of Rousseauian civil religion. By imputing a revolutionary conversion to the masses, state-sponsored Marxism becomes an orthodoxy that justifies continuing repression in the name of the revolution itself. This fundamentally liberal critique of imputed revolution was applied to Stalin

---

[13] See Talmon, *The Origins of Totalitarian Democracy.* See also Popper, *The Open Society and Its Enemies.*

in the 1950s. Subsequent revelations of the Gulag have revived it, and many neo-liberals now conclude that the "totalitarian temptation" is inherent in Marxism as a revolutionary creed, and perhaps in the idea of revolution in general.[14]

In rejecting the official orthodoxy of the Soviet Union, Western Marxists have maintained a faith in the possibility of authentic "revolutionary consciousness,"[15] as distinct from the imputed revolutions of the East. Over time disappointment in the apparent failure of the affluent working class to move beyond its corporate self-interest has led many would-be Marxists to extend the possibility of such revolutionary consciousness under "advanced capitalism" to other groups, and even to "the people" as a whole. For a time Western Marxists were fascinated with Maoism as an alternative to Stalinism — arguing that the long revolutionary struggle had created a transformation in popular consciousness before coming to power; that genuine revolutionary reeducation continued after power had been seized; and that "cultural revolution" would prevent the return of old inequalities, or the creation of new ones.[16] These arguments sometimes suggested that the model of "cultural revolution" was available to everyone on the Left — the psychic equivalent of the "long march" in the creation of revolutionary man, requiring above all a rejection of the values of industrial capitalism and an embrace of "revolutionary praxis" in everyday activity.[17]

As post-Maoist China began to espouse some of the values of industrial capitalism, Western Marxists have placed their hopes increasingly in a kind of "protestant reformation" within the catholic orthodoxy of international communism.[18] Relying on the early Marx, they suggest that those with a pure faith in the revolution yet to come can live in the present so as

---

[14] See, e.g., Revel, *The Totalitarian Temptation* and *Without Marx or Jesus*. See also Glucksmann, *The Master Thinkers*.

[15] The thought of Luxemburg and Trotsky for a time provided a Marxist pedigree for such a view.

[16] William Hinton's *Fanshen* was often cited as authority for this tendency.

[17] See, e.g., Boyte, *The Backyard Revolution*, and Bookchin, *Post-Scarcity Anarchism*. (For an academic counterpart cf. Unger, *The Critical Legal Studies Movement*.)

[18] Western Marxists have sometimes imagined such a "protestant reformation" as a form of "puritanism," and sometimes as a "liberalization." The former possibility is represented by the allure of Mao's cultural revolution to many in the 1960s and 1970s. The latter is represented by the current allure of Gorbachev, who combines the roles of Luther, Calvin, and the Pope. For an attempt to describe a "protestant" Marxism that evokes the appeal of both puritanism and liberalization, see Bahro, *The Alternative in Eastern Europe*. For an explicitly "Rousseauian" view of Marx as an anti-Statist, see Levine, *The End of the State*.

to be worthy of the future. Marxism then becomes a democratic counter-culture that celebrates the uncorrupted aspirations of defeated social movements.[19] The politics of culture has ultimately led Western Marxism back to Rousseauian democracy as a communitarian alternative to both class struggle and interest group accommodation.

When seen through the lens of Rousseauian democracy, Marxism appears as a revolutionary religion, and not as a method of political analysis. Writers on the USSR and China, whether sympathetic or not, rarely use the categories of political analysis that they would apply to non-Marxist regimes. Instead they debate whether the people *believe* in Marxism and whether this belief makes a difference in their identities and interests, much as another generation of scholars might have sought an explanation of European feudalism in the medieval belief in Christianity. In the West writers about Marxism are principally concerned with what it might mean to *be* a Marxist in one's everyday life under capitalism, much as an earlier generation of scholars debated whether the rise of capitalism was due to the efforts of some Protestants to find worldly proof of their own salvation. In choosing such approaches none of these writers employ a Marxian political analysis of the kind developed below.

In order to go beyond the politics of culture I believe that Western Marxism must finally exorcise the ghost of Rousseauian democracy, and with it the revolutionary mystique, as Marx himself attempted to do in the aftermath of 1848.

Democracy and class analysis

Marx originally developed class analysis before 1848 in order to assess the ability of public institutions to mediate the popular demand for democracy. In its earliest versions, culminating in the *Communist Manifesto*, the concrete problem for Marxian class analysis was to find a non-political majority whose interests and identity would cut across the political disorganization of civil society into groups.[20] As an object of such analysis,

---

[19] As we saw in chapters 1 and 3, the view of Marxism as a revolutionary mystique has been particularly prevalent in New Left studies of failed social movements in the West.

[20] Marx and Engels: "All previous historical movements were movements of minorities, or in the interests of minorities. The proletarian movement is the self-conscious, independent movement of the immense majority in the interests of the immense majority." (Marx and Engels, "The Manifesto of the Communist Party," p. 78.)

the class structure of a state would consist of those social cleavages that could not achieve democratic expression without a revolutionary breakdown in the regime itself.[21] Class analysis would thus show precisely which linkages between issues and identities a regime must depoliticize when it reproduces the kinds of cleavages on which its continued stability depends.

This formulation, however, remains ambivalent between two views of the relation between a democratic revolution and class analysis. The first is an essentially Rousseauian model of the revolutionary class as an expression of the General Will, suggesting that class analysis is an effort to find a democratic majority that is capable of overcoming its particular interests. Such a majority would transcend the divisive institutions of representative democracy in the name of a revolutionary counterculture based on direct democracy. The second is a model of how the non-revolutionary state can be transformed through the contradictions in its own mode of interest organization, suggesting that class analysis would identify those particular interests within democratic politics that are not effectively mediated by the official representation of groups. Such an analysis would point to the strategic connections between direct action within civil society and organized participation in political institutions. The first of these models of class analysis is part of what I have been calling "the revolutionary mystique"; the second adumbrates what I shall call "the critical theory of democracy" − a view of how the institutions of representative democracy organize and disorganize the social bases of political identity.[22]

The tension between these views remained with Marx throughout his life. Both appear in Marx's early critiques of Hegel's *Philosophy of Right* and of the Left-Hegelians − although the latter predominates as his thought progresses. While the critical theory of democracy clearly governs his analyses of 1848, the revolutionary mystique reappears in his celebration of the Paris Commune of 1870. Although Marx never left behind the creative tension between the utopian hopes that he shared with his contemporaries and his mature analysis of the politics of capitalist democracies, I believe that the latter view of class analysis, the critical theory of democracy, is Marx's most original and significant contribution to the broad tradition of political theory.

[21] Note Marx's earliest definition of the proletariat as "a class in civil society that is not a class of civil society" ("A Contribution to the Critique of Hegel's *Philosophy of Right*: Introduction" (ed. O'Malley), p. 141). Marx's language here is still caught up in the problem of finding a group in society that has universal rather than particular interests. For an interpretation of Marx along these general lines see Avineri, *The Social and Political Thought of Karl Marx*, ch. 2.

[22] See esp. chapter 9, below.

Marxist practice has undoubtedly benefitted from the effort to tie class struggles to democratic revolution,[23] but I believe that Marxist theory is based on the insight that these are not essentially the same. The right to democratic revolution is essentially a populist idea, based ultimately on a consent theory of government. According to this theory the collective obligation of citizens to obey the state is a voidable contract. From this it follows that the united people may withdraw their consent at any time. The mythic presumption of unanimity thus becomes necessary to the ideology of People's Revolution.[24] As a consequence, these revolutions tend to develop in similar patterns, even in very different historical circumstances, reenacting the democratic story of promise and betrayal that is the subject of our next chapter.[25]

In contrast to the theory of democratic revolution, Marx's view of class struggle does not originate from the theory of popular consent, but rather from the theory of just war. Although Marx hoped that class war would ultimately lead to a better world for all, he recognized that its intrinsic logic is ultimately zero-sum. Instead of assuming that "the people" are united, his mature method of class analysis allows us to see them as divided, identifying who benefits from social justice and at whose expense those benefits must come. Unlike revolutionary populism, and like military strategy, the logic of class struggle differs in different historical circumstances. The mature Marx believed that proletarian revolution, when it finally occurs, would not be the exercise of a democratic right of the whole people, but rather a final remedy for the counter-revolutionary injustice of the Party of Order. The result would be to place the state in a form of democratic receivership – the "dictatorship of the proletariat."[26]

Recognizing that class struggle is a continuing dimension of politics within formally democratic regimes, Marx came to see that popular democratic revolutions against authoritarian regimes occur only at specific moments of class struggle, and are always incomplete. Any effort to shoehorn

[23] The revolutions in Russia and China – made in the name of "people's democracy" – have also contributed greatly to the worldwide interest in Marxist ideas throughout much of the twentieth century.

[24] See, e.g., Norman O. Brown, *Love's Body*, chs 1 and 4.

[25] See also Walzer, "A Theory of Revolution."

[26] See Marx, "The Civil War in France," and Lenin, *The State and Revolution*. For subsequent discussions see Kautsky, *The Dictatorship of the Proletariat*; Balibar, *The Dictatorship of the Proletariat*; and Therborn, "The Dictatorship of the Proletariat and the Class Character of the State Apparatus." For a classic non-Marxist discussion of these issues see Schumpeter, *Capitalism, Socialism, and Democracy*, part 4.

class struggle into a more general theory of democratic revolution would therefore sacrifice much of the insight that can be gained from Marx on the altar of the revolutionary mystique. We should rather recognize that the ideas of revolutionary democracy and class war are rooted in different theoretical frameworks, and that Marx's own best thought is a painful effort to acknowledge this fact.[27]

Liberty, equality, fraternity

In Marx's youth the radical democratic language of the Jacobins in the French Revolution expressed the intellectual allure of the revolutionary mystique, much as the language of communitarian democracy does today.[28] The core ideas of Jacobin democracy are embodied in the French revolutionary slogan, "liberty, equality, fraternity." This slogan embodied both an inspirational ideal and an institutional analysis. As we shall see, Marx's lifelong struggle with the revolutionary mystique required him to come to terms with both aspects of Jacobinism.

We can begin to understand the roots of Marx's ambivalence toward democracy by examining each term in the Jacobin slogan, beginning with *liberty*. "Liberty" has a Roman origin, but its modern meaning is rooted in the medieval legal system where it combined a degree of immunity from royal law and the *privilege* to be a maker of private law for others. (The Latin word *privilegium* means private law.) To have feudal liberty was to be both a law unto oneself and the ultimate source of law for one's subjects, exercising a form of jurisdiction independent of the king's.

Equality, rather than liberty, was the core of the feudal meaning of "freedom." Freedom meant equal subjection to a common law, no matter how onerous in content. In feudal Europe the demand for liberty and the demand for freedom were thus politically antithetical: liberty was a demand by the aristocracy against the absolute powers of the king; freedom, a

---

[27] The difference between the concepts, and the temptation to conflate them, explains both the genius and the tragedy of Lenin and Mao. Their genius was to understand popular democratic revolutions according to the logic of class war. This positioned them to win the civil wars that followed from the revolutionary moment. Their tragedy lay in rationalizing an ongoing class war according to the logic of populist revolution. In doing so they fell victim to the revolutionary mystique of totalitarian democracy.

[28] For a critique of these tendencies in recent thought see Holmes, "The Community Trap." For a historical view see Yack, *The Longing for Total Revolution*.

demand by the middle classes to be protected by the king against the aristocracy.[29]

Before the French Revolution, the struggle over the state was largely understood in terms of the ongoing conflict between liberty and freedom in their feudal senses. Opponents of the monarchy argued that the royal authority was intrinsically despotic because it undermined the traditional liberties of the people, and that the centralized state should remain hollowed out by pockets of feudal autonomy. Supporters of the monarchy argued that equal subjection to the king would free people from their feudal lords, and that the rule of law should expand to fill the pockets of arbitrary private power.

The absolutist (or despotic) state can be seen as an effort by the king to mediate feudal conflict between liberty and equality by incorporating the privileges of the nobility under the royal law.[30] The revolutionaries in France did not, however, see the Old Regime as a hybrid resulting from a historic compromise between the king and nobility. Rather, they saw it as a singular expression of royal power in which the state was the source, and sole prop, of all feudal privilege. If France was suffering from the social disease of lingering aristocratic privilege, the cause of that disease was now perceived to be the political and military power of the king. On this diagnosis the cure would be to smash the royal state and seize power in the name of the people.[31]

This revolutionary vision of the Old Regime broke through the feudal contradiction between liberty and equality in a way that the Old Regime itself could not. In feudal terms the overthrow of the Old Regime accomplished two symbolic tasks at once: by overthrowing the despotic power of the central government it upheld liberty; by overthrowing feudal privilege it upheld equality before the law. But these achievements brought about a revolutionary shift away from the feudal conceptions of both liberty and equality — a shift that remains with us today.

---

[29] From the standpoint of those seeking their freedom under feudal law to be subject only to the law of the king was to be one's own man; to be subject to the private jurisdiction of one's master was to be another man's man.

[30] In some countries, such as England, the king accomplished this by creating from elements in the bourgeoisie a new, more dependent aristocracy, which lacked the traditional liberties. In France Louis XIV took the opposite path, choosing to make the maintenance of traditional feudal privilege dependent upon the power, authority, and largesse of the king. By paying this price he got the feudal aristocrats to give up their private armies and to become ornaments in the royal court at Versailles — the visible symbol of the Old Regime that the French Revolution overthrew. See, e.g., Moore, *Social Origins of Dictatorship and Democracy*, ch. 2.

[31] See, e.g., Paine, *The Rights of Man*.

In Jacobin France the core meaning of "liberty" changed from a power of law-making to a limitation on the effects of the law that is made. Instead of thinking of liberty as in part a form of sovereignty over others, post-revolutionary individuals would claim their liberty by assuming solely the point of view of a subject. Where feudal liberties were inherently limited to the few, post-revolutionary liberty is grounded in respect for an individual dignity enjoyed in principle by everyone in society.

"Equality" also underwent a reversal of definition. Where feudal equality had primarily defined one's status as a legal subject, the principle that citizens are sovereign would now make it possible to claim equality by assuming the standpoint of a legislator. Post-revolutionary equality defines one's status as a law-maker; so long as the state regards its citizens as equal sovereigns, it need not treat them equally as subjects.[32]

The French Revolution turned the feudal paradox of liberty and equality into a new paradigm; yet in doing so it also produced another paradox. As the basis of popular sovereignty, political equality implies a self-conscious refusal by majorities to accept the dictatorship of minorities. Why should the majority of the people enter politics unless they both know their own interests and are willing to rule the minority in those interests? Yet post-revolutionary liberty assumes that the majority will not rule the minority as the minority once ruled it. The liberty of all minorities will be worthy of respect now that liberty is based on universal principles of autonomy and dignity rather than the accident of traditional privilege. Post-revolutionary society should then be no less safe for former aristocrats[33] than for other political minorities. But how could a society that is safe for former aristocrats be compatible with a majority governing in its own interests? The new meanings of "liberty" and "equality" are no less in tension than the old.

Ideally, the potential contradiction between liberty and equality in the French Revolution would be resolved by the third term in the Jacobin revolutionary slogan – *fraternity*. The Jacobin conception of fraternity, however, also required a transformation in the feudal meaning of the term. The feudal meaning of "fraternity" referred to the medieval brotherhoods, the guilds. The existence of a common interest within each of these

[32] In the conceptual scheme described above, "freedom" is a floating term. After the revolution, individual freedom can no longer be sharply distinguished from liberty, since without a feudal aristocracy there is no need to differentiate between immunity from the state and from private law-makers. Yet collective freedom is still tied to a conception of political equality – a sovereign people is called "free" in a sense that resonates with the feudal meaning of the word.

[33] E.g., Alexis de Tocqueville, whose views are discussed in chapter 6, below.

fraternities presupposed the differentiation of the larger society. In contrast to the pluralism required by medieval fraternity, revolutionary fraternity evokes an ideal of unity,[34] representing the entire society as though it had a single corporate interest − corporate like a medieval brotherhood, but singular like a medieval king. In revolutionary fraternity, liberty and equality would become compatible insofar as the entire national community is valued for its own sake, and not for the sake of the particular interests of constituent groups.[35] Revolutionary fraternity imagines unanimity, representing any deviation or disappointment as betrayal. As we shall see, the dialectic of unity and betrayal, of promise and threat, became an essential part of the Jacobin legacy.[36]

The Jacobin imagination

The Jacobins were originally one among many political factions in the French Revolution, but in subsequent retelling Jacobinism came to stand for the politics of radical democracy, a politics that was ultimately based on the assumption that, through taking over the state, the united people could reorganize society in their own interests. In the Jacobin imagination democracy is the child of revolution: a democratic revolution both requires and creates popular unity; it occurs when a self-conscious and self-identified majority seizes the state in its own interest. Between the downfall of Napoleon and 1848, the Jacobin idea of radical democracy − of liberty, equality, and fraternity − had developed from contingent history into a powerful structuring myth, providing a narrative framework for interpreting the crisis of 1848 within a broader story of promise and betrayal.

The Jacobin story begins with the moment of promise. In the Old Regime the demand for democracy reflects the willingness of self-conscious victims to seize state power in order to use it as it had been used against them. Since democracy is motivated by the desire of the vast majority to reap benefits from the political system, the demand for democracy inevitably contains the promise of socialism − seen as a permanent, and self-renewing,

---

[34] See Norman O. Brown, *Love's Body*, ch. 1.
[35] Lacking fraternity, an alternative mediating idea must be found for liberty and equality to be reconciled.
[36] For a general treatment of this subject see Woloch, *The Jacobin Legacy*, parts 1 and 2.

revolution of the self-identified majority against the vested privileges of the few.[37]

According to the Jacobin story, however, the permanent revolution of the many against the few eventually must be betrayed so that democratic politics can be embodied in a set of stable institutions. In place of the revolutionary belief that all social power is an artifact of state power, the organized people are taught that the power the state had exercised against them was largely a consequence of entrenched social power, and that the state machinery, once in popular control, would not have the power to turn the tables on the enemies of the people. As political freedom is extended, the post-revolutionary public agenda is constricted and the restraints imposed by society on the state loom larger. The power of the state to transform society seems ever-diminishing as crucial political decisions remain in private hands.

This very betrayal of the Jacobin promise also forms the basis for an alternative view of political democracy, a view which makes a virtue of mass disillusionment with the state. Liberal anti-Jacobinism — the counter-revolutionary version of democratic theory — holds that the democracy *should* be what the people have found it to be — a means for stabilizing the state. According to this view, instability results when state power is taken over by a self-conscious majority that identifies its interests outside of the political process. This means that the practical function of a democratic process is not, as it would seem, to pit the many against the few, but rather to prevent instability by effectively *disorganizing* a would-be majority into minority groups. For the anti-Jacobin liberal the intrinsic value of democracy is to produce, not popular unity, but fragmentation: the unity of the "people" must be broken so that their liberty can be preserved.

Is political fragmentation the betrayal of popular unity, or the condition of democratic stability? Is democracy in essence a revolutionary or a counter-revolutionary idea? In the liberal account democracy becomes the counter-revolutionary ideology *par excellence*. When the masses learn that seizing the state apparatus leaves the state weaker than it seemed before, they come to participate 'responsibly' in politics. To do so they raise a political sociology on the ashes of the socialist promise. Rather than abolishing the political significance of one's social background, anti-Jacobin

[37] If the distinction between state and society was fully reflected in the self-consciousness of each individual, then there need be no contradiction between the democratic and socialist promises of the French Revolution: the state would become subject to the will of its citizens in implementing public values at the same moment at which all private individuals became equally subject to the state in matters of self-interest.

democracy makes social background the basis of political equality; the traditional identities of the Old Regime become the foci of political participation in the new.[38] The advantages of different individuals, however unequal, appear 'democratic' when they result from a process that treats the political rights of certain *groups* as intrinsically equal regardless of their relative size. In this model of democratic stability the will of the majority is no longer the autonomous power of a group. A majority, as such, would not know its interests except as an outcome of a political process that is valued for its own sake by those who participate in it. This transforms the desire to participate in representative institutions from a demand for advantage into a demand for recognition.

This tension in democratic thought became the key to Marx's understanding the kind of politics that the post-revolutionary state characteristically produces. Even in his early work, he recognized that "when the political state ... comes violently into being ... political life attempts to suppress its presupposition, civil society ... But it only manages to do this in *violent* contradiction to the conditions of its own existence, by declaring the revolution *permanent*, and for that reason the political drama necessarily ends up with the restoration of ... all the elements of civil society, just as war ends in peace."[39] Indeed, Marx's argument throughout his essay "On the Jewish Question" is that the political structure of the Old Regime had become the social structure of its successor. As a consequence, forms of social control once characteristically exercised by the political authorities would be increasingly relegated to the private sphere.

In the original Jacobin story, the revolutionary spiral ended in the ultimate betrayal: the coup of Napoleon Bonaparte who declared himself Emperor on the 18th day of Brumaire of the revolutionary calendar. His coup led ultimately to the consolidation of revolutionary political power by the bourgeoisie and the incorporation of the ideas of liberty, equality, and, to a lesser extent, fraternity into the political ideology of established institutions. The code of laws established under Napoleon redescribed existing social institutions as arguably consistent with the modern forms of legitimation announced by the revolution.[40] Through Napoleon the French

---

[38] Cf. Offe and Wiesenthal, "Two Logics of Collective Action: Theoretical Notes on Social Class and Organizational Form," pp. 67–71.

[39] Marx, "On the Jewish Question," p. 222.

[40] As a conqueror, Napoleon subsequently extended the ideals and legal system of the French Revolution across the face of Europe. From a Jacobin point of view there was, however, an unfinished quality to these regimes — absolutist in form, but grounded in a revolutionary ideology that was greeted by many as a liberation from feudal oppression.

Revolution had indeed declared itself to be "permanent" — an institutionalized struggle between the centralized state and the various elements of civil society. But, although in principle the revolution's ideals would remain at war with civil society, in practice each element in civil society would make its separate peace by rediscovering itself as a fulfillment of revolutionary goals.

Freedom and the modern state

Hegel was aware of himself as living and writing in the aftermath of the French Revolution and claimed to be the philosopher of a post-revolutionary age.[41] In the *Phenomenology* Hegel claimed that the supersession and spread of the French Revolution by Napoleon was the last *kind* of new event that would happen in the world. Later he argued that subsequent changes in regime must be understood as repetitions of Napoleon's success in institutionalizing the forces released by the French Revolution, or as failures to do the same. By this he meant that regimes would thrive or decay depending on whether their continuing existence is recognized as necessary to embody the ideals of the French Revolution. In Hegel's vision of a post-revolutionary state, there is a fundamental consensus on values, and a potential for conflict only over the degree to which they are realized in institutions.[42]

In order to make this argument, Hegel reinterpreted liberty, equality, and fraternity in a way that can be used to either criticize or describe any modern state. He argued that in response to these three demands of the French Revolution modern states claim to promote our welfare, show concern for our basic dignity, and allow us to achieve conscious national community. Moreover, the stability of any government will henceforth depend upon the degree to which it successfully benefits the people who live under it, respects their fundamental identities, and enables them to feel a sense of membership or belonging in a larger political order. He believed that this must be true of the state that is promised by the French Revolution, the state that actually emerges from it, and the states that must be realized by any counter-revolution that can succeed.

---

[41] See Hyppolite, "The Significance of the French Revolution in Hegel's *Phenomenology*"; Habermas, "Hegel's Critique of the French Revolution"; and Suter, "Burke, Hegel, and the French Revolution."

[42] Cf. Huntington's critique of populism as discussed in chapters 6 and 9, below, and the discussion of "the end of history" in Kojève, *Introduction to the Reading of Hegel*, ch. 6.

The permanent legacy of the French Revolution, according to Hegel, is that with the final overthrow of feudalism all modern states would take the realization of political freedom as their self-conscious goal. In Hegel's logical method, however, post-revolutionary political freedom would have two distinct moments. The universal moment of political freedom would be expressed by the ideals of the French Revolution — liberty, equality, fraternity. The modern state must embody these in itself so that we can feel free for ourselves. The particular moment of political freedom would consist of our demand for welfare, dignity, and community. The state must provide these for us so that we can feel free in ourselves.

The realization that these two moments are necessary to each other would represent the Idea of freedom. As we saw in chapter 2, Hegel believed that modern freedom is, at the most general level, a relationship between knowledge of the world and self-knowledge. Although acknowledging that one form of modern freedom is that of the individual who understands why he is misunderstood,[43] Hegel believed that a more satisfying conception of freedom would allow the individual to reconcile those parts of social reality that he is internalizing as a self and those parts that he allows to remain external as a fate. The first can be exemplified by ethics, the knowledge of the ideals and reasons that are capable of motivating our action from a first-person point of view. The second can be exemplified by social science, the knowledge of how our individual motives operate on us collectively as a causal force.

In developing his view of freedom Hegel was the first to articulate clearly the ideological role of market theory within the modern liberal state. He saw that the three post-revolutionary virtues that modern states claim to embody in and for themselves are also ascribed to the market — an institution that comes to be both distinguished from and incorporated in the state at this time. The first virtue that is claimed for the market in the years following the French Revolution is that through promoting liberty it maximizes utility — as a system it makes everyone better off. The market's second virtue is that by assuming equality it respects individual dignity — it is whatever results from allowing freedom of contract among autonomous rational actors who may not dominate one another. The third virtue of the market is that it automatically promotes community by creating interdependence through specialization.[44] Like the state, the market

---

[43] He can both explain and justify, but his explanations and justifications do not go together — his understanding of himself and his world may each be internally consistent, but nevertheless out of kilter with each other.

[44] The market does not, however, presuppose fraternity as a conscious motivation of rational actors.

puts itself forward as the concrete institutional embodiment of the three great universal values that apply to all politics after the French Revolution. Yet the two institutions give different pictures of how these values are to be realized. In the state they are to be realized as goals deliberately pursued; in the market as fate brought about by an 'invisible hand.'

The metaphor of the 'invisible hand' symbolizes the concern of the bourgeoisie with the transparency and opacity of political life. In 1776 Adam Smith argued that, if only we behave as egoists, we will do more good for our fellow man than if we try to be altruists. This happy formula is superficially appealing, but Smith nowhere says whether it is addressed to egoists or altruists, or how he expects it to persuade either. Is Smith giving self-perceived altruists a reason for treating *other* people as though they were egoists who do not respect altruistic motives? Or is he, rather, asking us to embrace our own egoism no matter what the altruistic consequences?[45] Does the market authorize us to identify with our selfish interests, while viewing the common good as a benign fate? Or does our *understanding* of the market (provided by the economist) dignify our selfish interest as an expression of a duty to promote the public good?

By placing Smith's argument in the context of state and market institutions Hegel is able to answer these questions so as to bring out the fuller implications of Smith's political economy. In Hegel's view Smith's argument is addressed to neither egoists nor altruists, but to businessmen and bureaucrats — each concerned with how his own activity is perceived by the other. The businessman will no longer understand his interests to be selfish when he recognizes the function the market performs in promoting the political values of welfare, dignity, and community. The economist's description of the state enables him to understand his self-interest as authorized by public policy that respects the liberty and dignity of individuals, while promoting their welfare. Likewise, the bureaucrat will no longer understand his interests to be selfless when he manages the economy. The economist's description of the market will enable him to see bureaucracies as having interests of their own, and public policies as inevitably subsidizing some social groups at the expense of others. In Hegel's interpretation Smith's arguments are addressed to neither the egoist nor the altruist, but to socially embedded individuals seeking fulfillment as either businessmen or public officials.

According to Hegel the modern relation between state and economy was the only realization that the political ideals of the French Revolution could

---

[45] I.e., even despite the fact that we cannot make the world better for ourselves without making it as good as it can be for everyone else.

have had. In this relation the state and the economy each appear, significantly, as part of the other. Liberty, equality, and fraternity become welfare, individual dignity and community once they are realized in institutions. The inevitable conflicts between these values can be avoided by selectively internalizing them as a self, or externalizing them as a fate, in the process of achieving self-understanding. Through this process we come to realize that our problems are necessary in order for us to understand the developed institutional order from within.

This means that the values realized in the modern state are not attributable to either government or markets, taken in isolation. Rather the state and the market must coexist in order for either to develop fully. Of course each of the ideals that we have called welfare, dignity, and community can superficially appear to be external to the state. But this is plausible only if we take the standpoint of the market, a concrete historical institution, and assume that it is natural— a version of the 'state of nature.' We could just as easily view these critical ideals as external to the economy.[46] But that would be plausible only if we take the standpoint of the state, a concrete historical institution, and assume that it is natural— a kind of a primordial national consciousness. For Hegel, both of these approaches were hopelessly one-sided. He argued that the ideals in question appear to be critical in the one sphere, only by appearing as fully realized in the other: they are the terms of self-analysis that a given institutional order makes available to us.

Group and individual in modern democracy

Hegel saw that, once realized in political institutions, the political democracy sought by the French Revolution must have two aspects: for itself it is a form of liberation and an exercise of popular power; in itself it is a form of co-optation and an imposition of social control. The post-revolutionary state would thus be an attempt to institutionalize the linkage between seeing government as a reflection of the will of the people, and seeing the will of the people as grounded in respect for law.[47]

This insight led Hegel to reinterpret the ideas of majority rule and political equality as they are actually realized in democratic institutions. The idea of majority rule became, ironically, something that bureaucracies could routinely assert to resist the demands of any particular private group

[46] This is the response of Piven and Cloward to the attack on the welfare state in the Reagan era. See chapter 6, below.
[47] See *Hegel's Philosophy of Right* (tr. Knox), paras 258, 274−4, and p. 294.

that challenges their official power. A version of political equality — the official respect for diverse social identities — could then become a substitute for majority rule as a rationale for popular "participation" in the representative institutions of government, such as legislatures and parties. Modern bureaucratic states, Hegel suggested, can realize the substantive democratic value of political equality without attaching much, if any, importance to the procedures of majority rule. In Hegel's corporatist model of democracy, group interests would be 'weighed' and group identities 'respected,' even if the votes of individuals are never really *counted*.[48] This view laid foundations for the modern argument that the fundamental value promoted by majority rule is equality of *respect* for the political identity of individuals — not equality of *results*.[49]

In rationalizing the Napoleonic state as the full realization of the French Revolution Hegel directly attacked Rousseauian democracy, which he believed to be the core of the Jacobin version of the revolutionary mystique.[50] Unlike Rousseau, who attacked both individualism and pluralism, Hegel argued that respect for individuals can be reconciled with majority rule by promoting the democratic equality of *groups*. He thus rejected the view, common to Rousseau and the radical Jacobins, that modern democracy would require us to relinquish prior social identities in order to take up the burden of citizenship. We can elaborate Hegel's argument as follows, drawing heavily on Marx's Hegelian critique of Bruno Bauer's essay "On the Jewish Question":[51]

(1) In a society with unequal rewards an individual cannot tell whether he is being treated as a political equal by looking only at his eventual place in the pattern of social distribution (any more than a student can judge the fairness of a competitive test by looking only at his grade). The isolated individual knows that someone must occupy the position that he eventually fills in a competitive world of scarcity.

---

[48] For recent discussions of these tensions in the light of issues raised above, see Schmitter, "Democratic Theory and Neo-Corporatist Practice," and Offe, "Political Legitimation Through Majority Rule."

[49] See, e.g., Dworkin, *A Matter of Principle*, chs 8–9.

[50] See, e.g., *Hegel's Philosophy of Right* (tr. Knox), para. 258. For discussions of the messianic implications of what I have been calling "the revolutionary mystique" see Talmon, *The Origins of Totalitarian Democracy*, *Political Messianism*, and *The Myth of the Nation and the Vision of Revolution*; and Yack, *The Longing for Total Revolution*.

[51] Marx's argument is in part that Bauer misunderstood the continuing role of primordial group identities in the political equality promised by formally democratic regimes.

(2) In order to determine whether the rules themselves are fair the individual must be able to assert an identity that is not fully determined by them. He must identify himself as a member of a social *group* that the political system purports to treat equally in distributing unequal rewards to *individuals*. By distinguishing between the social disparities that the system is prepared to justify and those that it is committed to correct, the individual can argue that the system discriminates against him as an individual whenever it has an unequal impact on the group through which he entered it.

(3) If group equality is the democratic foundation of respect for individuals, then the democratic citizen will not repudiate all of his prior identifications with social groups. As a self-conscious citizen, he will, rather, redefine some group identities as the basis of his participation in the politics of distribution that the state creates.

This essentially Hegelian conception of democratic equality allows for vast differences in the legitimate pattern of social stratification in ideologically democratic regimes. Hegel recognized that as the political relations of the old regime are transformed into the social structure of the new, identities that were once a basis of hierarchy can become a valued form of diversity. If, for example, a democratic regime is based on overthrowing hierarchy based on race it may nonetheless be able to legitimate inequalities in wealth that are consistent with treating racial differences as a valued form of diversity. Because regimes take their character from the revolutions that produced them,[52] democratic regimes will differ for historical reasons in the specific social distinctions they hold out as the paradigm of illegitimate hierarchy.[53] The range of social disparities that can be effectively challenged by assertions of democratic equality will in turn determine the range of social disparities that can be made arguably consistent with modern forms of legitimation.

As we shall see, mature Marxism begins, not with a return to the Rousseauian critique of liberal pluralism, but with both the Hegelian critique of Rousseau and the essentially novel Marxian critique of Hegel. Marx recognized that the Hegelian way of institutionalizing the appeal of democratic theory will not be equally effective for all combinations of group interests and identities.[54] The stability of non-socialist democratic

---

[52] Aristotle's *Politics* remains the best elaboration of this point.

[53] See Meister, "The Logic and Legacy of *Dred Scott*" and "Discrimination Law Through the Looking Glass," esp. pp. 969–88.

[54] For a recent account of some of the reasons for this see Offe and Wiesenthal, "Two Logics of Collective Action."

regimes depends upon politicizing only those social differences that suppress the contradiction between two aspects of the demand for democracy: that the results of government action should benefit the majority, and that formation of government policy should treat everyone as equals. Everything thus depends on how the majority identifies itself, and how it knows its interest. After the disappointments of 1848, however, Marx's approach to class analysis could no longer be an attempt to assert a universal basis of citizenship in a Hegelian world of interest group politics, and became rather an attempt to find the transformative possibilities of organizing certain groups around their own interests. In its mature form the class analysis of liberal capitalism is an application of what we shall call "the critical theory of democracy."

The critical theory of democracy will be the subject of the following four chapters. Chapters 7 and 8 trace the origins of that theory in Marx's joint critique of Hegel and the Left-Hegelians; chapter 9 explores its present-day implications. In order to fully appreciate Marx's mature use of his early discoveries, however, we must understand how his response to the revolutions of 1848 transformed his youthful commitment to Jacobin socialism and enhanced his suspicion of the revolutionary mystique. This is the subject of chapter 6.

6 Democracy and Deradicalization

The Jacobin legacy

In attacking the revolutionary mystique I am not arguing that Marx ever abandoned his commitment to revolution. Marx came of age in the midst of debate about the continuing significance of the French Revolution in post-Napoleonic Europe. In the *Communist Manifesto* Marx and Engels sought to bring this debate to a climax, boldly predicting that the coming revolutions of 1848 would fulfill the promise of 1789 by bringing both democracy and socialism. The failure of those revolutions to achieve either goal marked the death of Marx's youthful political ambitions and the birth of his mature achievement as a political theorist. Although Marx remained a revolutionary throughout his life, his thought developed increasingly around the question of what it means to be a revolutionary in non-revolutionary situations.

This chapter will explore the role of democratic politics in the modern state as an anticlimax to the Jacobin vision of revolution and class struggle. To do so, however, we must first describe the political expectations that were disappointed in 1848.

The bohemian political culture of Paris before 1848 bears a striking resemblance to the radical political culture of the United States in the 1960s and 1970s. In *A Sentimental Education* Flaubert describes an ambience in which new ideas and social experiments seemed to crop up everywhere, each winning its share of enthusiastic adherents. Art became self-consciously countercultural, setting itself in opposition to the academic conventions of the time. Socialist workshops were struggling to survive, and the idea of the "workshop" soon became a metaphor for all kinds of progressive activity.[1] There were experiments with alternative lifestyles,

---

[1] Tocqueville confirms this view of pre-revolutionary Paris in his *Recollections*: "It was those socialist theories ... that later kindled real passions, embittered jealousies, and finally stirred up war between the classes... [A] thousand strange systems

some of which aspired to a kind of economic self-sufficiency. The traditional family seemed on the verge of collapsing, to be replaced by communal arrangements grounded in the equality of the sexes. Religion seemed everywhere in disrepute, and yet burst out in surprising new forms where it was least expected. Liberation and participation were actively valued at the personal, cultural, and political levels.

Essentially a business, the so-called July Monarchy[2] had many clients but almost no constituency: even the regime's beneficiaries were fond of criticizing it on cultural and humanistic grounds,[3] and the best of those who worked for the government characteristically denied that they really supported the regime. Parisians moved freely between the counterculture and the establishment, and Paris itself had become an international city – a magnet for intellectuals (such as Marx) who came to learn the ideals of 1789 in the very place where those ideals were daily being betrayed. This was a world in which everyone of any sensitivity believed himself or

poured from the impetuous imaginations of innovators and spread through the troubled minds of the crowd ... [E]ach man had his own scheme ... One was going to abolish inequality of fortunes; another that of education; while a third attacked the oldest inequality of all, that between men and women. There were remedies against poverty, and against that disease called work which has afflicted man since the beginning of his existence ... There was great variety in these theories ... But all of them, aiming lower than the government and attempting to reach society itself ... adopted the common name of socialism." (Tocqueville, *Recollections*, pp. 93–4.)

[2] After the defeat of Napoleon, the victorious powers restored the Bourbon dynasty to the French throne, but with a new social face. The aristocrats had been dispossessed of their rural holdings as an immediate and lasting result of the first French Revolution, leaving an independent peasantry in the countryside. In the absence of a feudal aristocracy, the new Bourbon monarchy found a base of political support in a fragment of finance capital invested largely in agriculture. This produced a conflict with the interests of industrial capital. Investment in agriculture depended on high food prices; but high food prices in the city raised the cost of living and did not permit the low wages which investment in industry required. As a result of this conflict the Bourbon restoration was overthrown in July of 1830, and under the subsequent reign of Louis-Philippe (the so-called "July Monarchy") the industrial revolution in France began to take off. (See Marx, "Class Struggles in France," pp. 36–41.)

[3] "With us, when a government ... becomes unpopular, the members of the very class for whose sake it becomes unpopular will prefer the pleasure of joining with everyone else in abusing it to the enjoyment of the privileges it preserves for them. The old French aristocracy ... had already illustrated that rule; in the end it found it clever to criticize its own prerogatives." (Tocqueville, *Recollections*, p. 52, see also pp. 84–5.)

herself to be misunderstood, and in which self-professed radicals took consolation in the belief that they were living between revolutions.

In the years preceding 1848 there was every reason to believe that a major upheaval was imminent. Most thoughtful people claimed to be democrats — to be wholly in favor of the ideals of 1789 and fully aware of how poorly contemporary institutions measured up to those ideals. Even the forces of reaction believed that the spectre of Jacobinism haunted Europe, making everything seem possible — including communism. In Tocqueville's words, "the passions of the past were traditions, not feelings."[4] As Marx would later put it, "The revolution of 1848 knew no better than to parody 1789."[5]

The essential Jacobin legacy is the promise that democracy and socialism are one. Citizens who enter politics demanding the right to participate begin to demand, as well, the benefits that would come from that participation. Such citizens pose the question of whether democracy, "power to the people," means that the people should now rule in their own interests in much the same way they have been ruled in the interests of others. To this extent all first democratic revolutions (e.g. 1789) are socialist in the act. If the people could rule in their own interests, there would be no difference, ultimately, between the achievement of political democracy and the democratic revolution of the social order — the promise of "socialism."

The lesson for post-revolutionary Jacobins was that subsequent revolutions cannot remain democratic without also becoming socialist in principle: only a commitment to socialism could revive popular unity in opposition to the divisive counter-revolutionary strategies of liberal democrats. For Jacobins, however, a socialist revolution was simply a democratic revolution in which the majority could identify its interest outside of the political process, and beyond the stability of a particular regime. As Marx and Engels put it in the *Communist Manifesto*:

> All previous historical movements were movements of minorities, or in the interests of minorities. The proletarian movement is the self-conscious, independent movement of the immense majority, in the interest of the immense majority.[6]

In its Jacobin version the concrete problem for political analysis is the search for a non-political majority — a social group that can define the unity of the people around interests that are not essentially products of the

---

[4] Ibid., p. 30.
[5] Marx, "The Eighteenth Brumaire," p. 146.
[6] Marx and Engels, "The Manifesto of the Communist Party," p. 78.

political process. The post-revolutionary Jacobins with whom Marx associated in his youth[7] imagined that such a social group would represent the common interest as its own particular interest: it would be the part that represents the whole, or, put as another oxymoron, the universal class.[8]

Democracy between revolutions

For Jacobins and anti-Jacobins alike, the democratic story of promise and betrayal had yielded a single overarching lesson: that everything depends upon how one identifies oneself in entering democratic politics. This is the lesson with which both Tocqueville and Marx came to maturity — Marx as a young Jacobin in Germany, Tocqueville as a leading anti-Jacobin liberal in France.

Tocqueville believed that democracy had succeeded in America because the people had not made a revolution in order to gain political equality, but only to achieve independence. He believed, correspondingly, that democracy had failed in France largely because it was a product of social revolution based on class.[9] But, rather than resisting democracy, Tocqueville's lifelong project was to persuade the elites of France that democracy could become a technique of political stabilization as easily as a slogan for political revolution. The key to political stability would be to

[7] Especially the circle of Arnold Ruge, et al.

[8] For Marx's formulation of this notion see Marx, "A Contribution to the Critique of Hegel's Philosophy of Right: Introduction" (tr. Livingstone and Benton), pp. 252–7.

[9] Tocqueville's *Democracy in America* was addressed not to Americans, but to the French as part of the ongoing debate over the legacy of the French Revolution. He argued that since Americans had no feudalism to overthrow, democracy itself was not for them a revolutionary idea. They therefore valued political participation for its own sake, and not for the benefits that it could produce. According to Tocqueville, the ruling majority in America, lacking a preexisting identity that gave it a reason to seek political power, was able to identify itself only as a consequence of the political process.

Tocqueville's book about 1789, *The Old Regime and the French Revolution*, explored the paradox in using *revolutionary* means to establish democracy as a new basis of political *order*. Through the French Revolution "the people" entered politics already knowing what they wanted and thinking that they could get it by political means. Tocqueville argued that when a majority that is constituted outside the political process fights for entry to promote its interests, it will see politics as a mere surrogate for class war, rather than regarding the stability of the state as intrinsically valuable.

establish political equality from above before democracy is demanded from below. He believed that, if the establishment of democracy were not driven by the demand for equality, the people would come to value political institutions intrinsically, rather than as vehicles for pursuing their narrower self-interest.[10] In such circumstances the defense of democracy could be co-opted from the Jacobin Left by the forces of order. Democracy could then become a bulwark against revolution (as it was in the US), rather than a revolutionary ideology (as it was in France).

In the *Communist Manifesto*, written on the eve of the Revolutions of 1848, Marx and his collaborator Engels asserted that all previous history had been a history of class antagonism,[11] and that the French Revolution of 1789 had been democratic in name only.[12] They meant by this latter remark that the supposedly sovereign people had been enlisted to struggle on behalf of the bourgeoisie against the aristocracy, but that the resulting bourgeois government was placed in antagonism to its mass constituency. As post-revolutionary Jacobins, Marx and Engels argued that henceforth all democratic revolutions must also be socialist, aiming at the transformation, not just of the state, but of the society. Such a social revolution, they believed, was not only desirable but also strategically necessary. Without it the state's power would be hemmed in by hostile social forces. But in order to have a social revolution, Marx and Engels argued, the revolutionary 'people' must identify the enemy as the bourgeoisie — those who have property that can be used to control others. Immediately before the events of 1848, Marx and Engels wrote in the *Communist Manifesto*, "A spectre is haunting Europe — the spectre of communism." They concluded, "Let the ruling classes tremble at a communistic revolution. The proletarians have nothing to lose but their chains. They have a world to win."[13]

Like Tocqueville, Marx saw the emergence of the working class on the stage of history as signifying an important change in the character of democratic politics. A working class that understood its own interest at the moment of entering the political arena was, Marx believed, a new kind of social force. Now, and for the first time, the 'people' had a specific social identity through which they could identify themselves in advance. They

[10] Cf. Huntington, *Political Order in Changing Societies*.

[11] Marx and Engels, "The Manifesto of the Communist Party," p. 67.

[12] See Marx, "On the Jewish Question," and Marx and Engels, *The Holy Family*, ch. 6, esp. pp. 118–24, 134–6.

[13] Marx and Engels, "The Manifesto of the Communist Party," pp. 67, 98. Cf. Tocqueville: "Mentally I reviewed the history of our last sixty years and I smiled bitterly to myself as I thought of the illusions cherished at the end of each phase of this long revolution; the theories feeding these illusions; our historians' learned

could no longer be duped into valuing democratic politics for its own sake, nor could they be embarrassed into giving up the benefits that democratic politics could produce simply in order to prove to their former masters that they were responsible enough to rule. The youthful Marx concluded that the next great revolution would be a proletarian revolution against the bourgeoisie[14] in which the demand for democracy would be seen self-consciously as a vehicle of social transformation, rather than as a means of social control.

In sum both Marx and Tocqueville foresaw the oncoming proletarian revolution of 1848. Marx anticipated that in such a revolution the ideals of democracy would finally become weapons in the hands of the people, who would begin to realize the potential of democracy as a form of class rule. For Tocqueville this very possibility was a reason to fear the revolution, since the idea of class rule was inimical to the prospect that the political institutions thus established could be valued for their own sake. Marx saw in the coming revolution the promise of a democracy in which, at long last, the people would get what they wanted. Tocqueville saw a democracy achieved by revolution as making it less likely that people would want what they get. For this reason he doubted that a people who had once overthrown a government would ever be satisfied with its successor.

---

daydreams, and all the ingenious false systems by which men sought to explain a present still unclearly seen and to foresee the unseen future."

"The Constitutional Monarchy had succeeded the Ancien Regime; the Republic followed the Monarchy; the Empire the Republic; after the Empire the Restoration; then there had come the July Monarchy. After each of these successive exchanges it was said that the French Revolution, having achieved what was presumptuously called its work, was finished; men had said that, and they had believed it. Under the Restoration, I, too, unfortunately hoped for that, and I continued to hope after the Restoration government had fallen; and here was the French Revolution starting again, for it was always the same one. As we go on, its end seems ever farther off and hazier. Shall we reach, as other prophets as vain perhaps as their predecessors assure, a more complete and profound social transformation than our fathers ever foresaw or desired, and which we ourselves cannot yet conceive; or may we not simply end up in that intermittent anarchy which is well known to be the chronic incurable disease of old peoples? I cannot tell, and do not know when this long voyage will end; I am tired of mistaking deceptive mists for the bank. And I often wonder whether that solid land we have sought for so long actually exists, and whether it is not our fate to rove the seas forever." (Tocqueville, *Recollections*, pp. 83–4.)

[14] Marx and Engels, "The Manifesto of the Communist Party," part II.

The politics of anticlimax

The much-anticipated neo-Jacobin revolution finally began in Paris in February 1848. Instead of provoking a great struggle over the social order, however, the fall of monarchical government appeared almost as a foregone conclusion. Widespread suffrage, a new assembly, and even National Workshops were all established as though they had been planned long in advance.[15] The ripeness of the time was clear to everyone,[16] and events in Paris were a spark in the popular imagination that ignited the flames of national revolution throughout Europe.

Yet, in a significant sense, the French revolution of 1848 ended a few months later, in June, in what may have been the first self-conscious modern class war. This war was fought between those who had something to lose — standing side by side without social distinction — and the workers of Paris, who, as Marx and Engels would have it, had nothing to lose but their chains. In the end the workers were brutally defeated and slaughtered, despite fighting for over five days with remarkable tenacity and discipline against the combined forces of the professional military, the National Guard, and the Militia. Many of the friends of liberation who had embraced the revolution with open arms ended up fighting against the working class. As Flaubert's *A Sentimental Education* makes clear, the cultural consensus for change had been fostered by a coalition of those with incomes from elsewhere, those who controlled their own conditions of labor, and those who made their living in the old order by persuading others of the desirability of the new — the purveyors of alternative lifestyles.

The main political lesson that people who think they are radicals must learn from the disappointment of 1848 is what it looks like, and feels like, to become a counter-revolutionary. In the first moment — the February moment — virtually everyone of enlightened intellect identified themselves as radical republicans. And yet, when the second moment of revolution came — the June days — virtually no middle-class intellectuals found themselves on the side of the armed workers. Whatever their professed agreement with the workers' ideals, they rejected the politics of the workers who put those ideals forward, viewing such politics as either crazy or insincere. Between the best of times in February and the worst of times in June, intellectuals switched from the active voice to the passive voice in articulating their politics. Instead of describing political action as an opportunity for remaking their world to fit their ideals, they began describing

---

[15] See Tocqueville, *Recollections*, e.g. pp. 98ff., 125ff., 171ff.
[16] *Ibid.*, pp. 27, 39, 41, 52, 73, 83–6.

their politics as something that had happened to them. They spoke as if it had been merely inevitable that they would find themselves doing what was necessary — along with other like-minded, high-minded, people — once the revolution had gone too far.

Revolution and counter-revolution

In 1850 Marx and Tocqueville, the post-Jacobin and the anti-Jacobin, began to write histories of a revolution that both had anticipated — and in which both had been personally and politically disappointed. Both perceived 1848 to be the end of an age of democratic revolution, and the beginning of a new era of social revolution — the end of an era of struggle by the "people" for the common good in the name of *political* equality, and the beginning of an era of class war fought in the name of *social* equality. The Jacobin myth of a revolution in the name of the "immense majority" had decomposed. Both Marx and Tocqueville agreed that politics would now reflect social struggles between forces whose interests were fundamentally incompatible. Instead of producing popular unity, the next revolution would inevitably end with winners and losers among the "people."

According to both Marx and Tocqueville, the prospects for democracy in 1848 were critically determined by a new social actor — the Parisian working class. This social force was underrepresented in the political system, and it was poor, but most significantly it understood itself to consist of the working poor — an industrial (or industrializing) proletariat that differed in significant respects from previous movements that had taken the form of riots for the vote or for bread. In addition to these traditional demands the Parisian workers now demanded guaranteed work as a social right.[17] As Tocqueville remarked,

> [This] should not have surprised the world as much as it did. Had no one noticed that . . . the people had been continually . . . improving their condition . . . and that their importance, education, desires and power were all constantly growing. Their prosperity also increased, but not so fast, and it was getting close to the limit which, in old societies, cannot be passed, when there are many candidates but few places. How could it have failed to occur

---

[17] The workers of Paris believed that this right had been systematically denied by a political order that served the interests of financial markets, even when this meant allowing factories to be shut down. Cf. the defeated Humphrey-Hawkins Bill of the 1970s. Today factories are routinely shut down as a result of refinancing corporate debt.

to the poorer class, who were inferior but nonetheless powerful, that they might use their power to escape from their poverty and inferiority? For sixty years they had been working toward this end. At first the people hoped to help themselves by changing the political institutions. But after each change they found their lot was not bettered, or that it had not improved fast enough to keep pace with their headlong desires. Inevitably, they are bound to discover sooner or later that what held them back in their place was not the constitution of the government, but the unalterable laws that constitute society itself; and it was natural for them to ask whether they did not have the power and right to change these too, as they had changed the others. And to speak specifically about property, which is, so to speak, the foundation of our social order, when all privileges that cover and conceal the privilege of property had been abolished, and property remained as the main obstacle to equality among men, and seemed to be the only sign thereof, was it not inevitable ... that at least the idea of abolishing it should strike minds that had no part in its enjoyment?[18]

Tocqueville recognized that the demands of the new working class in a democratic age could be seen in two ways: as demands for equality, and as demands for victory. Working class demands for *equality* might fall within the outer limits of the liberal democratic tradition within which they were made. Nevertheless, Tocqueville saw a structural problem in the further extension of social equality, implicit in the passage quoted above. We can elaborate his insight as follows: the broad movement for democracy makes more and more players eligible for a limited number of prizes; under such conditions the number of losing contestants increases faster than the number of winners; this creates a growing constituency willing to challenge the terms of the game itself by adjusting the size and number of the prizes; yet since the value of the prizes lies largely in the social power they confer on the winners over the losers, the prizes are worth less as more people come to have them. (Political equality is thus sometimes experienced as inflation − a fundamental limit on the adaptive powers of liberal democracy.)[19]

As demands for *victory*, however, Tocqueville recognized that the claims of the workers to seize political power in their own interests would immediately burst the limits of the liberal democratic tradition, becoming nothing less than an effort to use the state to attack the cumulative social power that the prizes confer on the winners. All social struggles would

[18] Tocqueville, *Recollections*, pp. 94−5.
[19] Cf. Hirsch, *Social Limits to Growth*, and Ellis and Kumar (eds), *Dilemmas of Liberal Democracies*. This argument is taken up in more detail in chapter 12, below.

then become equivalent to the struggle to seize the state from finance capital, and thereby to break the advantages based on the ownership of accumulated wealth. In such a political climate no property would be safe insofar as it enabled its owner to exercise social power over others.

For these reasons Tocqueville saw the entry of the working class as poisoning the political process. He believed that class consciousness would polarize politics around the question of property — the accumulation of wealth versus the right to work. This would make the establishment of stable democratic institutions a more or less permanent impossibility, since no one would value them intrinsically but only as a means of promoting other interests. To defend democracy, Tocqueville realized, it would be necessary to suppress the socialist idea along with its protagonist, the working class. He believed that the fatal delusion of the democratic leaders of his time lay in thinking that they could moderate the forces they unleashed — thereby encouraging the workers' general aspirations while putting a brake on the workers' concrete demands.

In Tocqueville's account almost everyone who professed to be interested in democracy in 1848 was confused about what interests they were truly promoting.[20] Radical democrats, such as Lamartine, had put themselves forward, hoping to be able to control their constituents' demands. But while professing to be concerned for the Republic, these leaders encouraged people to act on the basis of envy.

> Society was cut in two, those who had nothing united in common envy, those who had anything in common terror. There were no longer ties of sympathy linking these two classes and a struggle was everywhere assumed to be inevitable soon. There had already been physical clashes with different results between the bourgeois and the people for these names had been revived as battle cries ... In Paris hardly a day passed without some attack or threat to the ruling classes' capital or income. Sometimes the demand was that they should provide employment without selling anything. Sometimes that they should let their tenants off their rent when they themselves had no

[20] "In this case the quality of imitation was so obvious that the terrible originality of the facts remained hidden. It was a time when everybody's imagination had been covered by the crude pigments with which Lamartine daubed his *Girondins*. The men of the first revolution were still alive in everybody's mind, their deeds and their words fresh in the memory, and everything I saw that day was plainly stamped with the imprint of such memories. The whole time I had the feeling that we had staged a play about the French Revolution, rather than that we were continuing it." (Tocqueville, *Recollections*, p. 67.)

other income to live on. The landlords bent as they could before this tyranny trying to get at least some advantage from their weakness by publishing it.[21]

Ultimately, according to Tocqueville, the radical democrats were unable to control, or to lead, the movement that they inspired. In his account, when a working class revolt began to take place in Paris between February and June of 1848, threatening to cut off the nation's jugular, all of France rose up against the workers. The organized social forces of French society then united in support of property, family, and religion as the institutional context in which ordered liberty must be rooted. By June, in Tocqueville's view, the "people" were truly united to oppose the power of a ruling class — only this time that ruling class was the proletariat.

Tocqueville's *Recollections* shows how inevitably, and despite their democratic pretensions, middle-class republicans chose the Party of Order when they could no longer dominate the forces that had swept them to power. The proletarian revolution that initially enlisted the near-unanimous support of the middle classes against an ever-receding enemy was subsequently defeated precisely because of its class character.[22] For Tocqueville the paradox of 1848 was that democracy itself became unpopular because it was tied to socialism. Although he believed the substantive value of democracy to be a legitimate revolutionary goal, Tocqueville argued that the sincere democrat, forced to choose sides, must defend political stability whenever democracy is sought as a means to other ends.

Marx saw the events of 1848 differently. Like the leaders whom Tocqueville criticized, Marx had originally called upon the working class to support a democratic revolution primarily as a means to achieve the further end of social equality. Yet, instead of describing the defeat of the revolution predicted in the *Manifesto*, Marx came to argue that 1848 signified the emergence of the bourgeoisie as a class-conscious political actor, finding its voice in the fear of a proletarian revolution that did not in fact materialize. The recognition that democratic mobilization could be harnessed to counter-revolutionary ends led him to doubt the automatic connection between democracy and socialism, an article of faith in his Jacobin youth. According to Marx, the premature unity of the bourgeoisie in 1848 had turned democratic politics on its head. For him the real story to be told was of an emerging counter-revolutionary idea of democracy — a phenomenon both described and reenacted by Tocqueville himself in the

[21] Ibid., p. 124.
[22] Cf. the recent popular antipathy to "big labor."

course of writing his *Recollections*. After 1848 Marx came to believe that undermining the bourgeois counter-revolution must become the long-range political project of democratic socialism between revolutions.[23]

In retrospect Marx saw the revolution of 1848 as a repetition of the sequence of the tragic events of 1789, but this time as farce.[24] The first French Revolution had been an unexpected democratic revolution that was constantly in the process of surpassing itself – of becoming more threatening to established order. The second was a self-described proletarian revolution so widely expected that it began with no opposition; yet, as soon as an independent workers' uprising finally occurred, this second French Revolution ended with almost no support. Both revolutions culminated in a Napoleonic Empire, willingly embraced by erstwhile bourgeois democrats.

Contrary to his own prediction in the *Manifesto*, Marx wrote the history of 1848 not as a conflict between bourgeois and proletarians, but as a story of fragmentation within both classes. The initial phases of the Revolution, he argued, reflected the convergence of three great bourgeois interests in civil society: finance capital, manufacturing capital, and agricultural capital. These three interests had been divided against each other as potential clients of the pre-revolutionary monarchy, and their convergence was first expressed as a demand for political democracy. When, however, the popular constituency mobilized by that demand threatened bourgeois interests the bourgeoisie reunited around the demand for order. To preserve

---

[23] Marx's introduction to "Class Struggles in France" describes his conclusion broadly: "With the exception of only a few chapters, every important section in the annals of the revolution from 1848 to 1849 carries the heading: *Defeat of the revolution*!

"What was overcome in these defeats was not the revolution. It was the pre-revolutionary, traditional appendages, the products of social relationships which had not developed to the point of sharp class antagonism – persons, illusions, ideas, and projects from which the revolutionary party was not free before the February revolution, from which it could be freed not by a *February victory* but only by a series of *defeats*.

"In a word: revolutionary progress cleared a path for itself, not by its immediate, tragic-comic achievements, but, on the contrary, by creating a powerful and united counter-revolution; only in combat with this opponent did the insurrectionary party mature into a real party of revolution." (Marx, "Class Struggles in France," p. 35)

Although Marx's analysis of 1848 as the coalescence of the counter-revolution still stands, his belief that this would clear the path for the final revolution must be viewed as wishful thinking.

[24] Marx, "The Eighteenth Brumaire," p. 146.

order the united bourgeoisie eventually acquiesced in a coup by a popular leader, Louis Napoleon Bonaparte, who mobilized the lumpenproletariat and the newly enfranchised peasantry as an electoral coalition against the Parisian workers. Instead of representing a united 'people' in a way that would divide bourgeois interests against themselves, the Bonapartist version of popular democracy represented a divided people to a united ruling class.

By eventually giving up its power to govern in order to continue to rule,[25] the united bourgeoisie forever stripped the revolutionary implications from its political rhetoric. The main consequence of 1848, according to Marx, was that the French bourgeoisie accepted its status as a permanent minority in democratic politics and abandoned the effort to promote its interests directly through majority rule. This freed bourgeois interests to embrace their role as pure clients of government, while acknowledging that the counter-revolutionary function of popular democracy is to divide the sovereign 'people' into groups. Henceforward, the bourgeoisie would hope to control the state by economic rather than electoral means – making its common interests appear to government to be a matter of necessity, and not an exercise of political will. According to Marx, the emergence of a class-conscious bourgeoisie out of a politics of factional division under the July Monarchy occurred at the moment the various factions perceived themselves to be governed by necessity rather than preference. Thereafter, a counter-revolutionary bourgeoisie would be able to understand what it was doing entirely in terms of what was happening to it.

In Marx's account of 1848 the unification of a bourgeoisie around its property interests came at the expense of its own political vitality. Having once again given up democracy rather than risk disorder, the bourgeoisie could no longer put forward a version of democracy that contained the promise of socialism. The bourgeoisie thereby exposed the illusions of 1789 to the scrutiny of the masses, revealing the class character on which its democratic ideology had always rested.

Political fate

The contrasting stories that Marx and Tocqueville tell about the fate of the Jacobin democrats in 1848 raises a deeper question: what is the relationship between a politics that is chosen and a politics that is necessary – between our political desires and our political fate?

[25] Ibid., ch. 4.

This is a question that applies equally to the main actors in the drama, and to the uneasy efforts of Marx and Tocqueville to be reconciled to the outcome. Their two political narratives of 1848 do not merely reveal that the values and beliefs of major protagonists had been hypocritical or insincere all along. Rather, the ironic unfolding of events brought many protagonists to realize a change in the relation between their ideals and their interpretation of reality. This was especially true of the narrators, Marx and Tocqueville. Neither was plainly insincere or hypocritical in their initial commitments to radical and liberal democracy, respectively. Yet both located these commitments differently after 1848. The stories they tell reflect their concern with the changing relationships between one's political beliefs and one's political identity.

The contrast between Marx and Tocqueville on 1848 allows us to think critically about how the same values and beliefs might be differently internalized or externalized as we identify ourselves politically over time. Writing near the end of his life, Tocqueville chose to internalize his liberal ideal of democracy, and to externalize his political analysis. Morally, he judged himself by the standards of internal sincerity and external responsibility, and he often described the relation between these two standards with situational irony. Writing near the prime of his life, Marx chose to question both his ideal of democracy, and his political analysis. Between 1844 and 1852 he had been intellectually preoccupied with the relation between the subjective and objective components of his Jacobin political identity. The disappointment of 1848 was clearly a turning point in Marx's view of the relation between political identity and political belief, and by confronting that disappointment he moved decisively beyond the Jacobin problematic of the *Communist Manifesto*, and into the modern world of ideological analysis. With the problem of ideology in mind we can examine the relevance of the democratic ideals of Tocqueville and Marx to the different standards by which they judged the aftermath of 1848.

Tocqueville directly uses his own ideal of liberal democracy to state clear standards for judging the conduct of individual leaders during and after the revolution. Do they really believe in democracy as a system of both liberty and equality – or are they merely fools, confused by events and trying to stay afloat in turbulent political waters? Do they act with sincerity and probity, or are they mere flatterers of the crowd? Tocqueville uses the same ideal of liberal democracy as a standard for judging events. Since this is ostensibly a democratic revolution, he is concerned with whether its proponents will succeed or fail in bringing it off. Will the revolution fail because the people themselves do not measure up – perhaps because they do not want democracy enough; or because they do not really want democracy at all, but only what they can get out of it?

Marx is less clear-cut in the standards he applies. He sees the revolution, not as a test of people's sincerity about the ideals that they hold, but rather as an emerging struggle of social forces. Those who read Marx from an idealistic point of view often find it difficult to tell from his historical writings just what he believes in. At first Marx seems to support the democratic movement, but he does so most strongly at the moment of its defeat. Yet his analysis also shows how the identity of a democrat can come to have counter-revolutionary significance, especially in times of apparent victory. In particular he argues that the revolution, which is defeated because of the promise of democracy, ends up being supplanted by a counter-revolution that is ratified through the entry into politics of a peasant vote, brought about by the extension of universal suffrage.[26] Is Marx for or against democracy? And is he 'sincere' in his willingness to accept whatever outcome democratic procedures dish up? Or is this merely the first betrayal of democracy by a 'Marxist' who appears to support it, just as later generations of Marxists who paid lip service to democracy betrayed it in deed?

Viewed as illustrations of their respective ideals of democracy, Tocqueville's account of 1848 is clearly the more satisfying. Yet viewed as reflections on the relation of political belief to political identity, Marx's account supersedes and encompasses Tocqueville's.

For Tocqueville 1848 was a time for responsible men to act responsibly. The serious question was the kind of person one will be shown to be under the test of events. He believed that by playing a part in these events a serious person can come to better understand his own motives.[27] As Tocqueville describes himself,

[26] See ibid., ch. 8. One gets some flavor of the politics of the peasantry by reading the description of Tocqueville's own political constituency in La Manche. In the *Recollections* he describes the peasants listening to his speech on the hilltop in 1848, and then voting unanimously for him as their representative to the Constituent Assembly. (Tocqueville was, of course, the descendant of the local feudal nobility, and would have been Comte de Tocqueville had there been no Revolution in France.) See Tocqueville, *Recollections*, pp. 108–20, esp. 119f.

[27] He is especially proud of the honesty of his own campaign speech in La Manche: "There are those who mean by a republic a dictatorship exercised in the name of freedom; who think that the Republic should not only change political institutions, but reshape society itself; there are those who think that the Republic should be aggressive and propagandist. I am not that kind of Republican. If that were your way of being one, I could be of no use to you, for I should not share your opinion. But if you understand the meaning of a republic in the same sense as I, you can count on my devoting my soul to a cause which is mine as well as yours." (Ibid., p. 112.)

I had no cause to defend except freedom and human dignity. To protect the ancient laws of society against the innovators by using the new strength the republican principle could give to government; to make the clear will of the people of France triumph over the passions and desires of the Paris working men, and in this way to conquer demagogy by democracy, such was my only design. Never has an aim seemed to me higher or clearer. I am not sure that the dangers to be faced ... did not make it even more attractive ... [A] touch of danger lends spice to most of life's actions.[28]

Although Tocqueville believed that in 1848 the demand for democracy had been corrupted at birth, he thought that an honorable man should act in the faith that democracy may be compatible with a respect for liberty, at least in theory. Yet as a realist he also knew that democracy cannot survive as a stable basis for political order if it is introduced to achieve equality. Tocqueville consequently believed that he was living through a time when it would be difficult for a good man to act well. His consolation was that, through action, he would come to understand better why his own motives must inevitably be misunderstood.

Marx begins his account of 1848 by seeing the demand for democracy as full of revolutionary potential. Yet once the working class is removed from the stage, he sees the extension of democracy as essentially a form of political repression and disorganization imposed from above. In writing about these events, Marx is partly concerned with how people such as Tocqueville became unable to act effectually, and devoted themselves instead to understanding why they were misunderstood. In his *Recollections* Tocqueville experiences the political reaction that Marx described in his account of the Party of Order in "The Eighteenth Brumaire." When Marx says that the bourgeoisie rallied behind the Party of Order without believing in it, Tocqueville shows what it is like to feel one's objective interests moving one's beliefs. His memoir reveals political reaction to be a form of disillusionment which at the same time gives release.[29]

This difference in narrative perspective largely explains why Tocqueville is so much easier to read than Marx. Of the two, Tocqueville is the first-order writer. The subject of his book is easy to identify. At one level the subject is Tocqueville himself: he wants to clarify his motives from his own point of view. At a higher level Tocqueville's subject is the revolution: why did it fail? If we ask rather, "At what did it fail?" Tocqueville's answer

[28] Ibid., p. 133.
[29] In some ways this resembles the release that radical intellectuals sometimes feel when they become disillusioned with the causes (or the people) they tried to serve. The difference is that Tocqueville never had any radical illusions.

is obvious: the revolution failed to create a stable state. The unity of Tocqueville's book lies in the implicit thesis that he was misunderstood for the same reason that the revolution failed — namely that the makers of the revolution were insincere and unrealistic in their ideals.

The state and the individual are thus the dual subject of Tocqueville's *Recollections*, as they are in most political histories. But the relationship between state and individual in such accounts can be of two distinct sorts: it can be a relationship of mutual recognition — "I recognize this state to be one that recognizes me as an individual"; or it can be a relationship of irony — "I am living in a political order that is illegitimate because I am misunderstood."

For Marx it is harder to answer the question: who or what is the subject of this book?[30] This is because there is a missing subject — the working class — which left the scene just before it was to take center stage. In "The Eighteenth Brumaire" everything is oriented toward the proletariat's absence — toward preventing the ultimate threat to property that a working class revolution proposes. Marx's writing thus appears to be history without a subject. It is *Waiting for Godot*, and not yet *The Passion* — the crucifixion and resurrection of the proletariat. But like many good histories without a subject, "The Eighteenth Brumaire" is really about subjectivity itself.

Marx is really writing about and against a conception of history that Tocqueville exemplifies — the view that history should be written using the techniques of dramatic irony.[31] By this I mean that the conventional historian takes the standpoint of a theatrical audience, looking at the action in the context of a backdrop scene that the actor does not see. The actor on the stage attempts to achieve a kind of reconciliation without knowing the scene, or backdrop, against which he acts. In such dramas the reconciliation often becomes apparent to those on stage only at the moment when the play is over. This reconciliation typically occurs when there are two situations, or subplots, each of which provides the background for resolving the other.[32] The tension between actor and scene thereby comes to full closure. Irony ends in reconciliation. But sometimes in drama the

[30] This is true of both "Class Struggles" and "The Eighteenth Brumaire."
[31] See Kenneth Burke, *A Grammar of Motives*, esp. part I.
[32] Situation comedies on TV use a particular version of this general formula. Their plots involve two problems, one in the background and the other in the foreground, and the characters typically represent distinct personality types. The dramatic reconciliation comes about by allowing each of these characters to realize that he or she did not know the full background of the others' conduct. When the background is revealed to them before our eyes, they realize collectively that their problems were "all a big misunderstanding."

final reconciliation is possible only for the audience, which sees the inevitability of an outcome that the characters on stage cannot see. This is a typical effect of good historical narrative. Here we see how actors attempt to reconcile themselves to the unseen backdrop that determines their success or failure, and also how the entire development of the drama is ironical given what the actors are thinking. In place of explanation, satisfying history, such as Tocqueville's, gives us an *ironic* perspective on the relation between the character and the background scene.

In the *Recollections* Tocqueville is the protagonist of his own history. As both an author and an actor he believes in ordered liberty, and the stable Republic which would protect it. Yet there is an inevitable backdrop of venal people who do not really believe in the Republic, but want it only as a means to something else. In such a scene it is clear to the author why he, and the state, will be misunderstood. The ironic twist in Tocqueville's story is that this initial misunderstanding is necessary to the final resolution of his plot: the unity of the people and their hypocritical leaders against the perceived threat from the workers of Paris. Tocqueville seems to suggest that such a resolution could not have occurred if the people had believed all along that they were acting consistently out of principle, rather than simply doing what was necessary. Instead of worrying about the inconsistency of being happily on one side in February and on the other in June, the people appear as dramatic characters who are betrayed in their principles but reconciled by their understanding of the events which take place under the guise of scenic necessity. Instead of creating the scene as an author, Tocqueville as memoirist describes his own reconciliation to the scene as an actor. He moves from seeing himself as the victim of inevitable misunderstanding to the sense of harmony that sometimes comes from muddling through. The book ends with him serving respectably in a government that itself inspired little respect.

For Marx, however, the story of 1848 is not of a popular revolution that went too far, but rather of the progressive deradicalization of democratic ideas. Instead of seeing the February revolution as an uprising of the organized Paris workers, he sees it as a moment of unity on the part of a previously divided bourgeoisie. Marx explains that everyone at first came forth as a republican because republicanism is the politics of the bourgeoisie at the moment when it feels its unity as a class. This had occurred once before in France — at the moment in 1789 when the bourgeoisie identified its particular position as the Third Estate with "the people" as a whole[33] — and was reexperienced in 1848 as a moment of warm fraternity

[33] For the classic expression of this view see Sieyes, *What is the Third Estate?*

in which the various divided interests of the bourgeoisie were again momentarily united, almost in the form of reminiscence. For Marx this element of nostalgia is as important as hypocrisy in understanding the imitative quality of the times. As soon as the revolution was set in motion, however, the sentimental unity of the bourgeoisie was jeopardized by the broader popular constituencies that it had to mobilize in order to challenge the state.

In Marx's narrative what eventually made the bourgeoisie unfit to rule was its struggle against its own revolutionary constituency. The new government, which needed more legitimacy than its predecessor, had less — and in defeating the workers it only discredited itself. As we have seen, Marx's story ends with the bourgeoisie as a client of a counter-revolutionary regime, promoting its interests, not through political participation, but in the guise of economic necessity. Whereas Tocqueville writes in the familiar voice of historical irony, Marx's voice is an uneasy balance between satire and prophecy.

Rebellion and reconciliation

The paradox of bourgeois democracy has been as important in the postwar US as it was in Paris in 1848. In both societies political upheavals had less to do with a war between competing creeds than with conflict about the fit between our democratic values and existing institutions. This pattern may be peculiar to the relation between bourgeois democracies and populist political cultures in which political conflicts often focus on whether institutions embody the values that justify them. Whenever such conflicts arise, sincerity becomes a salient political issue: competing political positions are then described as "idealistic" or "realistic," "activist" or "pragmatist," "outraged" or "disillusioned." Since these competing standpoints toward existing institutions are usually grounded in common values it is natural to ask whether the ideals of Jacobin or populist democracy are themselves inimical to the creation of political stability.

Tocqueville blamed the excesses of the revolution on an excess of democracy itself. He thought that democratic principles were destabilizing, leading people to believe that they could use democracy to establish crackpot socialist ideas, such as guaranteed jobs, national workshops, and the like. (Compare the "war on poverty.") But Tocqueville also saw how the emergent class consciousness of the bourgeoisie meant that anti-Jacobin democracy could itself become an ideology of stabilization. On this model stable governmental institutions would be accepted as the precondition for the realization of democratic ideals.

In the tradition of Tocqueville some of our most prominent conservative political observers tell us that the greatest threat to democratic *institutions* lies in the intensity of belief in democratic *values*. For example, Samuel Huntington argues that our populist democratic values are intrinsically biased against the consolidations of power necessary for stable government — they represent an "anti-power ethic." As a result, he says, our politics goes in cycles. At the extremes we move from the "hypocritical" stance that our institutions necessarily embody our values, to the "moralistic" stance that our values condemn our institutions. According to Huntington, we depart from these extremes only by becoming less committed to our values, or less critical of our institutions. In the one case we become "cynical" and in the other "complacent." Huntington stresses that the particular stage of the cycle we are in does not significantly depend on either the contents of our values or on institutional performance, but rather on variation in our commitment to those values and in our beliefs about how far they fit our institutions. The task of the true conservative democrat, according to Huntington, is to promote political stability by defending democratic institutions against cynicism and democratic values against complacency — without lapsing into either moralism on the one hand or hypocrisy on the other. As such a democratic spokesman for the party of order, Huntington takes as his model Alexis de Tocqueville.[34]

Huntington's cycle fits the pattern of responses to the American Welfare State by the democratic Left. In the 1960s and 1970s, writers such as Piven and Cloward invoked populist moralism against public welfare programs by suggesting that, as a device for "regulating the poor," 'big government' merely serves the interests of capital.[35] This argument implied that the core of the Welfare State should no longer be seen as a hard-won victory against the ruling class, but rather as a more or less effective means of social control. From such an analysis it followed that the spontaneous popular movements that had struggled to create the Welfare State were defeated at the very moment they became organized. By viewing organization as the death of democracy, Piven and Cloward argued that the apparent victories of "poor people's movements" were in fact moments of co-optation and that the true victories were in the brief moments of spontaneous revolt which shook existing power structures.[36]

[34] Huntington, *American Politics: The Promise of Disharmony*, chs 1–4. For earlier versions of his argument see "The Democratic Distemper" and "The United States."
[35] Piven and Cloward, *Regulating the Poor* (1971).
[36] Piven and Cloward, *Poor People's Movements* (1977).

The writings of Piven and Cloward before the Reagan era imply that every liberal reform is a defeat and betrayal of the social movement that fought for it. Their rhetoric provides a clear illustration of the American "anti-power ethic" that Huntington describes.[37] Since state power can only be exercised in the interest of the ruling class, Piven and Cloward suggested that true social democracy is intrinsically a challenge to state organization. Such a stance, however, raises serious questions about the goals of progressive movements. If socialism cannot be institutionalized in the state, it becomes nothing other than the struggle for socialism – a glorification of moments of popular protest within a democratic culture.

Piven and Cloward dramatically shifted their rhetorical ground when the consensus underlying the Welfare State came under widespread attack in the Reagan era. Newly jeopardized welfare programs now appeared not as instruments of social control, but as partial victories in the struggle for socialism that the socially dominant interests were bound to resist. Instead of being a capitalist tool, the Welfare State was now portrayed as the democratic critique of market society. As anti-Reagan activists, Piven and Cloward concluded that, given our unique democratic tradition, the "American road to socialism" lies in strengthening state institutions in the struggle to resist private power.[38]

In response to changing circumstances Piven and Cloward thus moved from arguing that democratic values cannot possibly be institutionalized to arguing that they are already embodied so far as possible in existing institutions that are now under attack. To Huntington this would merely constitute a cyclical shift from moralism to hypocrisy, signifying the ebb of "creedal passion" in the larger culture. For us it reveals the impotence and confusion of the democratic Left: our radical intellectuals tell us to regard every liberal reform as a betrayal of democracy, unless it has been defeated; they urge us to attack the Welfare State, until it is in retreat. In such a politics victory can never be claimed – when we are alive we are merely dying, but when we are dead we are immortal.[39]

The kernel of truth in Piven and Cloward's politics is Hegel's point that state institutions are *both* a means of engineering popular consent and an instrument of popular control over private power. From this one might conclude that democracy involves a twofold struggle: (1) to strengthen the

[37] This phrase comes from Huntington, *American Politics: The Promise of Disharmony*, pp. 38–9.
[38] Piven and Cloward, "The American Road to Socialism" (1983), and *The New Class War* (1982).
[39] I here adapt the criticism of Sheldon Wolin in Holmes, "On Reading Marx Apolitically," p. 113.

state against the high citadels of social power, and (2) to wrest at least some of this power back from the high citadels of the state.[40] Although this twofold view of democratic politics carries its own contradictions, as we shall see below,[41] radical democrats such as Piven and Cloward never see more than one side of the picture at a time. When the Welfare State is ascendant, they tell us that democratic power lies in the disbanded protests that created it; when the Welfare State is in decline, they tell us that democratic power lies in the ability of government to provide benefits. In both of their incarnations Piven and Cloward tell us that we *had* power, lost it, and must struggle for it yet again. Their reflexive conception of popular democracy invariably puts them in opposition to the majority. Yet their call to action is also an ideology that reconciles them to the inevitability of their own defeat.

The recent popular reaction against the leadership of our own radical democrats should not surprise us; it parallels the popular rejection of the Jacobin leadership in the aftermath of 1848. Marx describes the rhetoric of the Party of Order in the following way:

> One slogan constantly recurred, one theme always stayed the same, one verdict was always ready, whether it was a question of the right to petition, the tax on wine, the freedom of the press, trade, the clubs, or the charter of a municipality, the protection of personal freedom or the regulation of the state budget: the invariable word '*socialism*'. Even bourgeois liberalism was declared *socialist*, as well as bourgeois enlightenment and bourgeois financial reform. It was socialist to build a railway where a canal already existed, and it was socialist to defend oneself with a stick when attacked with a rapier.
>
> This was not merely a figure of speech, a fashion, or a piece of party tactics. The bourgeoisie correctly saw that all the weapons it had forged against feudalism were turning their points against the bourgeoisie itself, that all the means of education it had produced were rebelling against its own civilization,[42] and that all the gods it had created had abandoned it. It understood that all the so-called bourgeois liberties and organs of progress were attacking and threatening its *class rule* both at the social foundation and the political summit, and had therefore become '*socialist*'. It rightly discerned the secret of socialism in this threat and this attack.[43]

[40] See Walzer, "Dissatisfaction in the Welfare State" (originally published as "Radical Politics in the Welfare State").
[41] See chapter 9.
[42] Cf. Huntington, "The Democratic Distemper," and Bell, *The Cultural Contradictions of Capitalism*.
[43] Marx, "The Eighteenth Brumaire," pp. 188–9.

In telling the story of the aftermath of 1848 (including the period of reaction that Tocqueville did not live to see) Marx shows how the radical democrats eventually came to play the fool. "No party exaggerates," he says, "the means at its disposal more than the democratic party. No party deludes itself more frivolously about the situation." At another point, Marx describes the delusion of the petit bourgeois democrat, who represents no single faction of the bourgeoisie, and thereby thinks he represents the common cause of all.[44]

> [Because he forms] a *transitional class* in which the interests of two classes meet and become blurred, he imagines that he is elevated above class antagonisms generally. The democrats admit that they are confronted with a privileged class, but assert that they, along with all the rest of the nation, form the *people*. What they represent is the *right of the people*; what interests them is the *interests of the people*. Therefore, when a struggle approaches, they do not need to examine the interests and positions of the various classes. They do not need to weigh up the means at their disposal too critically. They have only to give the signal for the people, with all its inexhaustible resources, to fall upon the oppressors. If in the sequel their interests turn out to be uninteresting and their power turns out to be impotence, either this is the fault of dangerous sophists, who split the *indivisible people* into different hostile camps, or the army was too brutalized and deluded to understand that the pure goals of democracy were best for it too, or a mistake in one detail of implementation has wrecked the whole plan, or indeed, unforeseen accident has frustrated the game this time. In each case the democrat emerges as spotless from the most shameful defeat as he was innocent before he went into it, fresh in his conviction that he must inevitably be victorious, taking the view that conditions must ripen to meet his requirements, rather than that he and his party must abandon their old standpoint.[45]

This description could easily apply to the reflexive politics of Piven and Cloward today. Our radical bourgeoisie is still able to understand its politics in terms of the impossibility of its ideals. As a result, it has one coherent view of what it is doing, and yet another coherent view of what is happening to it. The conjuncture of these two views can allow the bourgeoisie to feel that it is somehow in control and at the same time non-responsible. In this way it is possible to accept the necessity of political repression while still continuing to regard oneself as a democrat.

---

[44] In America of the 1970s the slogan of "common cause" and the oxymoron of "the citizen's lobby" were among the delusions of this faction.
[45] Marx, "The Eighteenth Brumaire," pp. 179–80.

Politics and self-knowledge

Our comparison of the responses of Marx and Tocqueville to 1848 reveals a general problem about politics and political action: what is the relation between one's feelings and one's analysis? in what sense can we continue to believe in democracy while coming to accept the necessity of its failure? can we simultaneously achieve a coherent understanding of ourselves and of our world? Engaging in revolutionary politics, whether in 1848 or in 1968, inevitably leads one to question one's feelings of sincerity, single-mindedness, and purity of heart.

In writing his history Tocqueville was trying to achieve a retrospective clarity of motives by distinguishing between himself and the events that surrounded him. The beauty and power of his book consist in his attempting to maintain fidelity to his positions as both an actor and an observer, so that he can emerge with a coherent understanding of both what he did and what happened to him. Through his memoir he articulates both a self and a fate by internalizing one part of his social world and externalizing another.

Marx, in writing about the same set of events, addressed the impotence of those whose politics is only a form of communication striving toward the therapeutic ideal of being fully understood.[46] For such persons, Marx believed, it is usually enough to realize why they will be misunderstood in order to be reconciled to their fate. This of course is exactly what happened to Tocqueville.

In contrast to Tocqueville Marx's analysis of 1848 is centrally concerned with the displacements and tensions between how one explains the world and how one justifies oneself within it. Unlike other writers on democratic theory, Marx focuses on how we internalize our politics as action and externalize it as necessity, thereby coming to see our political life as at once transparent and opaque. Whatever one concludes about Marx's substantive political views, his is the only available theory that recognizes the possibility that we are victims of both false objectification and false subjectification. The former occurs when we project our own desires as external necessities; the latter when we introject external forces as our own wishes.

Marxism and Jacobinism

Thus far our discussion of Marx's ambivalent relation to democratic theory and practice in 1848 is an extension of the first three methodological points described in chapter 4 above: he is critical of the fact that both sides of the debate about democratic revolution are mainly concerned with overcoming the alienation of the theorist; he focuses on the contradictory ways in which democratic actors distinguish between the apparently objective and subjective factors in their situation; and he views democratic theory as an ideology that functions within the institutions that the theory purports to encompass.

Although Marx did not fully appreciate the concrete political significance of these insights until the events of 1848, the seeds of Marx's mature thought were present even in his early writings, where, in commenting on Hegel and Bauer, Marx explicitly recognized that the Jacobin distinction between state and civil society was deeply ambiguous. On the one hand, Marx argued, the boundary seemed real, even to those who believed that it should be overcome. On the other hand he recognized that each side of the boundary seemed to give a picture of modern life that was complete in itself: in one picture everything is the state, and we are always citizens; in the other there is only civil society, and we are always bourgeois. Even in his youth Marx saw that the distinction between state and civil society performed two theoretical functions – sometimes representing a boundary between two parts of a single whole and sometimes evoking two alternative views of the whole itself, as if seen in double exposure.

Despite this important insight, however, Marx's early writings still embraced the Jacobin illusions of the Left-Hegelians of his day by insisting in various ways that state and civil society must be treated as identical for purposes of critique. For example, he straightforwardly used Feuerbach's method of "transformative criticism" to argue against Hegel's archaic view of sovereignty. Where Hegel said that the sovereign must be a person, Marx argued that this conceals the truth that in the modern state the people must be sovereign.[47] Where Hegel had attacked the illusions of popular sovereignty by distinguishing between state and civil society, Marx, adapting Feuerbach, equated popular sovereignty and socialism by rejecting that distinction. Against Hegel's apparent view that modern governmental institutions necessarily embody democratic values, Marx flirted with the radical populist position that democracy, as spontaneous mass action, cannot possibly be institutionalized.[48]

In describing the aftermath of 1848 Marx largely abandoned the revolutionary mystique by recognizing, especially in "The Eighteenth Brumaire,"

---

[46] For a recent expression of this conception of politics, see Habermas, *Communication and the Evolution of Society.*
[47] See Marx, *Critique of Hegel's 'Philosophy of Right,'* pp. 20–40. This passage is far less sophisticated than Marx's discussions of Hegel's Executive and Legislature which immediately follow.
[48] Cf. the discussion of Huntington in chapter 9, below.

that the ongoing nineteenth-century debate between liberalism and socialism had arisen out of the ambiguous Jacobin legacy on the question of state and civil society. Both sides in this political debate saw the first French Revolution, for better or worse, as an incomplete attempt to transform the state and civil society at once. In the liberal view legitimate politics would largely consist of articulating and defending a boundary between state and society, public and private.[49] Illegitimate politics − political corruption − would then be defined as the conflation of public and private realms, such as typically occurs when private interests influence political judgments, or when politics intrudes upon private life. According to its liberal critics the French Revolution failed to establish a legitimate democracy because it was corrupted by the very social forces that it had unleashed. The liberal project in the aftermath of the Napoleonic state was to create a stable democratic order based on popular participation and social pluralism − an order that guaranteed respect for public and private interests, each in their proper place.[50]

In the socialist view the distinction between state and society was artificial; legitimate politics would largely consist of attacking that distinction wherever it appeared, thereby overcoming it in both theory and practice. The first French Revolution had failed, according to its socialist critics, because it did not root out of civil society the vestiges of private power that the revolution had promised to defeat at the level of the state: only when the state completed its takeover of society would society also be able to complete its takeover of the state. For Jacobin socialists the democratic project in the aftermath of the Napoleonic state was to act out and transcend the recognition that political and social power are ultimately indistinguishable.

Marx's mature response to the events of 1848 was in part a Hegelian critique of the tension between the liberal and socialist strands of post-revolutionary Jacobin thought. The message of the *Philosophy of Right*, written at the end of the Napoleonic era, was that the achievement of order is the implicit goal of all politics, whether revolutionary or not. In

[49] Marx pointed out in his essay "On the Jewish Question" that the paradigmatic boundary for American liberalism is the separation of church and state, but that liberal theory extends this principle of separation to civil society in general.

[50] For good recent statements of this position see Walzer, "Liberalism and the Art of Separation" and *Spheres of Justice*.

For an implicit liberal critique of the French Revolution see Tocqueville's discussion of the political significance of religion in America in *Democracy in America*. Marx makes use of these observations in his critique of Bruno Bauer in "On the Jewish Question." See also Marx and Engels, *The Holy Family*, ch. 6.

the modern state, as Hegel described it, the "people" is a creation of political institutions, and not vice versa. A main function of political representation in the Hegelian state is to organize and constitute a separate sphere of "civil society" as an idea in the minds of the people[51] – thereby inhibiting direct political action by social forces, and requiring even oppositional groups to work through officially recognized organizations. The failure of 1848 taught Marx the Hegelian lesson that, even if democracy or socialism are what a revolution demands, a democratic or socialist *state* will be the best it can achieve, and that a revolution that fails to achieve political order will inevitably be defeated by a party of order.[52] From that point forward Marx recognized that the revolutionary creation or transformation of political institutions presents a paradox: if the criterion for a successful revolution is whether it succeeds in creating a more stable successor state, the successor state will most likely reveal itself to be a more fully realized version of its predecessor – incorporating a broader range of elements from the Old Regime in a new, more self-conscious, form.

A version of the foregoing paradox was seized upon by conservative scholars in the 1960s and 1970s, who argued that the successful establishment of stable Marxist–Leninist regimes in the twentieth century had required the repudiation (however tacit) of Marx's own utopian socialism in favor of a renewed emphasis on building political institutions. According to these scholars, Marxism–Leninism had solved the problem of political stability because, despite the economic shortcomings of state socialism, the existence of a strong mass Party would preclude the possibility of oppositional movements that could destabilize a centralized regime. The clear conclusion was that the success of Leninism in creating exemplary Hegelian states owed little, if anything, to Marx's own political thought. Huntington stated this view most provocatively when he argued that, as a builder of political institutions, Lenin had more in common with Madison than with Marx, who was, according to Huntington, a political *naif*.[53]

---

[51] This would be true in both the ordinary sense of "Idea," and in the special Hegelian sense in which an "Idea" is not an abstract thought, but a reality, such as an institution, which could not be what it is without being understood ("realized") to be so from within. The thought is thus considered as part of the reality; the reality as thought-dependent. See chapter 2, above, and appendix 1, below.

[52] In chapter 9, below, these issues are discussed in relation to Huntington's view of the role of revolution in arresting political decay and advancing political development.

[53] See Huntington, *Political Order in Changing Societies*, pp. 334–43. These themes are taken up again in chapter 9.

From the standpoint of the late twentieth century, however, this view of Marxist politics has obvious deficiencies. The premise that existing Marxist–Leninist states are paradigms of stability, once widely shared by Left and Right, now seems to have grossly underestimated the possibility of organized oppositional politics within such regimes. Moreover, there is ample reason to doubt the view that in laying the foundation for a strong Hegelian state Lenin provides a political theory that is a clear advance on the original version of Marxism. I believe, rather, that Marx's own method of political analysis is relevant to understanding the internal politics generated by Hegelian states both East and West,[54] and that the recent emergence of destabilizing oppositional movements in authoritarian states – both "communist" and "anti-communist" – is consistent with a distinctively Marxian approach to political theory that is not merely the ideology of an existing "people's democracy."

In order to show how Marxian political theory goes beyond a Hegelian politics of reconciliation to the bureaucratic state we must now explore the institutional dimensions of his joint critique of Hegel and the Left-Hegelians. We shall see in the following three chapters that, although Marx began his political career as one Jacobin socialist among others, his originality does not lie in such populist critique of the Hegelian state, but rather in his method for analyzing the historical significance of popular movements within states that are creating civil societies on the Hegelian model – a process that we are witnessing today in the heretofore Leninist states of Eastern Europe and Asia.[55]

[54] Lenin himself might be plausibly reinterpreted as a more or less skilled practitioner of that method.
[55] For a recent discussion of this process see Keane, *Democracy and Civil Society*. See also Keane (ed.), *Civil Society and the State*.

7 Unity and Fragmentation

Classes and groups in modern politics

Did Marx underestimate or ignore the persistent role of groups other than capitalists and proletarians in the politics of the modern state? Most recent commentators on both the Right and the Left would agree with this charge. They believe that Marx's lifelong preoccupation with relations of exploitation in the marketplace blinded him to the other forms of oppression that exist in society, and hence to the possible emergence of social movements that are not directly based on class.[1] Writers who make this criticism frequently note that Marx seemed to take up the possibility of continuing fragmentation within social classes only in his last words on politics. Thus, the final chapter of volume III of *Capital* (entitled "Classes") breaks off speaking of "the infinite fragmentation of interests and positions into which the division of social labour splits not only workers but also capitalists and landowners ..."

I believe, however, that Marx's earliest writings on politics are also directly concerned with problems of group representation in the modern state, and that his mature concern for exploitation presupposes rather than ignores the phenomenon of group conflict based on premodern social

[1] Even in his analysis of class politics, critics say, Marx's focus on concentrated power in the economy led him to ignore the existence of dispersed power in the polity. For an attempt to adjudicate this and other issues see Lindblom, "Another State of Mind: Presidential Address, American Political Science Association, 1981." A recent contribution to this discussion suggests that a Marxian analysis of power in the economy can coexist with a Weberian analysis of state organizations and a Durkheimian analysis of political participation. (See Alford and Friedland, *The Powers of Theory*.) This brings the debate over the significance of Marxism back to a purely methodological level: do we seek to interpret conflicts in the superstructure in terms of contradictions in the base, or vice versa? which is more important – capitalism or democracy?

identities, which is a fact of modern politics in both developed and dependent states.[2] The present chapter takes up the first part of this argument. The second part must await my reconstruction of *Capital* in chapters 11 and 12, below. If my interpretation there is correct, the Marxian view that exploitation is required for social reproduction need not imply that all historically important conflicts are necessarily between exploited and exploiters. Once we recognize that the pattern of exploitation will not always overlap with the pattern of perceived oppression between groups, we can appreciate that the displacements between these patterns are as important in Marxian political analysis as the possibility of their convergence.[3]

If my position is correct, debates about Marxism should no longer be concerned at the level of theory with which identities and interests are most natural or fundamental — whether based on ethnicity, gender, or economic position — but rather with why certain group divisions become politicized when they do, and around what issues. Why do some historical differences between groups become politically salient, while others,

---

[2] Cf. Glazer and Moynihan, *Beyond the Melting Pot*, and Rudolph and Rudolph, *The Modernity of Tradition*. See, more generally, Benedict Anderson, *Imagined Communities*, on the modernity of cultural nationalism, and Nairn, *The Break-up of Britain*, on the resurgence of cultural nationalism in the motherland of both industrial capitalism and "collectivist democracy" (*pace* Beer, *British Politics in the Collectivist Age*). Many writers point out that in the third world the politics of communal recognition is not a throwback to 'primitive' roots, but rather a modern successor to the politics of anti-colonialism. See, e.g., Geertz, "The Integrative Revolution: Primordial Sentiments and Civil Politics in the New States," and "After the Revolution: The Fate of Nationalism in the New States." For a discussion of the persistence of cultural nationalism in Communist states before the Gorbachev era, see Connor, *The National Question in Marxist-Leninist Theory and Strategy*.

[3] At different moments what Marxists have called "class struggles" might relate to either of these patterns, or to both. The source of this ambiguity lies in the famous statement by Marx and Engels in the *Manifesto* that "[t]he history of all hitherto existing society is the history of class struggles" ("The Manifesto of the Communist Party," p. 67), and in the examples they use to illustrate this point (ibid., p. 68). Insofar as the cited relations between "guildmaster and journeyman" and between "lord and serf" are both hierarchical, both may seem "in a word" to be relations between "oppressor and oppressed," as Marx and Engels suggest. Yet the former example does not necessarily illustrate the theory of class exploitation (surplus extraction) which Marx later developed in *Capital*. For further discussion of the rhetoric of class struggle see chapter 12, below.

apparently as great, do not?[4] Why do some forms of group politics become bases of political cohesion, while others are a permanent source of conflict?[5] The challenge for Marxists is to avoid interpreting popular action in whatever form as a response to oppression simply speaking – thereby replacing a one-sided concern with the exploitation of labor with an equally one-sided concern for the cultural and political oppression of the 'new social subjects.'

In our contemporary world a Marxist analysis of politics should be helpful in deciding when and whether to support ideologically progressive demands that are not embraced by the victims of class exploitation, and how to regard demands of those victims that are not yet ideologically progressive. What makes such decisions especially difficult is that we cannot always trust our intuitions about what ideas and social forces are progressive to begin with – and that we rightly question who "we" are in thinking that our political identity is a matter of choice. These are precisely the problems Marx had to face when he began his concrete political studies in the 1840s.

In the present chapter I argue that, through his critical study of Hegel and Bauer, Marx developed a sophisticated understanding of the problem of political identity – an understanding that I believe informs the method of *Capital* and hence Marx's mature analysis of the role of the working class in capitalist democracies. To grasp this argument, however, we must first appreciate the degree to which Hegel anticipated much of modern thought about the joint emergence of individualism and group conflict in modern polities. We shall then see how, contrary to the usual view, mature Marxism is rooted in an approach to democratic politics well suited to analyzing the political differentiation of civil society under modern capitalism. The next three chapters lay the groundwork for a reinterpretation of the political argument of *Capital*[6] by showing how Marx's critique of Hegelianism – both Left and Right – poses the problem of political identity in its essential modern form.

---

[4] 'Communalism' does not explain why conflict between Muslims and Hindus has been politicized in India but not in Indonesia; nor does 'tribalism' explain why some nationalities in Africa kill each other, while others live in peace.

[5] Lack of a common language does not explain the persistence of riots in Belgium, but not in Switzerland; nor does religious heterogeneity explain why there is continued instability in Northern Ireland, but not the Netherlands.

[6] See part III, below.

Modernity and subjectivity

We have already seen that The *Philosophy of Right* is Hegel's effort to persuade us to stop wishing that we were happy — an accidental match between desire and achievement — and to recognize that from the standpoint of the state we are already free. Hegel believed that the substitution of freedom for happiness as the paramount concern of political philosophy completes the journey that Socrates began with his search for a standard of political value that transcends traditional morality. In Hegel's view self-conscious modern citizens, like Socratic philosophers, reject received tradition as an adequate basis for believing that existing institutions are good; yet, rather than following Socrates in judging institutions by an extrinsic standard of goodness, most moderns believe that internal legitimacy is the main political test that institutions must meet.

To be legitimate, Hegel argued, institutions must be recognized from within as the embodiment of choice — subjectivity lies at their essence. ("The principle of the modern world is freedom of subjectivity.")[7] For Hegel the central problem of modern politics is the recognition by the state of the subjectivity of its citizens.[8] This formulation shifts the proper agenda of political philosophy from constructing an ideal world to reconciling the tension between our inner and our outer lives as we find them.

[7] *Hegel's Philosophy of Right* (tr. Knox), addition, para. 273, p. 286. The passage continues: "Starting from this point of view, we can hardly raise the idle question: Which is the better form of government, monarchy or democracy? We may only say that all constitutional forms are one-sided unless they can sustain in themselves the principle of free subjectivity and know how to correspond with a matured rationality." For a general discussion of this topic see Kortian, "Subjectivity and Civil Society."

[8] The modern meaning of political freedom largely consists in a demand to have one's choices recognized by institutions that one believes to be legitimate. Although Hegel's State and Plato's Republic are both based on a social division of labor, the essential difference is that in the modern world the assignment of persons to roles must acknowledge their subjective choices. (See *Hegel's Philosophy of Right* (tr. Knox), para. 206. Cf. Foster, *The Political Philosophies of Plato and Hegel*.)

According to Hegel, this development lies at the root of Western philosophy. As a pre-modern, Plato was concerned with criteria for goodness in men and institutions, but as a philosopher he was also concerned with the central role of self-knowledge among these criteria. Faced with a declining traditional morality, Plato implicitly acknowledged the emerging role of subjectivity by arguing that the individual must know the good in order to be good, and that the best state would be ruled by those who pursue knowledge of the good for its own sake. Yet, living in a slave society, Plato saw no need to argue either that freedom was necessary for virtue, or that knowledge was necessary for freedom. As a modern, however, Hegel believes that freedom replaces goodness as the central ethical concern. (See Hegel,

Hegel sometimes explained the modern task of political philosophy by evoking a now familiar contrast between modern and traditional societies. Written from a modern point of view, Hegel's general account of traditional society attempts to capture the vanished possibility that we could be happy without worrying about whether we were free.[9] For the inhabitants of traditional society, as Hegel conceived it, there is no experience of being torn between the demands of different social spheres. Neither is there a tension between nature and culture: culture appears to be natural, and, through religion, nature itself becomes continuous with the cultural world.

As an idealized caricature of non-modernity this conception of traditional society would appear to be intrinsically stable and non-progressive, although Hegel's theory of historical progress assumes, of course, that some traditional societies carry the seeds of their own destruction. Traditional societies, thus conceived, lose their ahistorical character with the introduction of critical thought — as soon as traditional peoples consciously demand satisfaction from their lives, no particular culture will be enough for them.[10] Although acknowledging that some traditional peoples may have

---

Lectures on the History of Philosophy vol. 1, pp. 384–448, and vol. 2, pp. 1–117; *Hegel's Philosophy of Right* (tr. Knox), pp. 8–10, 123–4, 133, 267, 280.)

For other treatments of Hegel's relation to Greek thought see, e.g., Inwood, "Hegel, Plato, and Greek 'Sittlichkeit,'" and Shklar, "Hegel's *Phenomenology*: An Elegy for Hellas." See also Shklar, *Freedom and Independence: A Study of the Political Ideas of Hegel's 'Phenomenology of Mind.'*

[9] We should be less concerned about the accuracy of his image of traditional society than about its role in our conception of ourselves. The notion of traditional society is intrinsically a part of modern discourse, and can refer to virtually any stage in history for which it is currently fashionable to feel nostalgia.

[10] Although Hegel's view of traditional society is now widely dismissed, many of its basic assumptions about modernity are implicitly carried forward in our contemporary social science. Today, the business of anthropology is largely to describe 'traditional' societies to us moderns as culture, rather than as nature. In doing so it necessarily focuses on their particularity, teaching that, *contra* Hegel, traditional societies are everywhere different, and that culture is nowhere 'natural.' (For a dissenting view of such societies within anthropology see Wolf, *Europe and the People Without History*.) In describing what happens when such traditional societies modernize, however, historical sociology necessarily focuses on their common features, perhaps explained by a universal logic of modernity derived from Marx, Weber, or Durkheim. As a consequence of modernization the preexisting traditions often appear in retrospect as though they had been the organic unity that Hegel described. Typically, sociological studies of societies in transition supplement the interpretation of the indigenous culture with the recognition of subjective freedom and the cultural fragmentation that results.

been free without knowing it, Hegel argued that this is impossible for us: as post-traditional individuals our problem is precisely to *know* that we are free, even while being something in particular.[11]

In contrast with tradition, modernity is characterized by Hegel as the awareness that there are alternative cultural orders and that one's place in any given one is potentially arbitrary. Although this awareness originally appears as a form of enlightenment, it is also accompanied by a sense of loss. To modern men and women, each of the available cultural possibilities can seem limiting and particularistic; yet in rejecting such limitations modern consciousness is frequently reduced to an unsatisfying form of relativism, or to a barren search for universals. Whereas all traditional cultures contain specific rituals of self-interpretation, modern cultures, and those in contact with modernity, are characterized by a diversity of interpretive practices − religious, scientific, legal, artistic − which neither together nor separately exhaust the cultural meaning of any particular activity.[12] Hegel believed that the meaning of modern life can easily be swallowed up by its multiple interpretations with the result that our inner and outer lives will each seem arbitrary and capricious in relation to the other.

According to Hegel, all modern states in ceasing to rest on traditional authority must claim to embody the freedom of individuals to interpret the meanings of their own lives.[13] Once freedom becomes the self-conscious aim of political institutions, the dominant criterion of political value becomes immanent rather than transcendent.[14] Political philosophy must then set itself the task of making those institutions comprehensible from within,[15]

---

[11] To address this problem philosophy must recognize that reason is both objective and subjective − that in order to demonstrate necessity its conclusions must be understood to be necessary. A successful philosophical demonstration should give the feeling that we are compelled by rationality as though it were an external force, and yet that it expresses a conclusion that is fully our own.

[12] See, generally, Geertz, *The Interpretation of Cultures* and *Negara*.

[13] "What is to be authoritative nowadays derives its authority, not at all from force, only to a small extent from habit and custom, really from insight and argument ... The principle of the modern world requires that what anyone is to recognize shall reveal itself to him as something entitled to recognition." (*Hegel's Philosophy of Right* (tr. Knox), p. 294.)

[14] "So far as the authority of any existing state has anything to do with reasons, these reasons are culled from the forms of law authoritative within it." Ibid., para. 258.

[15] John Rawls has lately given a similar interpretation of his own theory of justice. (See Rawls, "Justice as Fairness: Political Not Metaphysical.")

thereby placing the post-traditional state firmly within the world of "mind" — a world that, as we have seen, encompasses everything that becomes what it is in virtue of how it is understood.[16]

The mixed blessing of the modern condition in the absence of fully realized political institutions has been vividly captured in recent years by the literature that describes the plight of post-colonial elites. This literature conveys the poignancy of feeling deracinated among one's own people, of translating between cultures while living within none, and of remembering what it was like to regard one's desires as natural. Post-colonial man has ceased to be happy by trying to be free, and yet realizes that he is not free, but only torn. But, although this story is often told as a critique of the colonial idea and of the resulting mentality of underdevelopment, the story is also emblematic of the modern condition more generally.[17] With feelings no longer grounded in a received community, we too perceive ourselves to be caught between possible forms of life, none of which fully expresses our nature; we too can often feel like displaced persons in our own society, and, stranded among the fragments of our culture, we too experience our unhappiness as a struggle to be free.[18]

As Hegel saw it, a philosophy that is adequate to the modern age must allow individuals to comprehend the universal significance of the demand for subjective satisfaction in their particular circumstances. Self-knowledge would then consist of a philosophical understanding of what it means to

[16] Of course Hegel did not believe that all institutions are fully actual. His analysis is equally relevant to pathological cases in which institutions fail to fully realize themselves. This might be true of a prison system in which the inmates do not understand what happens to them as *punishment*. Our ambivalence about the prison system in this country reflects our view of prison life as a subculture resembling a very bad boarding school with no recess or vacations. Only for middle-class offenders would such institutions constitute a punishment, rather than an extension of their social world. Yet these are precisely the offenders for whom we say that ordinary prisons would "do no good." (See, above, chapter 2, and the appendix 1, below, for a discussion of the non-pathological cases — e.g., a school that becomes more fully what it is by being understood to be the realization of its students' idea of an education.)

[17] Because the plight of post-colonial man is also quintessentially our own, the recent literature on new states in old societies bears strong similarities to Hegel's view of the modern state on the threshold of self-consciousness. See, e.g., Geertz, "The Integrative Revolution: Primordial Sentiments and Civil Politics in the New States."

[18] Cf. T. S. Eliot's *Four Quartets*, in Eliot, *The Complete Poems and Plays, 1909–1950*.

live at the intersection of multiple cultures, of multiple institutions, and thus of multiple interpretive frameworks. Hegelian political philosophy overcomes this multiplicity by providing a reflexive account of the practice of interpretation as itself the master practice of a culture centrally concerned with institutional boundaries.[19]

For Hegel the existence of the modern state itself makes his new conception of political philosophy both necessary and possible. He describes this philosophical project as a demonstration that "what is rational is actual and what is actual is rational"[20] — a formulation that is often misinterpreted. Hegel is neither trying to 'rationalize the actual' — to show that the world is ideal as it already is — nor to 'actualize the rational' — to urge that the world be made over to fit some ideal plan.[21] He is rather arguing that the actual world is partly constituted through our understanding of it as rational, and that through our greater understanding the world becomes both more actual and more rational.[22] This is true, he says, not merely of the natural world, but of any institutional framework that can function as a world for us.[23]

[19] For a recent effort along similar lines see Dworkin, *Law's Empire*.

[20] *Hegel's Philosophy of Right* (tr. Knox), p. 10.

[21] Rather than promulgating "still another" theory of the state, Hegel declared that the state already exists and therefore needs to be understood rather than reinvented. (Ibid., p. 4 ff.)

[22] "To recognize reason as the rose in the cross of the present, and thereby to enjoy the present, this is the rational insight which reconciles us to the actual, the reconciliation which philosophy affords to those in whom there has once arisen an inner voice bidding them to comprehend, not only to dwell in, what is substantive while still retaining subjective freedom, but also to possess subjective freedom while standing not in anything particular and accidental, nothing arbitrary and capricious, but rather in what exists absolutely." (Ibid., p. 12.)

[23] The preface to the 1821 edition of Hegel's *Philosophy of Right* defends this conception of political philosophy against the subjectivist delusions of students who had been inspired to political protest by a mixture of the ideals of the French Revolution and of German Romanticism. Hegel criticized the students for seeking to replace all institutional embodiments of social order with the subjective feeling of vitality, inspiration, and friendship. Such love of the "people," as Hegel saw it, was really grounded on a "hatred of law" on which the stable feelings of the people rest. (*Hegel's Philosophy of Right* (tr. Knox), pp. 5—7.) According to Professor Avineri, this preface was largely motivated by Hegel's desire to distinguish himself in the eyes of his superiors from Jacob Fries, a philosophy Professor whom Hegel believed to have egged on the radical students to protest the Carlsbad Decrees. See Avineri, *Hegel's Theory of the Modern State*, ch. 6, esp. pp. 119—22, 130—1.

In stressing the ways in which a political order becomes comprehensible from within, Hegel showed how the continuing existence of modern states has come to depend upon the internal politics they create. His writing does not, however, directly express what citizens already think and feel about the political divisions that move them, but rather attempts to capture the meaning of these intuitive experiences from the standpoint of the state — to describe what it looks like to the state for citizens to feel and act as they do.

Citizenship and social differentiation

Hegel believed that in modern states we realize our individual freedom by carving an overarching sense of personal identity out of the alternative frameworks of meaning that could be used independently to characterize the whole of our lives. Our problem, essentially, is to reconcile the demand that we act with integrity across our various social roles with our understanding of ourselves as operating within many different institutional spheres at once, each of which provides a set of plausible, and sometimes conflicting, categories for understanding the others.

Hegel puts this problem concretely in the *Philosophy of Right*, when he describes "the ethical life" of male citizens.[24] Through the institution of the family, Hegel argues, each man can understand what it means to grow up, become a citizen, and eventually start a family of his own. The family man sees his working life as an interval in his day and, eventually, as an interval between childhood and old age. Yet Hegel suggests that at another level each man also understands himself as part of the economy, and thereby sees himself as a jobholder, actual or potential. To economic man the life of the family is an interval in his working day and, eventually, in his working life. Finally, Hegel says, modern man understands himself to be citizen. His citizenship — a kind of master-role — reveals the universal significance of his particular roles in the family and the work force, allowing him to redescribe his social duties in both spheres as a basis for asserting political rights. The male citizen's implicit awareness of the state's standpoint toward his own interests lets him feel free as an individual while being someone in particular — raising his family, living in his community, and doing his job.[25]

Hegel believed that in the modern world the state enables males to see

[24] *Hegel's Philosophy of Right* (tr. Knox), pp. 105–55.
[25] See ibid., e.g. addition, para. 261.

themselves as individuals by giving them a point of view that unifies the multiple identities that make up their social life. By identifying himself as a citizen the individual can regard the conflicting social identities that threaten to engulf him as an occasion for free choice.[26] In this, and also in understanding such conflicting total perspectives as merely social, the perspective of the free individual resembles the perspective of the state as a whole. Just as citizenship gives the individual a standpoint from which to reflect upon his personal goals, stepping back from the various social groupings to which he belongs, the public ideology of the state differentiates it from the groups and institutions that make up civil society so that it can reflect on the public interests they serve. Throughout the *Philosophy of Right* the complementarity between the interests of the state and of the (male) citizen provides a privileged point of view from which individuals can understand their place in society seen as a whole.

In its strong Hegelian sense the modern citizen's interest in individuality is a demand that his life be seen to have integrity across institutional boundaries – the very integrity that is properly expected of him by others and by the state. This demand, which lies at the core of political equality, is more profound than the particular interests the modern citizen may assert through the political process, and can often defeat the arguments for majority rule. Nevertheless, throughout the *Philosophy of Right* the respect for individuality is presented as a philosophical issue that becomes politically salient only on rare, and sometimes tragic, occasions. Hegel believed that for the most part the modern state upholds the value of individuality through its very existence, suggesting that the state serves the interests of *individuals* in only a conclusory sense.[27] In the *Philosophy of Right* citizenship appears to be the only vehicle through which the modern state gives equal respect to the integrity of persons. The historical process through which modern states emerge plays no part in Hegel's account of the meaning of citizenship in the fully realized state, and within the bounds of Hegel's logical method there is little more to be said about political equality once the full extension of citizenship has been achieved.

Yet, writing in the aftermath of the French Revolution, Hegel was well aware that modern citizenship is often the result of a historical struggle for

---

[26] See ibid., para. 206.

[27] "Since the state is mind objectified, it is only as one of its members that the individual himself has objectivity, genuine individuality, and an ethical life. Unification pure and simple is the true content and aim of the individual, and the individual's destiny is the living of a universal life. His further particular satisfaction, activity, and mode of conduct have this substantive and universally valid life as their starting point and their result." (Ibid., para. 258.)

political equality.[28] Although the phenomenological form of this struggle tends to be similar from state to state,[29] its particular content varies depending upon the preexisting range of social differences at play in the process of political development — differences that may be based on such factors as religion, language, ethnicity, race, culture, or gender. In the process of political modernization (the "institution-building" described by political scientists)[30] these pre-political differences frequently become the constituent group identities around which the new political order is built.

The formal extension of citizenship alone will not be enough for individuals in such regimes who demand assurance that they are being treated as political equals across a multiplicity of social roles. To meet this demand the new regime must recognize the relevant prior grounds of social differentiation as a legitimate basis for asserting the equality of *groups* within the political process. Although based on ascriptive identities, these groups may not have existed as such prior to the political organization of civil society. The creation or redefinition of such groups in a form recognizable by the state is itself an achievement of the process of political development.

With growing frequency the modern state is called upon to give constitutional significance to the process of equalizing between the preexisting constituent groups in civil society.[31] In many political systems such group equalization is built directly into the legislative process.[32] In the US, group equalization is attempted mainly by the courts, and then only when constitutionally protected values of individuality are implicated.[33] Since Hegel, like Mill, saw the political process as, at once, a form of representation and of socialization, he might not have been surprised to see that issues of process and discrimination have become increasingly significant in developed modern states. In resolving such issues constitutional authorities, like Hegelian philosophers, find they must articulate the relationship between the forms of political representation and the modes of political socialization whenever the state is called upon to take positive initiatives to correct for the potentially repressive or discriminatory effect on individuals of the whole process by which desires are formed and recognized in the political system.[34]

---

[28] See chapter 5, above.
[29] See chapter 2, above, and appendix 1, below.
[30] See, e.g., Binder, "The Crises of Political Development."
[31] See Meister, "The Logic and Legacy of *Dred Scott*."
[32] See Lijphart, *Democracies*. Cf. Rae et al., *Equalities*.
[33] Cf. Ely, *Democracy and Distrust*, and Tribe, *American Constitutional Law*, for alternative approaches to these issues within an implicitly Hegelian framework.
[34] Cf. Fiss, "Foreword: The Forms of Justice."

162 The Critical Theory of Democracy

Citizenship and group identity

Hegel did not directly address the issues of communal politics in the *Philosophy of Right* (except in passing references to religion),[35] but he did anticipate some of the issues of gender politics in the *Phenomenology*. There Hegel argues that the tragedy of Antigone — her ethical conflict — reflected a lack of historical development in the points of view of both state and individual. Since her duties to her ruler were no less personal and arbitrary than her duties to her brother, she lacked a developed perspective from which to see her conflicting identities as merely social, and hence as partial. According to Hegel, the modern state provides just such a perspective, enabling the individual to live a multiply bifurcated life without tragic consequences. In the modern state, Hegel suggests, Antigone would see her problem as one of asserting (and cultivating) her sense of individuality.[36]

Although Hegel does not spell out what this would mean from the standpoint of the state, modern constitutional jurisprudence can help bring out the implications of his idea. Presumably, Antigone's potential disobedience would not automatically call forth a legal punishment from the fully realized state, but would rather raise the issue of whether the rule of law requires or forbids her punishment for an act of conscientious refusal. The modern legal system has the capacity to resolve such issues case by case. In some circumstances the state might find it necessary to punish her in order to uphold the rule of law, but in circumstances where respect for individuality itself is crucially at stake the state might even recognize that she has a *legal* right to civilly disobey.[37]

Hegel does not directly argue that a modern Antigone must assert her identity as a woman in order to achieve equality as a citizen, but the foregoing line of analysis could explain why many women in the modern state — especially those struggling to combine home and family with a full career and equal citizenship — might come to identify themselves politically as a group entitled to equality. Antigone's tragedy, as Hegel saw it, was that she could only be a good sister in virtue of being a bad subject, or vice

[35] See, e.g., *Hegel's Philosophy of Right* (tr. Knox), para. 270.
[36] Hegel, *The Phenomenology of Spirit*, chs 6.A, 6.C, and 8. For another discussion of the role of *Antigone* in Hegel's political thought see Shklar, "Hegel's *Phenomenology*: An Elegy for Hellas," pp. 83–7.
[37] Cf. Dworkin, *Taking Rights Seriously*, chs 7–8. (A somewhat different connection between Hegel and Dworkin is noted in Steven B. Smith, *Hegel's Critique of Liberalism*, ch. 4.)

versa. In facing her tragedy Antigone recognized that a belief that she was making a choice would be self-deception — a decision to achieve a consistent view of her own intentions by projecting the contradiction in her life onto the way in which *others* understand her.[38] She had no choice but to act out her role as a woman in her family, Hegel argues, because that role was more robust and ethically engaging than her as yet undeveloped identity as a political subject. The clear implication of Hegel's interpretation is that by taking the perspective of a developed legal system Antigone would have been able to see that she had choices about how to develop herself both as a woman and as an individual.

From a Hegelian perspective the post-traditional woman, like Antigone, is constantly faced with what appear to be choices between conflicting identities; yet her belief that she *has* to choose may often reflect, at the level of feelings, an objective set of circumstances in which she ultimately *cannot* choose. Insofar as her roles at home, at work, and in civil society are implicated in each other — providing alternative, but overlapping, conceptions of the *whole* of her life — all that she *really* chooses is which of these identities to regard as her self, and which as her fate.[39] If, for example, she sees her job mainly as a way to put the children through college, she can be reconciled to the possible failure of her career as something that might happen; if she sees childbearing as an interruption in her career, she can be reconciled to the possible breakup of her family as something that might happen. But, although she appears to have a choice between the demands of two competing spheres, she continues to live in both simultaneously, viewing her family life as her true self and her career as her fate — or vice versa.[40]

Those modern feminists who see the way out as political often rely on implicitly Hegelian arguments — beginning with the premise that liberation is not possible without accepting the necessity of tensions between family and career in a context of political equality. According to this line of argument, the woman who 'has it all' may look free to others, but even she will too often feel torn between the different aspects of what is, after all, a single life. The neo-Hegelian conclusion is that only by identifying self-consciously with the public identity of a "woman" can those who are socially disadvantaged by reason of gender achieve a self-realization that

---

[38] She might have avoided contradiction in her view of what she *does*, but only by interpreting what *happens* to her as an inevitable result of misunderstanding.

[39] For a recent view of this dilemma see, generally, Hewlett, *A Lesser Life*.

[40] For a recent feminist discussion of these issues see Markus, "Women, Success and Civil Society: Submission to, or Subversion of, the Achievement Principle."

overarches the conflict between family and job. By achieving political recognition specifically as "women" they enjoy the advantages and freedoms that citizenship itself provides for men in the Hegelian state. In this way women's liberation as a special form of citizenship could reconcile women to their everyday problems, enabling them to see these problems as what it feels like to look free.[41]

Through politicizing the differences between prior social distinctions, such as that between men and women, the modern political system satisfies our need to claim a standpoint outside the state at the very moment that we assert the political importance of our identities within it. The feminist citizen who addresses the state by identifying herself as a "woman" would be implicitly claiming to envision society as a whole, even while explicitly claiming to defend her particular interests within it.

The foregoing argument suggests that men who are citizens (and women who are also feminists) will be able to understand the problems that the modern state generates as inevitable tensions between family, job, and citizenship, and that, through appreciating those tensions, modern citizens will come to a mature sense of who they are and what they want. Such a conclusion would have been philosophically congenial to Hegel. His argument about the relation between individuality and citizenship directly applies only to those who enjoy the fullest citizenship available in a culturally homogeneous nation-state,[42] and presupposes that women will remain second-class citizens. Where citizenship is a product of a historical struggle for political equality, Hegel could have appreciated that many of the constitutional rights of citizens must be asserted through, rather than against, primordial social identities. His notion of citizenship was not based on abstract universalism, but on the infusion of particular identities with a universal significance for persons who will thereby come to regard themselves as individuals.

---

[41] For a defense of the implicit radicalism of Hegel's own view of the relation between the family, the economy, and the state see Westphal, "Hegel's Radical Idealism: Family and State as Ethical Communities."

[42] In *Hegel's Philosophy of Right* (tr. Knox), para. 274, he elaborates: "Mind is actual only as that which it knows itself to be, and the state, as the mind of a nation, is both the law permeating all relationships within the state and also at the same time the manners and consciousness of its citizens. It follows, therefore, that the constitution of any given nation depends in general on the character and development of its self-consciousness. In its self-consciousness its subjective freedom is rooted."

The differentiation of institutions and of groups

Our Hegelian account of the relation between individuality and group identity presupposes the existence of two forms of social differentiation — two senses of the term "pluralism" — which are commonly addressed in recent literature, but rarely together. These are, on the one hand, the differentiation of institutional "spheres" and, on the other hand, the differentiation of social groups.[43] In one sense modern men and women characteristically live out their lives in a plurality of social spheres — such as the economy, the family, the educational system — each associated with a distinctive category of institutional thought. When these spheres, or institutional categories, overlap, there is a need for a unifying perspective that allows one to live simultaneously within them, and to reconcile their often conflicting demands — the perspective through which one defines one's individuality as transcending one's social roles. In another sense, however, these individuals who live at the intersection of differentiated institutional categories must also identify themselves as members of differentiated social groups — men and women, white and black, Catholic and Protestant — in order to determine whether they are being discriminated against as citizens. Although specific lines of group division may be more closely associated with some institutional spheres than with others, group identities tend to become politically salient when they cut across several institutional spheres so as to express a standpoint from which to view civil society as a whole.

Hegelian pluralism recognizes the connection between these two forms of social differentiation. According to Hegel, the political importance of group identity is a product of the complex relations between institutional spheres, and the need to define one's individuality within them.[44] His argument is not merely the instrumental claim that individuals need to act through groups in order to assert themselves in a world of impersonal corporate entities.[45] Rather, Hegel suggests that persons need to imagine civil society to consist of groups as well as institutions in order to conceive

---

[43] Cf. Dahl, *Dilemmas of Pluralist Democracy*, and Luhmann, *The Differentiation of Society*. In separate works Michael Walzer has defended "pluralism" in both of these senses. (Cf. Walzer, *Spheres of Justice* and "Pluralism in Political Perspective.")

[44] A variant of this form of institutional analysis is Hegel's strained effort to rationalize the 'modern' political significance of primogeniture in aristocratic families. Cf. *Hegel's Philosophy of Right* (tr. Knox), para. 306, and Marx's commentary on this passage in Marx, *Critique of Hegel's 'Philosophy of Right,'* pp. 97–102.

[45] For interesting elaborations of this argument see the various contributions to Berger (ed.), *Organizing Interests in Western Europe*.

of themselves as individuals with an integrated understanding of their social world.

We can illustrate this insight by returning to some of the issues raised by contemporary feminism. From a neo-Hegelian standpoint the identity of woman has become politically salient, not because the point of view of gender is more fundamental or natural than other forms of social identification, but because women have come to invest their historic oppression with contemporary political meaning in order to comprehend their problems in living simultaneously at the convergence of many institutions, such as the family, the labor market, the educational system, and the state. Unlike the social theorist Michael Walzer, who sometimes argues that politics is the only institutional sphere that is properly concerned with the boundaries of the others,[46] Hegel perceived that political problems arise because each institutional sphere includes its boundaries with the others within itself, thereby offering an alternative environmental perspective on the whole of society. Because, as we have seen, the modern woman inevitably understands herself from all of these perspectives at once, she cannot escape the economic (career), personal (family), or educational significance of the choices she makes; her choices have such significance, whether she wants them to or not.

From a neo-Hegelian perspective, primordial social identities acquire modern political meaning at the junctures where differentiated institutions give fundamentally *conflicting* pictures of the value of the same activity. The institutional categories of family, economy, and education – to follow our example – each provide the individual woman with a model of fulfillment that can liberate her from the 'tyranny' of the others; yet each also provides a corresponding ground for criticizing the woman who seeks her liberation through the others. A woman's choices may thus be valued differently when her husband looks at the relationship between her education and employment and when her employer looks at the relationship between her educational qualifications and her role as wife and mother – and differently still when her teachers look at the relationship between her private life as a daughter/wife/mother and her career prospects. Rather than representing incommensurable 'worlds,' however, these different valuations often invoke common norms in virtually opposite ways. For example, a woman may be perceived to act self-indulgently from the critical perspective of family and career when she fulfills her educational potential by pursuing those subjects that have greatest interest for her in school; she may act selfishly from the perspective of school and family

[46] See Walzer, *Spheres of Justice.*

when she single-mindedly pursues career success. She may act self-destructively from the standpoint of school and career when she drops out to fulfill her perceived duties to her family.[47]

Faced with such conflicting valuations of the same choices, a modern woman could demand social equality by asserting that her identity as a woman is not exhausted by its meaning in any specific institution. She could plausibly imagine that institutions would be changed if the normative conflicts between them were as acute for men, and conclude that the social function of such conflicts is to subordinate her as a woman.[48] This conclusion would be easy to understand from a neo-Hegelian perspective: by identifying her problems as those of a woman the conflicted individual can grasp the unity of her life.[49] A feminist political consciousness would then enable her to understand herself as an individual living across institutional boundaries, while making it the business of the state to define the effect that one institutional framework should have on another.

Women do not, of course, differ from men in seeing themselves simultaneously from each of these institutional perspectives − just as slaves do not differ from masters in experiencing social contradictions; yet Hegel would not deem it an objection to the foregoing account of our contemporary women's movement that it merely interprets the significance of feminist politics for those who are already engaged by it. As a form of afterthought, Hegel's philosophical approach to modern institutions is content to comprehend the necessity of what actually happens in political life.[50] Under the historical circumstances of late twentieth-century industrial society, a neo-Hegelian could plausibly argue that conflicts between the ways in

[47] Cf. Hegel's discussion of Antigone in *The Phenomenology of Spirit*, chs 6.A, 6.C and 8, and Markus, "Women, Success and Civil Society: Submission to, or Subversion of, the Achievement Principle."

[48] See, e.g., MacKinnon, "Feminism, Marxism, Method, and the State: An Agenda for Theory."

[49] Hegel himself understood this, although he felt that the perspective of the free individual that becomes possible in the modern state would allow a woman to resolve and transcend such tragic contradictions between her ethical roles in society. Cf. *The Phenomenology of Spirit* (on "The Ethical Order") and *Hegel's Philosophy of Right* (tr. Knox) (on "Ethical Life"). For further discussion of Hegel's view of marriage see chapters 2 and 3, above.

[50] As we have already seen, Hegel believed that social science is inevitably part of its own time and place, and stands within the institutional reality it purports to comprehend. A theory that claims to predict which social movements will become politically salient in the future would be viewed by Hegel as part of the politics of the present, and beneath the level of philosophical self-understanding to which he aspired.

which the roles of women are described in various institutional frameworks make it necessary for individuals to identify as women (or with women) in order to grasp their social situation as a whole. These are the circumstances in which organized womanhood (the women's movement) would become a self-conscious social force capable of bringing about political change.

Living at the intersection of multiple institutions, the politically active feminist would be able to see her fragmented world as a totality from within. Her personal problems might then turn into the dilemma they already pose for the state: how to represent the contradiction between plural institutional spheres in society as a conflict between plural groups in the political system? Like the state itself, the neo-Hegelian feminist would posit the unity (or fragmentation) of the social formation as a direct relation between groups that appear and interact at the level of the political process. The political representation of groups then becomes the medium in which the contradictions between specific institutional spheres appear from the standpoint of both the state and individual. As Hegel puts it:

> Civil society is the [stage of] difference which intervenes between the family and the state, even if its formation follows later in time than that of the state ... [I]t presupposes the state; to subsist itself it must have the state before its eyes as something self-subsistent. Moreover, the creation of civil society is the achievement of the modern world which has for the first time given all determinations of the Idea their due.[51]

Assimilation and cultural nationalism: the Jewish question

The tension between the universal and particular aspects of Hegel's conception of citizenship in the modern state was hotly debated in Marx's

---

In the preface to the *Philosophy of Right* Hegel raised a similar objection to theories that offer an abstract justification of a political future based on one or another social identity: "As a work of philosophy, [this book] must be poles apart from an attempt to construct a state as it ought to be ... [I]t can only show how the state ... is to be understood ... To comprehend what is, this is the task of philosophy ... Whatever happens, every individual is a child of his time; so philosophy, too, is its own time apprehended in thoughts ... If [the philosopher's] theory really goes beyond the world as it is, and builds an ideal one as it ought to be, that world exists indeed, but only in his opinion, an unsubstantial element where anything you please may, in fancy, be built." (*Hegel's Philosophy of Right* (tr. Knox), p. 11.)

[51] Ibid., p. 266.

youth. This debate was occasioned by the rise of various forms of cultural nationalism — a phenomenon that some Left-Hegelians saw as a form of the human demand for self-determination that could not be met by abstract citizenship, and that other Left-Hegelians took as a betrayal of the promise of universal citizenship to liberate mankind from the bonds of social oppression.[52]

Moses Hess was one of many Left-Hegelians who came to suspect in the early 1840s that self-consciously assimilated nationalities would come to behave like corporatist interest groups in the modern state. He believed that, once the peculiarities of national communities have been incorporated into a cosmopolitan consensus, such communities would give up the hope of radically transforming society through the state in order to defend their narrow prerogatives as minorities in the political system.

This, as a socialist, Hess feared. Inspired politically by Mazzini, Hess came to argue that cultural nationalism was necessary in order to break the hold of the old universalizing empires that had enslaved not only individuals, but whole peoples. Inspired philosophically by Feuerbach, Hess consistently believed that a people could achieve egalitarian community only by celebrating and accentuating the particular cultural differences that distinguished it from other nations. Believing that socialism required nationalism, Hess concluded that the success of socialism in Europe would inevitably exclude such cultural minorities as the Jews. These excluded groups would need their own national homeland to achieve communal equality; Jews, for example, would first have to struggle for Zionism in order to achieve the kind of egalitarian community that established nations could create by struggling directly for socialism. (Hess believed, moreover, that establishment of a Jewish state would enable Jews living elsewhere to demand their civil rights as full political equals in multicultural Hegelian states — only by having a national homeland could Jews choosing to live outside be fully 'naturalized' as a minority group.)[53]

In contrast to the position of Hess among the Left-Hegelians, Bruno Bauer attacked the Jews for demanding civil rights by organizing around

---

[52] For a discussion of Hegel's view of nationhood see Pelczynski, "Nation, Civil Society, State: Hegelian Sources of the Marxian Non-theory of Nationality." For a provocative account of the power of cultural nationalism in determining political identity see Benedict Anderson, *Imagined Communities.*

[53] For a rich account of Hess, see Berlin, "The Life and Opinions of Moses Hess." See also Avineri, "Moses Hess: Socialism and Nationalism as a Critique of Bourgeois Society."

For a view of Marx's relation to his own Jewish origins see Berlin, "Benjamin Disraeli, Karl Marx and the Search for Identity."

their Jewish identity, arguing that in doing so they stooped to the level of their persecutors. He placed the burden on Jews, and presumably on other communal minorities, to base their political demands on a desire for assimilation that attacks the cultural particularism of the majority. Like recent opponents of preferential treatment for minorities, Bauer believed that such communal minorities discredit themselves unless they deny the political relevance of all group differences *per se.*[54]

Bauer concluded that Jews would truly liberate themselves from the kind of religious prejudice that lies at the root of the Christian state if they would renounce all religion and become atheists, instead of either asserting a right to their Jewishness or adopting Christianity. The Jews, Bauer argued, in taking this vanguard position on the question of religion might set an example of a kind of universalism that would transcend group interests and make way for a politics of enlightened individualism on the part of all citizens.

In his subsequent attacks on Bruno Bauer in "On the Jewish Question,"[55] Marx implicitly accepted Hess's point that demands for communal equality could be easily incorporated in the liberal state, without, however, embracing Hess's eventual conclusion that socialism would only be possible within national communities.[56] Before explaining the continuing role of communal identities in the modern state, however, Marx acknowledged that at the moment of its creation (as in the first French Revolution) the modern state may seek to suppress the preexisting social differences which it must later find ways of incorporating.

> Of course, in periods when the political state ... comes violently into being ... the state can and must proceed to the ... destruction of religion ... At those times when it is particularly self-confident, political life attempts to suppress its presupposition, civil society ... But it only manages

[54] See Bauer, "The Jewish Problem" and "The Capacity of Present Day Jews and Christians to Become Free." Most of the relevant passages from Bauer are quoted in Marx's various critiques. See Marx, "On the Jewish Question."

[55] See also the interesting elaboration of the debate with Bauer in Marx and Engels, *The Holy Family*, ch. 6; "A Reply to Bruno Bauer's Anti-Critique"; and *The German Ideology*, pp. 107–14.

[56] Avineri discusses Hess's influence on Marx's critique of Bauer in "Moses Hess: Socialism and Nationalism as a Critique of Bourgeois Society."

Marx later came to see Hess's populist communitarianism ("true socialism") as being in effect a reactionary ideological weapon against the progressive demands of the bourgeoisie. See Marx and Engels, "The Manifesto of the Communist Party," pp. 90–3; and *The German Ideology*, pp. 114–6, 455–70, 491–3.

to do this in *violent* contradiction to the conditions of its own existence, by declaring the revolution *permanent*, and for that reason the *political* drama necessarily ends up with the restoration of religion, private property, and all the elements of civil society, just as war ends with peace.[57]

Here Marx recognizes that despite the Jacobin origins of some Hegelian states, communal groups based on primordial social identities will eventually flourish alongside corporate groups at the level of civil society. As modern states mature, such groups will be recognized as social movements and, to a greater or lesser extent, accommodated along with other (corporate) groups. This essentially Hegelian point anticipates our effort earlier in this chapter to elaborate Hegel's theory of citizenship so as to make room for the constitutional importance of certain kinds of group identity in the modern state.

In the Hegelian state, Marx argues, "the Jew *acts politically* when, although a Jew, he demands civil rights."[58] This point had been missed by Left-Hegelian radicals, just as it has been missed once again by modern day liberals who criticize the "racism" or "communalism" of reverse discrimination programs.[59] Marx declared his independence of the Left-Hegelians in "On the Jewish Question" by noticing that the collective identities that determined social status in the old regime could in practice become the basis of organizing to demand individual equality in the new. Far from being abolished, these identities might be institutionalized in the modern state as the social basis of political participation.

> Bauer asks the Jews: Do you from your standpoint have the right to demand *political emancipation*? We pose the question the other way round: Does the standpoint of *political* emancipation have the right to demand from the Jews the abolition of Judaism and from man the abolition of religion? ... What is the relationship between *complete* political emancipation and religion. If in the land of complete political emancipation [the US] we find not only that religion *exists* but that it exist in a *fresh* and *vigorous* form, that proves that the existence of religion does not contradict the perfection of the state ... Therefore the *state* can have emancipated itself from religion even if the *overwhelming majority* is still religious.[60]

---

[57] Marx, "On the Jewish Question," p. 222.
[58] Ibid., p. 226.
[59] See Glazer, *Affirmative Discrimination*, and Isaacs, *India's Ex-Untouchables.* Cf. Meister, "Discrimination Law Through the Looking Glass."
[60] Marx, "On the Jewish Question," pp. 216–18.

Marx continues this passage by pointing out that the salience of religious differences in the politics of civil society is not an aberration in the secular state. Rather, he argues, the process of political secularization both presupposes and reinforces the significance of religious divisions at the level of society. Religion will continue to have political significance, Marx argues, even after it has been banished from "the province of public law." Indeed, the effect of secularization in the modern state is that religion "is no longer the essence of *community* but the essence of *difference*."

> The ... *displacement* of religion from state to civil society is not one step in the process of political emancipation but its *completion* ... The *dissolution* of man into Jew and citizen, Protestant and citizen, religious man and citizen is not a denial of citizenship or an avoidance of political emancipation: it is *political emancipation itself*, it is the *political* way of emancipating oneself from religion.[61]

In his critique of Bauer Marx thus returned to an insight deriving from Hegel on the role of the political representation of interests in the modern state: for itself representation is a means for the people to transform the state; in itself it is a means for the state to control the people. Marx recognized that the persistence and reproduction of certain group cleavages is not an accident of modern politics, but a necessary feature of modern politics − part of the dialectic through which more or less stable political institutions can be created on the basis of realizable democratic expectations.

> Political emancipation from religion allows religion − but not privileged religion − to continue in existence. The contradiction in which the adherent of a particular religion finds himself in relation to his citizenship is only *one aspect* of the general *secular contradiction between the state and civil society* ... Therefore we do not tell the Jews that they cannot be emancipated politically without radically emancipating themselves from Judaism, which is what Bauer tells them. We say instead: the fact that you can be politically emancipated without completely and absolutely renouncing Judaism shows that *political emancipation* by itself is not *human* emancipation. If you Jews want to be politically emancipated without emancipating yourselves as humans, the incompleteness and the contradiction lies not only in you but in the *nature* and the *category* of political emancipation.[62]

---

[61] Ibid., p. 222.
[62] Ibid., p. 226.

Unity and Fragmentation 173

Marx and the national question

In the foregoing passage we see once again[63] that Marx puts forward a Hegelian critique of the radical Left while at the same time apparently repudiating the Hegelian position. There is, however, little evidence in the critique of Bauer of Marx's own position on Hegel's view of modern citizenship. The meaning of "human emancipation," with its Feuerbachian resonances, is never elaborated in the essay — suggesting that at the time Marx's own position on cultural nationalism might not have been much different from the still-developing standpoint of his associate Moses Hess, whose views are briefly described above.

I find it significant, however, that Marx resisted every temptation to embrace Hess's emerging position on the national question. Throughout his critique of Bauer Marx stresses, not the need for self-determination by all communities, but the similarities between the treatment of primordial communal groups and ordinary corporate interests in the political organization of civil society. "The difference between the religious man and the citizen is the difference between the tradesman and the citizen, between the day-labourer and the citizen, between the landowner and the citizen."[64]

When Marx returned to "the Jewish question" in his contribution to *The Holy Family* he elaborated on the need to consider the demands of communal groups as part of the ordinary politics of developed states.[65] Bauer's equation of human emancipation with the emancipation of individuals from social groups concealed, according to Marx, the fact that modern states depend for their stability on the fragmentation of civil society into groups.

> The modern 'public system', the developed modern state, is not based ... on a society of privileges, but ... on developed civil society based on the vital elements which were still politically fettered in the privilege system and have

[63] Cf. chapter 3, above.
[64] Marx, "On the Jewish Question," p. 220f.
[65] Cf. the later debate between Lenin and Luxemburg on the national question in Luxemburg, *The National Question*, and Lenin, "The Socialist Revolution and the Rights of Nations to Self-Determination."

For an account of subsequent Marxist-Leninist attempts to grapple with the National Question see Connor, *The National Question in Marxist-Leninist Theory and Strategy*. For a different view of the origins of Marx's own view see Pelczynski, "Nation, Civil Society, State: Hegelian Sources of the Marxian Non-theory of Nationality."

been set free ... The state declares that religion, like the other elements of civil life, only begins to exist in its full scope when the state declares it to be non-political and thus leaves it to itself ... [T]o this very proclamation of their civil death corresponds their most vigorous life, which henceforth obeys its own laws undisturbed and develops to its full scope.[66]

Marx thus denied that the politics of the liberal state could be based on the atomistic individualism of the social contract, even after the feudal hierarchy of social groups is no longer officially recognized as a basis of individual dignity.

Speaking exactly and in the prosaic sense, the members of civil society are not atoms. The specific property of the atom is that it has no properties and is therefore not connected with beings outside it ... The atom has no needs, it is self-sufficient ... The egotistic individual in civil society may in his ... imagination ... inflate himself to the size of an atom ... [But e]very activity and property of his being becomes a need ... which transforms into seeking for other things and human beings outside him ... [A]s the need of one individual has no self-understood sense for the other egotistic individual capable of satisfying that need ... each individual has to create that connection ... [C]ivil, not political life is their real tie. It is therefore not the state that holds the atoms of civil society together, but the fact that they are atoms only in imagination ... but in reality beings tremendously different from atoms ... Only political superstition today imagines that social life must be held together by the state whereas in reality the state is held together by civil life.[67]

In the foregoing passages Marx suggests that political individualism and the fragmentation of civil society into groups can be mutually reinforcing grounds of constitutional unity in the modern state. This essentially theoretical point has been made about many modern political systems;[68] Michael Walzer restates it as follows in regard to the United States:

Americans are communal in their private affairs, individualist in their politics. Society is a collection of groups; the state is an organization of individual citizens. And society and state, though they constantly interact, are formally distinct. For support and comfort and a sense of belonging, men and women look to their groups; for freedom and mobility, they look to the state.[69]

[66] Marx and Engels, *The Holy Family*, pp. 116–7.
[67] Ibid., pp. 120–1.
[68] See, e.g., Glazer and Moynihan, *Beyond the Melting Pot*; Rudolph and Rudolph, *The Modernity of Tradition*, and Geertz, *The Interpretation of Cultures*.
[69] Walzer, "Pluralism in Political Perspective," p. 17.

As a form of modern constitutional politics, the demand for equality of individual opportunity is often inseparable from the demand that certain groups be treated equally in the distribution of unequal rewards to individuals. In most modern political systems the self-conscious individual does not repudiate his original group identity in order to claim his place as an equal citizen, but rather redefines that identity as the basis of his participation in the politics of distribution that the state creates.[70] Western political scientists have demonstrated again and again — as if performing a Hegelian ritual — that a politics that asserts the equal dignity of groups will also enhance respect for the fundamental differences between individuals. Mature individualism thus appears as the achievement of a modern political system, not its presupposition.[71]

Marx saw that the reason for this appearance goes to the heart of Hegelian liberal theory — the power of which he fully appreciated only in criticizing the Left. We must now turn to Marx's critique of the system of representation in the Hegelian state itself in order to develop his view of the role that groups of various kinds play in the political structure of civil society.

[70] As an assertion of rights *against* the political system, political equality must be based on social identities that are not exhausted by the beneficial interest one has in this or that public policy. The modern state can often reconcile individuals to unequal levels of welfare by equalizing for the kinds of prior group differences through which its citizens make constitutional claims for respect. See Ely, *Democracy and Distrust.*
[71] Cf. the suggestion in both Tocqueville and Mill that a politics that presupposes individualism in civil society is likely to produce mass despotism as its result, whereas a politics that presupposes pluralism in civil society is likely to produce individualism as its result.

8 Participation and Co-optation

The political representation of social groups

The conclusion of Marx's essay "On the Jewish Question" is that the post-revolutionary state, despite its grounding in the Rights of Man, does not really represent its citizens directly as individuals — stripped of their various social roles and group identities. The previous chapter demonstrates that this insight is fundamentally consistent with Hegel's theory of modern citizenship. For the most part Hegel assumed that, when the state is not defending the complex value of individuality as such, the subjective interests of individuals would have no privileged status in the political process. Lacking an objective social basis, those interests would appear as potentially arbitrary or capricious. Hegel argues that the modern citizen overcomes this apparent arbitrariness by connecting his subjective tastes and inclinations with institutional interests — such as those of his family, community, or profession — that he already has a responsibility to promote. Only by identifying with the interests of such recognized groups and roles in civil society would an individual have a plausible claim to have his interests respected in the political process.

The groupings through which citizens are to be represented in Hegel's state are not, however, the communal nationalities one sees in many states today, but rather the archaic orders and corporate entities of the medieval system of Estates. Although such traditional groupings may seem to lack relevance for the modern state, Hegel saw the point of representing them in wholly modern terms. He believed, like many recent writers, that representing citizens through corporate entities gives a form of recognition and respect to the subjective desires of individuals, while legitimating the occasional sacrifice of those desires in the public interest.[1]

---

[1] "The consideration behind the abolition of Corporations in recent times is that the individual should fend for himself ... Under modern political conditions, the citizens have only a restricted share in the public business of the state, yet it is

Writing in the midst of the liberal attack on medieval corporatism, Hegel clearly recognizes the need for the organized intermediation of public and private interests as a common underlying feature of developed modern states. The modern equivalents of the social interests that Hegel would represent in the state are not incorporated business firms competing in the marketplace – the "corporations" of today – but rather the functional associations that represent industries and professions (for example, the American Medical Association), and the public interest lobbies that represent the special constituencies or clienteles of government agencies and programs (for example, the National League of Cities in the United States, and the PTA.) Many political commentators argue that in the twentieth century such groups have had a more important influence on legislative policy-making than the formal constituency units through which individual citizens are organized in order to cast their votes in elections.[2]

Alone among the major political philosophers, Hegel anticipated these developments. Throughout the *Philosophy of Right* he denies, directly and indirectly, that systems of electoral democracy based on majority rule are adequate to perform the essential functions of political representation in modern states.[3] Hegel's philosophical argument that the fundamental interests of the individual and the state as necessarily coequal and mutually

---

essential to provide men – ethical entities – with work of a public character over and above their private business. This work of a public character, which the modern state does not always provide, is found in the Corporation ... [I]n fending for himself a member of civil society is also working for others. But this unconscious compulsion is not enough; it is in the Corporation that it first changes into a known and thoughtful ethical model of life. Of course Corporations must fall under the higher surveillance of the state, because otherwise they would ossify, build themselves in, and decline into a miserable system of castes. In and by itself, however, a Corporation is not a closed caste; its purpose is rather to bring an isolated trade into the social order and elevate it to a sphere in which it gains strength and respect." (*Hegel's Philosophy of Right*) (tr. Knox), addition, para. 255.

For a discussion of Hegel's corporatism in its own context see Heiman, "The Sources and Significance of Hegel's Corporate Doctrine." See also Poggi, *The Development of the Modern State*, chs 3–4.

[2] See, e.g., Schmitter, "Still the Century of Corporatism?" and "Interest Intermediation and Regime Governability in Contemporary Western Europe and North America."

[3] E.g.: "Despotism means any state of affairs where law has disappeared and where the particular will as such, whether of a monarch or a mob ... counts as law or rather takes the place of law; while it is precisely in legal, constitutional government that sovereignty is to be found." (*Hegel's Philosophy of Right* (tr. Knox), p. 180.)

grounded, implies that, only as a political analogue to the interests of the whole, do our claims 'as individuals' have greater legitimacy and universality than the interests of groups.[4] This suggests that citizen participation in the direct election of officials, or in deciding issues through plebiscite and referendum, can never satisfy the individual's need to be represented in the state.[5] Rather, Hegel argued, we must participate in politics through the mediation of the various social groupings from which we would step back in order to think of ourselves as 'individuals.'

> The circles of association in civil society are already communities. To picture these communities as once more breaking up into a mere conglomeration of individuals as soon as they enter the field of politics ... is ... to hold civil and political life apart ... and to hang the latter in the air, because its basis could then only be the abstract individuality of caprice and opinion, and hence it would be grounded on chance, and not on what is ... stable and justified.[6]
>
> ...
>
> Society is not dispersed into atomic units, collected to perform only a single and temporary act ... [I]t makes the appointment as a society, articulated into associations, communities, and Corporations, which, although constituted for other purposes, acquire in this way a connexion with politics.[7]

Instead of aggregating individual preference directly the developed Hegelian state will deem individuals to have been served whenever it aggregates all of the *group* interests through which they are represented. Like some recent social scientists, Hegel believed that by counting only group interests no relevant basis of individual preference would be excluded from the regulatory arena. Since the result of group representation can be construed to be the weighted sum of individual concerns, the separate representation of individuals in the policy-making process would be, at best, a redundant political formalism, and at worst, a source of confusion. Indeed, a main function of political representation in the developed Hegelian state is to nurture and preserve the groups in society that can mediate between the subjective interests of individuals and the needs of the government. Although the modern state is in some attenuated sense ruled by its 'people,' the constitutive role of the political process envisioned in the *Philosophy of Right* is to represent the 'people' to the state as *divided*, rather than *united*.

---

[4] Ibid., para. 258.
[5] Cf. the recent literature comparing legislative and plebiscitary democracy, e.g. Magleby, *Direct Legislation.*
[6] *Hegel's Philosophy of Right* (tr. Knox), para. 303.
[7] Ibid., para. 308.

Responsiveness and autonomy

According to Hegel, a successful government co-opts social interests by responding to them. In getting people to recognize that they have gotten what they want *because* they have organized to demand it, the state makes people come to want what they get *because* it is in the best interests of their organizations. Individuals thus learn to articulate the public values served by their private organizations, professions, and local communities. The recognition of these values by the state gives an ethical dignity to one's pursuit of one's own welfare through the associations of social life. This presupposes both that citizens can identify their interests outside of the political process, and that they must promote their interests through it.

The steel industry or the medical profession, for example, would represent private interests to the state as part of a public interest in promoting a strong economy or in improving public health. These interest groups would argue that the strength of the whole depends, at least up to a point, upon the strength of each of its interdependent parts − that the state strengthens itself in strengthening *them*. A Hegelian government could formally decide how much weight to give to directly competing private interests by emphasizing the functional interdependence of the conflicting groups in achieving some public purpose. When, for example, the Hegelian instincts of the state are reinforced by Keynesian economic theory, conflicts between high wages for workers and high profits for employers would be officially reconciled by appealing to the public interest in combining stable growth and low inflation − not by counting the numbers of individuals on the opposing sides of these issues.

How can the state 'represent' group interests without being 'corrupted' by them? The answer for Hegel (as for Tocqueville) was that the distinctive modes of participation in politics would teach groups to transform their particularistic private interests into the public (or universal) interests that the state could recognize in granting their demands. In theory and in law the public (universal) interests of groups to which the government claims to respond would simply not be identical with the private (particular) interests of groups that the state claims to resist.

A Hegelian conception of the public interest ties individuals to the interests of the state as both a material condition of receiving benefits and an ideological condition of demanding them. By officially recognizing the demands of organized interest groups the state would be 'responsive' to the subjective identities through which private individuals express their desires in the public realm. The public interest of the state would in this way become infused with private interests. Yet the Hegelian state would deny that it is thereby dominated by these interests. Rather, according to

Hegelian theory, the private interests of individuals are ideologically transformed into public interests through political participation based on group identity.

The everyday dialectic of politics in the modern state consists of manipulating the fine Hegelian balance between governmental autonomy and the need to be responsive to constituent groups. Thus, governments that are too responsive to private interests are typically accused of being 'corrupt,' while governments that are too autonomous in their view of the public interest are accused of being 'undemocratic.' The ongoing debate in American political science between disciples of Dahl and Lowi on the nature of American interest group liberalism can be characterized as a continuing effort to 'redress the balance' between responsiveness and autonomy.[8]

Bureaucratic policy-making, legislative oversight, and public opinion

Hegel himself tried to redress this balance at an institutional level by distinguishing between the functions of bureaucratic policy-making, legislative oversight, and public opinion in the modern state.[9]

Within a wide purview the Hegelian bureaucracy makes policy by dealing directly, but unofficially, with the various corporate interests that also find representation in parliament.[10] In some modern political systems the direct bargaining process between the state and functional interest groups can

---

[8] Dahl argues that the "dilemma" of pluralist democracy is to reconcile the "autonomy" of groups that seek to participate in politics with the ability of the state to "control" private interests. He suggests that resolving this dilemma may require changes in the organization of economic interests along decentralized democratic lines. Cf. Dahl, *Dilemmas of Pluralist Democracy*, and Lowi, *The End of Liberalism*.

[9] I shall not here comment on the extent to which my interpretation of the *Philosophy of Right* is in agreement with the previous literature. For further background, readers should consult works such as the following: Avineri, *Hegel's Theory of the Modern State*, ch. 8; Klaus Hartmann, "Towards a New Systematic Reading of Hegel's *Philosophy of Right*"; Ilting, "The Structure of Hegel's Philosophy of Right"; Kelly, "Hegel's America"; Pelczynski, "The Hegelian Conception of the State" and "Political Community and Individual Freedom in Hegel's Philosophy of the State"; Steven B. Smith, *Hegel's Critique of Liberalism*; and Charles Taylor, *Hegel*, ch. 16.

[10] Cf. *Hegel's Philosophy of Right* (tr. Knox), paras 288−9, 311.

become a surrogate for parliament altogether.[11] Elsewhere, the bypassing of parliament occurs only when the policy output or government benefit is easily divisible, for instance an exemption or subsidy, and can thus be directly distributed to groups one by one.[12] Although the scope of corporatist interaction may vary from state to state, the direct relation between the bureaucracy and corporate interest groups described by Hegel is invariably one of mutual responsiveness and co-optation.[13]

In contrast to the bureaucracy the Hegelian legislature would have virtually no policy-making function, but would, rather, be a vehicle for recognizing and respecting the primordial orders and corporate interests that make up the state.[14] Hegel forthrightly admits that for the most part

[11] Cf. Hegel and, e.g., Rokkan, "Norway: Numerical Democracy and Corporate Pluralism."

[12] Cf. Lowi, "American Business, Public Policy, Case Studies, and Political Theory," and Offe, "The Theory of the Capitalist State and the Problem of Policy Formation."

[13] Hegel says, "The corporation mind, engendered when particular spheres gain their title to rights, is now inwardly converted into the mind of the state, since it finds in the state the means of maintaining its particular ends. This is the secret of the patriotism of the citizens in the sense that they know the state as their substance, because it is the state that maintains their particular spheres of interest together with the title, authority, and welfare of these. In the corporation mind the rooting of the particular in the universal is directly entailed, and for this reason it is in that mind that the depth and strength which the state possesses in sentiment is seated."

Yet he is quick to add: "The administration of a Corporation's business by its own officials is frequently clumsy, because although they keep before their minds and are acquainted with its special interests and affairs, they have a far less complete appreciation of the connexion of those affairs with more remote conditions and the outlook of the state ... [O]ther circumstances contribute to the same result, e.g. close private relationships and other factors putting officials on a footing of equality with those who should be their subordinates, the rather numerous ways in which officials lack independence, and so on. This sphere of private interests, however, may be regarded as the one left to the moment of formal freedom, the one which affords a playground for personal knowledge, personal decisions and their execution, petty passions and conceits. This is all the more permissible, the more trivial, from the point of view of the more universal affairs of state, is the intrinsic worth of the business which in this way comes to ruin or is managed less well or more laboriously, & c. And further, it is all the more permissible, the more this laborious or foolish management of such trivial affairs stands in direct relation with the self-satisfaction and vanity derived therefrom." (*Hegel's Philosophy of Right* (tr. Knox), para. 289.)

[14] Ibid., paras 249–56, 295–320.

government could go on very well if the legislature never decided anything, and that most of what it does decide is formulated by the bureaucracy and proposed by the Crown. From the standpoint of the state the main function of the legislature is not to empower the people, but to represent the people to themselves in the mirror of politics. By participating in distinctively parliamentary forms of representation, Hegel argued, the people would recognize their interests outside such politics to have been merely social. The mere presence of the Hegelian legislature as a "moment" in the constitution implicitly represents the state to "the people" as the official form of organization for a society that would otherwise be fragmented into discrete corporate interests. By representing society as intrinsically disorganized in this way, the Hegelian legislature prevents what Hegel calls the "wild idea of 'the people'" from acquiring an appearance of unity that could threaten the stability of the state.[15]

Insofar as Hegel's legislature does not directly make public policy, the role that Hegel ascribes to the "legislative moment" in the modern state is similar to the role often ascribed in modern political science to the mass political party.[16] In competitive political systems mass parties function in parliament as if they were each separate "governments" with competing ideological claims to represent the whole of society;[17] and in single-party states the ruling party often performs internally the Hegelian functions of both political participation and social control without much reliance on either parliamentary forms or popular elections.[18] In neither case does the stability of the political regime necessarily require that the internal organization of the party be democratic, provided that the relevant social interests are somehow incorporated. Moreover, once the *policy-making* role of both legislatures and parties is sufficiently limited, it makes little difference in

[15] Ibid., paras 279, 301.

[16] Cf. the discussion of Huntington in chapter 9, below.

[17] See *Hegel's Philosophy of Right* (tr. Knox), paras 272–3, 298–300; and Pizzorno, "Interests and Parties in Pluralism."

The Hegelian equivalence between legislatures and parties can be illustrated by the history of the Indian National Congress. Before independence the Congress claimed, like a parliament, to represent the nation as a whole in the struggle to rid itself of the colonial occupier. After independence the Indian National Congress became the Congress Party. As such, it dominated the parliament of post-independence India into the 1960s by successfully incorporating a wide variety of social interest groups directly into the internal structure of the party itself. (On the role of the Congress Party in the early years of post-independence India see Weiner, *Party Building in a New Nation; The Indian National Congress*.)

[18] See, e.g., Huntington and Moore (eds.), *Authoritarian Politics in Modern Society*.

Hegelian theory whether the remaining *constituent* function of political representation is performed mainly at the level of the state, through parliamentary institutions, or at the level of civil society, through party organizations.[19]

In contrast to the politics of organized interest groups, the politics of 'public affairs' plays a subordinate, but essential, role in Hegel's state. At one level public institutions must strive to appear 'independent' of public opinion in their official decisions. Yet, if private citizens did not take an active interest in affairs of state, the public institutions could not claim to have a universal significance that distinguishes their activities from those of other organizations. The subjective recognition that the state's affairs are somehow public business is for Hegel a necessary part of what makes any particular set of institutions a state.[20]

Unlike the legislature (or the party), which represents the public as organized into groups, the institutions of public opinion (the mass media today) represent the unorganized people as a whole. In the forum of public opinion the "people" may appear to be more or less united, but only insofar as they are simultaneously denied official recognition by the state. Although such expressions of public opinion will usually have little bearing on public policy, Hegel believes they can be important as a harmless outlet for frustration, and even more important as a way of allowing individuals a subjective involvement with government's business as their 'public affair.'

> Public opinion is the unorganized way in which a people's opinions and wishes are made known. What is actually made authoritative in the state must operate in an organized manner as the parts of the constitution do. What is to be authoritative nowadays derives its authority, not at all from force, only to a small extent from habit and custom, really from insight and argument.
>
> The principle of the modern world requires that what anyone is to recognize shall reveal itself to him as something entitled to recognition. Apart from that, however, everyone wishes to have some share in the discussion and deliberation. Once he has had his say and so his share of responsibility, his subjectivity has been satisfied and he puts up with a lot.[21]

[19] For the distinction between these two functions of political representation, see Lowi, "Party, Policy, and Constitution in America."

[20] *Hegel's Philosophy of Right* (tr. Knox), paras 316–18, p. 294.

[21] He continues: "In France freedom of speech has turned out far less dangerous than enforced silence, because with the latter the fear is that men bottle up their objections to a thing, whereas argument gives them an outlet and a measure of satisfaction, and this is in addition a means whereby the thing can be pushed ahead more easily." (Ibid., p. 294.)

184 The Critical Theory of Democracy

Hegel clearly believed that a strong government can tolerate public opinion as a form of personal self-expression that makes citizens in turn more tolerant of their government[22] – but he also recognized that many real decisions that affect corporate interests will continue to be made outside the scrutiny of public opinion, and also outside the deliberative processes of the legislature itself.[23] For this reason the Hegelian legislature would have the function of conducting continuing public investigations of the direct dealings between the bureaucracy and corporate interests. By mediating between public opinion and the bureaucracy, the legislature would allow the people to take an interest in government – to view the government's business as their politics.[24]

The legislature, the bureaucracy, and the mass 'media' which mold public opinion, are separate and offsetting manifestations of the "public interest" in the Hegelian state. Each interacts with the other two in order to create "public affairs," and each mediates the claims of the others to represent the people as a whole. Yet Hegel readily acknowledges that the appearance of legislative oversight of the bureaucracy is more show than reality: the Hegelian legislature, as an organ of the state, 'evinces' itself by

[22] Ibid., paras 308, 315–20, and also paras 250–6.

[23] Political scientists often note the tendency of twentieth-century legislatures and parties to delegate oversight of the bargaining between social groups to bureaucratic agencies which are only loosely supervised by legislative committees. For a discussion of this phenomenon in the United States see, e.g., Lowi, *The End of Liberalism*.

[24] "The Estates are a guarantee of the general welfare and public freedom. A little reflection will show that this guarantee does not lie in their particular power of insight, because the highest civil servants necessarily have a deeper and more comprehensive insight into the nature of the state's organization and requirements. They are also more habituated to the business of government and have greater skill in it, so that even without the Estates they are *able* to do what is best, just as they continually *have* to do while the Estates are in session. No, the guarantee lies on the contrary (a) in the *additional* insight of the deputies, insight in the first place into the activity of such officials as are not immediately under the eye of the higher functionaries of state, and in particular into the more pressing and more specialized needs and deficiencies which are directly in their view; (b) in the fact that the anticipation ... of public criticism, has the effect of inducing officials to devote their best attention beforehand to their duties and the schemes under consideration." (*Hegel's Philosophy of Right* (tr. Knox), para. 301.)

"Estates Assemblies, open to the public, are a great spectacle and an excellent education for the citizens, and it is from them that the people learns best how to recognize the true character of its interest." (Ibid., addition, para. 315, p. 294.)

mediating between the government and the nation, thereby showing that their interests are not essentially opposed.[25]

There are many recent instances in American politics of the dynamic Hegel describes between the bureaucracy, representative bodies, and public opinion. For example, in the aftermath of Watergate a series of Congressional investigations 'exposed' the covert activities of the CIA to the media. These investigations revealed that the CIA had been pursuing its own 'particular' interests in conducting businesses abroad, playing 'dirty tricks,' and assisting 'our friends' abroad in assassinating 'our enemies.' The CIA defended itself by asserting the public interest in maintaining the secrecy of its operations, and arguing that the adverse publicity of the investigation had done more damage to the national interest than the abuses discovered.

The CIA was able to simultaneously strengthen its campaign against both the press and Congress in the forum of public opinion when unknown parties 'leaked' the official report of the joint Congressional Committee (the Pike Committee) to a television reporter (Daniel Schorr) shortly before its release. Supported by the professional ethics of journalism, Schorr resisted attempts by Congress to make him reveal his source — arguing that the press, as the 'unofficial representative' of the public, has a Constitutional right to protect the confidentiality of its sources against official investigations. This defense of the corporate interests of journalists implied that Congress, as the 'official representative' of the public, would have little legal power to maintain the confidentiality of its procedures against investigations by the press.

The constitutional conflict between Schorr and the Pike Committee placed the CIA in a stronger position to assert a public interest in frustrating Congressional interest in its operations. In effect the CIA, like Daniel Schorr, 'went public' with the institutional need to preserve its secrecy from the demands of Congressional investigators — thereby equating the CIA's need for confidentiality in its investigations with that of the media. With the growing support of the media, the CIA challenged Congressional

---

[25] "There may indeed be an appearance of opposition between them, but if they were opposed, not merely superficially, but actually and in substance, then the state would be in the throes of destruction. That the clash is not of this kind is evident ... because the Estates [i.e., the legislature] have to deal, not with the essential elements in the organism of the state, but only with rather specialized and trifling matters, while the passion which even these arouse spends itself in party cravings in connexion with purely subjective interests such as appointments to the higher offices of state." (Ibid., para. 302.)

oversight on the grounds that members of Congress could not be trusted to handle sensitive information pertaining to the national security. Public opinion (as formed and represented by the media) gradually came to see a 'threat to national security' in the attempts by members of Congress to 'abuse their role as representatives of the people in order to seek publicity, and promote their own petty careers.'

Eventually the President stepped in, using his direct relation with the media to put an end to the 'unseemly quarrel between branches of government that had become so damaging to American interests abroad.' Since the Presidency and the media are, respectively, the official and unofficial representatives of 'all the people' in Hegelian theory, these two institutions would tend to unite when quarrels between the legislature and the executive (or between party and bureaucracy) threaten to undermine public confidence in government.[26] As a modern-day Hegelian would immediately recognize, the political strength of both the presidency and the media lies ultimately in their ability to make patriotic appeals.[27]

In reading the *Philosophy of Right* Marx recognized that the principal function of legislative politics in the Hegelian state is to stimulate the subjective interest of citizens, and hence to make public institutions more comprehensible from within.[28] The 'publicly concerned citizen' – as depicted by Hegel – will try to make himself 'aware' of the goings on in government by following media accounts of investigations by the legislature

[26] For a discussion of the variable role of the media and the government in both representing the public interest and in stimulating the public's interest, see Meister, "Journalistic Silence and Governmental Speech: Can Institutions Have Rights?"
[27] See *Hegel's Philosophy of Right* (tr. Knox), paras 275–86, on the Sovereignty, and paras 314–20, on public opinion. A partial similarity between Hegel's view of the Sovereignty and public debates about the role of the "Presidency" in the US is cautiously noted by George Kelly in "Hegel's America," pp. 31–6.
[28] Yet even this political role of the legislature is for Marx largely a charade (as Hegel himself virtually conceded): "What was first intended to be the mean between two extremes now itself occurs as an extreme. ... This is a kind of mutual reconciliation society. It is as if a man stepped between the two opponents, only to have one of them immediately step between the mediator and the other opponent ... When the one extreme cries: 'Now I am the mean', then the other two may not touch it, but rather only swing at the one that was just the extreme. As one can see, this is a society pugnacious at heart but too afraid of bruises to ever really fight. The two who want to fight arrange it so that the third who steps between them will get the beating, but immediately one of the two appears as the third, and because of all this caution they never arrive at a decision." (Marx, *Critique of Hegel's 'Philosophy of Right,'* p. 88.)

of charges that the bureaucracy has mismanaged the public business, or failed to respect the rights of citizens. By inviting the citizen to reflect upon the boundaries between state and society, public and private, the official forms of political representation reconcile citizens to the need for differentiated organs of government to give competing embodiments of the public interest.[29] Our problems, insofar as they are political, once again appear to be the inevitable result of the categories in which we think about them.[30]

Public and private interests

In criticizing Hegel's account of constitutional politics Marx argues that the main difference between public and private institutions is subjective: the former are presumed to embody the interests of the state without further argument, and the latter are not. In order to create such a recognition, Marx argues, the state must somehow make people understand their politics as whatever goes on in the institutions that have been established explicitly and solely for the conduct of political affairs.[31] Marx thus came to see that the secret of Hegel's political institutions is ideological: like Tinkerbell they exist only for so long as they are believed in. In stating this as a criticism, Marx brought out the darker implications of Hegel's

[29] "A question attracts particular attention only when it becomes political, that is to say, either when it can be tied to a ministerial question, and thus becomes a question of the power of the legislature over the executive, or when it is a matter of rights in general, which are connected with the political formalism. How come this phenomenon? Because the legislature is at the same time the representation of civil society's political existence; because in general the political nature of a question consists in its relationship to the various powers of the political state; and finally, because the legislature represents political consciousness, which can manifest itself as political only in conflict with the executive." (Ibid., p. 120.)

[30] See, e.g., *Hegel's Philosophy of Right* (tr. Knox), preface, p. 12.

[31] According to Hegel, the public must take an interest in government affairs in order for government to be perceived to be acting in the public interest. Marx notes that the focus of public attention is expected to be the careers of public officials — the gossip that surrounds their successes, their failures, and their foibles. The celebrity of the government is, thus, an important, if unnoticed, dimension of the state Hegel wished to describe. For while Hegel regards "public affairs" as "complete without being the actual affairs of the people," Marx recognizes that "subjects do not need public affairs as their affairs, but public affairs needs subjects for its formal existence." (Marx, *Critique of Hegel's 'Philosophy of Right,'* p. 62.)

commitment to placing modern institutions fully within the world of "mind" – the world that must be understood to fully be as it is.

The ambiguity between the subjective and objective meanings of the word "interest" illustrates Marx's critique most clearly. So long as political institutions keep up people's interest in the state, Marx believed that Hegel would be committed to arguing that the state is serving the people's interest in an objective sense as well. According to Hegel, people take an interest in the affairs of the state mainly because they believe that the state, unlike other formally autonomous institutions, is directly interested in every aspect of social life. The people's interest in the state is thus the way in which they are indirectly interested in the very things that interest them directly. Today, in the United States the media's eagerness to report the reactions of presidential candidates to public opinion polls completes the Hegelian circle of reflexivity – suggesting that the people should somehow take a special interest in reports of the personal interest a candidate shows in his success in stimulating their interest. To the extent that polls themselves become the main media issue in political campaigns the people's interest in the interest of the state is truly what Marx calls "the *haut gout* of the life of the people – a ceremony."[32] According to Marx, "the illusion is . . . that truly public affairs are the affairs of the people." This, Marx says, is the "lie of constitutional states . . ." – ". . . that the state is the people's interest or the people the interest of the state."[33]

According to Marx, the reality behind this lie is that the special interests of government itself are set in a merely formal opposition to the particular interests in society that government agencies regulate or control. This opposition allows those who are engaged in the operations of the state to feel a sense of its autonomy,[34] even though the determination of the interests of public institutions might not differ in kind or content from the determination of the interests of any (other) grouping that belongs to the society at large.[35] In this sense, the public interest is no longer an external standard by which the performance of the state can be judged, but rather a reflection of the fact that the particular institutions that claim to embody the public interest are *regarded* as the state. Far from explaining why the state requires these particular institutions, Marx suggests that Hegel has merely explained why these institutions must rely on the ideology of *the state*, with all its moral resonance, in order to appear legitimate.

Thus, if we accept Hegel's premise that (1) the public interest can be

[32] Ibid., p. 65.
[33] Ibid., pp. 62, 65.
[34] Ibid., p. 49.
[35] Ibid., p. 46.

served only by a strong state; and (2) the state is strengthened when it appears to serve the public interest; it becomes objectively meaningless to question whether (3) a given political reform will *really* serve the public interest, or merely strengthen the state.[36] In asking such a question the force of the word "really" would be unclear from a Hegelian point of view, since the acceptability of political institutions requires their acceptance, and vice versa.

By denying us a conception of the public interest that is external to the state, Hegel has emphasized the significance of thinking of the state *as* what serves the public interest. Whether this means that the state is necessarily what it ought to be in virtue of what it is − or whether it means that a state that is not seen to be legitimate must ultimately cease to exist − is a question beneath the level of philosophy that Hegel would leave open to the vagaries of subjective politics.

The corporate interest of government

In turning his attention to the "private affairs" of the state − the business of the government bureaucracy − Marx noted that the "public interests" articulated by the Corporations are in Hegel's theory virtually indistinguishable from the material interests of the public agencies that regulate them. Ultimately, there would be little difference between the ways in which the Corporations and the bureaucracy seek to manipulate each other. As Marx puts it:

> The Corporations are the materialism of the bureaucracy, and the bureaucracy is the spiritualism of the Corporations. The Corporation is the bureaucracy of civil society, and the bureaucracy is the Corporation of the state ... The same mind that creates the Corporation in society creates the bureaucracy in the state. Thus as soon as the corporation mind is attacked so too is the mind of the bureaucracy; and whereas the bureaucracy earlier fought the existence of the Corporations in order to create room for its own existence, now it seeks to vigorously sustain the existence of the Corporations in order to save the Corporation mind, which is its own mind.[37]

Of what does the autonomy of Hegel's state apparatus then consist? In the autonomous state, says Marx, "the public affairs and their pursuit is a

---

[36] See Wolin, "Democracy and the Welfare State: The Political and Theoretical Connections Between *Staatsräson* and *Wolfahrtsstaatsräson*."
[37] Marx, *Critique of Hegel's 'Philosophy of Right,'* pp. 45−6.

monopoly" of the public officials. "Public affairs" then becomes the specific corporate interest of particular institutions that are recognized as the public institutions. But the autonomy of the state also requires that these institutions actively regard themselves as immune from the direct influence of any private forces in their determination of the public interest. It will thus be a major element of their policy to express the autonomy of the state from the corrupting influence of private power. In this limited sense, Marx admits, the interest of public institutions is formally equivalent to the public interest.

But the existence of bureaucracy implies that public officials must view their concern with the public interest as also a special interest — if only because they are professional citizens concerned with their careers. "In truth," says Marx, "private interest is their public affairs, not public affairs their private interest." Thus, Marx asserts, "the state interest is only formally the actual interest of the people, but is nevertheless present as a distinct form" — in effect the strengthening and perpetuation of the public agencies themselves.[38]

Marx believed that Hegel's discussion of the interaction between the bureaucracy and the Corporation came close to confessing that the bureaucracy rarely goes beyond the promotion of its own narrow professional interests in dealing with social groups. "The aims of the state are transformed into aims of bureaus, or the aims of bureaus into the aims of the state."[39]

The disorganization of civil society

In his Critique of Hegel's *Philosophy of Right*, Marx focused heavily on the ways in which the modern state gives official recognition to the needs

---

[38] Ibid., p. 65.

[39] The rest of this passage anticipates Weber: "The bureaucracy is a circle from which no one can escape. Its hierarchy is a hierarchy of knowledge. The highest point entrusts the understanding of particulars to the lower echelons, whereas these, on the other hand, credit the highest with an understanding in regard to the universal; and thus they deceive one another ... [A]uthority is the principle of its knowledge and being, and the deification of authority is its mentality. But at the very heart of the bureaucracy this spiritualism turns into a crass materialism, the materialism of passive obedience, or trust in authority, the mechanism of an ossified and formalistic behavior. As far as the individual bureaucrat is concerned, the end of the state becomes his private end: a pursuit of higher posts, the building of a career ... [H]is existence is the existence of the bureau. The state, then, exists only as various bureauminds whose connexion consists of subordination and dumb obedience." (Ibid., p. 47. Cf. Weber, *Economy and Society*, vol. 2, ch. 11.)

of corporate interest groups in both parliamentary and administrative politics. While recognizing that the transition to a free market might require the state to attack the monopoly privileges of the guilds and municipal corporations, Marx agreed with Hegel that the developed modern state would eventually set itself the problem of representing the public interests of industries and communities within the policy-making process itself.[40] Yet, through a careful reading of Hegel's text, Marx was able to give a critical reconstruction of the way in which a Hegelian system of interest mediation explicitly works to undermine the broadly democratic presumptions on which its legitimacy is based.

Marx notes that in a crucial passage Hegel describes the legislative body, like the bureaucracy, as a "mediating organ" that stands "between the government in general" and "the nation broken up into particulars (people and associations)." Without them the sovereign power of the state over society might "seem a mere arbitrary tyranny," or else the "particular interests of persons, societies, and Corporations" might appear isolated in their autonomy from the state and each other. Most importantly, however, (and in an apparent *non sequitur*) Hegel candidly admits that the forms of political organization through which the people are represented in the state "prevent individuals from having the appearance of a mass or an aggregate and so from acquiring an unorganized opinion and volition and from crystallizing into a powerful bloc in opposition to the organized state."[41]

In his extensive commentary on this passage Marx came to see Hegel's view of political representation as, essentially, a way of depoliticizing a mass public (for Hegel "the wild idea of the 'people'")[42] whose aggregate individual interests might otherwise polarize them as rich and poor. Where Hegel had described a process of interest intermediation for organized groups, Marx perceived the institutionalized "disorganization" of an effective political opposition.

[40] Cf. *Hegel's Philosophy of Right* (tr. Knox), paras 288–97, and Marx, *Critique of Hegel's 'Philosophy of Right*,' p. 45f.

[41] The actual passage in Hegel reads as follows: "Regarded as a mediating organ the Estates [parliament] stand between the government in general on the one hand and the nation broken up into particulars (people and associations) on the other ... [I]n common with the organized executive [bureaucracy], they are a middle term preventing both the extreme isolation of the power of the crown, which otherwise might seem a mere arbitrary tyranny, and also the isolation of particular interests of persons, societies, and Corporations. Further, and more important, they prevent individuals from having the appearance of a mass or an aggregate and so from acquiring an unorganized opinion and volition and from crystallizing into a powerful *bloc* in opposition to the organized state." (*Hegel's Philosophy of Right* (tr. Knox), para. 302.)

[42] Ibid., p. 183. See also pp. 180, 198.

To Marx the real revelation in Hegel's discussion of the Legislature is the existence of a latently "powerful bloc" to which the Hegelian state pays lip service. Insofar as this disorganized public can be manipulated from above, Marx recognized, "the mass is unable to make a move on its own and can only be moved by the monopolists of the organized state and be exploited as a powerful bloc." By giving the mass public "the illusion of its own objectification," the Hegelian legislature effectively preserves "the state from the unorganized aggregate [but] only through the disorganization of this very aggregate."[43] Marx concluded that the system of political representation in the Hegelian legislature is designed mainly to forestall attempts by organized social forces to exercise direct power over the state apparatus as a whole.[44] The very corporatist interests that would have such a major role in implementing public policy when working out of public sight with the bureaucracy would play a far less direct role in formulating public policy when openly represented in the legislature.[45] There is in the *Philosophy of Right* no conception of policy formation that reflects interests distinct from those of the institutions directly engaged in the bureaucratic process.

In his thoughtful (if somewhat convoluted) exposition of paragraph 302 of the *Philosophy of Right* (see p. 191 and n. 41, above) Marx laid the groundwork for his critical analysis of the kind of politics produced by the Hegelian state. In effect, he argued, the Hegelian legislature mediates between interest groups and public opinion — two alternative bases of the 'popular will' that are never adequately brought together in Hegel's theory.[46]

[43] Marx, *Critique of Hegel's 'Philosophy of Right,'* p. 68.

[44] In his *Critique* Marx acknowledged Hegel's point that the corporatist system of political representation might "prevent the isolation of the particular interests of persons, societies, and Corporations." According to Marx, however, particular groups could achieve political incorporation "first, by coming to an understanding with the interest of the state;" and, also, by turning their "isolation" into the special "political act" through which they come to understand that their own interests are merely social — as distinct from the public interests that the state embodies. (Ibid.)

[45] Claus Offe argues that in modern corporatism the state will have difficulty in resisting the direct participation of organized groups in the formation of public policy after giving them increasing responsibility for implementing it. (See, e.g., Offe, "The Attribution of Public Status to Interest Groups.")

[46] "According to Hegel, the direct participation of all in deliberating and deciding on political matters of general concern admits the democratic element without any rational form into the organism of the state, although it is only in virtue of possession of such a form that the state is an organism at all." (Marx, *Critique of Hegel's 'Philosophy of Right,'* p. 116.)

State institutions rely upon a conception of politics that holds forth the possibility of the conscious transformation of society from within. They cannot be merely autonomous from society in order to be legitimate, or even effective. In order to be legitimate institutions of *politics* they must appear to the public to take up its interest, and thus in their totality to represent the whole of a society to itself. But the way in which society appears to itself through the state is precisely as what is *not* the state. In the ideology of the state it appears for the first and only time as 'society' − a collection of private interests arising in family and civil life that become self-consciously aware of themselves as 'social' only in contrast to the state. To the extent that Hegel had provided an accurate description of the function of modern political representation Marx concluded that the "actual organized thought of the mass is not the thought of the state and cannot find its realization in the state."[47]

Marx's critique of Hegel

In the course of his study of Hegel's *Philosophy of Right*[48] Marx noticed two underlying reasons why the mutual transformation of private and public interests through the political process described therein must be illusory. The first is that the public interest, the interest declared by state institutions themselves, is a reflection of the differential power of groups in society. The second is that the differential power of groups in society is itself an artifact of state power, and the legal advantages it confers.

These two lines of critique reflect two distinct approaches to the relation of state and society, both of which are commonly identified with Marxism. The first approach is based on the premise that the state arises historically out of the struggles of social groups, and governs in the interests of the winners. Since, politically, some interests always rule, this approach takes

[47] The foregoing discussion is an exegesis of Marx, *Critique of Hegel's 'Philosophy of Right,'* p. 68f. (on *Hegel's Philosophy of Right* (tr. Knox), para. 302).

[48] I shall not here comment on the extent to which my interpretation of Marx's *Critique of Hegel's 'Philosophy of Right'* is in agreement with the previous literature. For a different view, or further background, readers should consult works such as the following: Avineri, *The Social and Political Thought of Karl Marx*; Berki, "Perspectives in the Marxian Critique of Hegel's Political Philosophy"; Hyppolite, "Marx's Critique of the Hegelian Concept of the State"; Ilting, "Hegel's Concept of the State and Marx's Early Critique"; McLellan, *Marx Before Marxism*, ch 5; O'Malley's "Editor's Introduction" to Marx, *Critique of 'Hegel's 'The Philosophy of Right'*; and Charles Taylor, *Hegel and Modern Society*.

it as axiomatic that the power of the state reflects the social power of the dominant social forces at a given moment in history.[49]

The second potentially 'Marxist' approach is based on the premise that the state necessarily affects the balance of power in relations between social groups. Social power is here depicted as a creation of the state which, despite its claim to treat all citizens impartially, can never be neutral among them at the level of civil society where members of social groups conduct their private bargains 'in the shadow of the law.'[50] According to this approach even the "free market" is historically constituted by a series of political decisions which have the effect of giving some individuals social power over others in society.[51] That power, exercised at the level of civil society, is a direct consequence of whether the groups to which those individuals belong are favored or disfavored by the state.

We can conclude from these two lines of Marxian criticism that there is a potential contradiction in Hegel's enterprise of distinguishing between state power and the social power of groups, but that there is also a potential contradiction in a total Jacobin critique of Hegel, such as Marx initially attempted. (1) A Jacobin critique of the representation of groups in Hegel's legislature would reduce the state to society by arguing that the political power of the state rests on the social power of dominant groups

---

[49] See, e.g., Marx and Engels, "The Manifesto of the Communist Party" and Marx, "The Critique of the Gotha Program."

[50] See, e.g., *Capital*, vol. I, ch. 8. In the *Holy Family* Marx wrote: "The contradiction between the democratic representative state and civil society is the perfection of the classic contradiction between public commonwealth and slavedom. In the modern world each one is at the same time a member of slavedom and of the public commonwealth. Precisely the slavery of civil society is in appearance the greatest freedom because it is in appearance the perfect independence of the individual ... Right has here taken the place of privilege." (Marx and Engels, *The Holy Family*, p. 116.)

[51] If, e.g., the capitalist's property right gives him an enforceable claim to recover the cost of harms that he suffers, and if his right to compete makes him immune from liability for harms that he causes, then the state, through its legal system, will have conferred considerable social power upon him. The effect of such decisions would be to extend legal protection to some interests that the capitalist may assert against other members of society (and even against the state), and to cut off legal protection for a range of social interests, perhaps equally serious, that the capitalist may harm as a result of his competitive advantage in the marketplace. (See, e.g., Morris Raphael Cohen, "Property and Sovereignty"; Commons, *Legal Foundation of Capitalism*; and Hale, "Force and the State: A Comparison of 'Political' and 'Economic' Compulsion," "Bargaining, Duress, and Economic Liberty," and "Coercion and Distribution in a Supposedly Non-Coercive State.")

which seek legitimation for their rule.[52] (2) A Jacobin critique of Hegel's bureaucracy would reduce society to the state, arguing that the balance of power between social groups is largely determined by legal advantages that can be politically enforced.[53] Attempting to combine these two critiques would imply on the one hand that the state is exercising the social power of some groups over others, and on the other hand that this differential social power is itself constituted by legal relations deriving from the state.[54]

To avoid this apparent contradiction Left-Hegelians of all eras have tended to emphasize one side of this Jacobin critique at the expense of the other. In our own century American 'populists' have attacked the power of private interest groups in the political process, and demanded that the people gain control of the state (seen as legislature). Meanwhile, 'progressives' have attacked the exercise of public powers in private life, and have demanded that the state (seen as bureaucracy) gain control of the balance of coercion in society. Neither of these viewpoints, however, captures the full force of Marx's critique of the Hegelian state.

In his critique of the *Philosophy of Right* Marx sought to avoid the contradiction between these two radical critiques by achieving a further insight into the structure of Hegel's state. Marx came to see that everything would depend, not on *whether* state and civil society were distinguished, but on *how*. Hegel's discussion of the state as legislature had represented civil society as part of the state; his discussion of the state as government had represented the state as part of civil society.[55] But, while Hegel had differentiated the institutions of the state in each of these two pictures, he kept the organization of civil society the same: a single set of organized corporate interests appears first as the clientele of the bureaucracy, and again as the constituency of the legislature. Hegel thereby assumed that the groups through which civil society would participate in politics would be the same as those through which civil society would be regulated by government.

This singular organization of civil society allowed Hegel to believe that there was no conflict between the demand for popular representation in parliament and the need for bureaucratic governability. The same corporatist

---

[52] As we shall see, below, this argument resembles the leftist critique of modern day pluralism.
[53] This argument resembles, as we shall see below, the leftist critique of modern day corporatism.
[54] A good summary discussion of these issues in regard to legal theory can be found in Robert Gordon, "Critical Legal Histories."
[55] See our discussion of wholes and parts in chapter 4, above.

organizations would both participate in legislative deliberations and assist the bureaucracy in implementing its policies. Marx found it ironic that Hegel had felt the need to describe civil society as having a single form of differentiation while implicitly confessing that it must be organized into groups twice over in relation to the state — once when the state governs social forces, and yet again when it represents them.

For Marx the formative problem of political analysis would be to define this potentially contradictory role of the distinction between state and civil society in modern systems of representation — to relate the political significance of one's social identity and the social significance of one's political advantages. Marx recognized that in Hegelian theory social and political power must be reducible to each other if we are to make arguments about the modern state, and distinguishable from each other if we are to make arguments within it. He formulated this by saying, "Hegel's keenest insight lies in his sensing the separation of civil and political society to be a contradiction. But his error is that he contents himself with the appearance of its dissolution and passes it off as the real thing."[56]

Corporatism and pluralism

Marxian political analysis thus begins with the insight that group politics appears twice over in Hegel's picture of the relation between state and civil society: once as a set of pre-political (or social) differences that constitute the state; once again, as a consequence of the legal and political advantages conferred by the state. The first version — constituent group pluralism — results from a historical struggle for domination that culminates in sharing state power, and is expressed by an ideology of equal respect. In this ideology the state springs from civil society, and depends for its stability on honoring the historical differences out of which it emerged. The second version of group politics — client group corporatism — results from a competition for advantages that derive from state power, and is expressed by an ideology of impartiality. In this ideology civil society appears as an artifact of the state, which in turn must mediate between the social interests it has created.

Today, "corporatism" and "pluralism" appear in the literature as separate concepts used to describe political systems in their entirety. While the definitions of these concepts is contested, most political analysts seem to assume that they are alternative modes of mediation between interest

[56] Marx, *Critique of Hegel's 'Philosophy of Right,'* p. 76.

groups and the state — that a given polity may be "pluralist" or "corporatist," but not both.[57]

The main distinction between pluralism and "neo-corporatism" in the recent literature rests on whether social groups engage in direct contestation with each other through the legislative process, or whether they each engage directly in policy-making with the appropriate agency of the state. While "neo-corporatist" regimes are often the political creation of ideological mass parties, they nevertheless identify and aggregate interests in a way that increasingly bypasses parliamentary democracy as a vehicle of policy-making. Policy is made rather by bureaucrats in direct partnership with corporate groups, which have a (virtual) monopoly in representing their respective social interests in the relevant policy arenas. In most accounts of neo-corporatism the following properties are also present:

[57] The recent distinction between pluralism and corporatism was originally meant to suggest a historical progression in the political representation of social interests. The first stage ("old corporatism") evoked the feudal Estates System in which collective interests were identified and represented on the basis of the ascribed social orders to which individuals were legally subject. The second stage ("pluralism") replaced the feudal corporations with the free market and the neutral state. In the pluralist stage, interests were identified in the "political marketplace" through unofficial voluntary associations, represented by competing ideological parties, and aggregated through parliamentary democracy. A third stage ("neo-corporatism") replaced *laisser faire* liberalism with the planned economy and the welfare state. (This progression is suggested in the seminal article on neo-corporatism in English: Schmitter, "Still the Century of Corporatism?" For the background historical argument see Maier, "'Fictitious Bonds of Wealth and Law': On the Theory and Practice of Interest Representation." See also Maier, *Recasting Bourgeois Europe*, for a discussion of the way in which corporatism was used to circumvent the destabilizing effects of parliamentary democracy in Europe after World War I.)

Recently, however, some scholars have argued that the pluralist model of democratic competition between interest groups may never have existed in large scale political systems. Against the conventional views of Dicey and others, these scholars claim that the high period of nineteenth-century parliamentary democracy and individualism was an illusion. Their evidence suggests that the apparent willingness of the state to be the neutral defender of individuals against groups was mainly a device for favoring some groups over others, and that *laisser faire* was mainly a preference for state regulation through private rather than public law. (For a reinterpretation of the era of *laisser faire* in the US see, e.g., Horwitz, *The Transformation of American Law*, and Hurst, *Law and Markets in United States History*. For the debate in relation to Britain see Arthur Taylor, *Laissez-Faire and State Intervention in Nineteenth-Century Britain*. Cf. Dicey, *Lectures on the Relation Between Law and Public Opinion*.)

competing interests are either frozen out of these decision-making arenas, or included only selectively; membership in such recognized corporate groups is either ascribed or compelled by the state, with little democratic control exercised by members over the group; and finally, public policies are implemented in a way that promotes state control over the groups, and group control over its members.

Calling a social order "corporatist" (as distinct from "pluralist") implies that the institutionalized relation between the state and organized social groups has become directly cooperative. In many cases there is also a suggestion that direct competition between such groups for both member support and official favor is negligible, and that the "political market" has failed because of the "monopoly power" exercised by certain groups — both in regard to their own members and in regard to specific arenas of public choice.

To many of its recent proponents the concept of "neo-corporatism" implies a democratic critique of modern relations between state and society. "Neo-corporatism" represents a negative model of what actually happens when the interest groups represented in the state acquire permanent organizations of their own. In this model some, more powerful, groups co-opt the state, while the state in turn co-opts weaker groups by controlling from above the forms of political participation. "Pluralism" in contrast represents the ideal model of interest group representation that is legitimated by conventional democratic theory.[58] In this model government is responsive to the give-and-take of equal social forces in the broadest possible arena.[59]

Marx learned from his critique of Hegel that both pluralist and corporatist forms of interest group participation occur in modern states, and that each form tends to describe itself as encompassing the other.[60] Even the apparently "pluralist" political system in post-New-Deal America has been criticized by McConnell and Lowi as having crucial features that others ascribe to "neo-corporatism" in Europe.[61] For them corporatism in practice

[58] Here economic interests are deemed to "float," even if the interests of communities must sometimes be recognized as more or less permanent bases of group identity.
[59] For a defense of "pluralism" as distinct from "corporatism" in this sense, see Walzer, "Pluralism in Political Perspective." On the relation of organization and co-optation see Piven and Cloward, *Regulating the Poor* and *Poor People's Movements*. See also Offe and Wiesenthal, "Two Logics of Collective Action."
[60] This suggests a potential continuity between the reality of interest-group politics in officially competitive political systems, and the forms of interest representation in non-democratic states. See, e.g., Huntington and Moore (eds), *Authoritarian Politics in Modern Society*, on interest representation in one-party states.
[61] See McConnell, *Private Power in American Democracy*, and Lowi, *The End of*

explains the corruption of an American polity that remains pluralist in theory; for others, the same paradox explains the regime's stability.[62] The two sides differ less in their description of how the system works than in whether it is a virtue or a vice that a mode of interest representation also functions as a form of political socialization.

As Marx would have seen it, the recent effort to distinguish between pluralist and corporatist regimes ought to remind us that modes of representation always have two sides. While the notion of "pluralism" stresses the role of group politics as a vehicle of political participation, the notion of "corporatism" stresses its role as a vehicle of social control. Some political scientists have recently begun to recognize both sides of this Hegelian picture by describing all forms of representation, whether "pluralist" or "corporatist," as modes of "interest intermediation."[63] This stresses the reciprocal relation between state policy formation and the articulation of group interests. According to the new model of "intermediation," interests are not merely inputs to the process of policy formation; they are also outputs of the way in which the process of representation channels, limits, and co-opts the range of societal demands.

Marx and group politics

I believe that a Marxian critique of the recent literature on group politics would track the logic of Marx's critique of Hegel's distinction between

---

Liberalism. See also Greenstone, "Group Theories," and Lindblom, *Politics and Markets*. For an argument that the US still conforms to the pluralist model, see Wilson, "Why is There No Corporatism in the United States?"

[62] See, e.g., Truman, *The Governmental Process*, and Dahl and Lindblom, *Politics, Economics, and Welfare*. For an overview, see Greenstone, "Group Theories."

[63] Such a progression can be seen in Schmitter's own continuing attempt to define the concept of "corporatism." See Schmitter, "Modes of Interest Intermediation and Models of Societal Change in Western Europe" (both corporatism and pluralism have state-dominated and society-dominated forms); "Reflection on Where the Theory of Neo-Corporatism Has Gone and Where the Praxis of Neo-Corporatism May Be Going" (the danger of dichotomizing between pluralism and corporatism); "Interest Intermediation and Regime Governability in Contemporary Western Europe and North America" (high corporatization promotes stability); and "Democratic Theory and Neo-Corporatist Practice" (corporatism lacks legitimacy in terms of democratic theory).

See also Panitch, "Recent Theorizations of Corporatism: Reflections on a Growth Industry."

state and civil society: what appears for itself as "pluralism," a way of representing social interests to the state, is revealed in itself (for the state) to be "corporatism," a way of co-opting social interests into a political regime. From this perspective the recent theory of neo-corporatism merely reflects the theoretical realization that all forms of political representation, beginning with pluralism, will always involve both participation and co-optation.[64] This suggests that the main rhetorical point of describing a particular state form as "neo-corporatist" rather than "pluralist" is to stress a gain in social control at the expense of political legitimacy.[65]

As we have seen, Marx recognized that the relative stability of the Hegelian state would depend upon its success in "disorganizing" the political participation of the public in order to produce both legitimation and social control. While Hegel thought that the same group organizations would serve both purposes, Marx saw that the autonomy of the modern state is grounded in its ability to distinguish in principle between the two models of the group division that make up the political organization of civil society, and to promise both liberal equality for primordial input groups and utilitarian impartiality for corporatist output groups. This means that a government would lose legitimacy if it sacrificed the sorts of

[64] See, e.g., Charles. W. Anderson, "Political Design and the Representation of Interests," and Offe, "The Attribution of Public Status to Interest Groups."

[65] Many recent commentators agree that without the integrating efforts of strong mass parties, the politics of neo-corporatism will be threatened with continuing disorder. This may be caused by an "overload" of demands by new corporate groups that claim direct entitlements from government; an uncontrollable growth of single issue or communal movements that seek to influence policy without sharing political responsibility for its implementation; or rank-and-file revolts within corporate organizations by members who are dissatisfied with the group as a contractual provider of services, and seek more meaningful forms of collective participation in group decisions. (These possibilities are sketched in Schmitter, "Reflections on Where the Theory of Neo-Corporatism Has Gone, and Where the Praxis of Neo-Corporatism May Be Going." Cf. Offe, "'Ungovernability': The Renaissance of Conservative Theories of Crisis."

Similar analyses have been given from different political perspectives. For an 'establishment' version of the "overload" theory, see Huntington, "The Democratic Distemper" and "Post-Industrial Politics: How Benign Will It Be?" For a social democratic view, see Walzer, "Radical Politics in the Welfare State," reprinted with a postscript as "Dissatisfaction in the Welfare State." For an optimistic discussion of communal and single issue politics as a way or reordering the political system see, e.g., Lowi, *The Politics of Disorder*. For an optimistic discussion of rank-and-file democracy in trade unions, see Sabel, "The Internal Politics of Trade Unions."

group claims that are deserving of equal respect; it would lose effectiveness if it gave deferential respect to the sorts of group claims that should be traded off to determine the public good. Both of these losses would eventually threaten the regime's stability.[66]

Marx's understanding of this dynamic became more sophisticated over time. In his early *Critique of Hegel* Marx frequently pointed to the apparent arbitrariness of the way in which the state determined which set of group differences it would fit into the models that we have been calling "pluralism" and "corporatism," respectively.[67] In his mature middle works Marx would notice that virtually any type of group could be made to appear as either a primordial constituent or a parasitical client of any given regime. (When, for example, Louis Napoleon successfully mobilized the French peasantry against the proletariat, Marx recognized that the effect of doing so was to convert the peasantry from a primordial constituent group of civil society into a corporate client of the political regime.)[68] In his late writings on politics Marx tended to argue that the political labor of disorganizing the "people" so as to be ruled may have the effect of either uniting or dividing the interests of ruling groups. The latter case provides the state with the ideological opportunity to assume the apparently impartial role of deciding between the interests of its corporatist clients in the name of the "people" whom it represents.[69]

Precisely because of the artificiality of the distinction between the two pictures of group division, Marx believed that location of a particular set of group differences in one or the other picture would reveal much about the character of particular regimes. Characteristically, his arguments took the form of reversing the ways in which a given regime attempted to articulate the distinction between corporatist mediation and pluralist representation. On the one hand he would typically describe the official picture of the corporate interests that are apparently ruled by the state as, rather, a distorted reflection of the divisions in the kinds of social interests that ultimately rule it. On the other hand he would describe the organization of the whole of society into communal or primordial groups that appear to rule the state as, rather, the political disorganization of the people in order to be ruled.[70] (This notion of "divide and rule" became especially significant

---

[66] See Habermas, *Legitimation Crisis*; Charles Taylor, "Legitimation Crisis?"; and Plant, "Hegel on Identity and Legitimation."

[67] Marx, *Critique of Hegel's 'Philosophy of Right*,' pp. 32, 72, 80–83, 112–14, and (generally) pp. 54 ff.

[68] See Marx, "The Eighteenth Brumaire of Louis Napoleon Bonaparte."

[69] See, e.g., Marx, "The Critique of the Gotha Program."

[70] This, as we have seen, was the argument of "The Eighteenth Brumaire." See chapters 5 and 6, above.

in later Marxist analyses of how colonial powers manipulated and politicized communal differences in order to consolidate their power over subject populations.)

Group politics and class politics

Marx began his political analysis of capitalist democracies by looking for a significant group identity that could not easily be incorporated or assimilated in the political organization of civil society — an identity that revealed the contradiction in the way in which the political order distinguishes between corporate and communal group. Hegel himself had admitted that the urban poor might constitute such a group,[71] placing local government at odds with both the central state and their corporate clients.[72] Others had

[71] See *Hegel's Philosophy of Right* (tr. Knox), paras 241–53. (See also Avineri, *Hegel's Theory of the Modern State*, pp. 147–54 and Plant, "Hegel on Identity and Legitimation.")

Hegel, ever fearful of direct mass action by the urban mob, saw the difficulty in incorporating the poor as a special interest in the state alongside others. After discussing the responsibilities of families, professions, and industries to educate and provide for their weakest members, he placed the remaining burden of policing and feeding the urban rabble on the local authorities. Hegel was ultimately pessimistic, however, about the state's ability to contain the problem of poverty — believing that sheer growth in the number of poor people would frustrate the effort of the state to incorporate them indirectly through family policy, professional training programs, and aid to local governments. He foresaw that the periodic eruption of the poor into mass direct action could threaten the stability of the state. To check such domestic unrest Hegel believed that it would be necessary for particular states to engage in occasional wars (*Hegel's Philosophy of Right* (tr. Knox), para. 324), and to promote economic colonization whenever possible.

In advocating colonialism as a solution to the political problem that poverty poses for modern states Hegel argued: (1) that acquiring colonies increases markets and also provides opportunities for emigration, (ibid., paras 246–8.) (2) that colonial wars involving foreign powers allow a state to promote national unity and encourage domestic sacrifice without immediate danger (ibid., paras 321–9, esp. para. 324) and (3) that the political independence of a former colony will not end its economic dependence, and may result in even greater benefit to the mother country (ibid., addition, para. 248). See also Hirschman, "On Hegel, Imperialism, and Structural Stagnation."

[72] Hegel did not see local authorities as arms of the central government, but rather as self-governing municipal corporations organized to provide a diversity of social

argued that the recognition of submerged nationalities, such as Poles or Jews, might require new forms of political community.[73] The initial appeal of the industrial proletariat to Marx was that it was just such a group — "a class *in* civil society that was not a class *of* civil society."[74] If the demands of the proletariat could not, *ex hypothesi*, be mediated by existing state institutions, Marx assumed that the immediate satisfaction of such demands would resemble the takeover of the state by society in a manner that would finally realize the Jacobin dream. Much of his life's work on the political significance of class was an effort to qualify and refine that assumption, as we shall see in part III, below. For the present, however, I wish to show the relationship between Marx's framework of class analysis and his effort to understand the transformative potential of new social movements in a developed Hegelian state.

Contrary to the assumption of most commentators, Marx's mature political analysis of the working class had two parts which are not inevitably linked: he argued (1) that socialism would serve the objective interests of workers as a class, and (2) that the achievement of socialism would require the democratic mobilization of workers as a group. Marx's first point arose directly out of his critique of the capitalist mode of production, and of the political issues it generates; the second, out of a highly specific scenario that he believed would arise from the organization of political participation around the group identity of "worker." Under this scenario

---

services on a territorial basis. Their willingness to provide social services for the poor would tend, he feared, to attract increasing numbers of poor people, thereby making it increasingly difficult for local government to also serve the needs of the families, industries, and professions that must be taxed to support poverty programs. At the higher levels of the Hegelian state, the political problem of poverty would thus appear indirectly as a potential conflict between policies that (a) strengthen the family, (b) promote the development of industries and professions, or (c) subsidize direct relief of the poverty programs provided by local government.

For a contemporary discussion of such problems in the Johnson administration see Peterson, "Federalism, Economic Development, and Redistribution." For a discussion of Nixon's aborted plan to replace the system Peterson describes with a program that would nominally strengthen the role of the family (The Family Assistance Plan), see Moynihan, *Maximum Feasible Misunderstanding*. One might also usefully compare Plant's "Hegel and Political Economy" part 2 (esp. pp. 110–13) with the modern analysis in O'Connor's *The Fiscal Crisis of the State* and with Lubasz, "Marx's Initial Problematic: The Problem of Poverty."

[73] See, e.g., Liebich (ed.), *The Selected Writings of August Cieszkowski*.

[74] Italics added. Marx announced this conclusion as soon as he completed his critical study of Hegel. See "A Contribution to the Critique of Hegel's *Philosophy of Right*: Introduction" (ed. O'Malley), p. 141.

the political organization of workers would ultimately provoke a counter-revolutionary (and anti-democratic) response. Marx believed that when the counter-revolution occurred the industrial proletariat would achieve the kind of class consciousness necessary for it to prevail in the ensuing struggle, and to subsequently rule in its own interests.

Although Marx argued that socialism cannot come about without the active support of the working class, he did not believe that socialism is whatever the working class happens to support.[75] Of course the conclusion of his own political analysis was almost always to support the politics of proletarian *groups* in non-revolutionary situations. But in such situations Marx recognized that these groups do not always represent the objective interests of workers *as a class* in the sense described in *Capital*; and he clearly did not believe that proletarian groups are necessarily immune from being co-opted as a distinct corporate interest in the state. Marx's fraternal quarrels with such groups were sometimes fierce, and his support – which was never automatic – reflected an analytical conclusion rather than a prior assumption.[76]

At a time when professed socialists in the West are acutely aware of the potential for co-optation of workers' organizations, and when professed socialists in the Third World routinely advocate the suppression of trade unions in the national interest, it is worth reminding ourselves of both the force and type of the argument that Marx actually made. We must recognize in particular that Marx's political lifework was a rigorous and disciplined

---

[75] His polemical writings and oratory frequently tend to show how the political significance of making certain demands may vary with the social base of the movement that makes them, and he sometimes suggests that particular demands are worth winning only if they are seen to be a political victory for the working class. See, e.g., Marx, "Inaugural Address of the Working Men's International Association" (written in 1864), and, of course, Marx and Engels, "The Manifesto of the Communist Party."

[76] In his approach to democratic politics Marx differed from the populists of his day and ours. In populist versions of democratic theory, political action would mobilize progressive forces around progressive issues. Raising class consciousness (political education), and advancing class struggle (political organization) would then go hand in hand – classical "agitprop." Marx did not accept this kind of essentialism in politics. Recognizing that apparently progressive ideas can be promoted by apparently reactionary groups, and that apparently progressive forces can be mobilized around apparently reactionary ideas, he did not believe that support for social movements can be given solely on the basis of either the ideas that they express, or of the social forces that they represent. (The goals of education and organization may be at odds.)

exploration of the linkages between the significance of wage labor in the capitalist mode of production and the variable role of organized labor in democratic politics.[77] This recognition will allow us to draw on Marx's account of the dynamics of capitalism to understand the relative significance of other group identities that come to be politicized.

Instead of relying on Marxist theory to explain why political protest occurs at all, the first task of Marxian political analysis today should be to explain why it takes a particular subjective form, given the objective forces it represents. This could provide a basis for deciding which movements to support around which issues as part of an overall strategy of political transformation. Will the apparently progressive ideas of a social movement become a threat to the working class because of the issues around which it mobilizes its social base (as when feminist ideas of comparable worth threaten blue-collar wage scales)?[78] Or can those ideas become a non-antagonistic basis for organizing the working class, and broadening its alliances (as when greater job equality for women promotes workplace safety)?[79] When does the practical experience of subjectively reactionary working class organizations provide the political education through which radical ideas are acquired? (Consider Catholic workers' movements in Latin America.) When does the reactionary ideology of workers' organizations express the degree to which they have already become a political base for official repression? (Consider the Boers in South Africa.)

My point here is not to qualify Marx's lifelong commitment to the working class movement, but rather to identify the question Marx thought he was answering in his political writings: 'Is socialism best advanced by supporting the democratic demands of workers' organizations, whether or not these political groups possess correct subjective (i.e. class) consciousness?' This question was particularly acute at a time when there were many self-consciously socialist groups that did not identify with the particular interests of workers' organizations – a situation that exists today in many Western and Third World countries. To understand our situation I believe that we must use Marx's method of analyzing the politics of workingmen's groups to analyze the political significance of other group movements that present themselves within the historical framework of capitalist democracy.

In this chapter I have argued that Marx's dual critique of Hegelianism and Jacobinism led to what we may henceforth call "the critical theory of

[77] See chapter 11, below.
[78] Or when environmentalism constricts the supply of lower-income housing.
[79] Or when environmentalism promotes awareness of toxic waste.

democracy." Stripped of its usual legitimating aura, this analytical use of the term "democracy" stands at the conceptual intersection of two types of group division: (1) those created when civil society officially participates in the state, and (2) those created when the state officially regulates civil society.[80] By directing our attention to the problematic *relationship* between the ways in which these forms of group interests are represented in and by the modern state, Marxian political analysis can serve as the basis for arguments both within and against the terms in which political conflicts typically occur.

Whatever its eventual conclusion, a Marxian political analysis of capitalist democracies is initially the study of the divisions that are displaced by the political work of distinguishing between the two forms of group division. Such an analysis alerts us to the specific institutional contradictions that find political expression in group conflict, and the material changes that give rise to those institutional contradictions. Once the material basis of these divisions has been located in the relation between wage labor and capital it will become possible for us to speak of the ways in which the state suppresses and mediates divisions between classes by articulating divisions within them.[81] As we shall see in chapter 9, however, the class analysis of capitalism begins with the critical theory of democratic group politics.

[80] As we have seen, Marx's "critical theory of democracy" also shows a contradiction within each of these types: (1) For some groups official participation means unofficial regulation, while (2) for others official regulation provides an occasion for unofficial participation.

[81] See chapters 11 and 12, below.

9 State and Society

A fable

In a metaphorical way Aesop's fable of the tortoise and the hare presents the basic elements needed to illustrate Marx's approach to criticizing the democratic rationale of institutional policies. Of course the race described in the fable is not a real institution, nor is the rule for determining the winner a fully articulated public policy. This is what makes the story a fable rather than a full ideology. But we can return to these important differences later, after first considering the fable as though it were an ideology.

Viewed as a democratic ideology, the fable is a story about the race that also has significance within the race. The institutional policy of the race is to distinguish between winners and losers on the basis of who crosses the finish line first. However, the runners are also identified, and identify themselves, as a tortoise and a hare. The fable tells us that, despite his apparent advantage, the hare is lazy and rests during the race. The tortoise, slow and steady, keeps on running and wins.

The moral lesson to be learned from the fable must puzzle many children. Is the point that the hare deserves to win, but doesn't? Or is it rather that the tortoise deserves to win because he crossed the finish line first, despite the fact that he lacks the quality the race is designed to measure? Does this mean that the race is really designed to reward effort? If so, why should the race reward the tortoise for trying hard in this particular instance, but not in other instances when he might try harder still? (Perhaps the tortoise always tries harder than the hare.)[1] Yet, if the race is really designed to measure speed after all, the fable seems to tell a story of simple institutional

---

[1] It will not do to say simply that the rules of the race reward *both* speed and perseverance. The rules do not reward the tortoise's perseverance at all, except when the hare decides not to run. Of course a fully handicapped race could reward both tortoises and hares in proportion to their previous efforts. But this would be a different policy, which would not reward speed as such, but only the relative improvement of each runner.

failure, or inflexibility.

Having come this far in our reconstruction of Marx, however, we can now see that these questions miss the point insofar as they ignore the function of the fable as an ideology that legitimates the institutional choice of the rule for determining the winner. While presupposing that the general distributive *impact* of the race will be to turn hares into winners and tortoises into losers, the fable is directly concerned with the *message* that the race conveys from a world divided into tortoises and hares to a world divided into winners and losers. As a legitimating ideology, the fable shows why the race must actually be run, despite the fact that we already know who is faster, thereby teaching tortoise and hare alike that they must run in order to win. Marxian analysis would begin with the recognition that in this ideology the relation between winning and running will be different for each.

Why does the tortoise run? There is certainly not an equal chance of his winning; but even if the criterion for determining the winner gives the advantage to natural speed, the race is not merely a device for rewarding the swift. The race is, rather, a device for making the tortoise run as fast as he can, and he would not do so if the hare did not run at all. The tortoise runs as fast as he can in order to make the hare beat him. The fable thus expresses the 'class consciousness' of the likely losers of the race, while directing it against hares rather than against winners as such. By denying the intrinsic superiority of hares over losers (indeed by equating the two identities), the message of the fable makes it possible for tortoises to accept the winners.

Yet, while the fable may thus express the potential moral *ressentiment* of tortoises, it is equally directed toward making hares feel more worthy of their gifts. The criteria for winning are intended to measure a quality that the hare has, but they are not just another, approximate, way of finding the hare. They are rather designed to make the hare run in order to win. The fable thus can also be read to reflect the 'class ideology' of the likely winners: they are the virtuous hares – those responsible enough to make the effort. As a message from winners to tortoises the fable allows a hare to believe that the race is a way of turning what is otherwise his natural advantage – fleetness of foot – into a prize that he can deserve because of a policy which serves the institution of the race itself. The prize is a reward that is given to the hare, if at all, because of his contribution to the running of tortoises.[2]

---

[2] Cf. the 'Protestant ethic' as articulating a relationship between divine grace and worldly achievement. As a work ethic, it reflects the moral resentment that

It is the (presumed) need for 'running' that informs the ideology of our metaphorical institution of the race. The deep point of the fable is that the ideology of the race neither selects winners nor measures speed, but rather distinguishes between these in order to get both tortoises and hares alike to run, and to get tortoises to run as fast as they can. By treating potential participants as if they were running only in order to win, the ideology of the race effectively gets them to want to win in order to run.[3] Yet it also allows all the runners to accept a world of winners and losers that is not based on intrinsic superiority, since the primordial difference between tortoise and hare has now become a basis of valued diversity without which the static society itself would not 'run.'[4]

This is not yet a full Marxist analysis of ideology, but it is a beginning. To go further, as Marx would have done, we need to leave the world of abstract fables, and deal with social reality. In the real world institutions do not appear singly. If the fable of the tortoise and the hare were part of a real world of multiple institutions, we would have to consider how the distinctions that the race draws between tortoises and hares, and between winners and losers, are reflected differently in the operation of other institutions, and how this in turn is reflected back in the form of contradictions in the running of the race itself. These contradictions would change the material conditions under which the institution of the race could effectively reproduce the activity of running by mediating the relations between runners. Understanding these changes will enable us to assess the

---

industrious capitalists might feel against idle aristocrats. But the Protestant ethic is also an ideological basis for accepting their own success in relation to those less fortunate. The rising capitalist thus sees himself as a 'tortoise' in relation to those who are allowed to win without running. But he is a reformed 'hare' in relation to all those who may run without winning. The difference in worldly success suggests that these unfortunates may simply lack divine grace. This is why their efforts are not rewarded.

The Protestant ethic has proven notoriously difficult to transplant in colonial environments. Here a person may become a 'hare' among 'tortoises,' and yet forever remain a 'tortoise' among 'hares.' See the discussion of colonialism and deracination in chapter 7, above.

[3] The subjective contradiction in the motives of the runners is transformed into a contradiction in what counts as justifying or explaining the rules. Which explains, and which justifies, the rules of the race − the desire to win, or the need to make people run?

[4] The objective contradiction in the identities of the runners is transformed into an ideological contradiction in what counts as justifying or explaining the results under the rules. Which explains, and which justifies, the expected identity of the winner − the equality of tortoises and hares, or their diversity?

historical significance of the issues through which discrete social groups act out the contradictions in their multiple institutional identities by asserting claims within the political process as a whole.

In a real world of multiple institutions a practitioner of Marx's method would want to know why something counts as a prize in relation to the race, and whether it conveys further advantages in this or other institutions. Is the race relatively dominant, autonomous, or subordinate with respect to hierarchies established elsewhere? Are these 'tortoises' and 'hares' merely the winners and losers of another contest? In the fable we assume that the differences between the tortoises and hares is biological and essential; in the real social world a consistent emulator of Marx would analyze these differences as historical and contingent – recognizing that the diversity of world cultures places few, if any, natural limits on the kinds of differences that could be used to fill the places of the tortoises and the hares, and on the kinds of criteria that could be used to distinguish between winners and the losers as we move across institutional boundaries.

As a materialist, a latter-day Marx would also want to know much more about the activity that we have been calling 'running.' Is it fundamental or peripheral to the survival of the social formation? What, if any, is its material role in the reproduction of this or other institutions? Do the crises within institutions sometimes reflect changes in the physical activity of 'running' itself? How does the social character of 'running' change with the relationship between institutions? How does the perceived importance of 'running' reflect the contradictions between institutions at any given time?

Public policy and democratic ideology

In modern states most public policies, like the policy in Aesop's fable, have both an impact and a message. A policy's *impact* consists of the *correlation* between the social differences that precede the policy and those created by it – what proportion of hares end up as winners? Assessing a policy's impact presumes that government is an external agent that will effectively benefit some social groups at the expense of others.[5] The *message* of public policies lies in how they articulate the *distinction* between the two types of difference that they purport to relate – what is the relation between winning, natural speed, and effort? Interpreting such a message presumes that government is both a divisive and a mediating force within society.

[5] This abstracts from the constitutive role of government in markets by describing the policy as external government intervention in preexisting market relationships.

In this dual conception of government, administering a given public policy is in large part a process of communication between two distinct pictures of social division: society as divided between the supporters and opponents of its policy, and society as divided between the victims and beneficiaries. A policy's message cuts across these divisions by relating, for example, its supporters and its victims, or its opponents and its beneficiaries – much as Aesop's fable legitimates the race by communicating between winners and tortoises, and between losers and hares.

Following the basic insights of Marx's critique of Hegel, we can understand the democratic legitimacy of a policy by analyzing the relation between the policy's impact and its message. Debates arise around questions such as the following: what is the message that the policy conveys from its supporters to its victims? is it one of respect or of contempt? what is the message that its implementation conveys from its beneficiaries to its opponents? does it effectively threaten to victimize them? The greater the overlap between supporters on the input side and beneficiaries on the output side, between opponents on the input side, and victims on the output side, the more suspect the policy is from the standpoint of critical democratic theory.[6]

This suggests that in constitutional democracies there may be a wide range of arguably pathological relations between the impact of a policy and its message. Sometimes impact and message reinforce each other, as when a policy of racial segregation conveys a message of racial superiority, while perpetuating the effects of past racial advantage; sometimes impact and message offset each other, as when protective legislation for women conveys a message of male superiority, while giving women legal advantages over men; sometimes a majority conveys its political contempt without gaining material advantage, as when it stigmatizes certain communities because of the past privileges of their members; sometimes, when a majority imposes large burdens on itself to bring about social change, it chooses to give its opponents the advantage of exemption – whether as a form of toleration or as a sign of weakness.

Whenever there is a sharp division between the supporters of a policy and its victims, the policy's democratic rationale becomes problematic. Here, the simple adherence to majoritarian procedures is not sufficient to establish the democratic legitimacy of the policy. There must also be resort to non-majoritarian institutions – the Courts in the United States, and, everywhere, the social scientists and myth-makers. These institutions have the task of adjusting, whether in theory or in practice, the substantive

[6] Cf. Ely, *Democracy and Distrust.*

relation between impact and message, and the work of these institutions should be a prime focus of Marxian political analysis.

From the standpoint of Marxian political analysis, the democratic rationale of a policy will fail to the extent that the policy itself is a transparent use of state power by its supporters to benefit at the expense of its victims. In this case the policy's victims become retrospective opponents because of the message it conveys, and its opponents become prospective victims because of its repressive impact.

Most often, however, a policy will include some victims among its supporters, and some opponents among its beneficiaries – the ostensible point of our fable of the tortoise and the hare. Insofar as a policy successfully divides its supporters and opponents along the same lines as its victims and beneficiaries, the policy's democratic rationale will be dialectical and changing. Here, the policy's implementation must be constantly reviewed to make sure that the advantages it confers do not reflect a political superiority of some constituent groups over others. Looking forward from adoption to implementation, the differential advantages conferred by the policy must appear to be in the public interest. Looking backward from implementation to adoption, disagreement with the policy must appear to reflect non-hierarchical diversity in civil society.

In such circumstances Marxian political analysis must turn to the ideological criticism of the social scientific and legal arguments that serve the modern state by giving public policy an arguably democratic rationale. In his lifelong examination of official materials Marx developed a sharp eye for contradictions in the efforts of public institutions to articulate the pattern of social differences that explain and justify their policies. Often (to put the point in his own Hegelian language) one basis of group differentiation serves as the "materialism" of state power, and another as the "spiritualism" of social advantage.[7]

Public ideology and policy science

Drawing on Marx's critique of Hegel I have tried to suggest thus far that each institutionally articulated policy projects a picture of the social world of groups 'outside' a given institution onto a picture of the social world of groups 'created' by that institution. The ideological function of public policy, whatever its merits, is to mediate between these two modes of

[7] See Marx, *Critique of Hegel's 'Philosophy of Right,'* pp. 45–8. Cf. Duncan Kennedy, "The Stages of the Decline of the Public/Private Distinction."

dividing society into groups. In analyzing public policy the "critical theory of democracy" attempts to put these two pictures of group identity back together in order to reveal any contradictions in a policy's democratic rationale. Such analysis takes its initial data from the theories through which institutions attempt to articulate the difference between the two pictures of group division on which their policies are based.[8] Since governmental institutions largely function by explaining society to itself, these theories can often be found implicitly in official documents (including judicial opinions), and more explicitly in the forms of social science on which these documents tend to draw.

The democratic rationale of public policy is often articulated in the welfare states of Europe through such official devices for group representation as consociational democracy and corporatism;[9] in the United States that rationale tends to be articulated most clearly by the courts. American courts will often explicitly demand such a democratic rationale for bureaucratic policy, using various theories of pluralism as an analytic device in public law litigation, much as they might use market theory as an analytical framework in private law disputes. In the course of judicial review of public policy these courts will frequently grant standing to virtual representatives of affected groups, while seeking to determine whether the publicly recognized interests of such groups have been adequately addressed in the course of bureaucratic decision-making. The applicable legal standards of administrative due process broadly require that group concerns be heard in forming and implementing public policy, and that a government agency be able to articulate the relationship between the group differences that justify its policy, and those that its policy justifies. When the courts come to fashion procedural remedies for breaches of due process they will often tend to *impose* a miniature version of democratic

[8] In the US, for example, we get one picture of social divisions when liberal political scientists wish to explain the influence of dominant social groups on state policy, and another when they wish to explain the influence of regulatory intervention on group differences. These two pictures are reflected in two largely separate empirical literatures: one focuses on the input side and describes electoral coalitions of groups based on symbolic issues, moral causes, and communal identities; the other focuses on the output side of government and describes the "capture" of policy-making agencies by special interest groups.

[9] See, e.g., Lijphart, *Democracies* and *Democracy in Plural Societies*. Cf. Offe, "The Attribution of Public Status to Interest Groups" and "The Theory of the Capitalist State and the Problem of Policy Formation."

pluralism onto the deliberations of agencies that have not adequately organized their own constituency groups in civil society.[10]

Yet, despite such procedural differences, the public policies of capitalist democracies are broadly similar in their theoretical rationales – if only because these policies are generally efforts to mediate between state and economy. The economic impact of every public policy must be assessed by considering it as a governmental intervention in the market that will effectively benefit some at the expense of others. The policy's political significance must be interpreted by considering it as a message from society as divided between the policy's supporters and opponents, to society as divided between the policy's victims and beneficiaries. Any policy thus assumes at least a loose sort of political sociology in the picture of group diversity that would justify its adoption, and a loose sort of political economy in the picture of group advantage that would be justified by its implementation.

Under the political ideology of most modern states, a successful democratic policy would justify the (economic) advantages it confers when these do not appear to reflect the (social) superiority of the groups that support it. As policy sciences, however, political economy and political sociology each have their own distinctive foundation in democratic thought. To paraphrase Marx's early critique of social science, our sociology implies its own economics, our economics its own sociology.[11] As a consequence, these theoretical disciplines may conflict with each other indirectly, even if each tries to remain within its own explanatory domain.

In its concern with public choice, for example, political economy has its own notion of democratic social inputs. This notion functions as an implicit 'sociology,' which tells us the expected advantages that would accrue to groups that define themselves in terms of the classifications through which policies are administered. The economist's theory of democracy promises that in deciding which interests will be sacrificed for the greater good the government will treat individuals as though their preexisting preferences were intrinsically fungible.[12]

[10] See, generally, Fiss, "Foreword: The Forms of Justice"; Frug, "The Ideology of Bureaucracy in American Law"; Jaffe, *Judicial Control of Administrative Action*; Tribe, *American Constitutional Law*, chs 3.17–3.19, 10.12–10.19, 16.47–16.57; Stewart, "The Reformation of American Administrative Law"; and Vining, *Legal Identity*.

[11] See chapter 4, above.

[12] See, e.g., Downs, *An Economic Theory of Democracy*; Buchanan and Tullock, *The Calculus of Consent*; and Barry, *Sociologists, Economists, and Democracy*.

Just as political economy has its own implicit sociology, so political sociology also has its own implicit notion of economic impact, which contrasts with that of the economists by focusing, not on resultant group identities, but on those that preexist a given policy. The 'sociological' theory of democracy promises that no primordial social group will be gratuitously sacrificed to another, regardless of relative size.[13]

In chapter 4 we described in general terms how institutional ideologies function by transposing the experience of objective and subjective contradictions into contradictions in what counts as a social explanation and in what counts as a social justification. We can now see this illustrated in the ways that ideas of liberty and equality function in the logic of public policy disputes. In disputes over public policy, democratic concepts such as liberty and equality function, alternatively, as either empirical hypotheses or normative constraints within the policy sciences. In most versions of political economy liberty is assumed empirically: results inconsistent with this assumption are then explained as forms of market failure or distortion, which should be corrected. In most versions of political sociology equality is assumed empirically: results inconsistent with this assumption are then explained as artifacts of discrimination or other forms of illegitimate social power, which should be offset. Public policy mediates between these two pictures of society by distinguishing between what needs to be explained and what needs to be justified in each.

Given these two conflicting forms of democratic social science – economic and sociological – it is not surprising that statistics may often become the preferred method for policy analysis. Essentially, statistics is a technique for comparing any two groups of unequal individuals by correlating the spread of differences within each group to the differences between them. By not questioning the construction of the alternative pictures of group difference that it compares, modern statistics mediates the contradiction between the two forms of democratic social science. So long as these two pictures can be kept distinct in everyday politics, statistics can show the degree to which one *explains* the other.

Public policy and social identity

Our abstract discussion of public policy has attempted to suggest that apparently discrete areas of institutional policy can be analyzed as micro-

[13] See, generally, Barry, *Sociologists, Economists, and Democracy*. For legal expressions of the 'sociological' approach described above see Ely, *Democracy and Distrust*, and Fiss, "Groups and the Equal Protection Clause."

cosms of the problems Marx saw in democratic politics. In articulating the rationale for its specific policies the state tends to present two distinct pictures of the divisions of civil society into groups. In the first picture, group claims express a demand by the group to be treated as an equal in resisting the selfish advantage of temporary majorities or other power blocs that hope to use control of the state to further their own interests. In the second picture group claims express a private interest in receiving the kinds of advantage that must be critically balanced against costs to others when the public interest is calculated.

This conception of the policy process envisions two basic reasons why group identity becomes politicized. New groups of the first sort would enter politics in order to claim respect, or to combat social domination. Such groups would be less concerned with what policies government pursues, than that those policies be administered in a way that shows equal respect to diverse constituent groups. New groups of the second sort would enter politics to lobby government so as to influence the choice of policy for their own benefit. They assume that any government policy will inevitably benefit some groups at the expense of others, and they hope to influence the policy-maker to decide that the balance of benefits justifies imposing the necessary costs on someone else.

But, as Marx saw, groups in politics are rarely so easily distinguishable on their face. The politics of gender in capitalist democracies illustrates how much depends on the state's success in distinguishing between the types of social differences that can be subsidized and those that must be equalized. In formulating family policies modern states frequently attempt to subsidize attitudes that are conventionally seen as female, even while claiming to avoid stereotyping women. Meanwhile, in their economic policies the same states frequently attempt to reward jobs that are demanding and inflexible, while claiming not to discriminate against persons for whom family commitments come first. In practice, however, the state cannot equalize between women and men in the labor market without having a non-neutral effect on the choice of women to work outside the home: by making new economic opportunities available to women who prefer them, the state inevitably raises the real and opportunity costs to women who choose the exclusive role of homemaker; yet the state cannot easily regulate family benefits and marital property so as to equalize between women who are homemakers and those who are wage earners without thereby giving male wage earners an advantage over females in the job market.

An example from American law will illustrate this problem. Allowing wives to automatically inherit the pension rights of their husbands as marital property without proving dependency, but not vice versa, is manifestly unfair to women workers: the pension benefits these women earn at their jobs are worth less to their families than those of their male colleagues. Yet treating men and women workers equally in this area would require either (1) eliminating the spousal benefit, (2) requiring both husbands and wives to prove eligibility on grounds that they were wholly dependent on the spouse during their working lives, or (3) diluting the average survivor's benefits by giving them automatically to all husbands and wives. Each of these possibilities would reduce the protection afforded to traditional housewives in the event of survivorship or divorce, and turn the decision not to work outside the home into a greater luxury or risk. Without an automatic right of survivorship a woman who chose to be a homemaker would either (1) not receive her husband's benefits, (2) not be certain of them if she had worked at any point in her life, or (3) be certain of receiving spousal benefits that would not be enough to live on if she did not have additional benefits on her own account.

In lobbying the state on this issue women's groups face a clear policy dilemma. If the state is to neutralize the choice between homemakers and career women, it cannot be neutral between working women and working men; yet if all women are to have a choice that most men do not have, there must be men at many income levels who can earn "family benefits" and a "family wage." Although most feminists would argue that women should have a choice, the policies of the state cannot avoid influencing the incentives of many married or divorced women, especially those with children, to work (or not to work) outside the home.[14]

The direction of influence one favors will depend upon whether one believes that having a career is a natural good that is denied to many women because of the cost of paid childcare, or whether one believes that full-time motherhood is a natural good that is denied to many women because of the economic necessity of supporting their children. This choice will inevitably divide women along cultural, educational, and economic lines.

Since the state cannot persuasively claim to be neutral on this basic choice of values, public policy-makers must unavoidably decide for which form of social diversity they are equalizing in effectively subsidizing either career women over housewives, or men who need to support a family over women workers who do not.[15] In giving an ostensibly democratic rationale

[14] These issues are taken up again in chapters 10 and 12, below.
[15] In the US the Equal Rights Amendment to the Constitution was defeated because of organized opposition from women's groups, despite strong initial support from overwhelmingly male legislatures courting the women's vote. In seeking to equalize the differences between women and men in the labor market the ERA

for their decision, policy-makers would typically call upon social science to paint two distinct pictures of social heterogeneity — the first organized around the group identities of women and men, the second around the preferences of women themselves for 'traditional' and 'non-traditional' roles.

These two pictures of social cleavage inevitably appear together in the same policy arguments, but whenever one is presented as a natural basis of social diversity the other is described as a mere artifact of past policy choice.[16] Thus, a policy argument in which the difference between men and women appears as a natural basis of social diversity might easily conclude that the state should eliminate the unequal advantages men have derived in the workplace as a result of women's performance of traditional female roles in the family. Yet a policy argument that stresses the naturally diverse preferences of women regarding traditional family roles might easily conclude that the state should endeavor to upgrade the dignity of the necessary tasks many women perform, perhaps by attacking the hegemonic gender-images that are used to devalue such tasks by men and women alike.[17]

The ideological role of the state in the area of gender policy is to articulate a distinction between those 'primordial' forms of diversity between men and women — and between women and women — that are to be regarded as the natural constituents of social life, and those 'artificial' divisions of labor between gender roles that are to be regarded as the regrettable but necessary consequence of public choice. In performing their ideological role policy-makers must consistently deny that this very distinction is itself an artifact of public choice — a denial that comes easily only so long as it both supports and conceals a contradiction in the political consciousness of women themselves.

From policy to politics

An authentically Marxian analysis of a policy cannot address the material question of who benefits at whose expense in the modern state[18] without

---

divided women among themselves. According to some surveys, many women feared that the ERA would reduce the level of economic protection for traditional housewives, and that it would force women into the labor market without significantly increasing net family income.

[16] Cf. the discussion above of tortoises and hares vs winners and losers.

[17] For an interesting discussion of a wide range of legal issues that also draws heavily on Hegel and Marx see Olsen, "The Family and the Market: A Study of Ideology and Legal Reform."

also addressing the ideological question of what identities will be politicized (or depoliticized) by the process through which the policy is adopted and implemented – of what groups will be organized (or disorganized) by the issues that the policy generates. This approach requires an initial focus on the changing and potentially contradictory ways in which political institutions articulate the distinction between the social divisions that would explain the policy, and the social divisions that the policy purports to justify. When, for example, a school system makes a policy decision to evaluate performance on the basis of standardized national tests this may mobilize groups of parents to argue that the school's policy has turned certain family traits, such as not speaking English at home, into *handicaps* which will come to explain poor performance. This argument implicitly recognizes that what makes a trait or difference in background a "handicap" is in most cases the policy decision not to treat it as a difference to be equalized for in the organization of tasks, or the distribution of rewards.[19]

Unlike one-sided Marxian analyses of the surface issues of modern politics – which have tended to reflexively demonstrate either that any given policy victimizes the working class, or that its apparent benefits in reality "co-opt" them[20] – a return to Marx's own critique of democratic politics would require us to investigate many possible relations between the question of who benefits at whose expense, and the question of who is co-opting whom. Emulating Marx's critical theory of democracy would allow us to take positions on the issues arising out of politics as usual – the politics of reform – and reopen Marxian analysis to the possibility that even counter-revolutionary forces may be co-opted by reform.[21]

The analytical approach developed in this chapter should enable us to go beyond the usual Marxist impulse to treat any given policy symbolically, as just another example of "typical" phenomena which are thought to be always and everywhere occurring – such as centralization, commodification,

---

[18] For a discussion of this question see Page, *Who Gets What From Government*.
[19] The issues described above are of course central to debates over "affirmative action" and "reverse discrimination." See, generally, Meister, "Discrimination Law Through the Looking Glass."
[20] See, e.g., the discussion of the influential work of Piven and Cloward in chapter 6, above.
[21] The bourgeoisie, for example, may sometimes lose its capacity for concerted and autonomous action as a result of the dependency of some of its elements on government subsidy. (On "class capacity" see Therborn, "Why Some Classes are More Successful Than Others.") Lenin well understood the possibility of partial co-optation of the bourgeoisie when he decided to enter the Provisional Government.

or labor force reproduction. Instead we can redirect our attention to the historical ironies in the kinds of constituencies that must be mobilized (or suppressed) for a policy to perform its "typical" function under concrete conditions. For example, in the United States, the critical theory of democracy might help us to understand why problems in the schools have recently tended to politicize questions of equality for American workers in a way that industrial issues have not.

If my suggestions bear fruit, a Marxian analysis of politics would not require us to look for class positions and interests alongside the identities and issues that are politicized by policy disputes. To follow Marx's example, however, we would need to go beyond the method of policy analysis that has been discussed thus far in order to explain how certain group identities within a political system provide a perspective from which it is possible to make claims against it. Why do certain social roles form the basis of group identities around which political mobilization becomes possible? How do the conflicts of group interests that are produced by public policy enter into the creation of those group identities that form the basis of political regimes?

Regimes and institutions

We have seen thus far how Marx's critique of Hegel's theory of the state can provide a technique for analyzing each policy arena as though it were itself a microcosm of a political regime. We must now apply this technique of policy analysis to the institutional structure of the regime as a whole. In doing so we must be concerned especially with how the politics of the regime reproduces the picture of social structure on which it depends. How far does it reproduce the kinds of cleavages and problems that explain its continuing necessity — so that its historical emergence is not an event in the past but a process continuously reenacted?[22] In what ways does this reproduction take place under changing conditions that create the new issues and identities that transform the structure from within? From what internal standpoint can we distinguish between the sorts of social conflict that sustain the regime, and those that undermine it?

To begin with, the unit of analysis here is not the class itself, but rather the political system seen as a relation between state and civil society. At

---

[22] See Rokkan, *Citizens, Elections, Parties*, ch. 1, for a non-Marxist account of how the pattern of cleavages reflected in the party structures of European countries can be seen to reenact the political history of those regimes.

the level of institutional analysis, class formation is not an assumption but a conclusion — an effect of political struggle rather than a cause.[23] A conscious politics of overt class conflict, when it occurs, must be explained, like any other political division, by an analysis of a particular configuration of institutions — at least if we are to be consistent with Marx's own method. Just as political antagonism is a consequence of the contradictory way in which market theory represents the value of labor in the mode of production,[24] so it is also a consequence of the contradictory way in which democratic theory represents the rights and interests of workers in the political system.

The late twentieth-century equivalent to Marx's earliest definition of his political project (dissolving the distinction between state and civil society not just in appearance but in reality) is to identify the real work of politics that goes into keeping the pluralist and corporatist paradigms of group division distinct under changing conditions. By superimposing these two models of group division, and ultimately connecting them, we can more clearly assess what kinds of group movements will weaken or strengthen the forces supporting a particular regime.

Class analysis, as Marx actually practiced it, is initially the study of the issues that are displaced by a regime's efforts to institutionalize the difference between pluralism and corporatism in civil society. Once we have grasped the institutional contradictions that find political expression in group conflict, the remaining task — addressed in part III, below — is to account for the material changes that give rise to those contradictions. In capitalist democracies class relations will then appear as the reality concealed by the political articulation of the two bases of group division in civil society, suggesting, as we shall see, that the political analysis of modern capitalism must interpret the argument of *Capital* through Marx's early critique of Hegel and Bauer.

[23] See, generally, Przeworski, "Proletariat Into a Class: The Process of Class Formation from Karl Kautsky's *The Class Struggle* to Recent Controversies," esp. pp. 367–70.

[24] Marx notes, for example, that Adam Smith measures the value of commodities in terms of the labor they embody, while measuring the value of labor in terms of the commodities it commands. "Political economy has ... never once asked the question ... why labour is expressed in value, and why the measurement of labour by its duration is expressed in the magnitude of the value of the product." *Capital*, vol. I, p. 173f. See also Marx, *Theories of Surplus Value*, part 1, ch. 3. These issues are discussed at some length in part III, below.

The ghost of Hegel

Unfortunately, the literature of American Marxism has not been concerned with political analysis in this sense. Rather, its dominant problem has been to attempt to explain the unexpected persistence and strength of the state.[25] As a result much of American Marxism has been mired in the kind of one-sided interpretations of the relation of state and civil society from which Marx himself broke lose in the 1840s. I believe that this problem has seriously afflicted scholarship on both the Old and New Left.

The Old Left characteristically accepted a Hegelian distinction between state and civil society in theory, while viewing persistence of a boundary between the two as a barrier to the historical advance of socialism. There were, however, two distinct views of how the distinction between state and society might be overcome in practice. (1) Democratic Centralists argued that the final struggle against entrenched vested interests in civil society should be carried out in the name of the state. (2) In contrast many Social Democrats insisted that the most urgent task of socialists would be to democratize the institutions of civil society so that they could be autonomous constituents of the political process. The New Left broke with this debate by repudiating the distinction between state and civil society in theory — and with it much of the socialist political agenda — arguing that either the state had already swallowed up civil society, or that civil society had swallowed up the state. Again there were two versions of this viewpoint (which we will number consecutively with those above). (3) Populists argued that civil society had already swallowed up the state, which would inevitably exercise its power in the interests of the socially dominant groups. (4) Cultural romantics (and Left Foucaldians) argued that the state had already swallowed up civil society, thereby replicating its repressive powers at the level of everyday life.

Within the framework of these alternatives the political evils of modern capitalism are, respectively, as follows: (1) the immunity of the private sphere from political control; (2) the limitation of democratic principles to the public sphere; (3) the control of public institutions by private interests; or (4) the extension of political surveillance and control into every aspect of life (the micropolitics of domination). Each of these diagnoses suggests a corresponding cure. The Leninist solution for (1) is to create a political base that could smash the resistance of private power to state control, and thus defeat the counter-revolution. This strategy would correct for the

[25] Recent efforts to turn this problem into a new paradigm are reflected in Evans, Rueschemeyer, and Skocpol (eds), *Bringing the State Back In*.

danger that a state apparatus in the hands of progressive forces would have less power than it had when it was used against them. The social democratic solution for (2) is to extend the principles of democracy from the state to the private sphere, thereby correcting for the danger that a powerful and effective state would serve the interests of only the vanguard party rather than the class as a whole. The populist solution for (3) is to limit the control of state power by elites, thereby relying on the purified state to protect its citizens from the control of social hierarchies. Finally, the cultural romantic solution for (4) celebrates and supports insurgent movements that resist the extension of state and market power to areas of communal life, relying on periodic spontaneous social uprisings to protect collective activities from both state and market control.

In the politics of theory, each of these positions can claim a Marxian heritage mainly in its opposition to the others. Although these approaches all lend themselves to empirical research, thus supporting the position of the Left in the academy, case studies from each of these perspectives typically prove to be repeated examples of the same point — which is generally an attack on one of the potentially contradictory relations of state and society noted in Marx's critical exposition of Hegel. For Marx himself, however, empirical work was not merely an occasion to illustrate a single general point of this kind, but rather a means of showing how the contradictions in the specific institutional distinctions between state and civil society have worked out in practice — strengthening or weakening particular institutions while creating new issues and the possibility of new movements.

Scholars loosely identified with the Marxist tradition are not alone in failing to exorcise the ghost of Hegel. Most contemporary political science remains at the level of the Hegelian distinction between state and civil society that Marx criticized. Within this implicitly Hegelian framework the theoretical alternatives are stark. If one accepts the validity of Hegel's distinction as an explanatory hypothesis, one can argue normatively that we need to redress the balance in favor of either the state or society. If one rejects the validity of Hegel's distinction as an explanatory hypothesis one can argue that the social formation has already been wholly infused with the attributes that Hegel ascribes to either the state or society. Curiously, debates both within and between the Right and the Left in American politics have generally tended to mirror these one-sided versions of the Hegelian view.

Mainstream American political scientists tend to argue that only by recognizing the distinction between state and civil society as a fact[26] can

[26] In mainstream American political science what Europeans call state and civil

we finally complete the takeover of society by the state, or of the state by society. In the study of American politics there are two basic versions of this view. (1) According to the first version, the outstanding task of political development is to complete the "conquest" of private power by the state — which is already presumed to represent the organized interests of the people as a whole.[27] (2) The second version says that the main task of political development is to complete the seizure of the state by a fuller range of social forces, through extending the principles of political democracy to the internal organization of underrepresented social groups.[28] In sharp contrast to the views dominant in political science, American political sociologists tend to believe (in common with the New Left) that the distinction between state and civil society is a myth. This general viewpoint also has two versions (which, to complete our picture, we will number consecutively with those above). (3) One version argues that we cannot speak of a state which is not simply the captive of certain social groups that exercise their power through it.[29] (4) The other version argues that in post-traditional society there is no such thing as a social organization that is not constituted and permeated by political power at every level.[30] Ironically, in both (3) and (4) the force of denying the distinction between the state and civil society in reality is often to reassert it in principle: (3) holds out the hope that the social power that controls the state can be curtailed by a vigilant politics; (4) holds out the hope that the political hierarchies that infect social life can be replaced by a revived communal spontaneity.

These four mainstream views, like their Marxist (and "post-Marxist") counterparts, tend to emphasize only one side of Hegel's description of group politics. Whenever one side of Hegel's view is put forward as the disease of modern politics, the other side is put forward as the cure — state institutions should either be more autonomous of social forces or more responsive to them; social life should either be more subject to bureaucratic control or more resistant to it. All four mainstream views thus hold forth the utopian possibility that change in either the state or civil society will achieve revolutionary goals without revolutionary breakdown,[31] but all would probably agree with Hegel that, whatever its professed ends, no

---

society are often referred to as "political institutions" and "social forces."

[27] See, e.g., Lowi, *American Government: The Incomplete Conquest.*

[28] See, e.g., Dahl, *Dilemmas of Pluralist Democracy.*

[29] See, e.g., Mills, *The Power Elite.*

[30] See, e.g., Foucault, *Madness and Civilization, The Birth of the Clinic, Discipline and Punish,* and *Power/Knowledge*; and Nisbet, *Twilight of Authority.*

[31] See, e.g. Dahl, *After the Revolution,?* and Lowi, *The Politics of Disorder.*

revolution can succeed at anything without establishing a stable state. (Nothing succeeds like succession.)

Political development and social movements

In mainstream American political science there is, however, a more rounded version of the Hegelian view of the relation of state and society – a view that marks a substantive advance in the Hegelian perspective. Just as Hegel had argued that modern politics was characterized by the demand that the "subjectivity" of persons be recognized in the state, so Samuel P. Huntington characterizes political modernity as a conjunction of "rising expectations" and a demand for "political participation." For him creating "strong political institutions" and "raising the level of [political] community" are virtually interdefinable.[32] Like Hegel and Tocqueville before him, Huntington sees such changes as both a potential threat to the stability of

[32] See, e.g., Huntington, *Political Order in Changing Societies*, pp. 24, 20. The flavor of this can be gotten from passages such as the following? "... [C]ommunity involves the relation of individual men and groups to something apart from themselves." (p. 10.) "The level of political community a society achieves reflects the relationship between its political institutions and the social forces which comprise it." (p. 8.) "Democrats are accustomed to thinking of governmental institutions as having representative functions ... Hence they tend to forget that governmental institutions have interests of their own." (p. 25.) "... [G]overnmental institutions derive their legitimacy and authority, not from the extent to which they represent the interests of the people or of any group, but to the extent to which they have interests of their own apart from all other groups." (p. 27.) "The capacity to create public institutions is the capacity to create public interests." (p. 24.) "The public interest is not something which exists *a priori* in natural law or the will of the people. Nor is it simply whatever results from the political process. Rather it is whatever strengthens public institutions. The public interest is the interest of public institutions." (p. 25.) "... [T]he autonomy of political institutions is likely to be the result of competitions among social forces." (p. 20). "Where the political system lacks autonomy [new] groups gain entry into politics without becoming identified with established political organizations or acquiescing in the established political procedures." (p. 21.) "... [I]f the society is to be a community, the power of each group is exercised through political institutions which temper, moderate, and redirect that power so as to render the dominance of one social force compatible with the community of many." (p. 9.) "In a complex society community is produced by political action and maintained by political institutions ... The degree of community in a complex society, then, ... depends on the strength and scope of its political institutions." (pp. 10–11.)

existing states, and a basis for a new, and more stable, political order.[33] Just as Hegel fears the "unorganized bloc" (and the "wild idea of the 'people'")[34] — just as Tocqueville hates the mob — so Huntington sets himself against "mass praetorianism," the threat of popular direct action in politics.

But Huntington is Hegel without illusions. In defending the autonomy of modern political institutions Huntington does not deny or conceal the two theories of group division that they mediate. Instead, he suggests that it is the historical task of the developing state to distinguish these two theories, and render them non-contradictory. This is done by expressly distinguishing between the institutions (such as parties) through which society participates in the state from below, and the institutions (such as regulatory agencies) through which the state governs society from above. Like Hegel, Huntington recognizes that both sets of institutions are (or might as well be) state organizations.

As a comparativist, Huntington realizes that his distinction between the two ways of institutionalizing group politics is not a natural property of the groups arrayed on either side, but an artifact of their treatment by political institutions. The general type of group division in which a particular group appears will depend upon which institutions have the task of bringing it into the political system. Moreover, the distinction between the two modes of group representation does not necessarily reflect the realities of political power. While the corporatism of client groups of the government apparatus is formally a supplicant to state power, it may actually represent the society as organized into the groups that rule the state for their own benefit. While the pluralism of constituent groups of the ruling party is formally the base of state power, it may actually represent society as organized into groups that seek protection insofar as they do not rule.

Those groups that will appear as 'primordial' often organize to enter politics because they can no longer accept a state in which a dominant group, even a majority, would use its power to oppress a subordinate group, especially if different political issues repeatedly divide people along the same lines. Whatever the original reasons for such groups to organize, however, what matters to the state is that they can be organized at all. Once their political organization in civil society is complete, such groups can be recognized as "participants" in the "political process." When such groups are organized to participate in politics on the input side, they may

---

[33] See, generally, Huntington, *Political Order in Changing Societies*, ch. 1 ("Political Order and Political Decay"), esp. pp. 32–92 (on the effects of modernization).
[34] *Hegel's Philosophy of Right* (tr. Knox), paras 279, 302.

eventually become satisfied with the premise that, in its policy outputs, the state respects their group rights by not discriminating against their individual members. There are in principle no scarcity constraints on the number of diverse groups that can be thus respected. Neutrality may be the ideology of the developed modern state, but because its constituent groups are often organized around past grievances, neutralization becomes its policy.

For client groups, on the other hand, there are theoretical limits to the number of interests that the state can serve. In the course of economic development not all client groups can be satisfied insofar as they raise issues in which some sectors of society must inevitably benefit at another's expense. Since the state cannot here be neutral even in theory, such corporatist groups will seek to capture the process by which it determines whose 'private' interest is in the 'public' interest. Even governments that have successfully 'bought off' subordinate groups with the expectation of continuing material improvements may find it difficult to do so when faced with periodic 'crises' in their economies.[35]

For non-utopian liberal theorists such as Huntington the problem of political development is to turn frustrated client groups into satisfied constituents − to get them to trade off benefits for respect. How is this possible? Huntington argues that ideally, social forces would become increasingly self-conscious as groups to the extent that they also become politically organized; they would then come to articulate the 'public' value of their interest as a group by finding means of promoting their interest that will strengthen the particular institutional interest of state agencies. The stability and growth of such agencies will usually depend upon their ability to justify their selection of the victims and beneficiaries of their policies according to rules. Huntington expects that social groups will come to accept an official monopoly of justification *by* the rules, if they are represented in the justification *of* the rules through some process of political participation.[36] The same groups would then be treated differently as inputs and as outputs (constituents and clients) of the political system, and their conception of their own interests would be correspondingly transformed. Instead of participating in politics in order to receive benefits, they would come to understand their demand for benefits as a means of participating in politics.

[35] For an illuminating discussion of the limits of working-class clientelism, see Przeworski, "Material Bases of Consent: Economics and Politics in a Hegemonic System."
[36] Unlike Hegel, Huntington seems to be as concerned with how such groups see the state as with how the state sees them.

The characteristic political issues in the modern states Huntington most admires concern the relative institutional supremacy of party and government. Such issues arise, he argues, because the ongoing activity of the party gives at least the appearance of according recognition to the subjective desires of the people — a recognition not otherwise available from the bureaucratic institutions of government. The modern mass party is an extra-constitutional body that has the specific function, not merely of contesting elections, but also of mediating between the government and social forces on a regular basis. From Hegel's own perspective the widespread supremacy of the party over parliament in many developed modern states might be seen positively as a modernization of the institutions of political representation, or negatively as the hegemony of part of civil society over the state. In either case the modern party system is a confession of the difficulty in Hegel's scheme of basing political community on common citizenship.[37]

According to Huntington the quintessential modern device for institutionalizing mass political participation is the Leninist party. By inclusively organizing a mass social base it creates the basis for a post-revolutionary government that is at once strong and stable. As we saw in another context, Huntington challenges Marxist political theory with the implicit notion that Lenin provides a Hegelian critique of Marx.[38] Huntington puts this point as follows:

> Lenin made Marxism into a political theory and in the process stood Marx on his head. The key to Marx is the social class; the key to Lenin is the political party. Marx was a political primitive. He could not develop a

[37] As we saw in chapter 8, Hegel thought that the modern function of parties could be performed by a legislative assembly. Such an assembly would not itself be a sovereign law-maker, and would not play much part in the formulation of policy, but would rather represent the organization of society as part of the state for the purpose of giving those who are governed the subjective satisfaction of participating in politics. In order to perform this function of "institutionalizing" participation, however, the legislative assembly would need to be an organized, stable, and continuing medium for popular participation.

In the light of modern criticism (beginning with Marx's) it is difficult to see how a constitutionally created parliamentary body can perform the function that Hegel ascribes to the legislature in stabilizing the state, given the infrequency of elections or other opportunities for political involvement by citizens. Such a function might be performed on a day-to-day basis, however, by a mass political party. (For useful discussions of the relation between party politics and democratic theory see Schattschneider, *Party Government* and *The Semi-Sovereign People*.)

[38] See chapter 6, above.

political science or a political theory, because he had no recognition of politics as an autonomous field of activity and no concept of a political order which transcends that of social class. Lenin, however, elevated a political institution, the party, over social classes and social forces.

. . .

Marxism, as a theory of social evolution, was proved wrong by events; Leninism as a theory of political action, was proved right. Marxism cannot explain the communist conquest of power in such industrially backward countries as Russia or China, but Leninism can. The decisive factor is the nature of political organization not the stage of social development.

. . .

Marxism is a theory of history. Leninism is a theory of political development. It deals with the bases of political mobilization, the methods of political institutionalization, the foundations of public order.[39]

According to Huntington, socialist revolutions succeeded in creating stable *states* by simultaneously broadening political participation and institutionalizing the avenues of participation as means of social organization and control. This technique, he argues, can be easily emulated by anti-Marxist movements, since its success has more to do with state-building than with socialism.

In this version of the Hegelian theory of development, strong government and the emergence of powerful social groups are intertwined: when groups organize to demand benefits from government, they can be governed through their organizations with the intermediation of political parties and state agencies. Huntington comes close to saying that public policy can only truly benefit groups when it simultaneously 'raises their consciousness' and co-opts them into the political system. Of course the political emergence of latent social groups may also destabilize particular regimes — what Huntington calls "political decay." But the Hegelian point is that any successor social movement that is able to govern would need a broader constituency, and a more stable base, than the one that broke down. To this extent the new regime would be 'more of a government' (Huntington) — a 'more realized state' (Hegel). This means in part that a successor government would recognize within its political system a more ramified and articulated picture of self-conscious social forces than the preceding regime had been able to accommodate.[40] For Huntington, 'real'

[39] Huntington, *Political Order in Changing Societies*, pp. 336–42.
[40] Although he is an American, Huntington tends to regard the United States as a politically underdeveloped state in this regard. In one of his works, American political institutions are characterized as "Tudor," and he believes in general these institutions are too decentralized, and that American political parties are weak and

reforms are not those that remove social problems, but rather those that institutionalize social problems as a way of broadening support for strong government as a *sine qua non* of effective social change.

In this theory the trick in political "development" is to solve the essentially ideological problem of mobilizing political participation on the basis of group identity, while simultaneously transforming the way in which groups understand their own interests.[41] The objective is to get these groups to serve the interests of public institutions, which is the only meaning Huntington attaches to the "public interest." Huntington assumes, however, that the greatest institutional interest of the state is stability, and that this often requires broadening the range of social forces served by government.

Huntington's formula for political stability is best understood through our interpretation of Hegel. To promote stability by expanding political participation, Huntington argues, government must necessarily institutionalize a difference between two kinds of group difference: one a set of social identities through which traditional hierarchy can be transformed into modern diversity; the other a set of group advantages produced by government policy — advantages now justified by the interest of public institutions rather than the claimed social superiority of those that benefit.

By turning some forms of inequality into recognized social diversity, and others into mere effects of public policy, neo-Hegelianism suggests that the modern developed state can mediate direct class conflict between the 'haves' and the 'have-nots.' As we have seen above, this theory of the state relies on political sociology to articulate the cultural differences for which it equalizes, and on political economy to quantify the differences in interest for which it optimizes. Thus Huntington contemplates that the distinctive traditions of workers or peasants may be respected in the ways that they are organized from above to enter the political process, even while the

---

under-inclusive. (See Huntington, *Political Order in Changing Societies*, ch. 2.) Huntington argues, moreover, that because American social movements have been characterized by eruptions of a moralistic "anti-power ethic," the normal development of US political institutions has been periodically interrupted by politics of "creedal passion." (See Huntington, *American Politics: The Promise of Disharmony*.)

Interestingly, Huntington's paradigm of a developed modern political system is the Soviet Union — pre-Gorbachev.

[41] Huntington would not think it matters whether such groups are also classes, because he would argue that even social classes enter the state as groups. In this respect Huntington would claim that his theory of politics is more general than Lenin's.

levels of real wages and prices will be set by the 'public' interest in controlling inflation, sustaining growth, and increasing accumulation under international market conditions.[42]

Marxian method and democratic politics

Is Lenin's theory of the party a continuation of Marx's critique of Hegel, or an anticipation of Huntington? I believe that the answer is self-evident in the writings of Lenin, and also of Mao. Both used Marxist analysis to project the combination of forces and events through which a revolution might be possible. Their Marxism allowed them to distinguish between those irreversible social changes that must occur before a revolution could take place, those that would occur through the act of revolution itself, and those that would become possible because of the revolution. For us the most significant point, however, is not that a belief in Marxism made them effective revolutionaries, but rather that their Marxism was a method of political analysis that proved equally useful to them before and after the revolution. Marxism allowed them to start from where they found themselves, to learn from what happened, and to decide what to do next. The important question for Lenin and Mao, and also for us in assessing their revolutions, is when and whether their Marxian analysis was right or wrong.[43]

The entire argument of this book suggests that a Marxian analysis of our own politics might take the work of Huntington as its initial data in much the way that Marx used Hegel.[44] Beginning with Huntington's update of Hegel's effort to institutionalize the demand for democracy, the

[42] This might involve considerable shifting of particular groups from a constituent to client pluralism. Huntington and his school see no necessary problem in a "developing" state that organizes a constituency of workers and peasants on the input side, while promoting the commercial interests of various client groups as an output. At points Huntington suggests that such a government (a version of the "deformed worker's state" in orthodox Marxist thought) has a good chance of political survival to the extent that it can use the techniques of mass politics to successfully represent the interests of its clientele to its constituents as an environmental (i.e. foreign) constraint on economic policy. (See Huntington, *Political Order in Changing Societies*, chs 6–7).
[43] See Lenin, *Selected Works* and Mao, *Selected Readings*.
[44] For a valuable critique of the entire field of "political development" studies in the US (including Huntington), see Gendzier, *Managing Political Change: Social Scientists and the Third World*.

critical theory of democracy would stress the potential contradictions in the way developed modern states distinguish between the two forms of group division on which they are based. In practicing Marx's method we would begin by showing how the distinction between state and civil society functions differently when civil society is represented as part of the state from the way the distinction functions when the state is represented as part of civil society. Just as political parties represent society in the state as something other than the state, so bureaucracies represent the state in society as something other than society.[45] In the one picture society appears as coalitions of communal groups that are primordially constitutive of possible alternative regimes. In the other, society appears as coalitions of interest groups that are clients of possible alternative policies.

Moreover, where 'political development' specialists focus on predicting the relative stability of regimes,[46] a Marxian analysis would recognize that political stability is not the only internal interest that any given regime serves. These other interests (such as capital accumulation) constrain the ways in which concrete regimes can reform themselves in order to produce a more stable political order and increase the appeal of more repressive options. As expounded in this book, Marxian analysis must therefore be especially concerned with the question of who is co-opting whom when the government accepts (or rejects) the demands that are made upon it.[47] Such an analysis would not regard the co-optation of emergent social movements as the normal form of 'political development,' while regarding the unmediated clash of group interests as the pathology of 'political decay,' but would, rather, be open to the possibility that the redistribution of benefits to emergent social groups may either incorporate them in the political system, or fuel their discontent. In analyzing the Leninist party, a practitioner of Marx's method could plausibly defend much of the party's

---

[45] This technique of analysis is used repeatedly in Marx's *Critique of Hegel's 'Philosophy of Right.'* E.g. (p. 78): "Here civil society effects within itself the relationship of the state and civil society, a relationship which already exists on the other side [i.e., within the state] as the bureaucracy."

[46] Often their purpose is to advise foreign investors.

[47] Thus, in his writings on France, Marx recognized that at different historical moments the extension of representative democracy may *either* co-opt or strengthen the autonomous organizations of the working class. He also recognized that the decision to repress democratic demands may mobilize counter-revolutionary forces behind the state, but that the failure of the government to co-opt the masses may also lead to a counter-revolutionary coup. Marx's lifetime of writing on democratic movements in France is a remarkable example of class analysis as the critical theory of democracy.

role in the period leading up to the Russian Revolution, while criticizing its stabilizing (and repressive) function in many socialist states.[48]

A Marxian analysis of politics must, thus, begin by acknowledging the full force of Marx's original insight. The distinction between state and civil society, between political institutions and social forces, is real — it cannot be dissolved in theory alone. But it occurs twice over — once within the state, and again within civil society: social forces participate in politics; social interactions presuppose a framework of political power. It is, thus, true both that the state swallows up civil society, and that civil society swallows up the state. Yet, it is also true that within each sphere institutions of state and civil society interact by distinguishing themselves from each other. Each is a whole in which the other is represented as a part.[49]

Our discussion over the last three chapters has moved from an implicitly essentialist view of different types of group differences as prior to the political order, to a structuralist view of the ideological representation of group differences in both sides of the relation between state and society. Beginning with a crude distinction between communal groups (sometimes referred to as 'primordial' identities) and corporatist interests, we have seen that the genius of modern politics allows the distinction between corporatism and communalism to be reversed with respect to particular groups, making it as difficult to incorporate the poor as Hegel feared, and as easy to incorporate the Jews as Marx predicted.

In explicating Marx's critique of Hegel we have gradually replaced our rough dichotomy between two types of group difference with a more sophisticated view of the way in which the state itself distinguishes between the kind of group differences that precede its policies, and the kind that result from its policies. This would allow us to ask, not only which groups are on each side of the picture, but what kind of picture each side is taken to be. We have seen that in the ideology of modern states, neither abstract model of group division can exist alone. Each qualifies and constrains the operation of the other. In order to make claims about the justice of the political structure as a whole, one must identify ideologically with the equality of a particular group within it; in order to promote the unequal advantage of a particular group, one must identify ideologically with the collective interests of the state. In his critique of Hegel Marx repeatedly notes the irony that we participate as citizens in government decisions only

[48] This is similar to the implicit position of Isaac Deutscher in his classic three-volume biography of Trotsky. (See Deutscher, *The Prophet Armed, The Prophet Outcast*, and *The Prophet Unarmed*.)

[49] Cf. Perry Anderson, "The Antinomies of Antonio Gramsci."

by asserting our particular interests; yet our political rights can be asserted only defensively — after the government has oppressed us as subjects.

Much of what I have described as Marx's approach to political analysis in the foregoing chapters may be read as a grudging defence of Hegel against radical Jacobinism — since it is indeed true that in important ways Marx believed that the Hegelian theory, critically reinterpreted, provides a fundamentally accurate description of politics in the modern state. Marx learned from Hegel that the idea of democracy in the modern state functions largely as a mode of organizing society. The ideology of organized democracy projects and 're-presents' two pictures of civil society — one before and one after the effects of state policy. According to this ideology, as we have seen, the state can only claim to act legitimately *within* a society that is capable of regarding the state as lying *outside* of it. For Hegel, the self-conscious organization of civil society "presupposes the state; to subsist itself, it must have the state before its eyes as something self-subsistent." The full development of a distinction between state and civil society, he believed, is the "achievement of the modern world."[50]

For Hegel, the specific function of representing the plural elements of organized civil society in the state "is to be sought in the fact that ... the subjective moment ... the private judgement and private will of the sphere called 'civil society' in this book — comes into existence integrally related to the state."[51] Our politics thus satisfies our need, as moderns, to understand and participate in the ways in which we are organized and disorganized from above. To the extent that we subjectively identify with the groups that the state recognizes, our politics will (from a Hegelian perspective) be democratic for itself; to the extent that we also attribute the political existence of those groups to a commitment by the state not to interfere with them, our politics will also be democratic in itself. Hence the importance of official respect for civil liberties in most 'objective' definitions of democracy — the definitions that we apply to countries other than our own. To exist both in and for itself in the Hegelian sense, pluralist democracy must make our fundamental political problems appear to be the inevitable result of the conflict between our desire to exercise collective control over the state apparatus and the autonomy of the groups through which we hope to exercise such control.[52]

In his critique of Hegelianism Marx recognized that this conflict is an

[50] *Hegel's Philosophy of Right* (tr. Knox), addition, para. 182, p. 226.
[51] Ibid., para. 301.
[52] "All democratic countries are also pluralist." Dahl, *Dilemmas of Pluralist Democracy*, p. 29.

inevitable result of distinguishing between state and society. The experience of professedly Marxist regimes in the present century has taught us that although abstract democracy is ideally the exercise of social control over the state, this ideal will be indistinguishable from its opposite, abstract totalitarianism, unless distinctively social interests can be defined as autonomous from the state. Concrete democracy, the politics of the Hegelian state, both articulates a distinction between state and society, and realizes the contradiction of doing so. According to Marx,

> Hegel is not to be blamed for depicting the nature of the modern state as it is, but rather for presenting what is as the essence of the state. The claim that the rational is actual is contradicted precisely by an irrational actuality, which everywhere is the contrary of what it asserts and asserts the contrary of what it is.[53]

Class analysis and the critical theory of democracy

Marx's critical theory of democracy as expounded in part II can take us considerably beyond Hegel's theory of politics, while still allowing us to be politically effective in the Hegelian states in which we live. As we have seen, both in general and through our continuing discussion of feminism, Marxian political analysis would allow us to ground political identity in institutional contradiction – a concept alien to Hegel, and highly powerful in strategic arguments that do not take the stability of the political regime as a paramount human good.

Once we have used the critical theory of democracy to grasp the concrete political meaning of a given social movement for a given regime, we can move beyond the perspective of the state in order to understand the historical processes that have placed institutions in contradiction. In doing so we will be retracing the path that Marx followed when he pursued the insights gained from his critique of Hegel's theory of the state into a critique of the theory of political economy – seen as an account both of the market as a discrete institution and of the process of historical transformation from one form of society to another.

In following this path, however, Marx never abandoned the objective of producing a concrete analysis that would give him a position within the surface conflicts of political life – a position from which he could intervene in politics while testing and improving his underlying view of institutions. There are, indeed, strong similarities between his approach to reading

[53] Marx, *Critique of Hegel's 'Philosophy of Right,'* p. 64.

Smith and Ricardo and his earlier reading of Hegel. As we shall see in chapter 10, Marx's critique of political economy takes the dual picture of social division on which that theory is based − division of labor and division of class − and shows how both sides of this picture are already part of each other. The argument of *Capital* is to a significant extent an elaboration and transformation of the approach to ideological criticism that Marx first developed in his early critique of Hegel.

Combining the critical theory of democracy with the critique of political economy, Marxian class analysis characteristically demonstrates that the effort of the state to distinguish between the division of labor and the division of class is part of the process by which the material relations between institutions change. The critical question for class analysis is how the policies of the state that reproduce group conflicts also affect the institutional contradictions that give rise to group demands. How does a political system that is stabilized by its public conflicts gain or lose control of the conditions under which those conflicts are reproduced?

The class analysis of democratic political consciousness is, thus, irreducibly diachronic. When we view the political system statically, there are only groups and institutions such as those described by Hegel. Marx's mature method of class analysis concerns the *dynamic* relation between group politicization and institutional change, connecting the contradictions within and between our institutions with the issues that are addressed in the public sphere.

Having come as far as we can with Marx's critique of Hegel, we turn next to his critique of political economy.

Part III
Political Materialism

10 Out of the Hall of Mirrors

Ideology and science

History has not been kind to Marxian economic thought. In developed capitalist countries the few mainstream economists who still take Marx seriously dismiss his method of argument as obsolete. Even those economists most sympathetic to the possibility of restating Marxian economics tend to conclude that his major hypotheses are generally unsupportable when reduced to precise analytical models.[1] At a time when even avowedly Marxist governments are shedding all pretence of respect for Marx's economic views, there would seem to be little further reason to study *Capital* as a source of insight into modern economies.

Yet a casual dismissal of Marx's economic thought would come at considerable cost to our overall project. Although the Marx presented in parts I and II would be a towering figure in social theory even if his substantive economic views were mistaken, no account of the present-day relevance of Marx's thought would be complete without addressing the economic writings that form the bulk of his life's work. Clearly, the critique of political economy has a special status in Marx's thought, giving

---

[1] See, e.g., Morishima, *Marx Economics*; Steedman, *Marx After Sraffa*; and Roemer, *Analytical Foundation of Marxian Economic Theory*, and "Should Marxists Be Interested in Exploitation." See also Leontief, "The Significance of Marxian Economics for Present-day Economic Theory"; and Samuelson, *The Collected Scientific Papers of Paul A. Samuelson*, vol. 3, part IV. Partial exceptions to the tendency describe above are Marglin, *Growth, Distribution and Prices*, and Foley, *Understanding 'Capital.'*

For a respectful presentation of the virtues of Marxian economics from the perspective of mainstream thought see Schumpeter, *Capitalism, Socialism, and Democracy*, ch. 3. For a classic critique of Marx (by Schumpeter's mentor) see Böhm-Bawerk, *Capital and Interest*, ch. 12. See also Samuelson, "1983: Marx, Keynes and Schumpeter."

him real stakes in the substantive issues that divide professional economists. How can we comfortably defend the continuing value of Marx's method of ideological criticism if Marx himself either abandoned or misapplied that method in his own major work?

An obvious way to rescue our account of Marx's method from the apparent defects in Marxian economics would be to invoke the commonly made distinction between ideological critique and positive science in Marx's thought.[2] This distinction is almost always used by Marxists to defend Marx's economic writings by emphasizing such non-Hegelian aspects as his effort to build operational models,[3] and his extensive empirical research.[4] Characteristically, those putting forward such claims tend to disparage Marx's phenomenological claims about the internal self-awareness of capitalist economies, and to ignore his continuing effort to restate the complex interrelations between the categories of economic thought using the techniques of Hegel's *Logic*.[5] In defending what I have called "Marxism as a method" it would be tempting to turn such discussions on their head

[2] There are at least two distinct versions of this view. The most common version, drawing heavily on statements by Marx and Engels in their various introductions to *Capital*, argues that classical political economy contained elements of both ideology and science, and that by dispensing with the ideology Marx was able to make concrete advances in economic science that are still unappreciated by economists mired in bourgeois ideology. With equally strong textual support, other commentators reserve the term "science" for Marx's own interpretation of capitalism as an historically grounded mode of production, arguing that non-Marxian economics is pre-scientific because it lacks key methodological concepts found only in Marx's thought. The former approach is exemplified in the works of Ernest Mandel, especially *The Formation of the Economic Thought of Karl Marx*, *Marxist Economic Theory*, vol. 1, and *Late Capitalism*. The latter approach appears in the works of Althusser and his school. See, e.g., Althusser, *For Marx*, and Althusser and Balibar, *Reading Capital*.

For accounts of the broader theoretical divisions between "scientific" and "critical" Marxism see Gouldner, *The Two Marxisms*, and Habermas, "Between Philosophy and Science: Marxism as Critique."

[3] For an interesting discussion about the relation between model-building and theories see Roemer, *Analytical Foundations of Marxian Economic Theory*, introduction.

[4] Those who defend a scientific Marxism rarely distinguish between the various paradigms of natural science with which Marx might have sought to make his economic theories conform – paradigms as diverse as geology, evolutionary biology analytical chemistry, Newtonian physics, and thermodynamics. For a vigorous recent defense of the affinity between Marxism and the claims of positive science see Timpanaro, *On Materialism* and "Considerations on Materialism."

by insisting that the enduring core of Marxism lies in his critical application of Hegel, and not in his flawed attempts at conventional economic analysis.

Dismissing Marx's economic writings in this way would not, however, be consistent with the overall approach to ideology set forth in part I and elaborated in part II. We saw at the end of part I that Marx's own approach to ideology was concerned with the relations between beliefs and the conduct that might confirm them in the mind of the believer: he recognized that ideology often comes true, and focused his analysis on the contradictory ways in which successful ideologies distinguish between how we explain what happens to us and how we justify what we do. In contrast those who rely on a distinction between ideology and science typically assume that ideologies are false, biased, incomplete, tending to conceal their own origins, and concerned primarily with the realm of 'values.' This preconception fails to grasp precisely the kind of ideology that Marx found in Hegel's account of modern thought as a body of more or less developed science that conspicuously included classical political economy. We have seen that the aspect of Hegelian ideology that Marx took most seriously was an acknowledged system of 'self-fulfilling prophecy' in which beliefs motivate behavior that creates the facts that confirm those beliefs.[6]

Throughout part III we shall find ourselves returning in different contexts to the claim that Marx's mature method of reading the political economists is a refinement and development of the approach to ideological criticism presented in the discussion of "wholes and parts" in chapter 4 and developed using the categories of state and civil society throughout part II. In analyzing

---

[5] "It is impossible completely to understand Marx's *Capital*, and especially its first chapter, without having thoroughly studied and understood the *whole* of Hegel's *Logic*. Consequently, half a century later none of the Marxists understood Marx!!" (Lenin, "Conspectus of Hegel's Science of Logic." p. 180.) For an effort to pursue this insight as a key to understanding the *Grundrisse*, see Rosdolsky, *The Making of Marx's "Capital."* Other discussions include Carver, "Marx – and Hegel's *Logic*"; Hyppolite, "On the Structure and Philosophical Presuppositions of Marx's *Capital*"; and O'Malley, "Marx's 'Economics' and Hegel's *Philosophy of Right*: An Essay on Marx's Hegelianism."

[6] Insofar as Marx sought to make social thought *scientific* in some normative sense, one would still need to decide what he meant by this beyond the introduction of new rigor and discipline into social analysis. Would a social theory become 'more scientific' in a Marxian sense when it acquires operational significance – the power to generate empirically falsifiable hypotheses? or internal coherence – the power to make sense of phenomena? or reflexivity – the power to explain itself? or historicity – the power to explain the origin of its subject matter? Hegel believed that an adequate scientific theory must embody all of these elements without acknowledging the possibility that some may be had only at the expense of others.

the conceptual categories of classical political economy Marx characteristically claims, for example, that production appears once over as part of the system of exchange, and then again, and quite differently, when exchange is seen as part of production. The repetition of this form of analysis over approximately five thousand pages – extending from the *Grundrisse*'s introduction to the concluding chapters of *Capital* – suggests that Marx's economic science is not necessarily distinct from his critique of ideology.

Materialism and social science

If Marx's economic thought is largely continuous with his critique of ideology, how can we account for the special status of economics in Marx's thought? May we now view his decision to pursue economic research as merely an arbitrary choice of specialization by a scholar whose method of analysis has a diversity of potential applications?

Anyone familiar with recent cultural studies can easily imagine what such applications might be. A latter-day Marx with a different research agenda might choose to analyze, for example, the contradictory ways in which the distinction between commerce and art is represented, first within commerce and once again within art;[7] or he might analyze instead the ways in which journalism is represented within fiction, and in which fiction is represented with journalism. Such possibilities arise because aspects of our approach to the relation of state and civil society in part II could be extended to the interpretation of *any* pair of connected cultural categories that are distinct, but in which each also represents the other as a part of itself. Armed with such an approach, academic Marxists could choose to pursue an analogy to what Marx meant by politics in every area of cultural discourse.

But although, as an academic Marxist, I too am attracted by this possibility, I would reject any suggestion that in applying Marx's method, as described above, there need be nothing special about economics.

To grasp the central importance of economic categories for our interpretation of Marx we must return to a fundamental premise of his critique of ideology – *materialism* – which has received little emphasis since we first introduced it in chapter 4. We said there that Marx's

[7] See, e.g., Benjamin, "The Work of Art in the Age of Mechanical Reproduction"; Lowenthal, *Literature and Mass Culture*; and Raymond Williams, *The Long Revolution*.

materialism committed him to the view that, although institutions reproduce themselves through actions that follow from belief, this process occurs under changing objective conditions that exist whether or not we are aware of them. In elaborating Marx's position[8] we went on to suggest that, when a system of institutions is reproduced under transformed conditions, the concrete linkages among those institutions are also changed in ways that are not necessarily reflected at the level of conscious thought.

Marx clearly believed that such changes in the relations between institutions at the 'material' level alter the significance of the accounts through which these institutions try to distinguish themselves from each other, even as they also claim to encompass each other. Because there is only a single material world in which we each live single lives, the contradictions between the overlapping descriptions of that world in different institutions can jeopardize the integrity of our experience. For this reason the existence of such contradictions imparts political meaning to certain grounds of identity that cut across multiple institutions. Within a given institutional framework, self-conscious politics is the activity of realizing that the meaning of received contradictions has already changed. Marxian politics (the kind he sometimes called "scientific socialism") requires one to grasp where one is in this process of change, so that one can perceive the contradictions that are about to become salient, and intervene in a social transformation that is occurring through human activity, even when the participants are not fully aware of it.

Without the premise of materialism the Marxist critique of ideology would tend to portray the concrete social formation as a hall of mirrors. All essences would be reduced to appearances, and all appearances to the mutual reflection of overlapping social practices or 'discourses.'[9] A Marxism lacking a dynamic material process such as "accumulation" could never explain why the patterns and outcomes of institutional overlap change over time. We would be left with a series of static pictures of the range of institutional contradictions that make political action possible at any given moment. Instead of showing a path of development, historical argument would consist of demonstrating the discontinuities between these pictures,

[8] This elaboration was based on the overall argument of Marx and Engels, *The German Ideology*, especially the lengthy discussion of Stirner.

[9] See, e.g., the discussions of Marxism and Post-modernism in Jameson, *The Ideologies of Theory*, vol. I, and *The Political Unconscious*, chs 1, 6. For additional perspectives see Nelson and Grossberg (eds), *Marxism and the Interpretation of Culture*.

suggesting always that particular outcomes are 'contingent' rather than necessary.[10]

Such a standpoint might satisfy the needs of the 'alienated intellectuals' described in chapter 4, but it would not fulfill the broader ambitions of Marxian theory. If Marx had believed that capitalist societies were driven entirely by their internal contradictions and distortions, only a misguided commitment to some philosophical ideal of consistency could have prevented him from embracing schizophrenia as a normal and desirable state of being. Living with and even enjoying contradiction would seem to present no intrinsic problem to those who — unlike the historical Marx — feel free to celebrate the plasticity of institutional forms. If realities could be multiplied as easily as institutions, analogies to politics would exist everywhere but real politics would fade from view: a genuinely 'post-Marxian' world would also be 'post-political.'[11]

Materialism provided Marx with a path out of the hall of mirrors and back to politics. Once he had set aside the naturalism of Feuerbach and the atomism of Democritus and Epicurus,[12] materialism became an approximate analogue in Marx's social thought to Spinoza's view of the underlying

---

[10] Note, however, that taking Marx's theory even this far would still allow intellectuals to tap the continuing power of Marxian thought to combat essentialism, reification, and false necessity in the human sciences. One might even imagine the development of a 'post-Marxian' research agenda, drawing fully on Marx's critique of Hegelianism, that could present itself as a full and flexible alternative to the dominant Weberian approach to social science as model-building. The goal of scholarship under such a paradigm would be to demonstrate contingency rather than necessity: contradiction would replace correlation as the dominant explanatory mode; and discontinuity would replace development as the key to understanding history.

For interesting suggestions along these lines see, e.g., Jameson, "Postmodernism, or the Cultural Logic of Late Capitalism" and "Marxism and Postmodernism." See also the extended celebration of "plasticity" and the attack on "false necessity" in Roberto Unger's explicitly post-Marxist work, *Politics*. The works of Foucault, although largely devoid of systematic theory, are partial expressions of the post-Marxian vision described above, as are those of Deleuze and Guattari.

[11] See Deleuze and Guattari, *Anti-Oedipus* and *A Thousand Plateaus*. Both works carry the subtitle, *Capitalism and Schizophrenia*.

[12] To trace this development see Marx, The Doctoral Dissertation, "Economic and Philosophical Manuscripts," and "Theses on Feuerbach"; and Marx and Engels, *The German Ideology*, part I.

identity of mind and matter.[13] In effect Marx believed that multiple institutions function as 'aspects' of a single social reality in much the way that Spinoza believed that thought and extension are 'aspects' of a single underlying substance. For Marx, "contradictions" in the relations between institutions (such as the state and the market) would 'reflect' (but not be directly caused by) changes in material reality in much the way that mental disturbance and biological disease appear as dual 'attributes' of a single substance in Spinoza's philosophy.[14] Materialism for Marx is at bottom the conviction that our multiple institutions are not distinct 'worlds,' and that there is underlying them a causal unity in the social formation.

Yet for Marx, unlike Spinoza, the core of materialism lies in the methodological presumption that nothing natural is eternal — that everything material must eventually pass away.[15] In stressing the transitory nature of the material world Marx disciplined himself to see matter not as substance, but as process — a process not reducible to the inertia of preexisting bodies. *Natura naturans*, as it functions in Marx's thought, might best be seen as a social analogue to combustion — a self-consuming process that both creates and destroys the condition for its own reproduction until it passes over into something else.[16] To understand a process as *material* in Marx's sense would require us to grasp how it produces the environmental changes through which it is both sustained and extinguished, and hence how it must exist and die in historical time. In this version of materialism

---

[13] Cf. the view of Lucio Colletti who argues that Marx's theory of ideology is essentially a Kantian critique of the dialectical materialism that Hegel developed from Spinoza. See Colletti, *Marxism and Hegel* and "Marxism and the Dialectic."

[14] See Spinoza, *The Ethics*, and Hampshire, *Spinoza*.

[15] I must here comment briefly on the passages in which Marx seems to speak of a future communist society as eternal. These passages are broadly consistent with my argument insofar as they are part of the rhetoric of 'de-eternalizing' capitalism by showing that it must die of natural causes, perhaps including the production and empowerment of its own "gravediggers." However, insofar as these passages are intended to suggest that the resolution of the class struggles in capitalism will inevitably result in the "end" of human history these passage are irreducibly messianic. This work (as chapter 5, above, suggests) is partly an effort to exorcise the "revolutionary mystique" from Marxian thought — a mystique that includes a tendency towards messianism which Marx himself never wholly escaped.

[16] In this respect Marx's materialism falls within the tradition of Jewish iconoclasm — the conviction that nothing natural is holy. If Marx's stress on the *created* (and hence ephemeral) character of material nature is metaphysically Jewish, his stress on *process* (rather than essence) is at root Heraclitean. See Schneidau, *Sacred Dis-*

both life and death appear as endogenous processes: the destruction of material processes is not always a result of external forces,[17] the self-perpetuation of those processes does not necessarily follow from their internal laws of motion, adequately understood.

Marx's materialism, as described above, commits him to the possibility of a scientific study of society without necessarily embodying any particular paradigm of science, and without necessarily distinguishing between the method of social science and the critique of ideology. Acknowledging that Marx might have drawn on his materialism to move in a number of different directions, we can briefly enumerate some of the ways in which he actually allowed his materialism to inform his critique of ideology − drawing on his various writings including his critique of political economy.

(1)   *Unity/Differentiation.* As we have seen, Marx was fundamentally committed to the view that a social formation functions as a single causal order, notwithstanding the multiplicity of institutions that it contains.

(2)   *Conservation/Balance.* Marx believed that in the material transformations of society nothing is lost. Just as energy and matter are conserved in scientific accounts of physical processes, Marx regarded it as a constraint on social theory that all inputs must be accounted for in the description of outputs.[18] Marx's adherence to the principle of conservation at the material level carries forward a notion essential to basic accountancy − the principle that the books must always balance in each period. In practice Marx paid special attention to the residual categories that social theories use to balance their equations. By tracing the ongoing presence of the residual elements needed to maintain the balance of any material process, Marx believed that one could understand the expansion or contraction of the process as a whole. Such complete accounting, however, does not preclude the possibility that some inputs or outputs will be wasted from the standpoint of social reproduction (see below). The point is that materialism presumes the existence of regulatory mechanisms through which the

---

content: *The Bible and Western Tradition,* and Norman O. Brown, *Love's Body.*
[17] Cf. Spinoza: "A thing has nothing in itself through which it can be destroyed, or which can negate its existence." (*The Ethics,* Part III, prop. 6.) I owe this reference to Norman O. Brown, "Revisioning Historical Identities" (unpublished ms). See also Norman O. Brown, *Life Against Death,* part 3, and Freud, *Beyond the Pleasure Principle.*
[18] Engels appropriately suggested in *Anti-Dühring* that the development of Marxism may have been influenced to some extent by analytical chemistry, and perhaps also by thermodynamics. (See also Timpanaro, *On Materialism.*) For the notion that social conservation and balance are as compatible with giving as with hoarding, see Mauss, *The Gift.*

material process continues over time, without presuming that its continuation is necessary or automatic.

(3)   *Reproduction/Death.* As we have seen, Marx believed that the continuation of a social formation as a material process must be explained rather than assumed, and that the explanation would partially consist of showing the degree to which the environmental conditions necessary for reproducing the social formation are endogenous[19] products of the social formation itself. This implies that the level of social reproduction is significantly constrained by the accumulated effects, both positive and negative, of the residual elements needed to describe the equilibrium of previous reproductive cycles. From Marx's materialist perspective the reproduction of a social formation may depend upon internal conflict (rather than a high degree of social solidarity or moral legitimacy),[20] and he recognized that the process of social reproduction might even come to require the intensification of such conflict over time. As a social formation dies of endogenous[21] causes, however, its conflicting elements − no longer harnessed and contained − can separately adapt to the new conditions for social reproduction.[22]

We are not here concerned to defend the rigor or completeness of these premises as an adequate account of materialism in social science; neither are we directly concerned with the relation between the methodological materialism that figures into Marx's critique of ideology, and other beliefs he may have held about man's symbiosis with nature.[23] As described above, Marx's materialism is independent of a commitment to naturalism, or an ontology that privileges physical objects, or any theory of human motivation that privileges biological needs. Within the Marxian critique of ideology, materialism functions rather as the constraint that competing

[19] This term is of course a matter of degree. Climatic changes, for example, are largely exogenous to the socially produced environment, and yet we now find ourselves adapting to a certain range of climatic changes that we recognize as unintended social products.

[20] In emphasizing the continuing ability to reproduce itself as the key to the unity of a social formation, Marx differed from non-materialist social theorists such as Weber (who stressed legitimation) and Durkheim (who stressed solidarity).

[21] Nothing in Marx's materialism rules out the death of a social formation from arguably exogenous causes such as drought, plague, deliberate extermination, etc.

[22] See Gerald A. Cohen, "Functional Explanation, Consequence Explanation, and Marxism;" Levine and Sober, "What's Historical About Historical Materialism?" and Levine and Wright, "Rationality and Class Struggle."

[23] For an effort to describe Marx's materialism as naturalism see, e.g., Venable, *Human Nature: The Marxian View*; cf. Schmidt, *The Concept of Nature in Marx.*

institutional perspectives must be treated as if they are describing one world – a world existing in historical time. Marx's methodological materialism commits him to treating the institutional ideologies that constitute our social nature *as if* they represented material systems subject to the constraints that he thought applicable to theories describing physical nature.

As actually applied, Marx's materialism functions less as an empirical assumption than as a heuristic device in the critique of social science as ideology.[24] Such an approach to ideology has little room for discussion of whether the theoretically based entities used to balance accounts, such as the accountant's notion of "good will" or the physicist's notion of "negative entropy" are 'real' in some pre-theoretical sense. In attempting to criticize particular analytical frameworks *as* ideology we could, for example, trace the accumulation of "good will" in accounting or the reduction of "negative entropy"[25] in thermodynamics until we reached the point of contradiction in our understanding of the world we know as a material system capable of reproducing itself.

Recent scholarship casting doubt on the logical positivist view of the history of science suggests that Marx may have been fundamentally correct in his view that the critique of ideology is continuous with the development of scientific knowledge.[26] Theories of combustion that posit the existence of phlogiston can be just as appropriately subjected to the constraints of materialism in Marx's sense as those that posit the existence of oxygen. Whereas the method of logical positivism would require us to look for evidence of the existence of either phlogiston or oxygen,[27] the method of ideological criticism suggests that we could proceed toward science by tracing the cumulative effect of either of these theoretically posited entities through our system of thought until we reached the point of a contradiction in the ability of that system to account for the reproduction of the world as it is known to us. As a candidate for ideological criticism a theory need not be scientifically true (empirically confirmed) in order to be materialist in the sense described above.

---

[24] In this respect the function of materialism in Marx's philosophy of social science resembles that of the regulative ideas of metaphysics in Kant's philosophy of natural science. Cf. Kant's proposal to test maxims of social conduct by treating them *as if* they were universal laws of nature. (Kant, *Critique of Pure Reason* (tr. Norman Kemp Smith), pp. 210f., 454ff., 515ff., 554ff., and *Fundamental Principles of the Metaphysics of Morals*, p. 47f.)

[25] Cf. such concepts as surplus value or industrial waste.

[26] See Kuhn, *The Structure of Scientific Revolutions*, and Quine, *Word and Object*.

[27] For a classic exposition of the logical positivist approach see Reichenbach, *Experience and Prediction*.

Materialism and economism

Marx's view of the relation between material and institutional change
relies on two metaphors that have been implicit in our general discussion
of materialism. These are the metaphors of *reflection* and of *causation*.

In conceiving of institutional change as a reflection of material change
Marx evokes an analogy between the way multiple institutions might
'reflect' the existence of a single causal order of society and the ways in
which Kant and Spinoza thought that the subjectivity of experience 'reflects'
the existence of a single causal order in nature. Just as it is a necessary
condition of experience that we reconstruct the subjective order as though
it were merely one among other possible perceptual routes through an
objective order of the world, so it is a condition of understanding our
insitutions as merely part of the social order that they each purport to
describe themselves as reflections of a unitary whole. At the level of social
explanation Marx's materialism, like Kantian critique, reflects the fact that
when our institutions tell us different stories we must act as though these
stories are the same.[28] Marx's materialism, insofar as it is based on the
metaphor of reflection, acknowledges the need to perceive the world in the
language of our institutions, rather than in the language of nature.

Yet in also drawing on the metaphor of causation Marx seeks to describe
discrete institutions as constituting the component parts of a material
whole, changes in which can explain the collisions of the parts.[29] Marx's
materialist premises, as enumerated above, enable him to argue that overt
social conflict is caused by the impact of material changes on a given
structure of institutional contradiction, and that under different material
conditions the conflicts that change society may be expressed at the level of
the church, the state, the market (and we might add, the family).[30] Marx's
thought about the causal relation between material and institutional change
resembles a layman's understanding of the geological forces that effect the
collision of plates in the Earth's surface. Here I have in mind the notion

---

[28] For a useful discussion of these matters in relation to Kant see Strawson, *The
Bounds of Sense*, part 2, ch. II.7 ("Objectivity and Unity"), esp. pp. 100−1, 104−5.
I owe this reference − and the point developed from it − to Jerome Neu.
[29] Marx here draws on a line of development from Spinoza to Hegel, rather than
from Spinoza to Kant. For a different view of these lines of development see
Colletti, *Marxism and Hegel*.
[30] See, e.g., Marx, *Capital* vol. I, p. 176: "The Middle Ages could not live on
Catholicism, nor could the ancient world on politics. On the contrary, it is the
manner in which they gained their livelihood which explains why in one case
politics, and in the other case Catholicism, played the chief part."

that, although the occurrence of the collision is caused by an underlying force, the form of that collision is determined by surface interactions of the plates, and its timing and intensity by the accumulated buildup of surface pressures.

Marx's materialism cannot be reduced at this general level to commonplace notions of economic determinism, such as the view that individual and group behavior is driven by material self-interest, or can be explained as if it were.[31] Marx believed in fact that the salience of market relations as the focus of institutional contradictions occurs only under concrete historical circumstances, specific to a particular level of capitalist development. Moreover, he imagined that under socialism economic determinism might cease to apply for reasons that he believed to be entirely consistent with his underlying materialism.[32]

There is, however, considerable room to argue that in explaining the capitalist systems with which he was fundamentally concerned Marx believed in some version of economic determinism. Whereas mainstream economists typically seek to explain collective outcomes as a product of *individual* choice under given market conditions, Marx often wrote as though *social classes* could be viewed as self-interested rational actors of the sort described by the classical economists. In making such arguments he was able to draw heavily on the views of Smith and Ricardo, who believed that individual economic interests are based in most instances on the factor market in labor, land, and capital. Continuing in this spirit, some of the best recent writers on Marxian economics have shown that signficant hypotheses about exploitation and class can be usefully restated in the language of methodological individualism and rational choice that underlies market theory[33] — suggesting that the market in productive

---

[31] For recent discussions of the theoretical genesis of market-thinking, see Dumont, *From Marx to Mandeville: The Genesis and Triumph of Economic Ideology*; and Hirschman, *The Passions and the Interests*.

[32] See, e.g., Marx, "The Critique of the Gotha Program."

[33] There is much to be said for such an approach. Rather than committing us to crude economic determinism, the method of rational choice allows us to abstract from the study of the market as a discrete institution alongside others while looking to market *theory* as a way of explaining behavior in contexts in which actual markets may or may not exist. A great deal of formal rigor can be gained by using such a method, and nothing of interest to competing approaches need be wholly left out of account: cultural differences may be built into the schedule of individual preferences that appear on the demand side; the historical level of material technology can affect the relative payoffs that appear on the supply side. Once all such factors are accurately accounted for in the initial description of decision matrices,

factors may have an intrinsic bias against those endowed initially with only their labor to sell.[34]

Despite the obvious power of such an approach, I believe that the methodology of rational choice is not fundamental to Marx's approach in *Capital* and that it does not exhaust the lessons of that work for modern observers of the market, seen as a discrete and functioning institution. Throughout his economic writings, Marx was less fascinated by the ways in which Smith and Ricardo prefigured rational choice,[35] than by the ways in which their theories of the *economy* appeared to satisfy the constraints of materialism as sketched above: Smith and Ricardo clearly thought of the political economy as a single causal order embodying differentiated unity; they observed a strict principle of the conservation of value in the process of production for exchange – and developed their notion of exchange value as a theoretical entity to express this principle in arguments designed to show a tendency toward equilibrium; growth and decline were explained by the economists as consequences of the conservation of value when equilibrium is reached in each cycle of production; and (assuming a fixed supply of land) the ability of the system to produce in each cycle the conditions of its own reproduction was limited by endogenous causes up to the point at which economic stagnation would be reached. As we shall see, classical political economy stresses the significance of the *produced environment*, and employs the heuristic of viewing material nature as if it were (increasingly) a social product.

The appeal of classical political economy for Marx closely resembles the more recent attraction of political ecology as a source of rigor in a social theory.[36] Both perspectives portray us as living in a *single world* in which nothing is lost. Because neither perspective purports to leave anything out of account in explaining how that world is transforming itself, both perspectives appear to be inescapable in their own terms. The revolution

---

social outcomes can be explained as the product of self-interested action by individual rational maximizers. For a recent critique of this approach see Wood, "Rational Choice Marxism: Is the Game Worth the Candle?"

[34] See esp. Roemer, *A General Theory of Exploitation and Class* and *Free to Lose*. See also Elster, *Making Sense of Marx*, introduction.

[35] That he clearly understood their use of this approach is evident from his discussion of ground rent and of the equalization of the rate of profit in Marx *Capital*, vol. III, chs 37–47.

[36] See, e.g. Forrester, *World Dynamics*. Cf. Georgescu-Roegen, *The Entropy Law and the Economic Process*. For a striking political statement of a conversion from a Marxian to an ecological perspective see Gorz, *Ecology as Politics*.

in economic thought that began with the physiocrats and Adam Smith allowed us to see that *everything* has an economic impact (there is a seamless web), just as the development in ecological thought in the twentieth century has enabled us to see the seamless web of our social and material environment. As a rigorously holistic social theory, classical political economy allowed for broader applications of Marx's method of materialist criticism than any other body of social science available to him. We should note, however, that the writings with which Marx was concerned viewed demography and social ecology as part of economics properly conceived, and that many of the insights yielded from Marx's critique of political economy relate to variables that most present-day economists do not accept as endogenously determined.[37] Without suggesting that classical political economy is superior in scope or power to its neo-classical successors, we can with some effort reconstruct the classical approach to political economy in a way that would allow us to apply some of Marx's insights to the concerns that underlie economic thought today.

Two principles of social unity

What is an economy? Throughout human history market relations — more or less formal systems of trade — have always existed between communities and have often existed within them. The achievement of the classical political economists was to redefine the domestic market that exists within modern nations as something more than and different from a system of trade, such as that between nations.[38] For Smith and Ricardo a market *economy* was conceived as a self-sustaining material system capable of reproducing itself at an expanded level through endogenous processes. In order to grasp what this breakthrough meant to the founders of modern economics we must reconstruct their basic paradigms of the unity of a social formation when viewed as a material process.

[37] See Marglin, *Growth, Distribution, and Prices.*

[38] Of course Smith and Ricardo strongly defended free market principles in international trade, but for somewhat different reasons than those used to support the removal of political restrictions on domestic markets. Modern economists who reject Ricardo's labor theory of value have been able to retain his theory of comparative advantage as a defence of specialization in international trade, and to assimilate it to the broader theory of marginal prices based on supply and demand, the existence of a consumer's surplus, etc. — all of which Ricardo would have rejected. See, e.g. Samuelson, *Economics*, ch. 34.

At this basic level social theories tend to proceed from root metaphors[39] that draw on analogies to interpersonal relations. One root metaphor of social unity extrapolates from the moral logic of 'side-by-side' relationships, such as those of cooperation, interdependence, and celebration. Another root metaphor of social unity extrapolates from the moral logic of 'face-to-face' relationships, such as those of domination, recognition, and worship. Since Plato's *Republic* these two root metaphors of social unity have been identified with their respective paradigm cases: the division of labor and the division of class.[40]

By invoking division of labor and division of class as paradigms of social unity, I wish to distance myself at first from the efforts of certain empirical social scientists to observe the degree to which a division of labor (functional specialization) or a division of class (overt antagonism) is increased or decreased within or among preexisting "reference groups,"[41] such as managers and workers.[42] As paradigms of social unity, division of labor and class division are not observed relations among preexisting groups, but rather distinct models for explaining how the underlying unity of a society results from its differentiation into groups.

The unity of a social formation may be explained as a *division of labor* by analogy with the way in which the distinct roles of a carpenter and a bricklayer might ideally interrelate in the process of building a house. Explanations of this type tend to represent social unity as based on the conscious or unconscious pursuit of a common goal or task and also on the functional interdependence that is achieved through the specialized activity of each participant in pursuing particular goals or specialized tasks.[43] In some divisions of labor the common goal coordinates the tasks of the participants as a transparent end-in-view. The members of a symphony

---

[39] See Pepper, *World Hypotheses*, ch. 5.

[40] For a discussion of the theoretical roots of these models see Foster, *The Political Philosophies of Plato and Hegel*.

[41] See Merton, *Social Theory and Social Structure*, chs 10–11.

[42] In their efforts to explain such observations these social scientists might invoke factors such as technological change or disparities in personal income, which would be treated as having only a contingent relation to the prior identification of these reference groups as the constituent elements in social change, described along the dimensions of antagonism (class) and interdependence (division of labor). (For attempts to discuss the issue of "intermediate class positions" from a Marxist perspective see Wright, "The Class Structure of Advanced Capitalist Societies," and Walker (ed.), *Between Labor and Capital: The Professional Managerial Class.*)

[43] The best treatment of this form of organization can be found in Durkheim, *The Division of Labor in Society*.

orchestra, for example, can hear the collective product while each plays his part. Sometimes, however, the common goal in a division of labor is opaque from the viewpoint of the participants – each contributes to it by trying to do something else. When Adam Smith describes the competitive marketplace as simultaneously a division of labor he knows that he must argue that social cooperation becomes the unintended result of individual competition through the operation of the "invisible hand." Both Hegel and Marx saw this argument as crucial to the recognition of the market as also constituting an *economy* – a self-sustaining causally unified system capable of reproducing itself over time. Since the competitive market "for itself" is "in itself" a social division of labor, competition can be defended as interdependence; private interest as public good.[44]

The paradigm of *division of class* is a different way of describing the unity of a social formation than as a division of labor. Instead of picturing individuals standing side by side performing different parts of a common task, it pictures individuals standing face to face; instead of giving us multiple parts of a single whole, the paradigm of class division gives us opposing perspectives on the same totality.[45] The type of social unity produced in class divisions could not generally depend upon functional interdependence, since in many cases it is clear that most of the necessary work is done on one side. When Smith and Ricardo describe the economy, not only as a system of production *for* exchange, but also as a system of production *through* exchange, they ascribe social unity to a set of face-to-face relations in which each party's action reflects a conception of the other's good. The mutually reflecting total perspectives of buyer and seller in the marketplace, and of capitalist and laborer in the workplace, are presumed to guarantee the reproduction of the economy as a material process.

[44] See Adam Smith, *The Wealth of Nations*, esp. chs 1–3; cf. Hegel's *Philosophy of Right* (tr. Knox), esp. para. 189.
[45] The prototypes of such 'face-to-face' relations are as varied as ruler/ruled, teacher/student, doctor/patient, master/slave, husband/wife, God/man. At stake in each such relation are the questions of whose *will* is being done, and for whose *good*. Since each standpoint toward the relation includes within itself an image of the good of the other, there is also at stake a question of progressive *development*. (In the relations above such questions involve, respectively, authority, education, health, liberation, love, and salvation.) The social unity created in 'face-to-face' relations depends on the extent to which in answering these questions each perspective on the unequal relationship incorporates the other, whether as a dialectic of love/acceptance or as a dialectic of domination/conflict. For a general discussion of related issues see chapter 2, above.

From the foregoing descriptions we can speculate that the paradigms of division of labor and division of class might be combined in some fashion to provide a more adequate account of social unity as a relation between wholes that appear as part of each other, such as we have described in the foregoing chapters. Plato seemed to recognize this possibility, at least implicitly, when in the middle of the *Republic* he gradually shifted from the metaphor of cooperation among specialized craftsmen (part and part) to the metaphor of mind over body (whole and whole) in describing the unity of ruler and ruled in a just society.[46] In modern social thought the same elision occurs. The relationship between rulers and ruled (or between managers and workers) can be seen as functionally interdependent parts of a larger activity, and also as structurally independent reflections of the same total activity. Combining our two paradigms in a modern context would clearly allow the possibility that both interdependence and conflict are necessary to the cohesion of particular societies.

This possibility is expressed in Marx's reliance on both analytical paradigms to describe the class structure of capitalist societies. Sometimes he describes class as a relation between ruler and ruled, oppressor and oppressed — a dichotomous relation of face-to-face struggle over the division of power. At other times he describes class as a division of labor, a functional interdependence of many occupational strata in the social creation of wealth. The former emphasis is often ascribed to Marx's effort to define class as a relationship of ownership, power, and control — especially over the means of production and subsistence; the latter to his effort to define it in terms of the tasks performed in the social process of production itself.[47] In eliding these two emphases Marx intends to suggest that conflict is necessary to the material reproduction of social formations when viewed as economies.

Value and distribution in market economies

Marx recognized that the historical emergence of a market economy from its feudal origins required a change in the social characteristics of both persons and things. Previously, the unequal status of persons had placed

---

[46] Cf. Plato, *Republic* (tr. Cornford), chs 1–10, 12–14, 18–23.
[47] For a seminal discussion of this tension see Stanislaw Ossowski, *Class Structure in the Social Consciousness*. For further developments see Giddens, The *Class Structure of the Advanced Societies*, and Parkin, *Marxism and Class Theory: A Bourgeois Critique*, ch. 2.

stringent legal and moral limitations on their ability to exchange things. Tasks were based on ascribed roles, and the motivation to produce things that serve the needs of others was presumed to exist mainly through the effects of custom, coercion, or altruism. For market relations to prevail in society, however, persons had to be treated as formally equal in the sense that each would be broadly entitled to refuse to produce for the benefit of persons of superior status. The differences between persons would then be ascribed to inequality in the value of — and hence the social power conferred by — the things these persons control.[48] In such circumstances enlightened self-interest would provide the most plausible explanation of the motivation of individuals to voluntarily cooperate for the social good, assuming of course that the notion that people are acting from choice is not significantly vitiated by grossly unequal wealth. Marx recognized in sum that the market economy described by Smith and Ricardo appears simultaneously as a social relation between person and person and a material relation between thing and thing.

There are two fundamental aspects to a market economy, once it has fully developed. Any market is, first of all, a system of exchange. In a developed market economy the whole of society appears as if it were a big store in which relations between persons are governed entirely by the relative prices of commodities. Once the social interactions between persons and things have been transformed in the manner described above, however, the market must also serve as a system of production. As such, the market economy represents society as if it were a big factory in which the relative prices of things are governed by the revenues that are circulated to persons in the productive process.[49]

Marx believed that the genius of Smith and Ricardo was to connect these two central aspects of the free market twice over: through a theory of value and through a theory of distribution. Each of these theories describes a different relationship between commodity exchange and the social division of labor. The theory of value describes production *for* the market, purporting to demonstrate that the relative prices of goods in circulation is proportional to the quantities of social labor embodied in producing them. Here the big store is redescribed as though it were the big factory. The theory of distribution describes production *through* the market, purporting to demonstrate that the cost of producing goods will be the

---

[48] The social power conferred by controlling things of unequal value assumes that those things are generally recognized to be mutually fungible.

[49] Given the classical economists' focus on agrarian capitalism, a "big farm" might be a more historically apt metaphor for capitalist production.

sum of the revenues paid to the owners of land, labor, and capital in the production process — what Marx disparagingly called the "trinity formula" of classical political economy.[50] Here the big factory is redescribed as though it were a big store.

The central thesis of classical political economy was that the theories of value and distribution would be equivalent. This meant that relative values of any two commodities for sale in the market would be proportional to the relative costs of producing each by means of the market. Smith and Ricardo believed that their account of the distribution of revenues and products in each cycle of production would explain how the market mode of production can reproduce itself over time, rather than exhausting itself at the end of each cycle.

Expanded reproduction and the stationary state

For Smith and Ricardo, however, the correspondence of exchange value and production cost was not a theory of how the price mechanism results in market homeostasis. In this respect they differed from the popularizers of market theory, such as Say, Sismondi, Bastiat, and Carey.[51] These "vulgar" economists argued (although somewhat differently) that in a perfect market, supply must always be equal to demand if prices are allowed to fluctuate freely. Say's Law, the vulgar equation of supply and demand, was designed only to explain how markets clear.[52] In explaining

---

[50] I.e., their view that the cost of production can be straightforwardly expressed as a distribution of revenues to land, labor and capital. Marx, *Capital*, vol. III, ch. 48.

[51] See, e.g., Say, *A Treatise on Political Economy*; Sismondi, *Political Economy and the Philosophy of Government*; Bastiat, *Economic Harmonies*; and Carey, *Principles of Political Economy*.

[52] By assuming that increased production is motivated by the desire of individual producers to reap windfall profits if prices do not fall, Say's Law merely proves that if prices fall far enough there cannot be overproduction in the market as a whole. Such an argument implies, however, that profits for reinvestment and growth are not necessary at the point of market equilibrium.

From both a Ricardian and a Marxian point of view, Say's Law is largely circular insofar as levels of both supply and demand are themselves to be determined by price. Say's Law does not explain the levels of supply, demand, or price, but rather assumes these and explains their interaction at given levels; it does not explain the cumulative economic value of the national product, but rather assumes this and describes the physical composition of that product at equilibrium. It does not explain how economic demands are themselves created (or changed) through the process of production, but rather assumes this and explains what people want

how markets clear, however, the vulgar economists were constrained to regard the growth and contraction of markets as largely accidental. Profits, like losses, were rather explained by temporary fluctuations in supply and demand that eventually balance out in a perfect market.[53]

In contrast Smith and Ricardo were centrally concerned to explain why markets tend to grow. They recognized the existence of a profit for reinvestment as a normal result of equal exchange in the market, and not an artifact of imbalances between supply and demand. For them the main challenge facing economic theory was to explain the difference between production increases that expand real economic wealth, and those that merely drive the value of commodities down. While the vulgar correspondence of supply and demand was part of a theory of market price, the classical correspondence of exchange value and production cost was part of a theory of market growth. Rather than describing a point of equilibrium in market prices, Smith and Ricardo set the parameters for the reproduction of market relations on an expanding scale. By their definition economic growth would consist of an increase in the level (and intensity) of employment in productive labor throughout the economy.

In describing the economy as a self-perpetuating system, Smith and Ricardo argued that the internal processes that caused economic growth would also come to limit it. The key to this argument lay in their recognition

as a response to what they can get, and what they can get as a response to what they want; it does not explain how economic value is accumulated at the end of each production cycle so as to reproduce and expand the market, but rather assumes that each cycle is a new gamble on the level of consumer and producer preferences; it does not even begin to recognize the periodicities and lags in the process of producing for a market.

Marx's fullest discussion of Say's Law (in the context of whether overproduction is possible) occurs in Marx, *Theories of Surplus Value*, part 2, ch. 17. See Foley, *Understanding 'Capital,'* pp. 146–8. Cf. Ricardo, *Principles of Political Economy and Taxation*, ch. 30. For a nuanced defence of Say's Law, see Schumpeter, *History of Economic Analysis*, pp. 615–25. For a characterization of Say's Law that bears a striking resemblance to Marx's, see Samuelson, "Concerning Say's Law."

[53] The existence of profits to be reinvested is not the same as the "consumer's surplus" that exists when supply and demand curves intersect. In the terminology of classical political economy the "consumer's surplus" would be a use value; profit would be a surplus exchange value. In neo-classical price theory the profit rate is built in as markup imposed by capital markets that affects how much of a commodity can be produced at a given price. The level of profit required by the producer thus appears as an exogenous fact, unaffected by the relative supply and demand levels for any given commodity. See Harcourt, *Some Cambridge Controversies in the Theory of Capital*, and Bergson, "A Note on Consumer's Surplus."

that continued economic growth changes the distribution of the national product. In the initial stages of a growth cycle, labor, being scarce, would generally receive a rising share of revenues paid out in production, thereby stimulating a rise in demand for wage goods.[54] Yet each cycle of growth would also increase the stock of accumulated capital that could set more labor into motion. Smith and Ricardo thus did not believe that in the long run the limits to economic growth would be set by the supply of either labor or capital, both of which could expand as a result of causes endogenous to the market.[55] As manpower[56] and capital stock increased with economic expansion, however, Smith and Ricardo recognized that non-reproducible resources, such as land, would become relatively scarce. The owners of those resources would thus be able to command a larger share of the value of the product in the form of economic rents.[57] As Ricardo explained, increased economic rents function not as a rise in production costs, but as a deduction from profits. When economic growth brings the rents collected on non-reproducible natural resources to the point where further investment is unprofitable, Smith and Ricardo believed that the economy would reach its "stationary state."[58]

According to the classical political economists, the core social conflict resulting from the stationary state was not between wage earners and capitalists,[59] but rather between capitalists and landlords — a conflict that

[54] Labor is never so well off as when the demand for it is increasing. See Adam Smith, *The Wealth of Nations*, p. 81, and Ricardo, *On the Principles of Political Economy and Taxation*, pp. 94–5, 98, 100.

[55] Adam Smith, *The Wealth of Nations*, bk 2, and Ricardo, *On the Principles of Political Economy and Taxation*, ch. 21.

[56] Unless otherwise noted, I shall use the words "man-hours" and "manpower" as a simplified way of referring to abstract, simple, social necessary labor power in the Marxian sense — and not as signifying a gender-specific activity.

[57] Ricardo, *On the Principles of Political Economy and Taxation*, p. 102.

[58] For a benign interpretation of the Ricardian picture of the end of economic growth see Mill, *Principles of Political Economy*, bk 4, ch. 6.

[59] Growth in agrarian capitalism, said Ricardo (chs 2, 5–6), would naturally lead to higher wages because of the rising labor-cost of producing a unit of food as the need arose to cultivate less productive land. This rise in wages, he projected, would be largely offset in the long run by the higher cost of subsistence. Smith argued (*The Wealth of Nations* bk. 1, ch. 8) that overpopulation in the stationary state would tend to keep real wages down. Although Smith and Ricardo disagreed about whether real wages would tend to be high or low in the stationary state, both believed that the actual money wage would fluctuate with the relative supply and demand of capital and labor, rather than with the labor-value of food. (Note that neither Ricardo nor Smith anticipates changing production techniques that could increase the marginal productivity of agricultural labor.)

both Smith and Ricardo saw as the real limit to growth in capitalist economies. Both Smith and Ricardo considered ground rent not the investment-backed expectation of a capitalist, but a political power to extract revenue based on claims originating in feudalism. According to Ricardo's theory that the value of commodities is proportional to the labor embodied in producing them, the market value of commodities would not be affected by rents − which appear, rather, as a deduction from profits. On this basis Ricardo argued that landlords on the more productive land are in a position to extract as rent most (or all) of the increased exchanged value of the crop as less productive land is placed under cultivation and the productivity of labor diminishes accordingly. This Ricardian analysis implied that, as the economy grows, rents tend to increase, thereby squeezing profits to the point where expanded investment would cease.[60]

In the class struggle between capitalists and landlords there is no doubt where the classical political economists stood. Both Smith and Ricardo believed that the lingering remnants of feudal political control over land were the main impediment to the growth of agrarian capitalism and the increased employment of productive labor in the economy at large.[61] For this reason they argued economic progress was greatest when rents could be kept low so that productive investment could be stimulated. The political implication of Ricardian economics was, above all, to curb the rise in rents by maintaining low food prices through imports.[62] Ricardo further suggested that, if taxes were levied entirely on land, there would be no detrimental impact on economic growth − the state would simply be supported by a form of surplus extraction (to use Marx's phrase) otherwise accruing to the landlord.[63]

In the 1970s some economists tried to develop a new awareness of the limits to the growth of capitalism by thinking of the world, rather than the

---

[60] Ricardo, *On the Principles of Political Economy and Taxation*, chs 2, 5, 6, 24. Cf. Adam Smith, *The Wealth of Nations*, chs 9, 11.

[61] We would be stretching a point, however, to argue that Smith and Ricardo anticipated that the increased *productivity* of agricultural labor would allow increased employment in manufacturing. For Smith and Ricardo increasing wealth was strictly related to growth in employment, rather than growth in productivity.

[62] Ricardo, *On the Principles of Political Economy and Taxation*, p. 126. Repeal of the Corn Laws was essential to this political program. For a Left-Ricardian view of this issue see Torrens, *An Essay on the External Corn Trade*.

[63] Ricardo, *On the Principles of Political Economy and Taxation*, chs 8, 10. For a general discussion of these arguments see Stokes, *The English Utilitarians and India*, ch. 2. Cf. George, *Progress and poverty*.

nation, as the relevant economic unit.[64] Like the classical economists, these modern writers attacked a mercantilist view of international trade, but unlike the classical economists they saw the world economy as a single mode of production based on an international division of labor. In the expanding world economy, they suggested, independent nation states are the counterparts of post-feudal landowners in classical political economy. Not only were these national actors initially perceived as anachronistic (if sometimes belated) beneficiaries of a bygone order; the energy crisis led many to the conclusion that OPEC (and other efforts at cartelization) could turn the political and territorial power over scarce and non-substitutable resources into the power to extract economic rents that would in the long run impede the process of capital formation in the developed world.[65] These ideas challenged environmentally conscious citizens to take a holistic − and anti-nationalistic − perspective on the new world economic order. Often this perspective consisted of arguing that the industrial development and high standard of living in the Western capitalist democracies had depended on the ability to extract irreplaceable natural resources at a cost that did not fully reflect what the value of those resources would be in an ideal world economy − conceived, roughly speaking, as an international market in which all countries had equal per capita purchasing power.[66]

[64] See, e.g., Donella Meadows et al., *The Limits to Growth: A Report of the Club of Rome's Project on the Predicament of Mankind*; Thurow, *The Zero-Sum Society*; "The No-Growth Society," a symposium in *Daedalus*, esp. Boulding, "The Shadow of the Stationary State." For a defense of the continuing theoretical relevance of Smith to this debate see Samuelson, "A Modern Theorist's Vindication of Adam Smith," esp. pp. 623–4.

[65] See Krasner, *Structural Conflict: The Third World Case Against Global Liberalism*.

[66] In the ideological debate on the global 'limits to growth' in the 1970s, environmentalism implicitly embraced the desirability of price inflation as a form of discipline in the use of those things that rise in value as a consequence of economic growth. (Extreme versions of this view described 'stagflation' as what it might feel like to become environmentally responsible at a global level.) In contrast global developmentalism − a foil for environmentalism − embraced the desirability of the full exploitation of existing resources in order to maximize employment by keeping real commodity prices down.

Although this debate between development and conservation was often coded as a conflict between two incompatible perspectives − the economic and the ecological − the main issues consisted of a conflict between two types of capital accumulation. Just as the value of an asset as capital declines if its future development is restricted, so the likelihood of its short-term development declines as its expected

The market and the factory

Marx based his mature critique of the classical political economists on conceptual moves that should be familiar to the reader who has come this far. After superimposing the economists' two pictures of the market − as a system of exchange and as a division of labor − he showed how each picture was already an essential part of the other. He was then able to show in a myriad of ways how exchange appears differently as part of the division of labor than it does when division of labor is described as part of the system of exchange.[67]

When the economists describe exchange between commodity owners, the division of labor appears not as a direct relation between persons, but as a relation between products, or, as we would now say, between industries. (Marx would come to describe this as "the division of labor in society.")[68]

---

value as capital goes up. As scarce environmental resources are conserved, those capitalists who own them may come to expect the present market value of their 'undeveloped' property to appreciate faster than the average capital investment. (We know, for example, that the very economic incentives that promote the conservation of existing oil reserves also raise the marginal return on exploration for new oil.) In arguments about conserving resources the present beneficiary of the interests of future generations is always some kind of capitalist.

The foregoing interpretation of the debate over developmentalism should not be surprising. A traditional defence of the capitalist in general is that he embodies the social interest in deferring consumption for the sake of preserving and expanding existing value, and quite often the greatest political supporters of conservation turn out to be the owners of scarce resources that rise in value as they become too precious to use. Ironically, the immediate victims of the environmental degradation allegedly required to maintain economic growth often become the villains. In the dialectics of political ecology we often find workers and the poor appearing as the political constituency for developmentalism − being all too willing to condone pollution because of the jobs it may preserve or create.

The *Daedalus* symposium on the "No Growth Society" gives a sampling of the mainstream debate on the desirability and inevitability of stationary state. Here, the anti-growth position is represented by Mishan and Boulding, and a moderate pro-growth position by Zeckhauser and Roberts. For alternative perspectives on these issues, see Enzensberger, "The Critique of Political Ecology"; Raymond Williams, "Problems of the Coming Period"; Bahro, *Socialism and Survival*; and Gorz, *Ecology as Politics*.

[67] The analysis of capitalism in terms of the fundamental contradiction between exchange and production is a dominant theme throughout *Capital*. See vol. I, esp. chs 7–15, 17, 19–22; vol. II, part 2, esp. chs 10, 11, and 16 (sec. 3); vol. III, part 7, esp. chs 49–51).

[68] The discussion above is based on *Capital*, vol. I, ch. 1, esp. p. 132; and chs

The classical theory of the market describes the ratios of exchange between the products of different specialized industries, for example between steel and cars. Its underlying conception of the division of labor implies that commodities are normally exchanged in proportion to the amount of social labor required for their production. According to Smith, a market is fundamentally a means of acquiring and allocating the social gains produced through specialization; the more specialization there is in the economy the higher the level of social interdependence.[69]

The second conception of the division of labor is concerned with the manner in which cars and steel are produced within their respective industries.[70] Marx came to describe this as "the division of labor in manufacture."[71] In the factory the worker does not sell his product to the employer, or to the next worker on the production line, but rather hires out the use of his labor-time.[72] As soon as the worker is hired the employer already owns the worker's product and will appropriate it directly, without going through a further process of exchange.

Within this second picture of the division of labor, as Smith himself admitted, jobs do not necessarily become more specialized and skilled. Even where the result of economic growth and investment is not merely to employ greater numbers of workers at the same task, Smith seemed to recognize that the result of introducing new techologies could be either to replace skilled with unskilled workers, or to employ fewer workers, even if those remaining had higher and more specialized skills. In either case the efficiency produced by expansion would come by raising the productivity of capital, and hence reducing the proportional return to labor as a cost of production.[73]

Although manpower is bought and sold on the market alongside other commodities, Smith and Ricardo did not derive its value in the same way as that of other commodities. In classical political economy commodities

---

13−15, esp. pp. 470−92, 544−53.

[69] Cf. the notion of "organic solidarity" in Durkheim, *The Division of Labor in Society*. See also Marglin, "What Do Bosses Do?"

[70] See Adam Smith, *The Wealth of Nations*, chs 1−3, 8−9.

[71] In order to focus more sharply on the critique of Smith, the discussion above compresses Marx's progression from the social division of labor to the division of labor in "manufacture" to the division of labor in the modern factory. See Marx, *Capital*, vol. I, chs 13−15, esp. pp. 470−92, 544−53.

[72] For a study of the linkages and crossovers between the two forms of division of labor see Williamson, *Markets and Hierarchies*, chs 3−4.

[73] Adam Smith, *The Wealth of Nations*, bk 1, chs 8−9.

other than labor derive their value from the labor time that went into producing them — not from the marginal equilibrium of supply and demand. Yet the value of labor time itself — the wage rate — is determined entirely by supply and demand.[74] Wages, according to Smith and Ricardo, depend in the short run entirely on the scarcity or abundance of workers in relation to the capital available to hire them.

Marx perceived that the existence of the division of labor in the factory cannot be wholly derived from the logic of increasingly specialized production for exchange. As a system of production, and not merely of trade, the Smithian market presupposes the availability of laborers who do not own commodities, or the means of producing them. Marx insisted that the emergence of a such a labor market must be explained independently as a result of historical changes in the social structure.[75]

Where the economists saw a single political economy, Marx saw two conflicting pictures of the market, based on two divergent models of the division of labor. In the first picture the division of labor in society appears as a system of exchange between the specialized producers of commodities. In the second picture the division of labor in the factory is the result of the need of the capitalist to invest and the need of workers to be paid.

Marx's method led him to see how each of these pictures seems to open a window in the other.[76] Within the picture of the social division of labor

[74] Smith occasionally suggests an alternative measure of the value of labor time — i.e., labor cost of producing the commodities necessary to command a unit of labor time. Ricardo, however, points out that this measure of the value of labor is not satisfactory. (See n. 76, below) Much of Marx's mature work exploits the tension between the labor theory of the value of commodities and the commodities theory of the value of labor. See chapter 12, below. See also Adam Smith, *The Wealth of Nations*, bk 1, chs 5, 8; Ricardo, *On the Principles of Political Economy and Taxation*, ch. 1; Marx, *Capital*, vol. I, p. 173f., and *Theories of Surplus Value*, part 1, pp. 67–77.

[75] See, e.g., Marx, *Capital* vol. I, part 8 ("So -Called Primitive Accumulation"); Robert Brenner, "The Origins of Capitalist Development: A Critique of Neo-Smithian Marxism."

[76] Looking at each picture through the window of the other, Smith offered a labor theory of the value of commodities, and (at moments) a commodities a theory of the value of labor — i.e., the measurement of market value of the wage-earner's time by the value of the commodities necessary to command it. Ricardo, however, recognized that the value of commodities in relation to each other is different from their value as capital in relation to labor — that wages are not merely a purchase, but an investment. For Ricardo (and for Sraffa) the worker is seen as in essence a

between industries, the wages of workers appear as an anomaly. According to Smith and Ricardo workers exercise their purchasing power only as consumers, buying some part of the social product but selling none of it: virtually everything they buy is used up, retaining none of its value for purposes of future economic exchange. The existence of this general category of consumers is clearly exogenous to a model of production based on exchange between specialized industries. Yet the efficient allocation of socially available productive labor obviously requires the maintenance of an adequate level of consumer demand.[77] This appears as a structural precondition, which is formally outside the picture of the division of labor between industries, but which can also be glimpsed within the picture through the window of wages.[78]

Within the competing Smithian picture of the division of labor in the factory, we can tell a parallel story. Standing alongside producers in his factory, the capitalist appears as an anomaly — appropriating the full value of the product while producing no part of it, at least in his capacity as capitalist.[79] From the standpoint of production in the factory all capital investments are purely exogenous — including the money advance by other capitalists in the form of loans, the materials that are purchased to be passed through the process, and even the money that the employer 'advances' to his workers in the form of wages paid before the product is sold. The preexistence of a pool of realized capital that must be accumulated — of money that must be invested in order to preserve and increase its value — appears as a structural assumption, formally outside the division of labor in the factory, which can be glimpsed within that picture through the window of theoretical arguments about the role of capital in the production process.[80]

---

machine that uses up a portion of the corn that it produces. By using corn, rather than labor-time, as the *numeraire*, Ricardo and Sraffa hope to avoid the circularity of Smith's theory by positing a single commodity in terms of which the value of labor itself can be measured. (See Sraffa, *Production of Commodities by Means of Commodities*.)

[77] See, e.g., Bleaney, *Underconsumption Theories*. Cf. Mandel, *Late Capitalism*.

[78] As we shall see below, the reproduction of an adequate level of consumer demand is not guaranteed by the microeconomic model of market competition between capitals, but is presupposed as a macroeconomic condition. See Keynes, *The General Theory of Employment, Interest, and Money*, and Samuelson, "Economic Theory and Wages."

[79] He may also have technical managerial expertise.

[80] As an investor the capitalist will expect to sell the product at a price that will yield an average rate of profit on *all* his costs. The level of expected profit necessary

Superimposing these two pictures, we can see the characteristic problem often noted by Marxist writers on the dynamics of capitalist development: expanding capitalism must on the one hand increase consumer markets in order to realize its profits, while on the other hand reducing the share of revenue paid out in wages in order to accumulate its profits. These two imperatives are potentially in tension — a tension on which many Marxist writers have based their projections of the evolutionary limits of capitalism itself.[81]

Our present challenge, however, is to connect Marx's critique of political economy with the identities that function at the surface of political life. In chapter 9 we saw that Marxian political analysis requires us to describe the cleavages of civil society twice over. We are now in a position to see that Marx's critique of political economy provides just such a dual description of the dynamic tensions in civil society.

Conflict and fragmentation

In thus far describing the market economy as both a mode of production and a mode of exchange we have presupposed two pictures of social division: the division of society into discrete product-based industries on the one hand, and the division of society according to ownership of the productive factors of land, labor, and capital on the other hand. The former division expresses the tendency of modern politics toward the differentiation and fragmentation of interests; the latter division expresses

---

to maintain an adequate rate of capital formation is largely a matter of politics and social structure that cannot be derived from the production function as such. It is, rather, presupposed as a macroeconomic condition of the microeconomic model of the competitive pricing of factors of production.

For a summary of the work of neo-Ricardian followers of Sraffa and Robinson on these issues, see Harcourt, *Some Cambridge Controversies in the Theory of Capital*. See also Kalecki "Political Aspects of Full Employment" and "Class Struggle and the Distribution of National Income"; Steedman, *Marx After Sraffa*, and Steedman et al., *The Value Controversy*. For a skeptical note on the "Cambridge controversies" see Sen, "On Some Debates in Capital Theory."

[81] On the question of whether Marx demonstrated the continuing possibility or the underlying impossibility of capitalism as a self-contained mode of production, see, the debate between Luxemburg and Bukharin: Luxemburg, *The Accumulation of Capital: An Anti-Critique*, and Bukharin, *Imperialism and the Accumulation of Capital*. See also, Lenin, *Imperialism, The Highest Stage of Capitalism*, and Mandel, *Late Capitalism*.

the counter-tendency of modern politics toward the homogenization and eventual confrontation of interests.

We can now put the foregoing point in more conventional Marxist categories. The view of civil society as organized through the competition among products is an expression of what traditional Marxists describe as the divisions within classes — the particular fractions of labor and capital that can be linked to form the economic base of particular regimes. In contrast the view of civil society as organized through the relation between the productive factors is an expression of what traditional Marxists describe as the divisions between classes — the fundamental conflict of interest between the owners of labor, capital, and land in the process of production. I believe that the form of political analysis adumbrated by the incomplete final chapter of *Capital* ("Classes")[82] would endeavor to relate the divisions within classes to the divisions between them — and hence to trace the mutually offsetting tendencies toward fragmentation and confrontation in modern politics.[83]

Even though mainstream economists no longer build directly on the classical conceptual foundations described above, we need not abandon the possibility of using present-day sources to carry out Marx's unfinished agenda. We must, however, shift our focus from the theoretical interests of academic economists to the practical interests of bureaucrats and lobbyists. Today the task of reconciling Smith's dual description of the market — as a division within classes and a division between them — falls directly to the bureaucratic agencies of the neo-Hegelian state.

Often this issue will find only indirect expression in the state apparatus. The diversity of industries, for example, is often made to appear in our political system as a pluralism of regions with different levels of employment and growth. Similarly, the potential conflict Smith described between wages and profits will find political expression as a tension between consumption and investment — often, more specifically, between efforts to stimulate aggregate demand and incentives to increase the productivity of capital. In countless areas, public agencies now address the ways in which efforts to equalize among particular industries will shift the balance between labor and capital investment, and the ways in which efforts to optimize the overall levels of labor and capital will create market imbalances between particular industries.[84] By emulating the Marxian reading of Smith and

---

[82] Before breaking off, that chapter concludes by noting "the infinite fragmentation of interests and positions into which the division of social labour splits not only workers but also capitalists and landowner." (Marx, *Capital*, vol. III, p. 1026).

[83] We shall return to this theme in chapter 12, below.

[84] See Musgrave, "Theories of Fiscal Crisis: An Essay in Fiscal Sociology."

Ricardo, we can see that just as the governmental regulation of industrial organization gives us a window on the relation of consumption and profitability across industries, so the governmental regulation of labor unions gives us a window on the competitive relations among and within industries.

In the United States, antitrust policy purports to regulate the effects of concentration in capital markets on the market in various commodities. The stated goal of antitrust policy is maintaining competition within industries in order to correct for the potential domination of producers over consumers in the marketplace and resulting inefficiencies. In practice, however, disputes over anti-trust enforcement have generally revolved around the relevant definition of the scope of the market for purposes of judging substitution effects between products, and the outcome of such disputes often has less to do with the interest of consumers and producers (which both sides will argue are identical in theory) than with the balance of political power between the consumer products and producer products industries.[85]

So pervasive are these arguments that one might conclude that the indirect goal of antitrust regulation in the United States is to equalize for the competitive disadvantages between (rather than within) industries. Whenever greater competition would damage an industry as a whole – leading to a profit squeeze, business failure, unemployment, disinvestment, and eventual reductions in supply – the government generally finds that industrial concentration is justified, even where the scope of consumer choice is significantly reduced.[86] Once legitimated under antitrust analysis, a given instance of industrial concentration becomes eligible for many kinds of protective regulation that enhance that particular industry's market advantage over foreign competitors and domestic substitutes. In the end the model of antitrust as the regulation of capital markets to protect consumers reduces to maintaining a legal appearance of industrial efficiency; industrial concentration need not be deemed harmful to consumers if each part of the larger organization keeps its accounts as though it were a separate profit center.

[85] See Hays "Political Choice in Regulatory Administration," pp. 124–54, esp. 136, 139.
[86] We are held to be in the presence of what was called in the early days of anti-trust regulation a "natural" as opposed to an "unnatural" corporate monopoly. For a valuable historical treatment of these subjects, see Chandler, *The Visible Hand*. For a theoretical treatment see Williamson, *Markets and Hierarchies*. See also Chayes, "The Modern Corporation and the Rule of Law," and Kaysen, "The Corporation: How Much Power? What Scope?"

The political problems posed by defining and regulating the scope of labor markets tend to mirror some of the issues in anti-trust regulation.[87] On the one hand the unequal economic conditions of different industries can be used to divide workers with similar job skills. Should workers therefore be organized for the purpose of collective bargaining on the basis of their industry — allowing each firm to maintain its own internal labor market? This approach would suggest unionization based on the division of labor in society — for example between autoworkers and farmworkers. On the other hand job categories in any given industry can be structured so that differentially competitive labor markets will divide workers in the same factory. Should workers therefore be organized for purposes of collective bargaining according to the external labor market for the tasks that they perform within each industry?[88] This approach would suggest unionization based on the division of labor in the factory — for example between mechanics and unskilled laborers.

In formulating governmental labor relations policy, both regulatory approaches have in practice been adopted piecemeal, and yet the difference between them often surfaces in paradoxes that resonate with Marx's critique of Smith and Ricardo. If government attempts to protect employment in depressed industries the effect will often be to subsidize internal wage differentials based on internal labor markets, even if this means tolerating a flatter wage scale for new employees than for those with accrued seniority benefits. If government attempts to reduce pay differentials between industries by regulating external labor markets, the effects on different industries will be unequal, as we see when raising the minimum wage leads to sectoral or regional unemployment.

The foregoing illustrations suggest the existence of countervailing tendencies toward both unification and fragmentation in the political relations among capitalists and workers. On the one hand, the market competition among capitalists and among workers tends toward the establishment of a uniform rate of profit and a uniform social wage, thereby increasing the tendency toward a confrontation between the conflicting interests of capital and labor as such — a point that Marx repeatedly stressed in his published

[87] In the United States the courts for a time applied anti-trust laws to regulate the activities of labor unions rather than businesses — in effect forbidding such techniques of labor organizing as the strike and the secondary boycott.

[88] See, e.g., Doeringer and Piore, *Internal Labor Markets and Manpower Analysis*; Edwards, *Contested Terrain*, chs 9–10; and David Gordon et al., *Segmented Work, Divided Workers*; Cf. Cain, "The Challenge of Segmented Labor Market Theories to Orthodox Theory: A Survey."

works. On the other hand, the heterogeneity of capitals and of labor markets leads to political linkages between fragments of labor and fragments of capital that reduce the level of direct confrontation between capitalists and workers in the state. The latter point was adumbrated (as we shall see)[89] in Marx's unpublished works on economics, but left tantalizingly undeveloped as his manuscripts broke off − except insofar as similar ideas appear in his historical writings.

In order to generalize Marx's approach to the critique of political economy we will need to give both of these tendencies their due. Although Marx himself stressed the developmental forces leading to the homogenization of both capital and labor,[90] we have seen throughout part II that his approach to analyzing modern politics consisted of overlaying two contrasting pictures of the division of civil society. We can now see that Marx's critique of political economy suggests that one of these pictures expresses the tendency toward political fragmentation resulting from the divisions within classes, and the other expresses the tendency toward political confrontation resulting from the division between classes. As the preeminent ideology of modern bureaucrats, political economy still expresses the absolute need of modern states to keep both forms of division in play.

A general version of Marx's critique of political economy must encompass the possibility that governments can succeed, as well as fail, in preventing either picture of the market from wholly erasing the other. In 1848 Marx and Engels predicted that liberal capitalist regimes would collapse when the dynamic need to develop single national markets in capital and labor led to the simplification of political conflict into a single antagonism − worker versus capitalist − that would render the market mode of production incompatible with majoritarian democracy.[91] We can now see that much of the public policy of modern states reflects and perpetuates a heterogeneity of labor and capital markets that partially offsets the simplification of political identity along the lines that Marx and Engels predicted.

Gender identity and the division of labor

The continuing possibility of democratic political alliances between fragments of different classes suggests that − except in the special case that

---

[89] See chapters 11 and 12, below.
[90] This stress is most apparent in *Capital*, vol. I.
[91] See Marx and Engels, "The Manifesto of the Communist Party."

Marx projected — an analysis of the market relation between wage labor and capital is only the beginning of a materialist account of modern political identity. Although we cannot here take up all of the bases of political identity that have recently been offered as alternatives to the traditional Marxist theory of class, we can attempt to illustrate a Marxian approach to the more general case by returning once more to the example of gender politics that we have pursued in earlier chapters.[92]

What is the relevance of Marxian materialism, as described above, to the politics of gender? From a conventional Marxist perspective the politicization of workers along gender lines is an instance of cross-class identification, like politicization of workers along racial, religious, or ethnic lines. The version of Marxian materialism sketched above, however, suggests that in a capitalist democracy the oppositional significance of any particular political identity — such as that of a woman, a black, or a worker — reflects changes in both the division of labor between industries and the overall composition of the labor force at the level of the relations between institutional frameworks — such as the family, the labor market, and the educational system.

The differential impact of changes in the structure of the labor market on men and women is now well known. In the immediate postwar era most male workers earning a "family wage" occupied a different position in the labor market from that of their wives.[93] Over the past two decades, however, many relatively well-paid career jobs in manufacturing industries have been lost, exported, or reclassified, and most of the new jobs created

[92] In recent years feminist scholars have made claims about the explanatory power of the gender division that fully rival the scope of traditional Marxist claims about the centrality of the division between wage labor and capital. See, e.g., MacKinnon, "Feminism, Marxism, Method, and the State: An Agenda for Theory;" and Hartsock, "The Feminist Standpoint: Developing the Ground for a Specifically Feminist Historical Materialism."

[93] The idea of extending the "family wage" to the working class was that the male "breadwinner" worked outside the home for a wage that was to be largely spent by the female "housewife" on goods that would be consumed in the course of her domestic labor. The essential difference between his work and hers was not that as a matter of fact the one was paid while the other was not, but rather that his work was intended to produce exchange value for the person who paid him (his wage was an investment) whereas her work produced only use value. Even if her work were paid, it would be a form of domestic consumption. And, if her work *had* to be paid, it must still be cheap enough for a worker to buy it out of his wages — or home life would again become a luxury available only to those who could afford to hire servants.

have been in the service sector — tending to be part-time, casual, and low-paid. As the "family wage" becomes a thing of the past for most male workers, the real purchasing power of the new two-income family does not much exceed that of the old "family wage" plus a "supplemental income." To unmarried female heads of households — an economic category that has vastly increased — the 'feminization' of the labor force has often meant the 'feminization of poverty.' The economic data for recent decades reveals that although a larger proportion of women are now earning incomes, there has been neither a proportional increase in the real level of consumption in society nor a proportional increase in the overall size of the national product.[94]

To a mainstream economist these phenomena might seem to reflect an accidental conjuncture between factors increasing the supply of women in the labor force, and factors increasing the demand for employees in the jobs that women typically perform. The general reduction in per capita earning power, combined with some movement toward greater gender equality in pay, has increased the proportion of women in the labor force.[95] If the increased supply of women in the labor force reflects both

[94] For a summary of relevant data see Lester Thurow, "A Surge in Inequality." See also Thurow, *Generating Inequality*, and Peattie and Rein, *Women's Claims*, ch. 4.
[95] The inflation and recession of the 1970s and early 1980s tended to drive women to take available jobs in order to maintain the real income of the family: "Recessions do draw more women into work ... But recessions also intensify the material pressures that reinforce the sexual division of labour. Women pay high penalties when they work, simply in order to maintain the family's previous standard of living. Their income is required to buy the same wage goods as before, so they can't afford market services to substitute for their own domestic labour. Employers have no reason to make concessions such as child care, since female labour is oversupplied as more wives are forced to seek work ... State service-cuts further increase the pressure on the household. The capitalist response to contraction — to attack the working-class standard of living — puts distinct limits on how far working-class families can recognize the division of labour within the household by aggravating the dynamics which created the rationale for the traditional division of labour in the first place. The more desperate women are to work, the more burdened by home responsibilities, the more difficult for them to organize against their employers, the more intractable income inequalities between men and women remain." (Brenner and Ramas, "Rethinking Women's Oppression," p. 63.) Cf. Barrett, *Women's Oppression Today*.

We must further note that women who are already obliged to work outside the home have a decreasing economic incentive to remain (unhappily) married insofar as the family has largely ceased to be a unit of savings and accumulation in the economy. Despite the reduced incentives of American women to remain married, the process of divorce often has differential economic consequences for women and men. See Weitzman, *The Divorce Revolution*. Cf. Hewlett, *A Lesser Life*.

the growing need of married women to work and the growing proportion of unmarried female heads of households, much of the increased demand for women in the labor force has come in the new low-paid service jobs, or the recently reclassified manufacturing jobs. The fact that these happen to be the jobs available as more women enter the labor force is partly coincidence, and partly a reflection of a preexisting sexual division of labor between industries, and within them.

But why is there a sexual division of labor in the economy, corresponding, however roughly, to the segmentation of the labor force between higher and lower paid jobs? A great deal of recent scholarship has been devoted to this question, almost all of it rightly rejecting biological explanations based on innate differences between the abilities of men and women. Of the widely accepted explanations, most focus on either attitudinal or institutional factors.[96] The attitudinal explanation is in essence that certain jobs have low pay or low status *because* they are typically women's – that stereotyping reinforced by overt discrimination tend to keep women out of traditionally male jobs.[97] The institutional explanation stresses the objective incentives that women have to seek and accept (in disproportionate numbers) jobs that have relatively low pay and status.[98] The implication of the institutional argument may be that women are hired at a discount in

[96] Most participants in this debate distinguish between taking a "culturalist" and a "materialist" perspective. Here, "culturalism" implies a stress on ideologies of dominance (such as patriarchy) that are not presumptively rational for the oppressed group, and that lose their hold as soon as their irrationality is realized. Feminist "materialism," in contrast, explains the acceptance of oppression as a rational response to circumstances that may, however, change. This is not, however, the specific sense in which I use the term "materialism" in the present chapter. Although I believe that my argument above is generally consistent with the view that economic exploitation is not the result of irrational behavior on the part of either its victims or beneficiaries, my stress on the importance of contradictory institutional frameworks attempts to capture some of the insights generally claimed by "culturalist" approaches.

[97] A stress on patriarchal attitudes plays an important role in the quasi-Marxist approaches to feminist issues in Barrett, *Women's Oppression Today*, and Heidi Hartmann, "Capitalism, Patriarchy, and Job Segregation by Sex."

[98] One version of this argument runs as follows: so long as women (whether married or unmarried) have the primary responsibility for domestic labor, and especially for the care of dependent children, they will be disproportionately inclined to seek jobs that are casual, part-time, or off-track; so long as there is a large supply of women willing to accept such jobs, predominantly female jobs will be paid less in both external and internal labor markets. See Brenner and Ramas, "Rethinking Women's Oppression."

the labor market because of their subordination in the family, that women
are subordinated in the family because they command lower wages in the
labor market, or – most likely – that the two areas of subordination are
structurally interrelated.[99]

My purpose here is not to resolve these complex issues, but rather to
suggest how a materialist analysis, in Marx's sense, might reveal the
objective sources of unity and fragmentation among women seen as an
oppositional group. Thus far, there have been three distinct elements in
our account of the material basis of gender inequality: the unequal distribution of men and women among available jobs, unequal pay in the jobs
that men and women typically do, and a general decline in the average real
incomes of wages earners.[100] Each of these dimensions has different implications for the possibility of uniting women around the issue of their
gender.

The need to equalize between men and women in the competition for
jobs[101] has tended to unite women during the transitional period in which
rates of participation in the labor force have become (once again) approximately equal for both sexes. Families tended to divide during this period
along generational and gender lines, as women – especially younger
women – came to resent increasingly their domestic roles and to identify
politically with the need to break the 'gender barriers' in every area of
endeavor.

The legal requirements of equal opportunity and of equal pay for the
same work may be enough to end, eventually, the sexual division of labor
in higher income professional and managerial jobs. Women who successfully
compete for such jobs can afford to have children, if they wish, by hiring
lower income women to raise them during the working day. (The people
whom they hire will generally be women who prefer or need the casual or
part-time character of the work.) But the income inequalities between
women that allow some to enjoy greater equality of opportunity in relation to
men imply that that others must necessarily rely on the welfare system and
the flexibility of their own conditions of employment to raise any children
they may choose to have.

The interests of lower income women are addressed directly by the issue
that is known in the United States as "comparable worth." Politically, the
notion of "comparable worth" challenges the idea that certain service and
manufacturing jobs can be paid less simply because the division of labor in

[99] This also seems to be the view of Heidi Hartmann. See Hartmann, "Capitalism,
Patriarchy, and Job Segregation by Sex."
[100] See Peattie and Rein, *Women's Claims.*
[101] State-mandated non-discrimination can be interpreted to require "affirmative
action." See *Johnson v. Santa Clara County.*

the family creates a large supply of women willing to take them. Within each industry the principle of comparable worth would limit the reliance on external labor markets to justify internal pay differentials.[102] Instead, there would be an effort to equalize between the wages scales in 'comparable' jobs that are in fact occupied by men and women in different proportions.[103]

The comparability of jobs that men and women do in different proportions would have to be based largely on factors such as educational credentials, experience, and responsibility. At the entry level, however, the educational system would become the prototype for the gender equality to be imposed on the labor market: equal pay for careers initially requiring equal educational qualifications, with further differentials based on the comparability of promotions and seniority up the line.[104] The stress on educational qualifications in the politics of comparable worth reflects the fact that women have achieved far greater equality in the educational system than in either the family or the labor market. (Presumably, few feminists would be interested in the principle of pay according to educational level in jobs not subject to gender stratification.)[105]

Unlike the politics of non-discrimination, the politics of comparable worth is a divisive issue for working women. Without comparable worth many single mothers could not earn enough to be the sole support of their families, unless their income was somehow supplemented by the state.[106] Yet, even if the movement for comparable worth has only limited success, the pressure for it will be used to justify keeping the pay differential in men's jobs from rising — thereby further accelerating the demise of the family wage. The politics of comparable worth will thus divide women who must work in order to live, and those whose relative need to work will depend upon the total family wage that can be earned by husband and wife together. From the standpoint of developing a gender-based political

---

[102] For a discussion of the general relation between internal and external labor markets see Doeringer and Piore, *Internal Labor Markets and Manpower Analysis*.

[103] Of course such a goal of equalization would be unnecessary if in fact men and women tended to do the same jobs in the same proportions. The only way, however, that such a result could be achieved through regulation of a labor market based on voluntary choice would be to pay women more in jobs in which women are underrepresented — a clear violation of the principle of equal pay for equal work.

[104] See Meister, "Discrimination Law Through the Looking Glass," part 7.

[105] Should accountants be paid more than baseball players, notwithstanding the labor market? Should professors be paid more than stockbrokers?

[106] Without comparable worth the feminization of the labor force is also the feminization of poverty.

identity these divisions will compound the effects of sacrificing the interests of women in male-dominated occupations for the sake of women in predominantly female occupations.

The respects in which the rise of feminism is an ideological reflex of declining per capita income will ultimately limit the extent to which oppositional politics can be organized around issues of gender before fragmentation sets in. So long as neither the employer nor the state can be made to effectively bear the cost of childcare, the political promotion of "family values" will become an increasingly salient issue for women who work for a wage. In the United States the policy issues of the future are likely to arise out of the decreasing ability of working families to support and educate their children out of their wages, and the perception that this will place higher demands on the welfare and distribution systems of the state.[107] The need to defend the opportunity of two-income couples to raise a family may once again divide women politically along class lines, and also on the issue of pro- and anti-natalism.[108] Such divisions among women may well undermine the status of feminism as a broad-based social movement, rather than a form of interest-group politics.

The foregoing sketch of a materialist analysis of the prospects of political confrontation and fragmentation along gender lines in the United States does not presuppose that the identity of 'woman' is less fundamental in modern politics than the identity of 'worker.' If my approach to Marxism is correct, one might attempt a similar analysis of the prospects of political confrontation around the identity of 'worker.'[109] As a general approach to political analysis in capitalist democracies Marxism should enable us to understand the limits on the capacity of the industrial proletariat to organize a basis of political identity that can swallow up the heterogeneity of capitals, just as we have here explored the material limits on the possibility of avoiding fragmentation through organizing around the identity of 'woman.' With this possibility in mind we must now turn to the special role that the relation between wage labor and capital plays in Marx's political materialism.

---

[107] See Balbo, "Family, Women, and the State: Notes Toward a Typology of Family Roles and Public Intervention." See also Hewlett, *A Lesser Life*, and Peattie and Rein, *Women's Claims*.

[108] See, e.g. Luker, *Abortion and the Politics of Motherhood*; Gimenez "Feminism, Pronatalism, and Motherhood"; and Blake, "Coercive Pronatalism and American Population Policy."

[109] Such a possibility was suggested in the discussion of public regulation of collective bargaining, above.

11 Class and Exploitation

Class analysis and political economy

"A class is a group of people who all relate to the labor process in a similar way."[1] So states a prominent Marxian scholar introducing a recent work on class and exploitation. Such assertions, often made as a preliminary matter of definition, are typical of writings on class by authors whose orientations toward Marxism may differ widely. Since Marx wrote we can hardly think of social classes without evoking the division between wage labor and capital, proletariat and bourgeoisie. Yet this automatic identification of class with economic relations marks a fundamental shift in the meaning of the word "class" in social and political thought.

Before Marx, the literature on class was concerned with who ruled in the political constitution. In the tradition of political thought emanating from Plato and Aristotle the paradigmatic classes were "the one," "the few," and "the many."[2] Presuming that in any political regime one or another such class must inevitably rule, the concern of the political theorist was to determine in whose interest and for what good each class must rule in order to be legitimate.

Discussions of wage labor, capital, and land were not part of the literature on class before Marx. Both Plato and Aristotle had argued that the political and economic organization of society should be kept distinct in principle, even though they each wrote single works (the *Republic* and the *Politics*) that encompassed both the relation of ruler and ruled in the state and the division of labor in production. Thereafter, politics and economics were rarely discussed together, and even in the period surrounding

---

[1] Roemer, *Free to Lose*, p. 5.
[2] Even the "people" could be a ruling class in this sense. See, e.g., Palmer, *The Age of Democratic Revolution*, vol. 1, ch. 1.

the French Revolution the literatures on the class division of politics and the social organization of production and trade were largely distinct.[3]

To say that economists before Marx were not concerned with the class basis of political constitutions is not, however, to say that their writings were apolitical. Mercantilism was concerned with the political aspects of international trade to the exclusion of those issues of production that we now regard as central to economics. The French physiocrats, as advisers to the King, saw land, labor, and capital as factors of agricultural production that could be differentially burdened by the tax policies of the state – and Quesnay's *tableaux* anticipate later developments in economic planning.[4] Although Smith and Ricardo defined economics as a distinct field of inquiry by assuming that the effects of the 'visible hand' of overt political rule could be distinguished from the natural economic forces that affect the relative scarcity and abundance of each of the factors of production, they were also directly concerned with minimizing the distorting effects of taxation and other state policies on the structure of prices.[5]

Writing after the French Revolution and the defeats of 1848, Marx was confronted with an expressly political theory of the state and an expressly economic theory of civil society. In his view each of these theories had two aspects: Hegel and Tocqueville had shown, as we have seen, that political institutions were both an expression of political equality and a way of organizing "the people" into groups; Smith and Ricardo described market institutions as both a system of exchange between (moral) equals and a social division of labor that in no way assumed equality of wealth. Marx believed that these two bodies of theory, taken together, could be seen as ironically complementary: to say that political legitimacy depends upon the official recognition of equal rights is to say that disparities in wealth and social power among groups can only exist outside the realm of politics in the world of consensual relations among individuals and groups.

Marx developed this insight by appropriating the word "class" to show how political power is embodied in the organization of economic production. He thereby turned the unofficial character of the social distribution of power and wealth into a new conceptual paradigm. As we have seen many times over, Marx recognized in his earliest work that political and economic institutions interpenetrate. In offering a *class analysis* of capitalism Marx

[3] A notable exception was Hegel's *Philosophy of Right*. See, e.g., Avineri, *Hegel's Theory of the Modern State*, ch. 7.

[4] See Samuelson, "Quesnay's 'Tableau Economique' as a Theorist would Formulate it Today."

[5] See, e.g., Schumpeter, *History of Economic Analysis*, chs 3–5. Cf. Marx, *Theories of Surplus Value*, part 1, ch. 2, and *Capital*, vol. II, chs 10, 19.

argued that the relationship between wage labor and capital is one of *exploitation* in which the capitalist appropriates the surplus value of the worker's labor through the normal operation of market mechanisms, much as Smith and Ricardo had contended that the parasitical state exploits productive economic agents through the coercive mechanisms of taxation. Unlike traditional political theorists who argued that the unjust domination of a class could lead to exploitation by means of state power, Marx saw modern class relations as a form of exploitation occurring normally through consent, but requiring occasional resort to overt domination, whether official or unofficial.[6] For Marx a significant degree of economic exploitation would be the essence of class rule, not a sign of its corruption.[7]

Although Marx's approach to class analysis connects politics and economics, it does not necessarily imply that individuals act in politics to pursue their economic self-interest, as vulgar versions often suggest. For Marx the underlying connection between politics and economics is not psychological, but rather structural: the mode of social reproduction is reflected by the relations between various institutions such as the state and the market in a way that becomes the basis of group conflicts in politics. This is Marx's *political* materialism.

Some of the most sophisticated debates in recent Marxian scholarship concern the relation between this political materialism − class analysis − and *historical materialism*[8] − the analysis of dynamic incompatibilities between relations of production and the emergence of new forces of production, especially technologies. Is class struggle or technological change the decisive factor in explaining the epochal transition from one mode of production to another? Are modes of production themselves best defined by the dominant technique of surplus extraction (class), or rather by the dominant organization of work (technology)?[9] Are classes and class struggle

[6] See, Przeworski, "Material Bases of Consent" and "Exploitation, Class Conflict, and Socialism: The Ethical Materialism of John Roemer."

[7] He also believed, as we shall see below, that some form of surplus extraction (exploitation in a technical sense) would continue to be necessary, even if there were no longer class-appropriation of the surplus (exploitation in a moral sense).

[8] For a somewhat different view of the distinction between political and historical materialism see Balibar, "The Vacillation of Ideology."

[9] See Gerald A. Cohen, "Forces and Relation of Production," and Robert Brenner, "The Social Bases of Economic Development." See also Gerald A. Cohen, *Karl Marx's Theory of History: A Defence"*; Elster, *Making Sense of Marx*, chs 5−6 and Roemer, *Free to Lose*, ch. 8. For a provocative view of how technological change today may be altering the meaning of class conflict at the point of production see Piore and Sabel, *The Second Industrial Divide.*

in Marx's sense a common feature of all societies, or only of capitalist societies?[10]

The literature that attempts to answer these questions generally uses a prior definition of class positions — based on either the distribution of property or the process of production — to test various hypotheses, such as the claim that classes so defined become collective actors or the more complex claim that strategies of class compromise explain the identities through which collective action becomes possible.[11] In stressing the strategic choices available to the occupants of various class positions, this literature has brought much clarity to our understanding of the micromotives of class conflict, and of the roles of class and non-class actors in specific historical conflicts. Unfortunately, this clarity has come at some cost to the interpretive power of Marxian theory insofar as one after another restated Marxian hypothesis based on a prior ontology of class positions has proven to be unsustainable, either at the level of abstract model-building or at the level of historical prediction.

Instead of viewing class conflict as a result of self-interested strategic action, structural Marxists tend to view the social construction of the political 'self' as intrinsically problematic, and to regard class identity as an *effect* of the ensemble of institutions that constitute a political regime.[12] The structural approach has the virtue of not presupposing fixed boundaries of class positions as a necessary precondition of class-based explanations of politics. Yet, if *everything* enters into the determination of class positions there is little remaining point in explaining social outcomes by reference to class conflict. Insofar as structural Marxism allows us to understand whatever happens in class terms, as a theory it is ultimately merely descriptive.

My approach in this chapter is to try to combine the advantages of both the strategic and the structural approaches to class. Having sketched in part II the varying divisions in civil society on which political conflict may be based, my hope in part III is to show how Marx's critique of political economy might help us to explain which conflicts are selected as the principal loci of social struggle over time. I share with structural Marxists

[10] The Lukácsian question that these writers attempt to answer using the techniques of rational choice is whether, or to what extent, classes "in themselves" ever become classes "for themselves." See, e.g., Elster, "Three Challenges to Class" and "Further Thoughts on Marxism, Functionalism, and Game Theory."

[11] See Roemer, *A General Theory of Exploitation and Class*; Wright, *Classes*; and Przeworski, *Capitalism and Social Democracy*, chs 4–5 (but cf. ch. 2 and its postscript).

[12] See Poulantzas, *Classes in Contemporary Capitalism* and *Political Power and Social Classes*.

the intuition that we cannot begin with an ontology of classes as discrete social groups that have the option of entering or withdrawing from mutual cooperation;[13] yet I also share with the Marxism of strategic choice the notion that "class struggle" cannot be meaningfully used to describe whatever actually happens, and that class analysis commits us to the idea that some part of a structure-in-conflict determines the outcome for the whole.[14]

I believe that an approach to class analysis rooted in the critique of political economy can be used to explain the emergence of ordinary group conflict, even where class struggle does not appear in a "pure" form. By focusing on why certain group divisions become politicized when they do, and around what issues, we can carry forward Marx's own attempt to analyze the contradictory ways in which changes in an underlying structure of social reproduction are reflected at the level of institutions and conscious practices. Political organization, including the formation of new collective actors, could then be explained as a strategic *outcome* of past conflicts, which in turn changes the historical conditions under which future conflicts can occur.[15]

Like most writers in the Marxian tradition, my view of class analysis stands or falls on a selective interpretation of the argument of *Capital*. Unlike most, however, I do not assume that class analysis must be an extrapolation of what would happen if the struggles described in volume I were carried out to their conclusion in a single-product, single-sector economy where primitive accumulation has run its course and prices remain proportional to values.[16] I stress instead the account in volume III of how the capitalist economy regulates its reproduction and expansion through the price mechanism, and the effects of the systematic divergence of price from value on the political significance of various social locations.[17] Even if Marx's political materialism proves to be largely specific to the rise

[13] Marx believed on the contrary that class relations are non-optional and that strategic alliances between groups are based ultimately on the systemic requirements of capitalist reproduction.

[14] See ch. 1, above.

[15] For a similar perspective see Przeworski, *Capitalism and Social Democracy*, ch. 2.

[16] According to this view *Capital* must be read as the theoretical background for the claims made in the *Communist Manifesto*, and not as a sophisticated reflection on the failure of at least some of those claims.

[17] My emphases in reading *Capital* are similar to those of the French "regulation" school, although I often differ with them at the level of concrete analysis. See Aglietta, *A Theory of Capitalist Regulation* and "World Capitalism in the Eighties," and Lipietz, *The Enchanted World*.

282 Political Materialism

and fall of capitalism, I believe that his analysis should hold great interest — both intrinsically and as a model of research into other cultural systems of material reproduction.

The project of *Capital*

Marx's overall thesis in *Capital* is that, unlike its predecessors, a market mode of production is driven by an internally generated need to create an economic surplus. Although the best-known arguments in *Capital* are primarily concerned with how surplus value can arise from the circulation of commodities,[18] I believe that the overall plan of the three volumes was intended to demonstrate that the particular commodities in which surplus is produced ("valorized")[19] must differ systematically from those in which it can be "realized" through sale, and must differ again from those in which it can be successfully "accumulated" as capital.[20] The process of valorization is described in volume I. The inherent disproportionality between valorization and realization is developed in volume II and elaborated in volume III. In volume III the dominant theme is the tension between the logics of valorization, realization, and accumulation. Taking full account of the posthumous volumes of *Capital*, we can see that the culmination of Marx's critique of classical political economy was to be an analysis of why prices cannot be proportional to labor value, given the effect of capital markets on the exploitation of wage labor. Unfortunately, Marx did not complete this plan, and published only volume I in his lifetime. Nevertheless, I think it is possible to trace the trajectory of the overall argument he wished to make, and to identify at least some of the crucial gaps left by his failure to complete his project.

Volume I of *Capital* abstracts from the effects of capital markets on circulation and accumulation in order to focus exclusively on the labor market. Unlike the later volumes it assumes that all commodities are exchanged in proportion to their labor values,[21] that all surplus value is

[18] See esp. vol. I, chs 4–6.

[19] In this use of "valorization" (referring to value-creation in the labor process) I follow Mandel and the new translation of *Capital*, and differ from writers, such as Rosdolsky, who use "valorization" to denote the process by which surplus value is realized in the sale of commodities. See Marx *Capital*, vol. I, pp. 252, 293.

[20] Marx describes the overall plan of *Capital* in the opening paragraph of volume III (p. 117).

[21] See e.g., *Capital*, vol. I, p. 269, n. 24.

realized, and that realized surplus value will be accumulated as capital on an increasing scale.[22]

Marx's "abstract" account[23] of accumulation in volume I is an effort to explain the endogenous causes through which a capitalist economy must both grow and die. As a materialist, he sought to root the limitations on capitalist development in its very principle of growth. While acknowledging that the expansion of capitalist production requires an absolute increase in the funds available both for buying raw materials (c) and for hiring labor (v),[24] Marx argued that the long-term effect of accumulation must always increase the proportional value of (c) in relation to (v).[25] This recognition of the growing importance of constant capital in the composition of the national product was an important correction to the arguments of Smith and Ricardo. They never fully integrated changes in the relative proportion of constant capital into their theory of natural price,[26] and attributed accumulation only to a growth in the wages fund. This growth, they thought, would both expand the size of the labor force and draw workers from unproductive to productive labor, even if there were no technological improvements in the productivity of labor.

Marx recognized that − even in Smith's description − the process of accumulation and growth inevitably increases productivity due to economies of scale, technical improvements, greater efficiency, and so forth.[27] But why, he asked, does the capitalist necessarily *seek* higher productivity, rather than merely increased production? Marx answered that, although the *amount* of surplus may continue to grow, this very growth decreases the ratio of the new labor input to the value of products passed through, squeezing the capitalist's rate of profit on production. Driven by the market to seek "more," to grow in order to stay in business, he is constantly forced to raise the rate of exploitation by lowering his labor costs per unit of output.[28] The capitalist can accomplish this objective through lengthening

[22] See, e.g., ibid., ch. 23.3.
[23] See ibid., p. 710.
[24] For further explanations of c, v, and s see "Accounting for Surplus Value," below.
[25] See, generally, vol. I, *Capital*, chs 24 and 25.
[26] See Wolff, *Understanding Marx*, chs 1−3.
[27] See Adam Smith, *The Wealth of Nations*, bk 1, ch. 1.
[28] For an interesting critical discussion of this argument at the level of micromotives see Elster, *Making Sense of Marx*, ch. 3.3.

the working day, reducing wages, or increasing the productivity of labor through new production techniques.[29]

To Marx higher productivity simply meant a higher intermediate product for the same new labor cost. The expected consequence of higher productivity is that in every working day larger physical quantities of raw material would be used. Assuming, as he does in volume I, that the production costs per unit of constant capital do not decline relative to the production costs per unit of wage goods, Marx inferred that the value of constant capital ("industrial consumption") must make up an increasing proportion of the national product. His overarching conclusion in volume I was that industrialization increases both the rate of exploitation and the accumulated value of constant capital.[30]

Marx's historical point, made repeatedly throughout volume I, was that the abstract process of accumulation both increases the market power of capital as a whole to command labor and accelerates the proletarianization of civil society.[31] The system could expand in this way, Marx thought, only up to a point at which "the integument is burst asunder."[32]

This abstract projection of the "historical tendency" of capitalist accumulation is based, however, on the explicit assumption in volume I that both capital and labor are homogeneous in each cycle of production, and that variations in the character of either occur only over the course of historical development. In the subsequent volumes of *Capital* such assumptions are progressively relaxed. Here Marx recognizes that surplus produced is not necessarily realized, that surplus realized is not necessarily accumulated, and that prices must deviate systematically from values in order for markets to clear.[33]

---

[29] Marx describes the lengthening of the working day as an increase in "absolute surplus value" and an increase in productivity as an increase in "relative surplus value." Because of the obvious natural limit on the length the working day, Marx attached far more importance to the concept of relative surplus value. See *Capital*, vol. I, part 4.

[30] This explains, as we shall see, why the rate of exploitation of labor (s/v) can increase, even as the average rate of profit ($s/c+v$) tends to decline. See, generally, ibid., vol. I, ch. 25 and chs 12–17. Cf. vol. III, chs 13–15.

[31] Which, however, begins with direct coercion. See ibid., vol. I, part. 8 ("So-Called Primitive Accumulation").

[32] Ibid., vol. I, p. 929. Cf. the "stationary state" of Smith and Ricardo.

[33] Marx acknowledges this simplifying assumption in various ways throughout volume I, e.g. at p. 269, n. 24. Note that in a capitalist market economy based on equal exchange there would be no crises within capital itself, but only the general contradiction between the logic of capitalist expansion and the need of capital to

These more realistic assumptions change the significance of volume I's abstract materialist vision of the birth, development, and death of capitalism. Instead of stressing the fundamental conflict between wage labor and capital, the historical focus of volumes II and III is on how the development of capitalism produces conflicts among capitalists themselves. The story here is not just one of the historically cumulative power of capital to create a labor force, but of its growing internal conflicts in the course of reproducing the conditions of its own success on an ever-expanding scale.

These conflicts occur on two levels. The first level has to do with the changing proportional balance in the physical outputs of the capital-goods and wage-goods industries required for the economy to reproduce itself on an expanded scale. Marx gives a detailed account of these problems in the management of aggregate demand and capital formation in volume II. The second level of conflict has to do with the existence of capitals with heterogeneous organic compositions in the same cycle of production – the subject of volume III.

In volume III Marx stressed that the products of heterogeneous capitals *cannot* in general exchange in proportion to their embodied labor values.[34] Anticipating later criticisms of Smith and Ricardo, he argued that:

1   if the relative *values* of commodities are proportional to the share of the socially necessary labor time that goes into their current production,
2   if the relative *costs* of producing commodities on the market are proportional to the average purchase price of labor *plus* materials (and rent), and
3   if competition in capital markets requires that the investor receive an average rate of profit based on his total production *costs*, then

---

reproduce both its labor force and its markets for the next round of production. Cf. *Capital*, vol. I, Part 7, intro., and *Theories of Surplus Value*, part 2, p. 513. See also Luxemburg, *The Accumulation of Capital*.

[34] If capital is allowed to flow freely to its most profitable use, Marx observed that the capital market will drive all rates of profit toward their social average ($s/c+v$), while allowing the organic composition of different capitals (c/v) to diverge from their social average. There will, thus, be a strong tendency toward a uniform rate of profit for capitals of different organic compositions. The equalization of the rate of profit among heterogeneous capitals requires that the relative prices at which commodities sell will diverge from the relative proportions of the social division of labor that went into the production of those commodities in the current cycle – if only because the working of capital markets makes the price of each commodity reflect the relative share of accumulated value that is passed through the production process. See *Capital* vol. III, part 2.

4   the exchange *values* of different commodities cannot be proportional to their relative market prices, unless current labor forms an identical share in the production costs on which the average rate of profit is figured;[35]
5   there is, however, no mechanism in classical economics that would lead one to expect that the proportion of labor costs to total costs would be identical in all spheres of production;
6   therefore things produced for a profit will not exchange on the market in proportion to the social labor embodied in their production.[36]

Two concepts of exploitation

The argument of volume II and III severely complicates the conclusions of volume I in ways that Marx never directly addressed. In volume I Marx proposed two main measures of the rate of exploitation (s/v) in capitalist economies. In the first measure v is based on the labor value of the money wage. Under this measure we would calculate the social rate of exploitation (s/v) as the ratio between the non-wage and wage portion of value added to the economy by a given unit of labor time.[37] In the second measure of exploitation the wage portion of value added (v) is equivalent to the labor value of what the worker can purchase with his wage.[38] Under this measure we would calculate the social rate of exploitation (s/v) as the ratio between unpaid labor time appropriated by the capitalist and the socially necessary labor time needed to produce the consumer goods purchased by the worker.[39] Marx used these two measures of exploitation interchangeably in volume I,[40] arguing explicitly that both techniques for

[35] See, Marx, *Theories of Surplus Value*, esp. part 2, ch. 10. Cf. *Capital*, vol. III, chs 1–3, 48; and vol. II, chs 1–4, 20–21.
[36] See e.g., Marx, *Theories of Surplus Value*, part 2, ch. 17; *Capital*, vol. III, part 7.
[37] For a lucid elaboration of this approach see Foley, *Understanding 'Capital,'* chs 2–3.
[38] This measure of v relates to what economists call the "real wage" – the rate of exchange between an hour of work and a physical quantity of consumer goods. The economist's "real wage," however, is an index of the worker's power to purchase goods at their market prices – not at their labor values. Unlike Marx, I believe that in the second formula for the rate of exploitation v should be based on the market prices workers must actually pay (the "real wage") rather than on hypothetical labor values.
[39] For a lucid elaboration of this approach see Roemer, *Free to Lose*, e.g. p. 20.
[40] Cf. *Capital*, ch. 6 and chs 19–22.

measuring the rate of exploitation are equivalent under the assumptions of homogeneous capital and labor.[41] As soon as the special assumptions of volume I are relaxed, however, these two measures of exploitation must diverge in ways that Marx himself did not seem to recognize.

We must here pause to trace the origin of this divergence — which will play a central role in my reinterpretation of political materialism. Even under the assumptions of volume I, Marx acknowledges that rising exploitation does not require a decline in real income. Marx's theory implies rather that if the productivity of labor rises fast enough, the physical size of the worker's consumption basket might increase even though a smaller portion of his working day is required to replace the labor time required to produce the goods that he consumes. In volume II Marx suggests that the productivity of labor can differ between the consumer-goods and the producer-goods industries.[42] This suggestion opens the possibility that the labor time required to produce a unit of essential consumer goods may decline more quickly than the social average — as when technological improvements in agriculture produced a decline in the labor value of food (and a rise in the working-class standard of living) that would have been unimaginable to Marx. In volume III Marx further stresses, as we have seen, that goods do not exchange in the market in proportion to the labor required to produce them. According to this argument, wage goods may actually be sold to the worker above or below their proportional value (measured in socially necessary labor time) — while still yielding an average rate of profit to the capitalist. The effect of different compositions of capital is compounded by changes in the value of money itself, whether as a result of inflation/deflation or of international trade.[43]

[41] In *Capital*, vol. I, ch. 18 ("Different Formulae for the Rate of Surplus Value"), Marx explicitly uses money wages and socially necessary labor as alternative formulations of the concept of variable capital. Marx says, e.g., "The capitalist pays the value of the labour-power itself (or, if the price diverges from this, he pays the price) and receives in exchange the right to dispose of the living labour-power itself." (Ibid., p. 671.) In the light of volume III (which Marx had already drafted), such statements are genuinely confusing. Some of this confusion results from Marx's desire to both criticize and transcend Adam Smith's view of value as both the quantity of labor embodied in a product and the quantity of labor commanded by it. See Adam Smith, *The Wealth of Nations*, chs 7, 8. Marx attempts to address the issues raised by Smith's dual definition of value in various texts, e.g. *Capital*, vol. I, p. 173f., vol. II, pp. 285, 302–3; vol. III, chs 14–15, 37, 49–51, and esp. p. 978; and *Theories of Surplus Value*, part 1, ch. 3.

[42] Technically, this is a difference in what Marx terms the "composition of capital" ($c/c+v$).

[43] For tantalizing suggestions along these lines see *Capital*, vol. I, ch. 22.

Once we incorporate the arguments of volumes II and III into the analysis of exploitation in volume I, we can see that the proportion of the working day required to reimburse the capitalist's expenditure on the money wage is no longer identical to the number of man-hours required to replace what the average worker consumes. Measuring the changing rate of exploitation using the labor value of money would focus on the fraction of the value added to the economy by an average unit of productive labor time that the worker actually receives in wages.[44] Measuring the changing rate of exploitation using the labor value of wage goods would focus on the fraction of the labor force employed in the wage goods sector.

These two measures do not necessarily covary – the relative levels of employment in the production of capital and wage goods do not predictably rise and fall in direct proportion to changes in the average value that the employment of a unit of labor power adds to the national income. In the one measure the level of exploitation would fluctuate with the average productivity of a dollar invested in labor – the changing labor value of money; in the other measure the level of exploitation would fluctuate with the relative productivity of the producer and consumer goods sectors, with the divergence between the price and value of wage goods in the market, and with the changing purchasing power of money in the consumer goods sector.

By sharply distinguishing between the two possible ways of describing the value of the money wage we can potentially combine the virtues of both of Marx's approaches to exploitation. Focusing on the labor value of the money wage reveals the proportion of the worker's time directly appropriated by the capitalist in the process of production. Focusing on the labor value of the commodities the worker can purchase (or more appropriately on the real wage) reveals the effect on exploitation of unequal exchange – the deviation of prices from labor values.[45] In grounding the

[44] Technically, one could multiply the money wage by the labor *value* of money – the (fractional) hours of national employment represented by each dollar of national income. The result would be a pure fraction representing the amount of social labor the worker receives for each hour he works. See Foley, *Understanding 'Capital,'* p. 36 and *Money, Accumulation, and Crisis*, pp. 6–10.

[45] According to some writers, the paradigm of exploitation lies in Marx's description of the relation between capital-intensive and labor-intensive industries both at home and abroad. In this view the exploitation of the worker by the capitalist would be a special case of unequal exchange, such as that which occurs in neocolonial relations of trade. See Amin, *Unequal Development*, and Emmanuel, *Unequal Exchange*. For a discussion of these works in relation to other views see Brewer, *Marxist Theories of Imperialism*. For Marx's own discussion of unequal exchange between capital- and labor-intensive industries see, esp., *Theories of Surplus Value*, part 2, chs 10, 15–16. Cf. *Capital*, vol. III, ch. 1.

measure of exploitation on the disparity between two aspects of the money wage, I am attempting to find the intersection between the 'productionist' emphasis on the labor process and the 'exchangist'[46] emphasis on the realization process: productionism is reflected in the relation of the value of the money supply to the aggregate level of productive employment; exchangism is reflected in the value of the commodities that the worker can purchase with the money he receives. Although I believe that the labor value of the money wage is more useful than the real wage in setting the baseline for differential rates of exploitation in different economic sectors, I shall tentatively suggest that the degree of disparity and convergence between the two measures might prove useful in Marxian political analysis. My argument on this latter point, although directly critical of Marx, will also be a kind of homage insofar as I am carrying forward his method of critique. We shall see in essence that Marx implicitly gives two disparate pictures of capitalism − each a partial reflection of the other − and that the apparent contradictions between them might yet provide a useful framework for political analysis. Before proceeding with this argument, however, we must return to Marx's theory of surplus value from the perspective of the whole of *Capital*.

The critical theory of income accounting

Marx developed his theory of surplus value to explain how, at the level of the economy as a whole, capital can continually create new value through the circulation of commodities. The general form of the theory of surplus value is introduced in volume I to express the macroeconomic components of continuous growth in a market mode of production. In the subsequent volumes the theory of surplus value is elaborated to express the problems that result from realizing that growth in the market price of commodities, and accumulating it in the market price of capital.

Marx's formula for surplus value is notoriously ill-adapted to the categories of modern neo-classical economics because − like Smith and Ricardo before him − Marx does not distinguish between what we would now consider the micro- and macroeconomic aspects of his project. For this reason modern commentators seem to be uncertain as to whether Marx would see his theory as a competitor to modern notions of price (which are based on the equilibrium of marginal utilities and costs) or to modern notions of growth (which deal in terms of relations among aggregates included in national income accounting). If Marx's theory of surplus value

[46] This distinction derives from Baudrillard, *The Mirror of Production*.

is presented as an alternative to the theory of price at the microeconomic level, economists can plausibly question the advantage of using a shadow system of economic measurement based on labor-time, which may prove to be wholly independent of observable prices denominated in money. If Marx's theory is a competitor to the notion of "value-added" commonly used in public finance and national income accounting, then one may reasonably ask why the unit of account should be based on man-hours rather than money prices.

I believe, however, that in its underlying conception Marx's theory of surplus value is usefully orthogonal to the distinction between macro- and microeconomics that prevails in present-day theorizing. To translate Marx's seemingly anachronistic framework into modern terms we must recognize that a Marxian discipline in economic theorizing today does not consist of disregarding money values, but rather of using the ratio between the aggregate monetary value of the national product and the total hours of paid productive labor[47] to analyze the ways in which costs are actually accounted in order for markets to clear at the microeconomic level. This suggests a simple approach to measuring the value of abstract, simple, socially necessary labor[48] for purposes of economic analysis: we can simply divide the money value of NNP (total value added net of depreciation)[49] by the total number of paid hours of productive labor[50] —

[47] I here follow Foley, *Money, Accumulation, and Crisis.*

[48] For an account of these concepts see Rubin, *Essays on Marx's Theory of Value*, chs 8–9, 13–16.

[49] The Net National Product includes both wage goods and the investment of new capital in the 'end products' of the production cycle. Yet it excludes the portion of the total prices of all goods and services sold in the process of production that simply preserve and pass on the value of existing capital, as well as the proportion of gross investment required to offset depreciation. The latter is added back in computations of Gross National Product. See Samuelson, *Economics*, ch. 10.

[50] A useful discussion of productive labor for this purpose can be found in Fine and Harris, *Rereading 'Capital.'* In my current thinking about this subject, however, I am uncertain as to how far the 'value-added' approach to the theory of surplus value affects the relevance of recent Marxist debates about productive and unproductive labor — particularly in regard to the growth of the service sector. Although there is surely a continuing need to distinguish between surplus-producing and surplus-absorbing activities, I am no longer sure what to make of the distinction between productive labor and necessary unproductive labor within the theory of surplus value as restated above. (For a discussion of this issue in the context of economic planning in the welfare state see Gough, "Productive and Unproductive Labour in Marx.")

assuming *ex hypothesi* that every hour of productive labor is of equal value for this purpose. The result of such a calculation will be a magnitude of the average *money value of labor* for the entire economy — measured in a particular currency (such as dollars/hour) — and reflecting only the aggregate value added in the current cycle of production, the total social labor time, and the money supply.[51]

By taking the reciprocal of the money value of labor, we can derive the *labor value of money* (man-hours/dollar) which can be used to express the macroeconomic significance ("value") of the worker's wage as a capital investment, taking account of the current state of the money supply and productive technology. This "wages" approach to the value of labor power has the advantage of leaving open for investigation the separate question of the real purchasing power of the wage — whether the worker is able to buy wage goods in the market above or below their value.[52] The *surplus* for the economy as a whole would simply be the difference between the money value of the social wage and the total value added (NNP) in each production cycle. Assuming that modern price theory provides an adequate account of the ratios at which commodities must exchange, we can expect the portion of the total social surplus realized in the sale of a given commodity to deviate significantly from the portion of the total social

[51] The formulations above, and in the following paragraph, are based on Foley, *Understanding 'Capital'* and *Money, Accumulation, and Crisis*. Unlike Foley, however, I shall argue that there are at least three possible points to performing such a calculation. (1) By comparing the social value of an hour of labor (its average productivity) with the price of labor (the wage) we can measure the average rate of exploitation at a given level of output and prices. This was Marx's main concern. (2) We can measure deviations from the average rate of exploitation as the social surplus is redistributed from product to product through the price system. (As we shall see, Marx himself did not notice the importance — or even the possibility — of unequal rates of exploitation.) (3) We can calculate the changing relationship between the social labor time represented by the money the worker earns and what mainstream economists call his "real wage" — the time he must work to purchase a fixed quantity of wage goods. This allows us to discuss, as Marx did not, the effect on the worker's standard of living when wage goods are sold above or below their value, and the differential effect of inflation in the prices of wage and capital goods on both the standard of living and the rate of exploitation. Points (2) and (3) will be particularly important when we take notice of the effect of international flows of commodities, capital, and money on the rates of exploitation and standards of living in different countries.

[52] We shall take up this question in chapter 12, below.

labor time absorbed in the production of that commodity.[53]

Marx's approach to surplus value, as interpreted above, is a critical theory of income *accounting* that directly relates the monetary value of the national product to the levels of (productive) employment in each 'industry.'[54] Marx presupposes, virtually as a matter of accounting convention, that surplus value in his sense is both transformed and conserved in the market. By "transformation" of surplus value I mean that surplus value created ("valorized") in the production of one commodity will often be "realized" in the sale of another commodity, and that the surplus value thus realized will often be "accumulated" through investment in yet another commodity. (For example, value produced by industrial labor may be realized in the high price of crude oil and invested in real estate.) By "conservation" of surplus value I mean that in a closed economy (such as

---

[53] We shall not here explore, as an alternative approach, the use of mathematical techniques to measure the total output of society using labor inputs. Such techniques have been developed by Sraffa, Leontief, Morishima, Steedman, etc., and hold considerable interest for those wishing to attack the dominance of ideas based on marginal utility in modern economic analysis. The essence of such arguments is to hold the *real wage* constant as measured in a standard physical quantity of consumption goods.

The approach endorsed here (after Foley) starts and ends with the money economy, and measures the difference between the money value of the hourly wage and the value added by an hour of labor. Under this approach it is entirely possible that the labor value of the real wage will not be proportional to the labor value of the money wage. One practical advantage of Foley's approach is that workers receiving the basic wage can be described as exploited because of the ratio between the value of their pay and the social value of their labor time − even if their labor time is not employed in activities that create surplus value.

Cf. Foley, *Understanding 'Capital,'* ch. 6; Samuelson, "Understanding the Marxian Notion of Exploitation." Note that Samuelson, replying to criticism of that essay, attempts to demonstrate that within the Marxian framework of volume III real wages could be expected to rise as profits decline, notwithstanding Marx's extrapolations in volume I regarding the growing immiseration of labor. See Samuelson, "The Economics of Marx: An Ecumenical Reply," p. 280. (These points are anticipated in Samuelson's early essay, "Wages and Interest: A Modern Dissection of Marxian Economic Models," pp. 349−52, and developed further in "Marx without Matrices.")

[54] In the sentence above, "industry" does not refer to a firm, but rather to a competitive location in the social division of labor. Although the rubber industry, the steel industry, and the auto industry presently remain a major focus for large corporate firms that compete over their entire product line, the production of telephones and radios would constitute separate "industries" in the sense employed above, even though both commodities may be products of large industrial conglom-

the world economy) the total surplus value will be necessarily equal to the difference between the total monetary value of the net product and the total wages paid for productive labor.

Marx's use of the theory of surplus value to account for income flow in the current cycle of production directs our attention to the way in which the economy as a material process must always function as a social division of labor, notwithstanding the effects of accumulated capital on the proportions in which things actually exchange. Such an approach allows us to express, at least hypothetically, the proportion of aggregate economic growth that can be attributed to the production of each commodity before the abstract value added to the economy is systematically redistributed by the price system.

What I am calling Marx's "critical theory of accounting" is the economic counterpart to the "critical theory of democracy" described in part II as the Marxian alternative to the Hegelian theory of the state. Just as Marx used the critical theory of democracy to assess the differential impact of policies and regimes on their constituent groups, I am suggesting that he also used his theory of surplus value to focus on how changes in the market relations between things effectively redistribute social power and advantage among the persons who depend upon producing or consuming those things. Like the critical theory of democracy, the critical theory of income accounting represents society as divided twice over — as a relation between the market prices of commodities, and as a relation between the persons supported by producing those commodities. Marx's critical theory of income accounting — complementing his view of democracy — can give us a politically relevant perspective on the economic impact of public policy within civil society that is different from the perspective of the state itself, and that provides significant insight into how political identities are formed around economic interests.

In my view Marx's theory of surplus value is not a method of economic calculation that (for better or worse) is wholly autonomous from the price system, but rather a basis for performing a political critique of the system of prices necessary for markets to clear — regardless of whether those prices are explained in classical or neo-classical terms. By recognizing that Marxian categories apply critically at the level of income accounting — for the firm, the household, and the nation — we can use Marx's method to assess the demographic (and hence political) significance of what happens when markets clear, both at the level of price equilibrium and at the level of general equilibrium between the marginal rates of saving and investment.[55]

---

erates that are not direct competitors in many of their activities.

[55] Although I was not aware of their work in earlier drafts of this approach to *Capital*,

Accounting for surplus value

Viewed as an approach to income accounting, Marx's theory of surplus value begins by abstracting from the heterogeneity of commodities and capitals and divides the 'national product,' viewed as a single commodity, into three distinct components.

1 Marx referred to the value of the invested capital that is simply preserved in the production of the commodity as "constant capital" (c), in order to distinguish it from value added.
2 Marx referred to the part of value added that the capitalist pays out in current wages as variable capital (v).
3 The accounting difference between the net value added to the national product in the production of the commodity and the cost of the capitalist's investment in materials, fixed capital, and wages $(c + v)$ is the "surplus" value itself (s).

Let us suppose that an employee puts nuts and bolts together so that his employer can sell the assembled product. From the standpoint of the individual employer the initial purchase of the unassembled parts is a cost, a part of his total investment on which he must expect to make a profit. From the standpoint of the economy as a whole, however, the money the employer spends on nuts and bolts does not produce added value – it rather preserves old value.[56] The constant capital that passes through the production process will appear over and over again as an investment in new production in the accounts of each individual capitalist; but in the accounting of national income constant capital will appear in each stage of production, not as value added in the production process, but only as value preserved.[57]

---

the writings of Foley and Lipietz bear a strong affinity to my argument, and have helped me to clarify the final draft. See Foley, *Understanding 'Capital,'* and Lipietz, *The Enchanted World.* Foley mentions (p. 69) similarities between the Marxian reproduction schemes and basic accounting conventions – a point anticipated in Paul Sweezy's exposition of the resemblance between the Marxian formula for surplus value and the main categories of corporate and national income accounting. See Sweezy *The Theory of Capitalist Development*, p. 63. See, generally, Foley, *Money, Accumulation and Crisis*, pp. 6–14, and *Understanding 'Capital,'* chs 3–5.
[56] Stated in Marx's technical vocabulary the transaction either realizes value that has been previously created or accumulates value that has already been realized.
[57] This point of view was confirmed in the theory of national income accounting and

Variable capital represents the capitalist's wage bill as an investment that will be returned to him when the commodity is sold. Unlike his investment in raw materials (a major component of constant capital) that must rise in direct proportion to the amount that he produces,[58] the capitalist's investment in wages can be seen as "variable" because "[it] both reproduces the equivalent of its own value and produces an excess, a surplus value, which may itself vary, and be more or less according to circumstances."[59]

This statement can be misleading. According to Marx, the total value added at each stage of production (or in each period of national income accounting) depends upon how efficiently the capitalist uses the labor power he purchases while passing through his costs in fixed capital, materials, and wages. The fact that value added will in the general case exceed these fixed costs by a variable amount led Marx to conclude that, unlike constant capital, the value of labor power is variable inasmuch as it is worth more to the capitalist ($v + s$) than it is to the worker (v). Recent writers have pointed out, however, that the same 'variability' might be imputed to constant capital which, as a "value in process," might be said to be worth more at the end of a production cycle than at the beginning. As accountants, we might impute such a transformation to a rise in the replacement cost of inventory (using LIFO); as economists we might argue tendentiously that money invested in raw materials has the same capacity to expand in value that Marx ascribed to money invested in wages.[60]

The largely metaphorical character of Marx's description of variable capital as "self-expanding" does not pose serious difficulty for the description of surplus value given here. We distinguished the value of c and v largely for the purpose of isolating the surplus — which Marx saw as that part of the national product that is redistributed in the transformations of the relative values of commodities through which markets eventually clear. Even if we do not place much weight on the designation of v as "variable"

---

growth principally developed by Simon Kuznets. See, e.g., Kuznets *Modern Economic Growth*. On the difficulties the classical economists had in accounting for constant capital in their theory of natural price see Wolff, *Understanding Marx*, chs 1–3.

[58] I here leave aside the effects of waste reduction, etc., as a way of economizing on the use of constant capital.

[59] Marx *Capital*, vol. I, p. 317.

[60] John Roemer argues forcefully that there is nothing special about labor power in the theory of surplus value; technically, constant capital is also 'exploited' in the production process insofar as a surplus is produced. See Roemer *A General Theory of Exploitation and Class*, ch. 6, and "Should Marxists be Interested in Exploitation."

capital, from the standpoint of our critical theory of accounting we will need to distinguish between intermediate product on the one hand, and the wage and non-wage components of national income on the other. Our purpose in performing such an analysis is not to discover again and again the factor of production that *causes* the surplus,[61] but, rather, to critically redescribe the price system – a set of economic relations among things – as also a political relation among the persons who depend for their employment upon producing those things.[62]

The analytical framework of volume III[63] allows Marx to express the notion that some commodities may contribute to the surplus produced in the economy, even when they are not produced at a profit, while other commodities may allow their sellers to realize a profit substantially in excess of the social surplus created in their production. Surplus value is, from a Marxian perspective, the core of microeconomics when seen from a macroeconomic point of view.[64] Because of the divergence of price and value, the total amount of surplus produced in a single enterprise or industrial sphere appears only at the level of the economy viewed as a whole, and only from the point of view of all investors seen as a class. Marx believed, however, that in the process of circulation, surplus value may come to be distributed variously in the form of rents and interest (and perhaps in tax benefits for excess depreciation) – which appear in the accounts of the individual entrepreneur as costs. The entrepreneur's individual profit is thus only a component of the surplus that he produces

[61] Many Marxist scholars who resist viewing the surplus as a joint product of constant and variable capital nevertheless persist in suspecting that labor power that is not employed in the conversion of raw materials is, prima facie, unproductive. See, e.g., Baran and Sweezy, *Monopoly Capital*.

[62] Marx expresses a similar viewpoint when he says: "The historical conditions ... [for the existence of capital] ... are by no means given with the mere circulation of money and commodities. It arises only when the owner of the means of production and subsistence finds the free worker available, on the market, as the seller of his own labour-power. And this one historical pre-condition comprises a world's history." (*Capital*, vol. I, p. 274.)

[63] See also Marx, *Theories of Surplus Value*, part 2. Although these works were published posthumously, they were in fact composed before the final draft of volume I – which makes repeated mention of the simplifying assumptions that allow the micro- and macroeconomic perspectives to be collapsed into one. See, e.g., *Capital*, vol. I, p. 269.

[64] See esp. Marx, *Capital*, vol. I, parts 3–5. See, generally, Marx, *Theories of Surplus Value*, esp. part 2. For a non-Marxist effort to discuss microeconomics from a macroeconomic point of view see Okun, *Prices and Quantities*.

(although it may be augmented by any previously unrealized surplus deriving from other commodities that he realizes in the sale price of his commodity).

The components in the value that a given commodity contributes to the social product as a whole are expressed by Marx in the formula $(c+v+s)$ — suggesting that the existence of an economic surplus is necessary for even the simple reproduction of the system. By building the basis for systemic growth into his initial description of the capitalist economy as a whole, Marx is able to describe how it is possible for such an economy to reproduce itself through the operation of capital and commodity markets, while at the same time transforming the conditions under which it does so. These transformations are the necessary results of the way in which the market system must redistribute value between commodities in the course of reproducing itself on an expanded scale. Marx's argument in *Capital*, volume I is intended to show only how it is possible for capitalism to work as an engine of social growth and transformation, albeit in a way that is ultimately doomed to destroy its own conditions of success in reproducing the relation of wage labor and capital. In the remaining volumes he is concerned with the ways in which the equilibrating functions of commodity and capital markets introduce divisions between different capitals in the process of displacing surplus value from one to another.[65]

The reader should be warned that my approach to this issue, while not entirely novel, is unusual. Given the notorious difficulties posed by *Capital*, volume III, many would-be Marxist economists have despaired of beginning with value and ending with price (the so-called "transformation problem") or of beginning with price and ending with value (the "inverse transformation problem.")[66] As a result of the generally acknowledged difficulties in Marx's own solution to the transformation problem[67] recent work in Marxian economics has tended to divide — like its mainstream rivals — between macroeconomic and microeconomic variants.

[65] Such divisions within capital, and their effect on its underlying relation with wage labor, make the continuing success of a capitalism that has not run its course seem less automatic. For our present purpose, however, it is necessary only to see how Marx's framework for analyzing surplus value leaves room for these historical possibilities.

[66] For a useful survey see Samuelson, "Understanding the Marxian Notion of Exploitation." Cf. Foley, "The Value of Money, the Value of Labor Power, and the Marxian Transformation Problem."

[67] These difficulties have been generally acknowledged since Bortkiewicz first pointed them out. A clear statement of the central issue can be found in Sweezy, *The Theory of Capitalist Development*, ch. 7. For recent discussions see, e.g., Foley, *Understanding 'Capital,'* ch. 6, and Wolff, *Understanding Marx*, chs 5−6. See also, Marx, *Capital*, vol. iii, chs 8−10.

Macroeconomic Marxism is represented by such writers as Baran and Sweezy.[68] In their restatement of Marx the formula $(c+v+s)$ refers to the composition of the national product rather than the relative values at which individual commodities are exchanged on the market. By taking a highly restrictive view of what constitutes investment in productive labor and a consequently expansive view of the surplus-producing power of modern productive processes, they are able to describe the major macroeconomic problem of late capitalism as the absorption of excess surplus. In this they do not differ much from maverick liberal economists[69] except insofar as their Marxist roots lead them to place a growing majority of wage earners on the side of those who live off the surplus rather than produce it.[70]

Microeconomic Marxism is more recent, and more diverse. One strand – typified by the neo-Ricardians centered in Cambridge, England[71] – seeks to develop a microeconomic algebra of price based on either physical inputs or "dated labor time" that can serve as an alternative to marginalist theories of the pricing of capital and labor in the production function. Another strand is typified by American economists, such as Roemer,[72] who would deny that Marxism provides a basis for any *methodological* critique of mainstream economics, but who believe that politically important Marxist theorems can be proven using unimpeachable modern techniques. Both of these strands are alike in rejecting the significance of a critical distinction between value and price.

My suggested approach – the critical theory of income accounting – attempts to sidestep the problem of translating between monetary and physical measures of value, while preserving the point of Marx's own desire to distinguish value from market price. Instead of attempting to algebraically transform dollars into pure labor power or pure labor power into dollars, I would begin and end with the monetary values of commodities. These monetary values would, however, be measured in two ways: (1) in

---

[68] See Baran and Sweezy, *Monopoly Capital*; Baran, *The Political Economy of Growth*. Foley's approach is also explicitly macroeconomic. See Foley, *Money, Accumulation and Crisis*, pp. 1–6.

[69] See, e.g., Galbraith, *The New Industrial State*.

[70] If many proletarians are engaged in surplus-absorbing labor, they would seem to share important interests with the bourgeoisie who live off surplus value that they do not produce. Thus, the argument that a majority of wage laborers are not exploited in Marx's sense would seem to offer, at least implicitly, an explanation of the absence of overt class war in advanced capitalism.

[71] See, e.g., Steedman, *Marx After Sraffa*.

[72] See Roemer, *Analytical Foundations of Marxian Economic Theory*.

relation to what proportion of aggregate value added is attributable to the commodity; and (2) in relation to what proportion of aggregate employment is attributable to the commodity. Comparing these magnitudes would measure the effect of the relative values accumulated in the prices of commodities on the political relations among interest groups engaged in democratic politics.

Reading *Capital* backwards

My reconstruction of Marx's argument suggests that, were it not for major difficulties in terminology and exposition, *Capital* could be read most profitably in reverse order, beginning with *Theories of Surplus Value*,[73] and moving backwards from volume III of *Capital* to the discussion of the commodity form in volume I. In pursuing this path we would both begin and end with the phenomenology of the market as a system of exchange in which values are accumulated after being realized in the relatively inflated or deflated prices of certain assets.[74] By the time we reached the beginning of volume I the underlying structure of the market system would have been revealed through the materialist analysis of the ways in which revenues must be distributed if the process of production is to be controlled by capital markets. Although I do not here propose to follow such a path through the labyrinth of *Capital*, I can attempt to summarize the main lessons we might learn from reading *Capital* backwards.

The first lesson is that, although the general formula for surplus value expresses the fundamental unity of capital in relation to wage labor, the displacement of surplus value through the price system reflects divisions within capital. By reading the volumes in reverse order we would encounter the direct conflict between capital and wage labor in volume I only after reading about the various conflicts that occur within capital.[75] As suggested in the previous chapters, political struggles over state policies are frequently an expression of conflicts within capital.

The second lesson we would learn from reading *Capital* in reverse order

---

[73] *Theories of Surplus Value* should be read from part 2, ch. 17 in more or less reverse order through the discussion of productive and unproductive labor at the beginning of part 1.

[74] Cf. Lipietz, *The Enchanted World*.

[75] These conflicts may be between what Marx called (in volume II) the two "Departments" of production – the capital goods and the consumer goods industries; they may be conflicts among the various industries in each Department; or they may be competitive conflicts within industries.

is that we should pay close attention to disproportionalities between the valorization of surplus in production, the realization of surplus in sale, and the accumulation of surplus in investment. In the economy as a whole Marx clearly thought that cumulative lags and gaps in the process of expanded reproduction lead to periodic crises of overproduction, under-consumption, or underinvestment.[76] Marx also believed, however, that it is normal under capitalism for the same commodity to represent different proportions of the total surplus as it passes through the stages of production, realization, and accumulation.[77]

A third lesson is that the combined effects of unequal rates of exploitation and an equalizing rate of profit mean that, as a general matter, part of the surplus value created in the more labor-intensive processes of production will tend to be realized in the market price of goods created in the more capital-intensive processes of production. The former will tend to be sold below their value; the latter will tend to be sold above their value − a point that Marx developed at length in the writings eventually published as *Capital*, volume III and *Theories of Surplus Value*, part 2.

There are, however, two further complications related to this insight, which Marx did not address. The first is that the deviation of price from value − although grounded in different organic compositions of capital (c/v) − may also have a differential effect on the prices of wage goods and capital goods. As we shall see, Marx's account of surplus value is consistent with the possibility that in some national economies wage goods may be sold below their value and that investment goods may be sold above their value − allowing workers to reach a relatively high standard of living without ever coming close to being capitalists. The second complication concerns the possibility that under the conditions described in volume III

---

[76] For an analytical reconstruction of his arguments see Foley, *Understanding 'Capital,'* chs 5 and 9, and *Money, Accumulation, and Crisis*. See also O'Connor, *Accumulation Crisis*, chs 3−7, *The Fiscal Crisis of the State*, and "The Meaning of Crisis."

The reader should note, however, that my argument above (and in the following chapter) does not presuppose that capitalism will die prematurely of pathological causes, such as crises, rather than as a consequence of its 'normal' course of development; nor does my argument stress the pathological forms of capitalist "underdevelopment," rather than the problems arising out of the supposedly normal forms of capitalist development. In choosing these emphases I once again follow Marx's own example.

[77] For example, a given commodity, such as a gourmet delicacy, may sell for more than the value of the labor used to produce it, and yet have little value as a capital investment for the end-purchaser.

the rate of surplus extraction might prove to be markedly different in different industries – suggesting that there might be a continuum rather than a sharp distinction between the employment of labor to produce surplus and the employment of labor to absorb it.[78] Is Marx's overall argument in *Capital* consistent with his assumption of a uniform rate of exploitation in a capitalist economy?

Heterogeneous labor

Marx introduced the assumption of a uniform rate of exploitation in volume I as an adjunct to his argument that the historical tendency of capital intensification is to economize on labor, and hence to raise the rate of exploitation.[79] To simplify this argument, he assumed, as we have seen, that the organic composition of capital (c/v) is homogeneous throughout the economy at a given moment. On this assumption, Marx argued that labor power must also become increasingly homogeneous as competition between workers tends to result in a uniform wage and a uniform working day. He was thus able to conclude that in an economy at any historical moment the average rate of exploitation (s/v) may also be treated as a uniform rate of exploitation. If, however, we relax the assumption that the organic composition of capital is homogeneous, why must we continue to assume the existence of a homogeneous rate of exploitation of labor in all industries?

In the later volumes of *Capital* there is no mechanism that tends toward a uniform (as distinct from an average) rate of exploitation. Individual capitalists are not motivated to maximize the rate of exploitation as such, but rather to maximize their rate of profit. The competition among heterogeneous capitals that tends to equalize the rate of profit could easily allow for differential rates of surplus extraction (exploitation) in different industries. Where both mainstream and Marxist economists have traditionally argued that different wage levels between industries are explained by different skill levels among workers, we might argue instead that the

---

[78] Cf. Baran and Sweezy, *Monopoly Capital*.

[79] Although Marx's argument is highly plausible under the historical conditions specific to early capitalist development, at the level of a general theory of capital there is a possibility of "reswitching" between labor-saving and capital-saving forms of investment. See Harcourt, *Some Cambridge Controversies in the Theory of Capital*, ch. 4.

distribution of skilled and unskilled workers among industries is explained by the ability to pay different real wages.[80]

The possible need to incorporate a variable rate of exploitation into the general formula for capital coheres with recent theories of the segmentation of industrial labor markets. According to these theories different industries tend to hire from different labor pools. Although these different labor pools, like different capitals, are still subject to changes in general market conditions, they will be so to markedly different extents.[81]

We thus see a stratification of industries according to their investment structure, roughly corresponding to a stratification of the work force according to its political culture.[82] Different industries, and different firms within them, will pursue investment strategies based on their expected ability to control the price of their product over time. These strategies will determine the extent to which firms rely on stable variable (labor) or constant (capital) costs in the production process, and also the proportions in which they hire long-term, highly paid, skilled employees, or casual, poorly paid, unskilled employees.[83]

In a highly segmented labor market workers will receive very different consumption baskets, depending on the relation between external labor pools and the internal labor market of the firms that employ them. Some jobs allow workers to achieve a middle-class standard of living, and even accumulate personal savings for the purpose of future consumption during retirement. Others jobs presume that workers can partially depend upon

[80] Some parts of such an argument are anticipated, I think, in Sabel, *Work and Politics*. See also Edwards, *Contested Terrain*, and David Gordon, et al., *Segmented Work, Divided Workers*.

[81] Cf. Thurow, *Generating Inequality*, and Cain, "The Challenge of Segmented Labor Market Theories to Orthodox Theory: A Survey."

[82] See Berger and Piore, *Dualism and Discontinuity in Industrial Societies*, and Sabel, *Work and Politics*. Cf. Cain, op. cit., and Hechter, "Group Formation and the Cultural Division of Labor."

[83] According to Sabel, firms that have a highly skilled, highly paid, work force with low capital investments are most vulnerable to market fluctuations. These are typically small firms providing expensive craft skills and services that it is not worthwhile for larger firms to bring in-house. Larger firms that operate in highly fluctuating market environments tend to develop investment strategies geared to being able to lay off marginal casual employees without idling capital investments. Firms that depend upon skilled employees to run complicated machinery are generally located in markets with constant or steadily growing demand. See Sabel, *Work and Politics*, ch. 2. See also Berger and Piore, *Dualism and Discontinuity in Industrial Societies*, part I, "An Economic Approach" (Piore), pp. 13–81.

government transfer payments, public consumption, or the income of other family members.

Observers, such as Sabel, note that workers in a segmented labor market may develop systematically different career expectations, both within their firms, and between industries.[84] Some jobs create a lifelong career commitment that can only be breached at great cost to worker and employer alike. Other jobs rely on the willingness of a part of the labor force − by choice or necessity − to accept casual or part-time employment, perhaps in return for a higher short-term wage. Often these divisions in the labor force correspond to gender divisions, ethnic divisions, or recency of immigration.[85] Sometimes divisions in the labor force reflect more personal differences in choice and opportunity.

Although high wage workers in capital intensive industries are still exploited in Marxist terms − perhaps more highly − they may not feel solidarity with casual workers in service industries who receive substantially lower real wages (even if these workers are their wives). The conditions of class compromise may simply be different for industries with different capital structures, and hence different rates of exploitation.[86] And, while it would be wrong to say that the workers in different industrial sectors exploit (extract surplus value from) those in other sectors, this would be a more plausible claim about the companies for which they work, and clearly true of the capital market generally, insofar as it presupposes an unequal exchange of commodities.

Given the clear relevance of heterogeneous labor in today's capitalist economy, we must ask whether Marx was nevertheless committed to the existence of a uniform rate of exploitation throughout a given economy at a given stage of development. In his commentary on *Capital*, Paul Sweezy questions the validity of assuming a constant rate of exploitation, but views such an assumption as a harmless simplification[87] − perhaps because Sweezy recognizes that a variable rate of exploitation is unnecessary to explain the divergence of prices from values that is the main concern of Volume III.[88]

I believe, however, that although Marx occasionally acknowledged the

[84] See Sabel, *Work and Politics*.
[85] See, e.g., Hechter, "Group Formation and the Cultural Division of Labor."
[86] For discussion of class compromise see Przeworski, "Material Interests, Class Compromise, and the Transition to Socialism"; Przeworski and Michael Wallerstein, "The Structure of Class Conflict in Democratic Capitalist Societies."
[87] See Sweezy *The Theory of Capitalist Development*, p. 65.
[88] James O'Connor first pointed this out to me.

existence of variable rates of exploitation,[89] he had important reasons for not revising his theory accordingly. In order to argue that the equalization of the rate of profit requires a *transformation* of surplus value Marx wished to distinguish the surplus created in the production of a commodity from the surplus realized in its market price. Yet, unless the rate of exploitation were uniform across the economy, he had no way to isolate the surplus value (s) embodied in a single commodity without basing his calculation on its market price.

Working in the mid nineteenth century on the classical model of capitalism as it exists within a single nation-state, Marx had little practical reason to resolve this problem. He did not anticipate the role of state regulation in the management of consumer demand in national economies, and he underestimated the ability of workers to reduce wage competition through collective action − at least for so long as the effects of immigration and job exportation could be limited. Because Marx expected the growing homogeneity of capital and labor to place the perpetuation of capitalism in conflict with the needs of stable democracy, he indefinitely postponed the project of explaining the stability of capitalist democracy as a product of the fragmentation of capital and the heterogeneity of labor.[90] Yet this is clearly the situation in which we find ourselves today. Is a Marxian approach to economics still meaningful, except as a special case of capitalist development that was never typical, and is now impossible?

A Marxism for markets

I believe that Marxism can be made relevant once more by stressing the role of money in national and world economies. The labor theory of value, as I interpret it here, is an essentially political approach to the labor value of money under historically given conditions of capitalist production, and not a description of the ratios at which commodities exchange in the market. We shall here consider the significance of a Marxian approach to surplus value in the politics of national economies.

In any national economy we can divide the value added (in a given

---

[89] See, e.g., Marx, *Capital*, vol. III., p. 368.
[90] And because he shared with Smith and Ricardo the view that capitalist production occurs within national economies, Marx did not fully grasp the possibility of an international division of labor − a global market where capital, commodities, and jobs can flow freely between national economies in which the labor value of money differs widely. For further reflections on this topic, see chapter 12, below.

currency over a given period of time)[91] by the number of man-hours worked in paid productive labor, in order to derive the *average* value added to the economy per hour of labor. We would then know the average (not the marginal) productivity of labor at the relative prices that prevail under existing conditions of capital formation. By subtracting the value of money wages (v) from the total value added we could derive the surplus (s) and calculate the rate of exploitation in the production of the *average* commodity. But what is the significance of these averages for political analysis?

My tentative answer (at this point untested) is that these averages constitute a matrix for measuring the price structure of the capitalist economy against the ideal of social democracy − the mode of production viewed as a pure division of social labor to which each citizen contributes equally over the course of a lifetime. As an interpretation of Marx, this approach is based on the obvious fact that the market prices of exchange *actually do* tend to reflect the average value added of a dollar of capital. If market mechanisms are already in place to reduce deviations from the average value added by an invested dollar of capital,[92] it would seem reasonable from a political perspective to measure the effects of capital markets in amplifying deviations from the average in accounting for the value added by investing in an additional hour of labor. I believe that Marx's valid political insight in his critique of Smith and Ricardo was to transpose the labor theory of value to the level of social averages, but that he erred in attempting to complete (and not merely to criticize) the classical theory of natural prices in the market.[93]

Marx does not, however, straightforwardly give us the conceptual tools we would need to perform the type of analysis I am suggesting here. In order to meaningfully apply a value-added approach to the critique of political economy we would need to compare the ratio of value added to wages for the *average* commodity with the same ratio for *each* commodity. For this purpose we would not use the rate of exploitation (s/v), but a variant of the formula for surplus value that I believe Marx does not consider − $(s+v)/v$. In this formula the component of value added ($s+v$)

[91] In the United States we would use the net dollar value added per year − or (with suitable adjustments for trade imbalances) the NNP.

[92] In a perfect capital market any remaining deviations would simply reflect differences in risk.

[93] For an approach that stresses Marx's effort to complete the classical theory of natural price, see Wolff, *Understanding Marx*. For a viewpoint that sharply distinguishes the theoretical bases of aggregate and relative prices see Lipietz, *The Enchanted World*, and Foley, *Money, Accumulation, and Crisis*.

would be derived from the sale price of each commodity at every stage of production,[94] just as it is in the calculation of the national income as a whole. The magnitude of the markup at each point of sale would indirectly reflect the proportion of the capitalist's non-labor costs (c).[95] We would thus have a measure of how the capitalist's need to receive at least an average rate of profit on his entire investment in production $(s/c+v)$, combined with the need to pay above or below average wages, accounts for deviations from the social average in the measurement of $(s+v)/v$ for individual products.

Note that my approach to finding the variation in the rate of exploitation among different industries depends on comparing the amount that a unit of labor power adds to the *price* of the commodity to the amount that the average unit of labor power adds to the NNP. By assuming that value added is $(s+v)$ — backing out non-labor costs (c) — we have sidestepped Marx's problem of isolating (s) for each commodity. But have we successfully eliminated the problem, or have we merely located the variable rate of exploitation in the realization rather than the production of surplus value?

My approach would indeed seem to suggest that workers in industries that can overcharge for their products will (all else being equal) tend to be 'exploited' more than workers paid the same money wage in industries that undercharge. Such a possibility reflects the fact that for the individual capitalist the ability to pass through a price increase in raw materials can have the same effect as a productivity increase in reducing the proportion of his total revenue that must be paid out in wages: in either case he will be processing a higher value of constant capital for each unit of variable capital.

But should it not make a difference to the worker whether this change in the organic composition of capital in a particular industry comes from a productivity increase or merely an increase in the *price* of materials? Of course the particular means of bringing about productivity gains, such as

---

[94] We would of course deduct from the sale price the costs of materials and fixed capital that are passed through.

[95] According to Marx the average rate of markup is $s/(c+v)$ — a quantity algebraically equal to the average rate of exploitation (s/v) multiplied by the average composition of capital $v/(c+v)$. (See Foley, *Understanding 'Capital,'* p. 45.) The approach taken above does not, however, presuppose that surplus is always increased by increasing the organic composition of capital (c/v), and would thus seem to avoid the "reswitching" (or "double switching") phenomenon — a theoretical possibility that neither Marx nor classical economists seemed to anticipate. See Harcourt, *Some Cambridge Controversies in the Theory of Capital*, ch. 4.

speedups on the assembly line, are often onerous to workers in a way that the passing through of price increases is not. But at the highly general level at which we are now speaking, we must recognize that *some* productivity increases are brought about by new tools that do not make the job any harder, and that resulting price reductions can stimulate demand to a degree that allows preexisting levels of employment to be maintained or increased.

My approach to the issue of exploitation reflects Marx's own ambivalence about capitalist development. As we have seen, he clearly argues that under capitalism productivity gains necessarily increase the rate of exploitation of labor — that exploitation is highest in capital-intensive production. This argument coheres with his view of capitalist development as being good for humanity in important respects (socialism in itself but not yet for itself). Yet the foregoing argument does not cohere with Marx's apparent assumption that increased exploitation in his technical sense will necessarily be bad for the worker. I believe, however, that the latter assumption is not universally true as it applies to Marxian exploitation in the technical sense. The industries that employ a disproportionate number of workers per unit of value added are not likely for that reason alone to be more egalitarian in their distribution of revenues, nor is the standard of living enjoyed by workers in such industries necessarily higher. In today's capitalism workers in labor-intensive industries buy the products of workers of capital-intensive industries, and vice versa. The relative standard of living for workers in labor-intensive and capital-intensive forms of production will depend on how far they are paid above or below the prevailing wage, and on what they can buy with their wages. Beyond this one cannot generalize about labor-intensive production in a manner that will be equally valid for skilled craftworkers and migrant farmworkers.

The real reason that my approach may seem counterintuitive lies in the common, but false, assumption that exploitation cannot increase unless the real wage falls. Whether an increase in the nominal price of his product lowers the real income of the worker will largely depend upon the relative prices of the goods that workers buy with their wages. When world oil prices soared in the 1970s, Middle Eastern Oil workers may have been more heavily exploited in my technical sense — even though their real incomes rose strikingly because of increased wages and the increased purchasing power of the currencies in which those wages were paid. When other industries passed on these increased costs, the rate of exploitation also increased, even as real wages fell. The conservation of surplus value on a world-wide scale led to adjustments in the relative rates of exploitation in different industries through changes in the labor value of money in different countries. I take it as a virtue of my approach to capitalist exploitation that it makes visible the redistributive effects of inflation, both nationally and internationally.

The foregoing argument suggests that, especially in the context of international markets, comparative standards of living become important to the analysis of exploitation. To complete our political analysis of differential exploitation we must once again take account of the real wage, after having excluded it from our technical definition. One plausible way of doing so would be to superimpose on our account of differential exploitation based on the labor value of the money wage an account of exploitation based on the purchasing power of the money wage. The degree of disparity or convergence between these two accounts could potentially reveal something of the prospects for forging alliances between segments of the labor force – both between and within national economies.[96]

There are of course various complications that would need to be addressed before a critical theory of income accounting, such as I propose, could be carried out. In ordinary accounting practice, as I understand it, businesses tend to charge a markup on their rental expenses, but not on their interest expenses. I would probably want to consider both current rent and interest as part of the value added to the economy by each commodity, rather than viewing these as costs that are simply passed through. In taking this approach I recognize that some of the "value added" in my sense might be reflected on a business's books as costs rather than as markup. The effects of tax accounting on real and nominal production costs in countries such as the US raise further complications.[97] In general, however, my approach would allow empirical researchers to take advantage of the correspondence between the value-added statistics used in national income accounting and the figures reported to governments that collect a value-added tax.[98]

[96] For further discussion of the relevance of this argument to international markets see chapter 12, below.

[97] Although I would include a socially average rate of depreciation on fixed capital within the category of constant capital that is passed through the production process, any cash flow resulting from tax-motivated "accelerations" in the costing of depreciation in the US should probably be included in "value added," seen from a Marxian point of view. No doubt there are many such issues that would need to be addressed before my proposal could be carried out for any given country using currently available data.

[98] Being part of a long tradition of Marxian autodidacts in economics, I do not see myself as the person best equipped to test the feasibility and utility of the interpretation of Marx proposed above. (See Paul Samuelson's assessment of Marx in "Economists and the History of Ideas," pp. 1512–15. See also Robinson, *An Essay on Marxian Economics*.)

Although I venture this highly tentative reinterpretation of *Capital* partly for the purpose of stimulating further discussion among open-minded professional economists,[99] I believe that the approach taken here could have real advantages for the purpose of carrying forward the project of Marxian political analysis under conditions of advanced capitalism. The most important advantage would be to replace the emphasis on the rate of exploitation as such[100] with an emphasis on *disparities* in the rate of exploitation. By analyzing these disparities we could, perhaps, grasp the political effects of economic development in modern capitalism – a development in which surplus value tends to be more highly realized in some sectors of the economy while surplus population is more heavily absorbed in others.[101] When investment and population tend to flow in different

[99] Development economists are already concerned with the measurement of per capita NNP, and welfare economists with indices of inequality such as the Gini coefficient. (These perspectives are thoughtfully combined by Amartya Sen, e.g., in Sen, *On Economic Inequality* and *Resources, Values, and Development*, parts 4 and 5). I attempt to reconstruct a Marxian reading of economic data in the hope of stimulating economists to develop techniques of disaggregating their analysis of economic inequality. Richard Musgrave has suggested to me that a non-Marxian economist might pursue my suggestion by comparing the Gini coefficients of the value added in the production of each commodity. Such data would allow analysis of the degree to which an individual's economic interests are tied to the industry in which he shares the value added, and the degree to which his economic interests are common to those of other individuals at his income level across the society. (For Professor Musgrave's own views on these issues, see Musgrave, "Theories of Fiscal Crises: An Essay in Fiscal Sociology," esp. pp. 370–2.)

[100] From the standpoint of an idealized social democracy a high rate of exploitation (i.e. economizing on labor time) could be intrinsically desirable, provided that there were also effective social control of investment decisions and an equitable allocation of consumption decisions between the individual and the social spheres.

[101] "The same causes that have raised the productivity of labour, increased the mass of commodity products, extended markets, accelerated the accumulation of capital ... these same causes have produced ... a relative surplus population ... of workers who are not employed by this excess capital on account of the low level of exploitation of labour at which they would have to be employed, or at least on account of the low rate of profit they would yield at the given rate of exploitation.

"If capital is sent abroad, this is not because it absolutely could not be employed at home. It is rather because it can be employed abroad at a higher rate of profit. But this capital is absolutely surplus capital for the employed working population ... It exists as such alongside the relative surplus population." (Marx, *Capital*, vol. III, pp. 364–5.)

directions[102] there is a problematic relationship between capitalist development and democracy – a phenomenon we see reflected today in the simultaneous feminization of the labor force and of poverty.[103]

Although I cannot say whether my suggested reinterpretation of political materialism would produce politically interesting results, I believe that it constitutes a plausible extension of Marx's own thought. The approach presented here extrapolates heavily from passages in volume III where Marx seems to acknowledge the disparity between the two measures of exploitation that he equates in volume I.[104] In these passages I believe Marx comes close to basing a political analysis on certain aspects of this disparity – superimposing the conception of exploitation based on the paid and unpaid portion of the economic value added by an average unit of labor on the conception of exploitation based on changes in the proportion of aggregate social labor time that goes into producing consumer goods. Marx steps back from such an approach for a variety of reasons – some related to the state of capitalist development in his time, some to the problems in his view of the relations of prices to value. In the foregoing proposal I have attempted to generalize Marx's approach to analyzing the *changes* in the pattern of capitalist exploitation – focusing on the disproportionate realization of the surplus in some products, and the disproportionate numbers of workers employed in producing others. My account of class and exploitation would direct our attention to the distortions and imbalances between the rise and fall in the relative prices of commodities and the rise and fall of employment in the production of those commodities. If the details of such an analysis could be worked out, we would have a powerful tool for assessing the differential effects of economic change on the identities though which populations participate in politics – effects that could be measured against the matrix of an ideal social democracy based on the equalization of value added for analytical purposes.

[102] "The increase in the absolute number of workers, despite the relative decline in the variable capital laid out on wages, does not take place in all branches of production, and does not take place evenly in the branches where it does. In agriculture, the decline in the element of living labour may be absolute." (Ibid., vol. III, p. 372; cf. vol. I, ch. 25, secs 3–4.)

[103] See chapter 10, above.

[104] See esp. Marx, *Capital*, vol. III, ch. 15. E.g. (p. 368) "Since the development of labour productivity is far from uniform in the various branches of industry and, besides being uneven in degree, often takes place in opposite directions, it so happens that the mass of ... surplus value ... is necessarily very far below the level one would expect simply from the development of productivity in the most advanced branches."

As an approach to analyzing modern politics,[105] my reading of *Capital* draws heavily on Marx's conception of capitalism as a form of socialism "in itself" – an idealized expansion of the social division of labor.[106] In taking this approach I set myself apart – I think in distinctively Marxian ways – from other approaches to analyzing exploitation in capitalist market economies. Above all, I would distinguish my approach from the discredited approach of international Communism, which claimed to seek the end of exploitation as such. I do not know what such a claim would mean in theory – apart from a return to subsistence or an end to scarcity. In practice the claim has meant that exploitation is "ended" when surplus is appropriated by the state which can then act to enforce high rates of saving throughout the economy in order to invest more heavily in the production of capital goods. I would also distinguish my approach from the Left-Ricardian views of Proudhon and others, who believed that wages should be equal to value added – that labor time should be the unit of currency.[107] My view that the existence of a surplus is both necessary and desirable is based on Marx's own critique of Ricardian socialism in *The Poverty of Philosophy*, a work that figured heavily in the development of his mature economic writing. Finally, I would distinguish my approach from that of recent liberal defenders of the market, such as Ronald Dworkin. Where these writers defend the market as a way of economizing on the use of resources (capital) through equalizing opportunity costs,[108] I suggest in the Marxian tradition (perhaps influenced by Rawls)[109] that we should view the economy as though it were a division of labor among equals, and that the burdens of exploitation in creating collective wealth should be equalized as far as possible.

I am of course acutely aware of putting forth my interpretation of *Capital* at a moment in history when Marxist-Leninist states are moving to

[105] By this I mean the forms of politics described in part II, above.
[106] There are numerous passages that reflect this conception. E.g.: "The development of the productive forces of social labour is capital's historic mission and justification. For that very reason it unwittingly creates the material conditions for a higher form of production." (Marx, *Capital*, vol. III, p. 368.)
[107] See, e.g., Bray, *Labour's Wrongs and Labour's Remedy*; Hodgskin *Labour Defended against the Claims of Capital*; Proudhon, *System of Economical Contradiction; or The Philosophy of Misery*; and Thompson, *Labour Rewarded. The Claims of Labour and Capital Conçiliated* and *An Inquiry into the Principles of the Distribution of Wealth Most Conducive to Human Happiness*. For further discussion of this point see appendix 3, below.
[108] See Dworkin, "What is Equality?" parts 1 and 2.
[109] See Rawls, *A Theory of Justice*.

reintroduce market mechanisms governed by the political logic of civil society. Although I cannot here do justice to the issues raised by these developments, I would assert that *Capital*, as interpreted here, is more relevant to analyzing political issues posed by emerging market economies in such states than it was to the failed efforts to construct a centrally planned economy. I can only hope that as perestroika brings the socialist states in Asia and Eastern Europe into the global capitalist economy, the Marxian tradition of political analysis will not be altogether lost. Indeed, I believe that my proposed interpretation of political materialism, if it proves to be a coherent and feasible project, might cast considerable light on the politics within and between states as capital markets become increasingly global and efficient.[110]

---

[110] Recent technology has made the movements of international capital and money markets virtually instantaneous – a fact that may directly or indirectly bear upon the validity of many of Marx's arguments in volume III.

12 Thinking Through *Capital*

Balance and equilibrium

In order to grasp the present-day significance of Marx's overall argument in *Capital* we must return to the metaphors of conservation and balance that underlie economic thought.[1] These metaphors are basic, I believe, to accounting practice at every level – the household, the firm, and the nation. We have already seen[2] that the fundamental economic premise in the writing of Smith and Ricardo is that the sum of the relative values at which goods must exchange must balance against the sum of the separate costs paid out in producing those goods. This is the classical equivalence of value and distribution.

When the classical political economists argued that the exchange value of a commodity in the market is equivalent to the sum total of the wages, rent, and profit that had to be paid out to produce it, they clearly intended their formulation to refer to both the aggregate national product (NNP) and to any single commodity produced for sale on the market. As we saw in chapter 11, classical political economy was simultaneously a theory of macroeconomics (concerned with the aggregate components of economic activity) and a theory of microeconomics (concerned with the marginal returns on the factors of production). Today, however, mainstream economics[3] generally distinguishes, as pre-Keynesian economists did not, between

---

[1] For a useful discussion of the role of these assumptions in *Capital* see Wolff, *Understanding Marx*, ch. 6.
[2] Chapter 10, above.
[3] I here refer to the "neo-classical synthesis" – i.e., Keynes as transmitted through Hansen and enshrined in Samuelson's classic textbook. Hansen claimed that Samuelson was the first to use the word "macroeconomics," but Samuelson himself later gave the credit to Laurence Klein. Cf. Samuelson, "Alvin Hansen as a Creative Economic Theorist" and "Rigorous Observational Positivism," pp. 220–1. See also, Samuelson, "The General Theory" and "A Brief Survey of Post-Keynesian Developments."

the microeconomic theory of price and the macroeconomic theory of employment and growth. This change occurred in two phases: the marginalist revolution and the Keynesian revolution.

Shortly after Marx published volume I of *Capital* professional economists[4] began to reject the distinction between use value and exchange value on which Smith and Ricardo had built the theories that Marx criticized.[5] In classical political economy use value was a measure of subjective satisfaction or utility derivable from a good; exchange value a measure of the sacrifice (or disutility) required to produce the good. The point of this distinction for the classical economist was that, unlike use value, the magnitude of exchange value could be defined independently of the distribution of goods in society — and that misguided efforts to maximize use value (subjective satisfaction) through redistribution of wealth could have negative effects on the aggregate level of exchange value.[6] In classical political economy exchange values are based entirely on relative production costs of different commodities — sometimes taking account of changing marginal costs of the different factors of production, but never of the changing marginal demand for the product. The marginalist revolution in economic thought became possible when "use values" were introduced in the form of *marginal*, rather than aggregate, utilities. This innovation allowed the development of an elegant theory of market prices based on supply and

---

[4] I here have in mind the work of Menger, Jevons, and others — culminating in Walras and Marshall. See Schumpeter, *History of Economic Analysis*, ch. 5. For useful discussions of the marginalist revolution from a more or less conventional Marxist perspective see Meek, "The Marginal Revolution and its Aftermath," and Sensat and Constantine, "A Critique of the Foundations of Utility Theory." See also, Robinson, *Economic Philosophy*.

[5] Because I am concerned with elucidating Marx's method I shall often speak in terms of the distinction between exchange value and use value which he derived from the economists that he was criticizing. However, as we shall see below, a major point in Marx's critique was to show how the force of this distinction is inverted in the analysis of the labor process under capitalism. Cf., e.g., Marx, *Capital*, vol. I, chs 1–3 and 6.

[6] This point does not of course follow from the mere definitions of "use value" and "exchange value." Although a social distribution of wealth that maximizes aggregate use value would not necessarily maximize aggregate exchange value, most theories of distributive justice assume that a reduction in the size of the total social product (measured independently of distribution) would have a negative effect on the prospects of raising the aggregate level of social satisfaction through redistribution. (This assumption rules out the existence of intense and widespread preferences for distributional equality, even at the cost of all other satisfactions.)

demand, or more precisely, on the equilibrium of marginal costs and marginal utilities.

The marginalist approach to the scientific study of markets removed mainstream economics from its grounding in the enterprise of accounting for national income — the wealth of nations.[7] Although the new focus on marginal rather than aggregate utilities enabled economists to describe efficient resource use in the market, the resulting theory did not suffice to bring aggregate levels of investment and consumption into ex ante balance for the economy as a whole except under conditions of full employment. This point was grasped by Keynes, who attempted to bring economic theory back to the level of generality sought by Smith and Ricardo by focusing on the equilibrium of macroeconomic aggregates.[8]

Ever since the insights of Keynes were absorbed into mainstream economics, textbook descriptions of national income accounting have embodied the basic premise of Smith and Ricardo that the total value of the goods produced in each cycle (net national product) must be equivalent to the total revenues paid out in the process of production (net national income). In contemporary macroeconomic thought the components of the national product are conventionally categorized as consumer goods (C), investor goods (I), and government expenditure (G).[9] As noted above, Keynes did not believe that under the marginalist theory of prices (which he fully accepted) the national account would automatically balance on an ex ante basis, unless there happened to be full employment.[10] He thought, however, that such balance could be created artificially by using the spread between government taxation and expenditures to regulate the marginal rates of

[7] Cf. Adam Smith on accumulation (in *The Wealth of Nations*, bk 2), and the accountant's notion of net worth.

[8] Keynes, *The General Theory of Employment, Interest, and Money*.

[9] For the purpose of the discussion above we shall leave out the complications caused by inflows and outflows of foreign investment, trade imbalances, etc., and treat the national product as though it were identical with the net domestic product. This simplification has the defect of setting aside the important question of whether expanded reproduction is possible in a closed capitalist system. See, e.g., Luxemburg, *The Accumulation of Capital*, and Kalecki, "The Problem of Effective Demand with Tugan-Baranovski and Rosa Luxemburg." The importance of the interaction between global and national economies will be considered below.

[10] See Keynes, *The General Theory of Employment, Interest, and Money*, ch. 3. Keynes was no more a believer in Say's Law (aggregate supply necessarily equals aggregate demand) than Marx or Ricardo. Cf. Ricardo, *On the Principles of Political Economy and Taxation*, ch. 20, and Marx *Theories of Surplus Value*, part 2, ch. 17.

saving and investment — and hence the general level of wages and profits in the economy as a whole. Overall equilibrium at full employment would be achievable in the economy, said Keynes and his followers, but only as a result of effective government intervention in the general case.[11] The modern "neo-classical synthesis" seeks to combine the insights of Keynes' general theory of employment and growth with the insights of marginalist price theory — the two revolutions in mainstream economic analysis that have occurred since Marx wrote.[12]

Circulation and distribution

Now that we have sketched the divergence in modern economics between micro- and macroeconomic approaches, we can say something more about the potential relevance today of Marx's critique of theories that were superseded soon after he wrote. I believe that Marx's critique is not merely orthogonal to the distinction between macro- and microeconomics — a position he shared with Ricardo — but also that Marx's theory of surplus value foregrounds the conflicting pictures of the economy as a whole that today find expression in the largely unfilled gap between the two levels of theorizing. Marx's mature critique of political economy is, as we have already suggested, an effort to problematize the relation in classical political economy between the circulation of commodities and the distribution of revenues. Marx introduces this problem in *Capital*, volume I by asking the simple question: how can new value be added to the economy as a whole through the simple purchase and sale of commodities? He posed this question because he believed that economists, beginning with Smith and Ricardo, had systematically confused the determination of the value of capital as a commodity with the determination of the value of the commodity as capital.[13] What does this mean?

[11] See, e.g., Samuelson, "The Theory of Pump-Priming Reexamined." For Keynes' discussion of some of the political implications of his views see Keynes, *Essays in Persuasion*, secs 2, 4, and 5, and *The End of Laissez-Faire*. The standard Marxist critique of Keynes is Mattick, *Marx and Keynes*.

[12] For an interesting, if technical, discussion of the tensions and complementarities between pure neo-classical, neo-Keynesian, and neo-Marxian models, see Marglin, *Growth, Distribution, and Prices*.

[13] This is the major concern of volume II of *Capital*. It is, also, the essence of the opening argument of volume I regarding the commodity form (see esp. chs 4—6), and recurs at the conclusion of volume III (see esp. chs 58—61).

Put simply, every item that is purchasable as a commodity must be capable of circulating on the market at a price that establishes its value in relation to all other commodities. But every commodity can also be viewed in the system of exchange as an investment, an asset which can ultimately realize for its owner a profit on the money used to purchase it. So every capital investment has a value as a commodity, and every commodity can in theory be valued as a capital investment.

According to mainstream economists, the market must be viewed both as a circulation of commodities and as a circulation of capitals. In the former picture market competition functions to equalize the prices realized by different owners of the same commodities. In the latter picture the effect of market competition is to equalize the profits returned on different investments representing the same quantity of capital.[14] Yet these same economists believe that we can equate these perspectives to describe the economy as a single system of circulation — a material process of the sort described in chapter 10.

Marx proposed that we describe this material process of circulation as follows: a Commodity is exchanged for Money which is exchanged for a Commodity which is exchanged for Money, and so on, *ad infinitum*. This can be abbreviated C-M-C-M-C-M etc. In describing the circulation of commodities and of capitals as a single system, the classical political economists undertook to prove two propositions. (1) Looking at any given segment C_1-M-C_2, the economists argued that the exchange value of the two commodities must be equivalent: $C_1 = C_2$; the money is merely a medium of exchange. (2) Looking at any given segment M_1-C-M_2, the economists argued that M_2 may be greater than M_1 (why else would someone buy something in order to sell it?). The commodity is merely an investment; the money, expanding capital.[15]

For Marx the puzzling relation between (1) and (2) as descriptions of a single material process, concealed the secret mainspring of capitalist production itself. When commodity is traded for commodity, such a transaction occurs at a ratio at which exchange values are in theory equivalent. The parties would then agree to make the transaction only if they both believe they will gain in use value. Yet Marx believed (as did Smith and Ricardo) that in order for the market to produce new value as capital there must

---

[14] See, e.g., Marx, *Capital*, vol. III, ch. 50 ("The Illusion Created by Competition"), esp. pp. 1003ff.

[15] See ibid., vol. I, chs 4–5.

Look

also be a gain in exchange value — not merely a "consumer's surplus."[16] He thus argued that even where every commodity is exchanged for its equivalent, there has to be (at least?) one commodity that could be purchased for money but which, unlike all other commodities, expands its value in the process of circulation. Because the expansion in the value of capital is the mystery that needed explanation, the commodity that can raise the exchange value of others without increasing its own cannot be capital itself. Marx concluded that this commodity had to be labor power.

Consumption and investment

As we have already suggested in chapter 11, this search for an element of "self-expanding" value was misleading and unnecessary. One might just as well say, as most sympathetic expositors of Marx now do, that surplus is produced when money is spent to purchase and employ the necessary factors of production.[17] The real insight in Marx's theory of surplus value does not lie in his bravado act of lifting the veil on the mysterious character of human labor power, but rather in his critical anticipation of modern views of the relation between consumption and investment.

Marx's underlying point was that the reproduction of a capitalist market economy depends upon a disanalogy between the worker's expenditure of wages on consumer goods and those expenditures of revenue that can be considered as investments. Expenditures on capital goods [18] alongside cash and unsold product are presumed to retain their value as assets throughout the transformation (M-C-M). (The foregoing reflects the accounting practice of carrying inventory on the books as an asset alongside cash and unsold

[16] When two commodity owners trade in a perfect market (C-M-C), they are assumed to give each other goods of equivalent exchange value in order to enjoy a greater use value from their subsequent holdings. This conceptual foundation of classical political economy resembles the argument in neo-classical theory that there will be a "consumer's surplus" in terms of aggregate social utility when all goods are exchanged at their marginal price. See, e.g., Bergson, "A Note on Consumer's Surplus," and Samuelson, *Economics*, pp. 438–40. Cf. Foley: "Neo-classical economic theory, since it acknowledges only the pursuit of use-value [C_1-M-C_2] as an ultimately rational end of human activity, cannot conceptualize capital accumulation [M_1-C-M_2] as a self-determined phenomenon, and in its place studies economic growth driven by changes in external variables like population or resource availability." Foley, *Money, Accumulation and Crisis*, p. 11, n. 3.

[17] See, e.g., Foley, op. cit., p. 10 and *Understanding 'Capital,'* chs 3, 5.

[18] And, as it happens, on many luxury goods, although this parenthetical point is not part of Marx's argument.

product — so that the financial statement can reflect a 'snapshot' view of the circuit of capitalist production.) In contrast the worker's expenditure of wages on the means of subsistence consists of the purchase of commodities that do *not* generally retain their (exchange) value in the process of use. In the "dismal science" of classical political economy the goods that the worker buys out of wages (such as food) would be necessary for his survival, but they would not constitute the means of production that could either make the worker self-sufficient outside of the market, or allow him to sell his own products in the market — thereby appropriating a part of the surplus for himself. In describing the reproduction of wage labor as a social relationship the theories of Smith and Ricardo presume that the worker will not generally be able to resell the stock of wage goods that he purchases before he uses them up,[19] and that the workers purchase of the means of subsistence is not an investment.

Of course the generalization that capitalists buy exchange values and workers buy use values need not be true in every particular instance where labor power is hired for a wage. Smith and Ricardo both recognized that capital may be spent to hire labor power for purposes of consumption rather than production. (Expenditures on servants or on doctors tend to create use values, but not exchange values — and at least the latter expenditures may be deemed as necessities.)[20] It would also have been consistent with classical political economy to admit that wages may occasionally be spent to purchase goods that preserve their value. (In advanced capitalism many workers have even been able to buy homes that appreciate over time.)[21] At the other end of the developmental spectrum Smith's comparative historical framework could have accommodated easily the phenomenon of "mixed" capitalist development — in which workers, supported in part by a subsistence economy, can directly appropriate and circulate use values that are not purchased with wages.[22]

[19] Wage goods may be used up either through consumption or waste.
[20] See Adam Smith, *The Wealth of Nations*, bk 2, ch. 3; and Marx, *Theories of Surplus Value*, part 1, ch. 4
[21] However, high mortgage indebtedness, a byproduct of rising real estate markets, often increases the pressure on workers to 'moonlight' etc. — thereby having a positive effect on what Marx would call "the absolute rate of surplus value."
[22] In cases where the goods produced in the capitalist sector are largely exported, a growing subsistence sector may allow a rate of exploitation of wage labor that is relatively high for non-capital intensive forms of production. (See, e.g., Geertz, *Agricultural Involution*.) If, however, there is also a growing internal market for produced commodities, some workers who are not dependent on their wages in order to live may be able to invest in means of production, and thereby become artisans.

These qualifications, although important, should not obscure the basic fact that in the process of producing commodities for sale on the market the capitalist appropriates a value that is greater than his expenditure, and that the worker must spend his wages on commodities that do not hold their value in use. The latter point follows in the theories of Smith and Ricardo from the near tautology that in an economy producing for internal markets the labor force would not be rehired if wages did not create an effective demand for the production of new wage goods. In Keynesian theory the main source of increased effective demand in a closed market economy would likewise come from higher wages (and expanded employment). For Keynes, however, this conclusion is based on the contingent fact that persons with a lower income have a higher marginal propensity to consume when their income is raised, a premise of market psychology that has nothing to do with whether these low-income people are also producers, rather than merely recipients of transfer payments.[23] Given this premise, Keynes believed that there were no mechanisms (apart from deliberate government intervention) that would bring the marginal propensity of consumers to save into equilibrium with the marginal propensity of capitalists to invest so as to satisfy consumer demand at stable prices. For Marx, however, the relative inability of workers to save was inextricably connected to the ability of capitalists to invest and accumulate.

Marx's point was that in a normally functioning capitalist economy workers must always have the need to return to the labor market in order to live.[24] If the inability of workers to save[25] were viewed as simply a

---

[23] Keynes, *The General Theory of Employment, Interest, and Money*, chs 10, 18, 19.

[24] To say that this phenomenon is *explained* by the high initial prices that workers must pay for certain consumer goods that retain a relatively low value in use is simply to redescribe a structural necessity of capitalism in terms of the prices that reflect it — a return to what Marx called "vulgar economics." Although such vulgar explanations might direct our attention to contingent problems — such as the existence of manipulative business practices or other market failures — the techniques of vulgar economics tend to obscure the extent to which the continuing survival of an economic system that produces commodities for sale on the market depends upon the reproduction of the basic relationship between wage labor and capital.

[25] Although pensions for workers now fulfill one of the prime purposes of individual saving, the promise of a future pension (vesting upon retirement) cannot in general be viewed as accumulated wealth during the worker's productive years, and tends to increase rather than diminish the incentive to keep working. We

consequence of low real wages, as Keynes believed, Marx would respond that capitalism cannot survive high real wages without a constant influx of new labor from the reserve army of the unemployed. Although there is now considerable evidence to support such a response,[26] I believe that Marx's view is also consistent with the position that rising real wages would not necessarily reduce the gap between purchasing consumer goods and investing in capital goods.[27] Even if the economy grows to the point where some workers can save for future consumption out of present wages, orthodox Marxian analysis suggests that such savings would be unlikely to constitute an accumulation of capital for the workers.

Marx himself explained the necessary inability of workers to accumulate using the language of classical political economy. He argued that when capital is invested in labor power the use value of the capitalist's purchase is identical to the exchange value added to the product.[28] The value of the worker's labor to himself, however, is measured only in terms of what he can buy with his wages. As we have seen, the goods that he buys are not an investment; they cannot usually be resold at a gain,[29] and any surplus of use value usually takes the form of waste. The commodities produced for the consumer market can thus be expected to hold their value as capital only so long as they can be used to command new labor power. In order to maintain his purchasing power the worker must return to the market where his labor can again be commanded by capital in the form of commodities.[30] To put the point in Keynesian terms: economic development (growth in the value of the national product) occurs to the extent that the workers depend on new wages to purchase newly produced consumer

---

should also note that not all workers hold jobs that would make them eligible for future pensions; that pension programs tend to vanish in the process of corporate restructuring; and that an increasing proportion of the new jobs that have been created in the US economy do not offer pension benefits.

[26] This analysis would tend to be confirmed by the increasing reliance on guest workers in countries where the indigenous labor force has a high standard of living, and also by the creation of a two-tier wage structure as increasing numbers of women enter the labor force in low-paid service industries. For a discussion of the relation between this wage structure and issues of international competitiveness in the production of manufactured goods, see Thurow, "A Surge in Inequality."

[27] See Hirsch, *The Social Limits to Growth*.

[28] Less the depreciation on fixed capital. For Marx's argument on the use- and exchange-value of labor-power, see, e.g., *Capital*, vol. I, ch. 6.

[29] Nor can they generally double as means of production, or as payments-in-kind for subsistence labor, as they do in some underdeveloped economies.

[30] See esp. Marx, *Capital*, vol. I, ch. 6.

goods; economic stagnation occurs to the extent that workers survive through the recirculation of existing use values.

The importance of this insight may be illustrated by a brief mention of the pathological forms of capitalist development. Urban ghettos or barrios with high rates of unemployment (and underemployment) are characterized by the development of "involuted" systems for the extraction of increasing use value out of goods with diminishing exchange value. The elaborate social mechanisms required for circulating and consuming use values appears to the larger economy to be a form of 'waste,' since little exchange value is realized for the effort put in. Yet through such mechanisms an ever-more-rapid circulation of a fixed (or slowly growing) stock of wage goods is able to support an ever-larger population, albeit at a near-subsistence level.[31] To the Keynesian theorist of capitalist development the existence of such involuted subeconomies means that the value of the annual national product is less than it would be if available labor power were 'fully' employed to meet the current and expected demand for wage goods which would be 'fully' consumed in a given product cycle.[32]

The Marxian analysis of saving and investment casts considerable light on the social significance of modern Keynesian efforts to redistribute

---

[31] The interdependence, and the frequent proximity, of heavy industry and the ghetto may be an urban counterpart to the relation the anthropologist Clifford Geertz describes between plantation and peasant agriculture in Java. In his examples the use of labor-saving techniques in the production of export goods (e.g. sugar and coffee) are symbiotic with the use of population-absorbing techniques in the production of subsistence goods (e.g. rice): increased productivity in the export sector is supported by greater complexity in the subsistence sector. Geertz describes the resulting societal pattern as overpopulation and developmental involution − a classic paradigm of economic "stagnation" as opposed to "growth." (see Geertz, *Agricultural Involution*. Cf. Marx, *Capital*, vol. III, ch. 47.)

[32] Many twentieth-century Marxists have stressed the centrality of pathological forms of capitalist development (often called "underdevelopment" or "dependency") in analyzing the root problems of capitalism. Such views tended to presuppose, either implicitly or explicitly, the existence of external pressures on capitalism in the form of ideological and political competition from Marxist-Leninist states to control the economic development of the Third World. The analysis undertaken above, however, takes no position on the likelihood that capitalism will die (or decline) prematurely because of its tendency to develop pathological forms that would enhance the appeal of Marxist-Leninist regimes in developing countries. By giving primary emphasis to the problems arising out of the normal development of capitalism, I follow once again the example of *Capital*. (For examples and discussions of dependency theory see Brewer, *Marxist Theories of Imperialism*, and Owen and Sutcliffe, *Studies in the Theory of Imperialism*.)

income in order to manage aggregate demand. According to the account given above, such redistributions of revenue would not constitute redistributions of wealth. Money is a form of wealth — as Marx learned from Smith and Ricardo — only when it can be spent on things that preserve and expand its value as capital. Thus, the employer's ability to spend his money on labor power in order to produce national wealth depends upon the extent to which the worker who receives that money as wages circulates it back to the capitalist through the purchase of consumer goods. Insofar as the objective of Keynesian redistribution is to stimulate consumer demand, the higher money wages that pass through the worker's hands are not a form of increased wealth; consumer goods — whatever their utility — do not preserve and expand their value as capital.

Marx's critique of political economy suggests that an increase in the revenues available to workers, rather than equalizing wealth, may simply shift certain commodities which once had value as capital to the status of ordinary consumer goods.[33] If Marx is correct, the effort to redistribute spendable income to workers in the name of social equality is likely to result in an inflation in the initial price of many consumer goods, and an equally rapid reduction in their retained value once they are the property of the consumer. The lowered effective utility of revenues that have been redistributed reflects the fact, already noted, that consumer goods can keep their value as capital for only as long as they are useful in commanding new labor. Consumer price inflation is one way the demand for social equality is reflected in the phenomenology of the market.[34]

Disappointment in the real distributive effects of economic growth tends to produce a gestural politics of cultural movements based on the celebration

---

[33] Such a shift would occur insofar as goods that were once valuable as capital investments cease to confer significant social power over others. An expenditure on higher education, for example, may have diminishing returns as an investment in human capital to the extent that such qualifications become common. (Eventually, a B.A. degree might become a form of consumption, personal or social, rather than an investment.) Similarly, those now receiving significantly higher nominal incomes tend to find that such income levels do not buy the standard of living they once did because, being more widespread, they cannot be used to command human labor in the form of service. A frequent concomitant of capitalist development, along with higher salaries for parts of the middle class, is that the high cost of service tends to lower the retained value of many luxury goods initially purchased at a high price, such as cars and stereos. (As urban real estate rises in value, efficiency apartments in prime locations can have higher resale value than large houses with high maintenance costs.) See Hirsch, *Social Limits to Growth*.

[34] See Hirsch and Goldthorpe (eds), *The Political Economy of Inflation*.

of alternative life-styles. The classical spawning ground for such counter-cultural movements is the lumpenproletariat. When the commodities in which surplus is realized vary sharply from those in which it is accumulated, there is a large pool of wasted commodities that retain some use value after their exchange value has been largely exhausted. These commodities become the material base for supporting counter-cultural movements which may identify abstractly with the plight of the working poor while remaining materially tied to the continuation of the system of accumulation that produces the waste off which they live. Such counter-cultural movements can embrace a variety of elements – religious revivals, xenophobia, pacifism, communitarianism, attacks on the corruption of urban life. Whatever their other elements, they frequently contain a strong element of opposition to the human cost of industrial society. Just as earlier opponents of capitalist industrialization did so on the basis of a romantic rediscovery of rural values, today, broad-based social movements (such as the Greens) have opposed industrial development because of its human toll in alienation and pollution.[35]

Planning and regulation

We have seen that according to Marx, the picture of the market as a circulation of commodities (C-M-C) and as a circulation of capitals (M-C-M) are not automatically equivalent. Each appears embedded in the other as a set of macroeconomic assumptions about the distribution of revenues between wage labor and capital, and about the division of the product between consumer goods and capital goods.[36]

---

[35] The English romantics believed that "civilization" (industrial capitalism) needed to be offset by a self-conscious resurgence of the national "culture" which it naturally tended to choke off. Indeed, Samuel Taylor Coleridge – in *On the Constitution of Church and State* – proposed a scheme to institutionalize the existence of a mass counterculture as a religious organization with parishes and a "clerisy" that would have functioned much like the cell-structure and cadres in a Leninist party. For a general discussion of romantic anti-capitalism see Raymond Williams, *Culture and Society*; cf. his more recent "Problems of the Coming Period." For a presentation of "green" ideology see, e.g., Capra and Spretnak, *Green Politics: The Global Promise*.

[36] Marx discusses these contradictions from a microeconomic perspective in parts 1 and 2 of *Capital*, vol. II ("metamorphoses" and "turnover" of capital), and from a macroeconomic perspective in part 3 ("The Reproduction and Circulation of Total Social Capital").

In volume II of *Capital* Marx developed insights about the circulation of commodities and capitals from his materialist perspective in order to show that the capitalist market can indeed work as a unified system of circulation, but only on the basis of certain macroeconomic assumptions about the composition of the national product and the distribution of national revenues. He demonstrated that as the system reproduces and expands itself through the process of circulation of commodities it will systematically change the proportions of capital goods and consumer goods that must appear as end products of *this* round of production in order for the *next* to get underway. Periodic crises arise, Marx argued, because the distribution of the total revenues from both of these "departments" of production do not guarantee a stable market for their products in the next round.[37]

Mainstream economists following Keynes, Kalecki, and Leontief have explicitly returned to the concerns of the classical political economists in developing a theory that deals with both microeconomic equilibrium between the prices of commodities and the macroeconomic distribution of revenues between the capital and labor that would be necessary to provide a stable rate of growth. They demonstrate (in somewhat different ways)[38] that not all points of market equilibrium in the prices of commodities are also points of equilibrium in the social rates of investment, savings, and consumption. According to most mainstream economists (until quite recently),[39] the state should be called upon to regulate the economy so that price equilibrium is compatible with general equilibrium − the rate of investment necessary to maintain a "warranted rate of growth."[40]

Given the need to reconcile two contradictory pictures of the market − as a circulation of commodities on the one hand and of capitals on the

---

[37] I shall not attempt to summarize Marx's reproduction tables here. For good elementary discussions see Foley, *Understanding 'Capital,'* ch. 5. See also Tarbuck, "Editor's Introduction" to Luxemburg, *The Accumulation of Capital, − An Anti-Critique*, and Mandel, "Introduction" to Marx, *Capital*, vol. II. Mandel attempts to apply these schemata in his *Late Capitalism*.

[38] Kalecki moved directly from a grounding in Marxism toward conclusions about general equilibrium that Keynes arrived at by making a break with his training and background. See Samuelson, "Marxian Economics as Economics."

[39] I here refer parenthetically to the "rational expectations" school, which argues that government efforts to regulate the economy are futile in a world of low information costs. If Marx were alive today, he might note that this new approach to economics reflects the emergence of computer technologies that have drastically lowered information costs on a world-wide scale, making the operation of global capital markets virtually instantaneous.

[40] This concept was contributed by Harrod.

other — the state will have a continuing problem of regulation.[41] Following the path of the pioneers mentioned above, the macroeconomists who advise the governments in developed capitalist economies have seen their task as generating policies that address the problematic relation between the values of things (prices) and the distribution of resources (between investors and consumers) that is concealed in the general formula of market circulation criticized by Marx.[42] To economic policy-makers steeped in the market, political decisions that change the relative prices of commodities and those that change the relative return on investments are *both* essentially redistributive. When these debates are seen from a Marxian perspective even "deregulation" is a regulatory policy, at least insofar as it allows rising commodity prices to subsidize capital markets.

At the level of public policy, debates about regulating the economy occur in the language of "equalization" and "optimization" discussed in part II, above. Once we grasp that we are again dealing with two divergent pictures of the divisions in civil society we can see that the political dilemma of the policy planners is real: on the one hand the government cannot treat all investors as 'primordial' equals who cannot be sacrificed in the political process without allowing commodity prices to fluctuate in ways that sacrifice some industries; on the other hand the government cannot treat all existing industries (and their employees) as the primordial equals who cannot be sacrificed in the political process without regulating commodity prices in ways that sacrifice some investors in the capital market. Using the framework developed in chapter 11, we can restate this point as follows: government cannot treat the hourly value added by the employees in each industry as 'politically equal' while also treating as 'politically equal' the expected return on each dollar invested in capital markets.

---

[41] For the mainstream view see, e.g., Samuelson, "The Theory of Pump-Priming Reexamined." This view is subjected to critical scrutiny in O'Connor, "Scientific and Ideological Elements in the Economic Theory of Government Policy"; Claus Offe, "Social Policy and the Theory of the State," and "Competitive Party Democracy and the Keynesian Welfare State"; and Therborn, "The Theorists of Capitalism." The work of Fred Block is also relevant in this regard. See, e.g., Block, "Postindustrial Development and the Obsolescence of Economic Categories" and "Political Choice and the Multiple 'Logics' of *Capital*."

[42] See, generally, Santomero and Seater, "The Inflation-Unemployment Trade-off: A Critique of the Literature." (Some of the techniques Leontief developed for achieving a balance between the different "departments" of capitalist production may be viewed as successors to the schemata developed by Marx in *Capital*, vol. II. See Leontief, "The Significance of Marxian Economics for Present-day Economic Theory," and Samuelson, "Marxian Economics as Economics.")

The foregoing description of the political issues posed by modern theories of the national economy is close to the surface of policy debates.[43] If the state perceives its constituent interest groups as preexisting national industries, it will attempt to equalize among these industries through incentives and restrictions aimed at inducing capitalists to either retain or increase their investment in spheres of production that do not (or would not without government intervention) earn the generally expected rate of profit.[44] Governments typically seek to justify such interference with capital flow on the grounds that the short-term perspective of capital markets can have a distorting impact on long-range economic planning which requires maintaining intact the basic social division of labor. If, on the other hand, the state acts to treat all capitals as equal, however invested, it will have to make policy decisions that, at least implicitly, sacrifice certain preexisting industries. Governments typically seek to justify a general subsidy to new capital formation by arguing, on grounds of efficiency, that markets turn opportunity costs into real operating costs once assets are fully capitalized.

Actual economic policy, responding as it must to particular issues, is in practice a 'trade-off' between these two approaches. Moreover, there will always be market economists ready to remind government that it could never really succeed were it to adopt either of these approaches to the exclusion of the other. Their theoretical point is that government cannot aim to control the aggregate values of commodities without also having a deleterious effect on the efficient allocation of marginal investments; and that it cannot allow capital markets to control prices without systematically upsetting the balance in the composition of the national product.

Under either broad policy orientation available to government, however, the striking fact is that capitalists as a class cannot lose. Whatever the state does some capitalists will benefit, either as commodity owners or as investors (owners of money). The only question is which capitalists will benefit more. And, as we have learned in recent years, many capitalists can benefit either way from changes in government policy insofar as finance-driven managers have the option of either 'capitalizing' or 'expensing' their costs.[45]

---

[43] For a further attempt to theorize some of these issues see Offe, "'Crises of Crisis Management:' Elements of a Political Crisis Theory."

[44] Of course the state as capitalist could also nationalize the loss − so-called "lemon socialism."

[45] There is often a great deal of flexibility in whether an enterprise's losses are charged to its operating budget or its capital account. A business that is 'fully leveraged' on the basis of expected earnings will normally show an operating loss

This latter point is an important political consequence of the foregoing analysis. If, for example, the government tries to stimulate aggregate consumer demand, the capital market has a choice of response. It can either shift capital into new production in order to meet increasing demand; or it can redirect investment into hard assets which will tend to rise in price. In the latter case capital markets would tend to view investments as commodities – 'hedges' on inflation, which grow in scarcity faster than consumer demand can push up the overall price scale.[46] This tendency to speculate, combined with the relative underinvestment in new production, results in what is sometimes called "stagflation" – low growth and rising prices.[47]

Under such an economic scenario the return on capital in the economy as a whole would increasingly take the form of interest, rents, and acceler-

---

unless actual earnings meet or exceed expectations. Such a loss would reflect the fact that the continuing 'overhead' of interest costs make the business 'too expensive' to run at its fully capitalized value. If, however, the business were to be sold or refinanced at a lower capitalized value, profitability would return, assuming that everything else remains the same.

[46] The flight of capital into unproductive investments was an unintended result of the Great Society programs conceived by the Left-Keynesians in the 1960s. As a consequence of a low demand for productive domestic investments, the modest equalizing effects of the income maintenance programs introduced by government were largely offset by the rising real cost (lower value) of many consumer necessities through the 1970s.

A decade of capital flight into hard assets was rewarded when the investment incentives of the Reagan era allowed businesses to refinance existing assets and take a larger share of their income-flow tax free in the form of investment credits, stepped-up depreciation, accelerated depreciation, etc. Throughout the 1980s businesses were in effect repurchasing preexisting assets at a higher capitalized basis – at first through tax sheltered limited partnerships, and eventually through highly leveraged buyouts based partly on the prospects of raising cash through the sale of undervalued assets. Thus, tax policies that had the stated rationale of drawing finance capital into new productive investments led rather to the recapitalization of existing assets at their inflated value. The increased deficit resulting from lower income tax rates is the political price that democratic politics has exacted for the other tax benefits to investors that were designed to bridge the gap between manufacturing and finance capital. (For occasional prescient comments on the capitalization of productive assets see Marx, *Capital*, vol. III, chs 26–32.)

[47] For a variety of perspectives on this issues in comparative perspective see Lindberg and Maier (eds), *The Politics of Inflation and Economic Stagnation*. For a quasi-Marxist attempt to address some of these issues in the British context see Rowthorn, "Conflict, Inflation, and Money." For a comparative perspective see the essays in Hirsch and Goldthorpe (eds), *The Political Economy of Inflation*.

ated or stepped up depreciation, which is often merely a tax deduction for the appreciation of assets that have a rising replacement cost. Because these forms of financing can be fully and favorably 'expensed' in the operating budget, they appear as higher costs of production, which have the effect of raising product prices, squeezing (taxable) corporate profits, and creating a financial basis for seeking wage reductions. As domestic production costs increase, nominal prices are raised wherever possible, and jobs exported where price increases prove to be impossible. Meanwhile, real profits decline in manufacturing relative to the return on other investments; real wages are driven down as investors threaten to cease production and take their returns in the form of economic rents; and unemployment remains high (in secular terms) as more finance-driven employers are willing to carry out such threats.[48]

Regimes and parties

My argument about the role of the state in the economy has two sides. The first is that the state cannot fail to act in the interests of capital as such. The second is that in doing so it tends to divide capitalists as a class, rather than uniting them. From the perspective of political materialism the historical changes in capitalism can generally be explained from within by the divisions within the capitalist class that result when the state responds to the problems caused by the fundamental contradiction between wage labor and capital.[49]

In achieving a political perspective beyond that of the state itself Marxian analysis must also have two sides. It must always explain the interests that unify competing capitals around the need to maintain a high average rate of social exploitation. But it must also analyze the effect of the divisions

[48] The foregoing description focuses only on the national economy, leaving aside the relation to international capital markets, which will be taken up below.

[49] Third-World Marxists might thus tend to describe the relation of divisions within classes to the divisions between them as the "leading" and "principal" contradictions of a social formation. The notion of "contradictions among the people" in this literature generally refers to the politicization of salient differences among groups — a subject that Western literature tends to describe as the politics of pluralism. (See, e.g., Mao Tse Tung, "On the Correct Handling of Contradictions Among the People" and, more generally, "On Contradiction." For an extension of these ideas in an African context, see Cabral, "Brief Analysis of the Social Structure in Guinea.")

within capital on the identities through which individuals participate in politics.

The relation of divisions between classes to divisions within them is crucial to understanding the identification of individuals with political parties in modern regimes. Although Marx had little to say about parties in his economic writings, his historical account of 1848 describes how the unofficial parties of Orleanist France coalesced – despite internal differences on social issues – around the competing interest of finance, manufacturing, and landed capital.[50] In offering this analysis Marx laid the foundation for understanding the politics of institutionalized mass parties as grounded in competing alliances between fragments of wage labor and fragments of capital. This fragmentation occurs as a reflection of two forms of contradiction that are critical to Marx's understanding of capitalism: the first is the contradiction explored in this chapter between viewing capital as commodities and commodities as capital; the second is the contradiction discussed at the end of chapter 10 between identifying the interests of workers with the social division of labor between industries and also with the market in labor power as such.

The existence of such intra-class fragmentation creates the possibility of inter-class alliances over a wide range of issues. Because such issues divide workers among themselves as potential constituents of a regime while dividing capitalists among themselves as potential clients, there arise various possibilities of compromise between the resulting class fractions.[51] Thus, a conservative party in power can show that it is 'responsive' by creating a clientele among a subset of the poor (perhaps the 'neediest'). These it may aid directly through the circulation of commodities with wasting investment value (such as 'food for work,' 'payment in kind,' and so forth). In contrast a progressive party in power can show that it is 'responsible' by creating a constituency among a subset of capitalists (perhaps the most 'productive' or 'technologically innovative'). These it may aid directly through the infusion of capital (or tax advantages) for purposes of expansion and research. By using such techniques it is possible for parties in power to create political regimes.

---

[50] See Marx "Class Struggles in France" and "The Eighteenth Brumaire of Louis Napoleon Bonaparte." For further discussion see chapter 6, above.

[51] For provocative discussions of the relations between economic policy issues and the stability of regimes see Offe, "Competitive Party Democracy and the Keynesian Welfare State" and "Social Policy and the Theory of the State." See also Przeworski, "Social Democracy as an Historical Phenomenon." For valuable discussions of the logic of class compromise see Przeworski, *Capitalism and Social Democracy*, and Offe, "Legitimation Through Majority Rule?"

Extrapolating from our account of Marx thus far, we can infer that the issues that divide capital in its relation with wage labor will prove to be particularly salient as a basis for mass mobilization in electoral politics around the divisions in bourgeois economic interests. The cleavages around which oppositions organize into permanent parties are directly relevant to the role of the state apparatus in managing the economy as a whole, and require a concerted effort to exercise some control over state policy.[52] These differ from the 'valence' issues that all parties attempt to reflect in response to changing cultural currents.[53]

From a Marxian perspective, American commentators in the pluralist mainstream are wrong in their frequent assertions that mass political parties are accidental coalitions of communal, corporatist, and ideological interest groups. Rather, what characterizes party politics as distinct from interest-group lobbying is a standpoint toward government regulation of what we have been describing as the contradiction between circulation and distribution. In the United States during the 1980s polls showed that although both Republicans and Democrats were internally divided over a wide variety of "social issues," the parties coalesced around the difference between a supply-side Keynesianism that sought to stimulate investment and a demand-side Keynesianism that sought to stimulate consumption.[54]

How does the organization of party coalitions around the politics of consumption and investment bear on the various possible forms of political identity contemplated in this book? Of course the answer to this question will differ for each asserted basis of political identity. Nevertheless, we can sketch how such answers might be sought by returning once again to the illustrative example of feminist politics.

[52] For a discussion of the links between fiscal policy and electoral politics during an earlier period, see Tufte, *Political Control of the Economy.*

[53] For a discussion of the various bases of cleavage around which party structures are organized, see Burnham, *The Current Crisis in American Politics.* Similar issues are discussed in a comparative perspective in Dalton, Flanagan, and Beck (eds), *Electoral Change in Advanced Industrial Democracies: Realignment of Dealignment.*

[54] Between 1936 and 1984 the Democratic Party sought to unite those sectors of the economy whose reproduction depends upon publicly generated revenues — ranging from Southern textiles, to Midwestern industry, to Northwestern aerospace. (Midwestern agriculture was briefly part of this coalition during the heyday of Public Law 480.) At the level of policy, the Democrats during this period consistently favored selected sectors of the domestic economy through expenditures, direct aid, acceleration of consumer demand, tied foreign aid, and protection where necessary. Distinctively Democratic programs largely consisted of windfalls to particular

Our discussion of gender politics thus far suggests that the feminization (or, rather, the historical 'refeminization') of the labor force is reflected in the degree to which consumer goods and public consumption provide many of the use values once produced by domestic labor. In the United States since World War II domestic labor has been commodified to the extent that the need for domestic service has been replaced by labor-saving devices. Insofar as such devices have been cheapened relative to other wage goods, the woman worker can afford to buy herself out of domestic labor with her wage. Domestic labor has also become socialized to the extent that the state provides services, such as care of the dependent elderly, that free many women to reenter the labor force at middle age.

But women have still not been able to enter the labor force on equal

---

industries – ranging from the TVA to the Space Program and federally funded private medical care for the poor and elderly. These programs were generally intended to stimulate the economy as a whole by subsidizing an area of governmentally accelerated growth. While actively pursuing such policies, Democrats resisted imposing the world price of food, energy, and raw materials on American consumers whenever this threatened to curtail high industrial employment.

The Republican Party during the same period typically united those sectors of the economy that are most sensitive to interest rates and inflation, such as Northeastern finance capital and Western agriculture and ranching. At the level of policy, Republicans tended to support the operation of private capital markets as a way of setting the relative prices of industrial commodities, and to oppose governmentally subsidized windfalls to particular sectors. Yet as capital markets became increasingly multinational, distinctively Republican policy came to oppose the interests of the national bourgeoisie on a range of critical issues – especially the desire for an "industrial policy" that would support selected domestic manufacturing industries through trade protection, price subsidy, and maintaining artificially low domestic costs for materials that are in high demand abroad. Although such resistance to the national bourgeoisie may have been detrimental to the Republicans during the period of American hegemony in the world economy, because of this resistance the Republican coalition was eventually joined by Midwestern agriculture and Southern oil and gas, as these have come to depend less on government subsidies and more on the ability to impose rising world prices on domestic markets. As American industry becomes increasingly subject to world capital markets outside its control, the typical Republican programs of private tax relief and investment credits have also found increasing favor with those voters seeking to protect jobs in declining industries, although not with those voters who have already lost jobs. With the growing internationalization of American capital the regulatory policies of the Republican coalition has come to dominance at the level of national politics, leaving the Democrats largely in control of state governments where the interests of the national bourgeoisie still predominate.

terms insofar as the domestic labor of childcare has been effectively neither commodified nor socialized. Even if biology need not determine for long which parent must care for the child, the continuing segmentation of the work force along gender lines will reflect (in various distorted ways)[55] the prevailing sexual division of labor within each family with children. If one parent, generally the mother, must still bear the larger share of responsibility for the care of dependent children, this will tend to mean, as we saw in chapter 10, that one parent will be more willing to accept marginal employment than the other (unless both can somehow earn enough together to buy out their joint childcare responsibilities by hiring domestic labor).

The analysis here and in chapter 10 suggests that a demand for greater equality between the sexes — and the desire to abandon traditional household roles — may be the ideological embrace of the increasing difficulty of supporting a family on a single income. In this sense feminism, at least within the working class, is the progressive face of the decline in per capita real wages which it reflects, and which is experienced by everyone as a rise in the cost of living.

Once we have understood the material basis of feminist political identity, an important question for Marxian analysis will be the degree to which feminist identity can become the basis for cross-class political alliances. We have already seen in previous chapters how the policy responses to feminism may be dividing women in ways that could well undermine the reproduction of its own social base as a movement. In chapter 9, for example, we explored the contradictions in the state's policy of equalizing between male and female workers, on the one hand, and between female workers and female housewives, on the other. Our account of "political materialism" in chapter 10 allowed us to consider the extent to which women are subordinate to their husbands in marriage because of economic inequality in the labor market — and the extent to which women suffer discrimination in their job classifications because of family responsibilities. Now we must briefly consider whether at the level of parties and regimes the refeminization of the labor force signifies an increasing mobilization of a 'women's vote' in the political process.

The issues here reflect the changing relation between the structure of the new employment opportunities created by capital investment and the real

[55] Family issues can often arise very indirectly in the segmentation of the workplace: e.g., through the issue of whether women capable of childbearing should have the 'right' to compete for jobs that might endanger unborn children (and the related issue of whether occupational safety standards may be appropriately satisfied by the condition that women of childbearing age do not fill such jobs).

purchasing power of the average wage.[56] Combining these factors accentuates the link between gender inequality in the household and the workplace while politicizing the tension for women between employment issues and consumer issues. Women, identified as such, might perhaps be mobilized in the short term to perceive a difference between political parties along these lines: one party might briefly appear to be a stronger voice for equality between the sexes in employment; another, against the forces driving homemakers into the labor market. A Marxian political analysis on this level could explain the structural significance of a differential women's vote (the so-called "gender gap") should it arise, while seeing it as a short-term reflection of the differential ability of parties to respond to the ways in which women would benefit from greater equality with men at work, and/or suffer from the declining ability of their husbands to support their families.

Money, products, and people in the world economy

We cannot conclude our reinterpretation of Marx's political materialism without briefly sketching some of its implications for the emerging world capitalist economy. Chapter 10 has already suggested that the state of theorizing about global economics in recent decades bears a resemblance to the ways in which Smith and Ricardo conceived of the existence of a national economy.

The neo-Smithian aspects of the theories of the world-economy that matured in the 1970s were not confined to those who approached these problems from a liberal environmentalist perspective. Some social scientists, such as Immanuel Wallerstein, synthesized various tendencies in theories of dependency and imperialism in order to push the notion of a capitalist world economy back to the origins of capitalism itself. Wallerstein argued that capitalism was in essence, and from the beginning, based on an international division of labor between what, from the standpoint of traditional Marxism, would appear to be capitalist and pre-capitalist modes of production.[57] Other writers, such as James Kurth, have described the global division of labor as a "products cycle." In any given economy,

[56] See, e.g., Thurow, "A Surge in Inequality."
[57] See Immanuel Wallerstein, *The Modern World System*, vols I and II, *The Capitalist World Economy*, and *The Politics of the World Economy*. Wallerstein's view has been strongly, and I think persuasively, criticized from a Marxist perspective as a "mirror image" of Smith's approach to the economic development of

according to this argument, there is a life-cycle for the leading industrial sector (such as textiles or automobiles). The resulting path of capitalist evolution is a movement from one boom sector to another, as less developed countries take over production of the commodities that were previously exported by more developed countries. At any given moment in history, Kurth suggests, the world market will represent an international division of labor in the production of commodities (such as textiles and automobiles) corresponding to the relative level of capitalist development in each country.[58]

Although none of the diverging theories of a capitalist world economy as a division of labor has thus far achieved dominance over the many plausible neo-mercantilist alternatives,[59] there is no doubt that we are living in an era when the relation between free global markets in capital and commodities on the one hand and the prerogatives of regional or national political actors on the other are high on the agenda of economists and political scientists. Many who once thought otherwise, now believe that Adam Smith and "export orientation" are better guides than Karl Marx and "import substitution" to the problems that have hitherto been the province of development economics.[60] Whatever one's position on these questions, there is increasing reason to recognize that Smith and Ricardo are indeed relevant to the moment of conceptualizing a global world order as an "economy."

Because of the renewed relevance of Smith and Ricardo, mainstream economic thought has not been able to avoid confronting indirectly the kinds of problems that Marx addressed. The conception of political materialism developed in part III enables us to distinguish between those commodities in which the value of capital is realized, those commodities in which it is accumulated, and those commodities that absorb a disproportionate share of the population in their production. In our present

individual nation states. See Brenner, "The Origins of Capitalist Development: A Critique of Neo-Smithian Marxism." Cf. Skocpol, "Wallerstein's World Capitalist System: A Theoretical and Historical Critique"; Laclau, "Feudalism and Capitalism in Latin America"; Brewer, *Marxist Theories of Imperialism*.

[58] See Kurth, "Political Consequences of the Product Cycle: Industrial History and Political Outcomes." See also Gilpin, *U.S. Power and the Multinational Corporation Foreign Direct Investment*.

[59] See Gilpin, *The Political Economy of International Relations*, for a balanced assessment of the state of debate. For a conservative view of the present-day 'wealth of nations,' see Tucker, *The Inequality of Nations*.

[60] Cf. "The Poor Man's Burden: A Survey of the Third World," *The Economist*, and Griffin and Gurley, "Radical Analyses of Imperialism, the Third World, and the Transition to Socialism: A Survey Article."

circumstance the structure of *Capital* can be a model of theory building, but much of the substantive analysis will have to be redone. The type of analysis that Marx attempted in volume I would now need to directly incorporate the existence of heterogeneous labor and capital, and hence of variable rates of exploitation. The type of analysis that Marx did in volumes II and III would have to address the flows of capital, currency, commodities, and workers across the boundaries of national economies that still maintain discrete political and monetary systems.[61]

A new Marxian analysis of global capitalism would call our attention to strategic political questions that are left ambiguous from the perspective of individual states operating uncritically in an environment of given market prices.

1   Where is the global surplus being *produced*? In the low-wage economies that increasingly manufacture the world's consumer goods? Or in the high-wage economies that increasingly demand imported wage goods to offset the constantly rising costs of domestic production?
2   Where is the surplus being realized? In the price of consumer goods imported from the Third World? In the price of capital equipment exported to the Third World? Or in the economic rents charged by those with political control over scarce non-reproducible resources?
3   Where is the surplus being *accumulated*? In unproductive assets in the declining manufacturing economies? In new production in the developing economies? In the appreciating value of resources that grow scarce as the world economy expands?

The answers to such questions would be critical in linking the identities that are politicized within nation-states to an emerging civil society that is partly national, and partly trans-national.

In carrying out the research agenda suggested by such questions the recognition of a variable rate of exploitation (in Marx's technical sense) would be crucial. The logic of capitalist production in a global division of labor is to produce where the labor value of money is high and to sell where the money value of labor is high. When we shift our focus from the national to the world economy the question of the labor value of money comes to the forefront. In discussions of the national economy the value of money varies only over time, much as the rate of exploitation varies only over time in traditional Marxist theory based on volume I. When we turn

---

[61] In carrying out this project, the analyst would have to address such puzzling concretizations as the "duty free zone" − a space of production that is part of the labor market of one economy and the commodity market of another.

to the integrated world economy, however, we can see a wide variance in the labor value of money existing simultaneously in a single cycle of production. The ability of international capital to exploit the variance in the labor value of money magnifies the variance in the rate of exploitation that we have already noted in national economies.

The fact that exploitation now occurs across monetary systems must play a central role in the project of revising *Capital* suggested above. Any present-day return to Marx must account for the degree to which a worker's product may be sold in the currency of a foreign country while his wages are spent in the currency of his own country — often to purchase goods that are not sold at their world market price. One possibly fruitful approach to this problem, already suggested in chapter 11, would be to superimpose an analysis of differential exploitation based on the purchasing power of the money wage on an analysis of differential exploitation based on the labor value of money — modernized versions of the two measures of exploitation that Marx himself failed to adequately distinguish in his writings. The degree of disparity and convergence between these two measures of exploitation might reveal something of the impact of world markets on class fragmentation within national polities. Perhaps more importantly, however, such an analysis might indicate the changing possibilities and limitations of political alliances between class fragments across national boundaries.

Finally, the research agenda that I am proposing must address the relations between national and international political economy. In the present world economic order, national boundaries remain a barrier to the mobility of labor, but they are no longer a significant barrier to the mobility of capital, commodities, and currency.[62] Weak bourgeoisies increasingly rely on changes in the value of local currencies — often combined with stringent IMF conditions — to raise the average level of exploitation to internationally acceptable standards. These changes in the average would be reflected in the labor value of each country's currency, but the differential effects of these changes would only be revealed by examining changes in the real wage in different sectors of production.[63] In our contemporary

[62] The work of Fred Block addresses aspects of this phenomenon from a post-Marxist point of view. See Block, "Cooperation and Conflict in the Capitalist World Economy" and *The Origins of International Economic Disorder*. For an ambitious attempt at an integrated Marxian theory of the linkages between national and international economies see Aglietta, "World Capitalism in the Eighties."

[63] The existence of different, and interrelated, productive sectors with different real wages can also occur within a single monetary system, and is often a significant factor in national politics.

world, inflation-based changes in the rate of exploitation result to differing degrees in both class confrontation within national units and pressure for immigration between them. A renewal of Marxian analysis in our present situation could be expected to provide a political interpretation of the linkages between the sectoral sources of immigration in the 'sending' economies and the sectoral targets of immigration in the 'receiving' economies.[64]

The issues addressed by my proposed reconstruction of Marxian economic analysis are close to the surface of the politics of developed capitalist countries. At the level of economic policy-making our domestic politics often takes the form of a conflict of interest between those industries that benefit from greater integration with world markets and those industries that suffer when this results in higher production costs and shrinking domestic markets. At the level of electoral politics these issues appear as a choice between a foreign policy based on nationalism (the old economic imperialism of high domestic wages, cheap imported materials, and protectionism) or multinationalism (the new world-order of job exportation, higher world prices for raw materials, and free trade).[65]

In developing countries full integration into a global world economy poses different political questions. Should economic development focus on labor-intensive forms of manufacturing for foreign markets, or on the importation of high technology to manufacture for domestic markets? If the first path is pursued, the growth in the labor force creates a high consumer demand for goods that can only be provided through imports. If the second path is pursued, the developing economy can substitute for imports, but without creating the downward linkages that absorb the excess supply of labor.[66] Issues of fiscal and monetary policy are also

---

[64] An interest in such questions is not of course a unique property of Marxism. See Hirschman, *Exit, Voice, and Loyalty* and *Essays in Trespassing*, chs 8–12, and Rokkan, "Dimensions of State Formation and Nation-Building: A Possible Paradigm for Research on Variations within Europe."

[65] For non-technical presentations of some of these issues see Reich, *The Next American Frontier* and *Tales of a New America*.

[66] The pathology of capitalist "underdevelopment" occurs in the special case when goods produced in a labor-intensive sector are sold below their value in the markets that purchase them, while the workers who produce them must purchase wage goods above their value. Often such arguments conclude that workers in low-wage, high-exploitation, labor-intensive industries are partially supported by the use values contained in traditional subsistence goods or created through collective consumption based on either the family or the state.

critical to many developing countries: to what extent should they rely on foreign debt, thereby potentially subjecting their currencies and macroeconomies to direct international controls?[67] For some developing countries a further issue arises: should the economic surplus be reinvested to expand indigenous modes of production, or should capital accumulation take the form of investment in the economies of developed countries?[68]

Finally, we must try to envision the special problems that will emerge as failed socialist economies – especially those with highly disciplined labor forces and massive pent up demand – are somehow integrated into world capital markets. As I write, these developments are still too inchoate to be adequately grasped. Some might argue that a capitalism that develops out of indigenous socialism would have few of the historical defects of the forms of capitalism that developed out of feudalism.[69] Others might argue that, whatever the internal rationales for introducing economic incentives to increase productivity, the actual capitalist development that occurs in state socialist countries will probably come about from an infusion of foreign capital and commodities, resulting in massive inequalities based on windfalls and profiteering at the same time that the bulk of the labor force is being increasingly disciplined and denied its social safety net. If the latter argument is correct, the increasing autonomy within civil society of a capitalist class tied to foreign markets could result in deepening internal conflicts of the sort Marx himself discussed. Pursuing a Marxian analysis of such conflicts, we might expect such societies to face once again a political

---

The model of 'underdevelopment' contrasts with 'normal' capitalist development in which the real purchasing power of the hourly wage increases, although not as rapidly as the productivity of an hour of labor-power. For the contrast between the 'developmentalist' and 'underdevelopmentalist' interpretations of Marxist theory, cf. Warren, *Imperialism: Pioneer of Capitalism*, and Immanuel Wallerstein, *The Capitalist World Economy*.

[67] See, e.g., Sachs (ed.), *Developing Country Debt and the World Economy*.

[68] I have in mind, for example, the investment of the revenues realized through the sale of Middle Eastern or Latin American oil in capital markets in the US and Europe, and in real estate in such cities as London, New York, and Miami. When developing countries accumulate capital in the form of international investments, their ruling elites will tend to acquire a growing stake in maintaining stable capital and commodity markets in the developed economies – even if this mean limiting the neo-mercantilism of cartels such as OPEC.

[69] See, e.g., Robert Nozick's fable of how capitalism develops in a hypothetical socialist society when Wilt Chamberlain is allowed to charge people who wish to see him shoot baskets (Nozick, *Anarchy, State and Utopia*, pp. 161–4). Cf. Gerald A. Cohen, "Robert Nozick and Wilt Chamberlain."

choice between a renewed form of social democracy[70] and various manifestations of cultural nationalism on a mass scale.

Bringing history back in

There are of course ways of reviving Marxian theory other than that presented in this book. We have already engaged at various points the recent claims of "rational choice Marxism" to restate an intelligible, if not a generally defensible, version of Marx's views.[71] There have also been significant recent efforts to recover the utopian elements in Marxian thought as a basis for counter-hegemonic political mobilization in the present.[72] These writers build on precisely the messianic elements in Marx's theory of democracy that I have tried to exorcise, while rejecting the analytical dimensions of Marxism on which I have tried to build. Finally, and most importantly, there have been significant efforts to revive Marxism through renewing the technological determinist theory of history. These arguments suggest, with increasing plausibility, that we are in the throes of a worldwide transformation of the mode of production brought about by a fundamental change in the technological character of the forces of production.

Although there are many possible versions of such an argument, there is one in particular that resonates with Marx's own optimism that the capitalist mode of production will produce the material basis of its own transformation. According to this argument, the technology of the first industrial revolution brought us centralized and dehumanizing forms of industrial organization − whether imposed by a Henry Ford or a Joseph Stalin. Yet the internal needs of capitalism have also led to the creation of technologies for processing information that are transforming (and linking) the modes of production on a worldwide scale. Although the outcome of these developments is by no means preordained, some are seizing the

---

[70] See, e.g., Nove, *The Economics of Feasible Socialism*. From a somewhat different perspective Michael Burawoy suggests that struggles for workplace democratization in Eastern Europe may in fact constitute the first steps of a transition *to* socialism. See Burawoy "Should We Give Up on Socialism?" and the more detailed studies cited therein.

[71] For a debate about the degree to which the strategic choice approach to Marxism constitutes a reconstruction or an abandonment, see Burawoy, "Marxism without Micro-foundations," and Przeworski, "Class, Production and Politics: a Reply to Burawoy."

[72] See, e.g., Bahro, *From Red to Green*, and Laclau and Mouffe, *Hegemony and Socialist Strategy*.

moment of transition to suggest that the technology of the computer revolution makes possible (requires?) a new organization of production based on the model of craft industries. The political implication of such an argument is that decentralized and democratic forms of industrial organization may make the distinction between centrally planned and market economies increasingly irrelevant.[73]

One can only speculate on the implications of the latter argument in interpreting the apparent collapse of centralized state socialist approaches to industrial development. Are we seeing the triumph of capitalism, as many suggest? Or do the forces of history at work in the world rather portend the irrelevance of much of the traditional capitalist political agenda at precisely the moment when we seem to lack a credible alternative? Whatever the answers to these questions, even mainstream commentators in the popular media now recognize that the world is in the grip of historical forces that can no longer be contained by the political agenda of any existing regime.

Although I believe that a return to long-range historical theorizing of the sort Marx occasionally practiced[74] may be necessary to give an aerial view of our present situation, I am also convinced that in living on the ground of history we need the kind of Marxian analysis suggested in this book. The main plan of this work has been largely limited to presenting Marx's method of political and economic analysis. As a result my claims about the relationship between state and society – and about the various contradictions within society – have been mainly structural. To illustrate my broad claims, however, I have occasionally tried to make some political arguments, and these have been, at least partly, historical.

Effective political argument generally requires that we be able to locate ourselves, not merely in a structure of institutions, but also at a moment of its development; rhetorically, such arguments tend to be about 'what time it is'. The *Communist Manifesto* and the other manifesto literature in the Marxist tradition present political arguments which are historical – not in the sense of viewing history as a set of objective forces that work apart from human agency to bring about their inevitable result – but rather in the sense that they identify and address the social forces through which a

---

[73] For a cogent statement of the methodological thesis of technological determinism, see Gerald A. Cohen, *Karl Marx's Theory of History: A Defence*. For an interesting application of a version of technological determinism to the present transformation of capitalist economies, see Piore and Sable, *The Second Industrial Divide*.

[74] For a useful discussion of Marxian historiography see Vilar, "Marxist History, A History in the Making."

given structure of institutions *becomes* historically contingent.[75] A Marxian political argument would present a midstream view of the scenario of events that must take place in order for these experiences to provide a critical standpoint toward the structure of institutions as a whole. Once the Marxian argument has been put forward, the institutional response to it acquires a moral significance, either as the progression of the projected scenario, or as the price that institutions must pay in order to prevent that scenario from taking place.

The foregoing view of the rhetoric of Marxian political argument allows us to locate the concerns of more traditional Marxist accounts of class with which we began this book.[76] One part of the standard account emphasizes the aspect of *class struggle* in all political events. This form of political argument expresses the original Marxist insight that at revolutionary moments workers are able to interpret and appropriate the objective significance of past history as a conflict over who is to benefit from the exercise of state power in a zero-sum situation. A second part of the standard account is the development of workers' *class capacity* to engage in political organization. This form of political argument expresses the Leninist insight that militant class politics is not sustainable in the long run unless the groundwork has been laid by a class party.[77] A third part of the standard account is that class analysis is the study of the emergence of *class consciousness*. This expresses the insight (put differently by Lukács and Gramsci) that at revolutionary moments workers develop a distinctive sense of cultural community.[78]

---

[75] For discussions of the relationship between historical rhetoric and political argument see, e.g., Kenneth Burke, *A Grammar of Motives and a Rhetoric of Motives*; White, *Metahistory* and *Tropics of Discourse*; Jameson, *The Political Unconscious: Narrative as a Socially Symbolic Act* and "Symbolic Inference, or, Kenneth Burke and Ideological Analysis."

[76] See chapter 1, above.

[77] For a useful discussion of class capacity see Therborn, "Why Some Classes are More Successful than Others."

[78] An available counter-hegemonic culture with a prophetic vision of the future can become the basis of such an emerging class consciousness, and no revolution can succeed unless its historical agent has such a vision, or rapidly develops one. In the 1960s, debates within the New Left focused on whether Marxism itself could function as the distinctive political tradition of a social group – the working class – which is, uniquely, the product of capitalism.

The well-known Anderson–Thompson debate addressed these issues in the British context. See Edward P. Thompson, *The Making of the English Working Class* and "The Peculiarities of the English," and Perry Anderson, "Origins of the Present Crisis," "Socialism and Pseudo-Empiricism," and *Arguments Within English Marxism*.

As a simultaneous account of class conflict, class capacity, and class consciousness the standard Marxist view of political argument projects the moment of revolution backwards onto the politics that might lead up to it. This rhetoric reflects the fact that once Marxist–Leninist revolutions have been attempted it is generally possible to go back and discover after the fact the progressive emergence of class consciousness, the increasing assertion of class interests, and the prototypes of autonomous organizations of workers.[79] Marxist historians, aware of this rhetorical possibility, have sometimes tried to play a role in the revolutionary process by preserving the historical memory of class struggle 'between revolutions.'[80] But Marx's own experience teaches that revolutions do not always happen, even when they are expected.

My approach to Marxian political argument does not privilege revolutionary situations, and is hence more general than the standard account described above. In non-revolutionary situations I believe that Marxism allows us to learn about the structure of social institutions through their reactions to arguments that play out contradictions in their moral logic. The relation between political argument and political analysis is then continuing and interactive – the analysis must inform the argument, so that responses to the argument can provide precisely the kind of new information through which the analysis can be advanced. I believe that Marxism is unique among approaches to politics in requiring that concrete political strategy be planned in a way that will allow one to learn from whatever happens next. Marx's understanding of the unity of theory and practice requires that effective political practice also function as experimental social science – as a way of simultaneously changing and probing an institutional structure from within.[81]

The end of history?

If Hegel is correct in supposing that philosophy is its own time apprehended in thought, then something must be said in conclusion about the timeliness of a book offering a new interpretation of Marxian philosophy. This work

[79] See, e.g., Marx's discussion of the Paris Commune in Marx, "The Civil War in France."

[80] For critical comments on aspects of this historiography see chapters 3, 5, and 6, above.

[81] Gramsci was perhaps suggesting a similar approach to Marxian analysis when he referred to the need to fight "the war of position." See Gramsci, *Selections from the Prison Notebooks*, "State and Civil Society."

comes to completion two hundred years after the first French Revolution in a year when we are witnessing the death or abdication of the various Marxian movements that have kept the revolutionary mystique alive in its second century.[82] In 1989 the death of organized Marxism (and the consequent irrelevance of Marxian thought) has been proclaimed in the mass media throughout the world. The thinkers addressed in this book who are now deemed worthy of sympathetic reconsideration (especially in eastern Europe) are Adam Smith, Tocqueville, and even Hegel.

There is indeed growing evidence that Hegel is the man of the hour for those modern intellectuals who are undaunted by the esoteric.[83] Some scholars are now attempting to keep alive the political agenda of the New Left, not by reinterpreting Marxism, but by developing an implicitly (or explicitly) Left-Hegelian critique of modern institutions.[84] Other theorists celebrate the worldwide debacle of Marxism as a vindication of the thinker Marx most clearly sought to supersede — Hegel.

In a daring recent article one conservative theorist — presently employed by the US State Department — has argued that the twentieth-century defeat of both fascism and Marxism has brought about "the end history" in the sense that Hegel described after the triumph of Napoleon at the battle of Jena: henceforth, the argument goes, there will be no serious rivals to liberal capitalism as a framework for modern political life; all actual states will be more or less liberal, and more or less capitalist.[85] I shall not pause here to criticize the particular defects of this argument.[86]

[82] For evidence of the death of the revolutionary mystique in interpretations of the French Revolution itself see Furet and Ozouf (eds), *The Critical Dictionary of the French Revolution*.

[83] For samples of the growing trend to reinterpret institutional politics from a variety of Hegelian perspectives see "Hegel and Legal Theory Symposium," *Cardozo Law Review*.

[84] For an implicit Left-Hegelian perspective see, e.g., Wolin, *The Presence of the Past: Essays on the State and the Constitution*. For an explicit Left-Hegelian perspective see, e.g., Isaac Balbus, *Marxism and Domination: A Neo-Hegelian, Feminist, Psychoanalytic Theory of Sexual, Political and Technological Liberation*.

[85] See Fukuyama, "The End of History?," which purports to be an application of the Hegelian thesis as articulated by Alexandre Kojève in *Introduction to the Reading of Hegel*, ch. 6, n. 6.

[86] Among these defects are: its interpretation of Hegel on the state; its simplistically idealist interpretation of world history; its highly adventitious link between liberal political philosophy and the international consumer society made possible by global capitalism; and its skewed identification of Hegelian states with the Protestant ethic. Some of these criticisms are noted, often as sympathetic qualifications, by Fukuyama's conservative critics. (See "Responses to Fukuyama," *The National Interest*.)

For our purposes the important point is that the "end of history" in Hegel's sense signified the cessation — except as empty ritual — of struggles for recognition based on issues of political identity.[87] I believe that we are living at a moment when the politics of identity is reemerging in new forms, and with new urgency, in Eastern Europe and perhaps throughout

---

Of particular interest is the argument by Fukuyama's mentor, Allan Bloom that the international triumph of liberalism should be seen as an opportunity to philosophize on the meaning of "the good life." Bloom's argument, while seeming to gently chide Fukuyama for confusing the good life with the availability of mass consumer electronics, implies that the success of capitalism in 'delivering the goods' may be merely an exoteric argument for a political philosophy that has other esoteric appeals for the cognoscenti. In his own introduction to the English translation of Kojève, Bloom suggests that the "end of history" requires the end of "historicism" and a "reconsideration of the classical philosophy of Plato and Aristotle, who rejected historicism before the fact." See Kojève *Introduction to the Reading of Hegel*, pp. x-xii. Cf. Strauss, *Natural Right and History*.

[87] Alexandre Kojève (1959): "Hegel was right to see ... [in the Battle of Jena] ... the end of History properly so-called ... What has happened since then was but an extension in space of the universal revolutionary force actualized in France by Robespierre-Napoleon ... One can even say that, from a certain point of view, the United States has already attained the final stage of Marxist 'communism,' seeing that, practically, all the members of a 'classless society' can from now on appropriate for themselves anything that seems good to them, without thereby working any more than their heart dictates. ... [S]everal voyages of comparison made between 1948 and 1958 ... gave me the impression that if the Americans give the appearance of rich Sino-Soviets, it is because the Russians and the Chinese are only Americans who are still poor but are rapidly proceeding to get richer ... I was led to conclude that the 'American way of life' was the type of life specific to the post-historical period, the actual presence of the United States in the World prefiguring the 'eternal present' future for all humanity. ... [F]ollowing a recent voyage to Japan (1959) ... I had a radical change of opinion on this point ... 'Post-historical' Japanese civilization undertook ways diametrically opposed to the 'American way' ... [I]n spite of persistent economic and political inequalities, all Japanese without exception are currently in a position to live according to totally *formalized* values ... This seems to allow one to believe that the recently begun interaction between Japan and the Western World will finally lead not to a rebarbarization of the Japanese but to a "Japanization" of the Westerners (including the Russians). ... [W]hile henceforth speaking in an *adequate* fashion of everything that is given to him, post-historical Man must continue to *detach* 'form' from 'content,' ... no longer in order actively to transform the latter, but so that he may *oppose* himself as a pure 'form' to himself and to others taken as 'content' of any sort." (Kojève, *Introduction to the Reading of Hegel*, ch. 6, n. 6 pp. 160–2). Cf. Offe, "The Separation of Form and Content in Liberal Democracy."

the world. After the long stasis of the Cold War, "history" — in Hegel's sense — seems about to begin again.

But to understand the "history" that lies ahead, Hegel is not enough: we must return once more to Marx and to materialism. Both the politics of identity and the claim that we have reached its "end" are rooted in the kind of Hegelian idealism that Marx rejected — the view that political struggle is ultimately an expression of the universal need to overcome alienation. According to this view, there would be no internal limits to the universal human need for recognition on the basis of one or another ground of difference, unless that need can be channeled out of the political sphere and rendered harmless in the infinite divisions of the economic and cultural marketplace. Materialism gives a different perspective on the sources and limits of the politics of identity, requiring us to analyze the grounds of unity and division that arise from the emerging contradictions of a capitalist social formation. If politics in the forseeable future is likely to take the form of contesting groups and values struggling for recognition — and struggling also over the scope and meaning of the 'political' itself[88] — a materialist analysis such as that suggested above could enable us to see such politics as symptomatic of the internal transformation of world capitalism into something new.

The Marxian moment

No one reaching the end of a book like mine should lightly scoff at the pretensions of those who would recast current issues in the recondite vocabulary of Hegelian thought. With the consolidation of a single global economy[89] the world is entering a new era, and epochal thinking is once more appropriate to our condition.[90] I do not, however, believe that my argument for the present-day relevance of Marx is untimely, except as 'afterthought.' A developed capitalist world economy made up of more or less liberal polities with democratic ideologies is, roughly speaking, the world that Marx would have expected to result from the logic of capitalist development. Although not all of Marx's tentative expectations in *Capital*

---

[88] See, e.g. Maier (ed.), *Changing Boundaries of the Political: Essays on the Evolving Balance Between State and Society, Public and Private in Europe.*

[89] The distinction between "first," "second," and "third" worlds is rapidly becoming obsolete.

[90] See, e.g., Paul Kennedy, *The Rise and Fall of the Great Powers*, and Olson, *The Rise and Decline of Nations: Economic Growth, Stagflation, and Social Rigidities.*

volume III have been fulfilled, the world social order we are presently entering should form a home domain for the development of concrete analyses along the lines initiated by Marx. There was little in Marx's own work to support the now-crumbling historical efforts to impose "communism" either from the outside or as a revolutionary intensification of the process of capitalist development in particular countries. As the external threats to world capitalism diminish, however, Marx would have expected its *internal* contradictions to deepen. The much-celebrated "unravelling" of communism in Eastern Europe may yet portend a transformation in the nature of capitalism as well.

I believe that for those who would retain a critical perspective on the emerging world order there is now an unprecedented opportunity to start over again with Marx. For the better part of the twentieth century Marxian thought has been constrained by its respect for the efforts to apply Marxist categories to societies with weak states and pre-capitalist economies, and by its admiration for the revolutionary achievements of Lenin, Trotsky, Mao, and Castro under the banner of Marxism. This is not the place to assess those achievements and their impact, both for better and for worse, on the study of Marx. We may note, however, that the Protestant reformation now taking place in the Leninist church has eliminated whatever arguments there were – based on solidarity and history – against rethinking the most basic premises of Marxism. What has died is the revolutionary mystique, and in its absence the issues addressed by Marx himself take on an urgency they have lacked since Lenin.

I believe, moreover, that the particular interpretation of Marx offered in this book is strengthened by the recent revival of academic interest in the immediately pre-Marxian strands of modern thought – Hegelian, Smithian, Tocquevillian. The more self-consciously and explicitly contemporary thought resembles the precursors of Marx, the stronger my argument for returning to his method of critical analysis as a way of addressing the literature of our time. My effort to reinterpret Marx thus requires and participates in the current revival of interest in his predecessors: I can think of no time in recent history – not even the defeats of 1848 – when the lifelong lessons Marx derived from his joint critique of Hegel and the Left-Hegelians have been more relevant.

To say that Marx is more relevant than ever in our neo-Hegelian world is not to argue that Marx was some kind of prophet whose every statement must be read as an esoteric prediction of our current situation. I have suggested, rather, that Marx's own work remained incomplete in his lifetime, and that much of what he accomplished needs to be done over again. My basic premise is that, whatever the particular defects of Marx's view – and they are many – we have no better example of the type of social theorizing that is needed today. No other thinker rivals Marx as a guide to understanding the politics of states which must view the capitalist economy as global and environmental, and I believe that his materialist method of addressing the theories of his day is a propitious guide for discovering the structural fissures in a world that only seems to be on the verge of understanding itself. The widespread perception that liberal democracy is triumphing through the global integration of the capitalist market persuades me not that Marx has nothing more to teach us, but rather that the Marxian moment is now.

Appendices

Appendix I The Hegelian System

The discussion that follows is a schematic summary of some of the philosophical issues covered in chapters 2–4 of the main text, and is intended to assist readers who may be unfamiliar with Hegelian terminology.

The phenomenological method

The argument of the *Phenomenology of Mind* is, superficially, an effort to redescribe the experience of coming to know yourself as both a subject and an object at the same time. Hegel uses a genetic account of consciousness to characterize both the maturation of a child into a self-comprehending individual and the development of world societies toward a point where respect for individuality is part of their way of life.[1] At both the individual and collective levels, Hegel characteristically argues that the achievement of self-consciousness requires a simultaneous transformation of the self and the world – the self so that it can better understand, and the world so that it can be more understandable.

Hegel's phenomenological method addresses the relationship among three ways in which we experience our thought. Firstly, there is *consciousness* – the experience of thoughts in our heads. Secondly, there is *self-consciousness* – the awareness of ourselves as thinking. Finally, there is the experience of the difference between consciousness and self-consciousness – this Hegel called the experience of *alienation*. It is through alienation that we are conscious of the difference between our consciousness (the contents of our minds), and our consciousness that we are conscious (of being the self who is conscious). (See figure 1.)

[1] Phenomenological development, then, represents the development of consciousness in both the individual and in history. Like subsequent biological theories, its thesis is that ontogeny (the development of the individual) recapitulates phylogeny (the development of the species).

Figure 1.   Phenomenology: Subjectivity vs. Objectivity

Alienation
becomes Absolute Knowledge

Consciousness	**Self-consciousness**
"I" for "me"	*"me" for "I"*

According to Hegel, the very birth of conscious experience is also the experience of embodiment. As expounded by Kojève, Hegel's fundamental argument rests upon the following insights into the problems of being simultaneously subject and object.

1   The possibility of desire presupposes that our access to material objects is largely mediated by the actions of others; inasmuch as material need is also a form of social dependency, even our most primitive needs must be recognized as desires by others before they can be satisfied. Self-consciousness begins when we too recognize our needs as desires. By recognizing our desires for things in the world, we have already internalized the standpoint of the other.

2   The recognition of desire organizes our thought simultaneously into a system of self and other, and of inner and outer. These two distinctions are elaborations of the underlying distinction between subject and object. They are not the same, but are linked as follows: in *thinking* of our own needs we cannot help but conceive of them in the same terms in which we would conceive of another person's needs for such objects; we thus become aware of others as having needs competitive with our own through the same mental act by which we distinguish between our inner lives and our awareness of the external world. The conscious externalization of a material world is for Hegel simultaneous with the unconscious internalization of our social dependence upon others.

3   If internalizing the other is the root of our psychological independence, then the role of philosophy for Hegel will be to reconcile our knowledge of the external world (the world as external) with a greater recognition of the self as a social construct grounded in our dependence on others. In Hegelian phenomenology relations between subjects are mediated by their needs for material things, and the individual awareness of relations among things is inherently intersubjective — that is, socially constructed.

4   The conscious self in Hegelian phenomenology is in the world, but is not identical with the world. We are each subjects who are regarded as objects by subjects who are not ourselves. The role of philosophy in

this predicament is to make the relation between our inner and our outer life seem less arbitrary and capricious by grounding it in a coherent account of the relation between self and other.[2]

The logical method

Hegel's *Philosophy of Right* uses his logical method to derive the *freedom of the individual* from the moments of our Concept of what it means to *live a life*. The central argument of the *Philosophy of Right* derives the Idea of the individual from the universal and particular moments of the Concept of the will.[3]

1   Hegel first argues that *for itself* the will is experienced as something *universal*, which means that it is not tied to any particular content. In the abstract we are capable of willing anything. This *moment of negativity* is the starting point of all of Hegel's logic. In the present context it means that our will (i.e., our subjectivity) is first experienced as the possibility of negating our present existence in our imagination. According to Hegel, our *immediate* experience of freedom[4] is that we can always change our mind.

2   Hegel next argues that *in itself* the will is experienced as something *particular*. This refers to the experience of having made up our minds. There would be no point in feeling free to be anything if we could not also feel free by being something in particular. Hegel described such determination of the will as a *negation of the negation*. The fact that we have made up our minds, when we could have chosen otherwise, is recognized by others as constituting a real commitment. Correspondingly, we respect the will of others by respecting the choices they have made, however arbitrary these may appear. As the negation of a negation the *positive* will differs from both negativity and mere "being." The positivity of our will (the will in itself) is for Hegel identical with our will as it would appear *for another*.

[2] For good discussions of the opening arguments of the *Phenomenology*, see Kojève, *Introduction to the Reading of Hegel*, "In Place of an Introduction," and Charles Taylor, "On the Opening Arguments of the *Phenomenology*."

[3] In German the word Hegel uses is "*Begriff*," sometimes translated as "notion," but translated as "Concept" in the Knox edition of the *Philosophy of Right*. See Knox's "Translator's Foreword" and Hegel's introduction, in *Hegel's Philosophy of Right* (tr. Knox).

[4] I.e., our experience unmediated by any particular choice foregone.

3   The Idea exists both in and for itself. It *actually* becomes what it appears to be in virtue of being *realized* to be so from within.[5] According to Hegel, the Idea of the individual is the realization of the first two moments of the Concept of the will through which we experience our subjective freedom. *For* itself the realization of individuality requires a respect for the universality of the chooser. *In* itself the realization of individuality requires a respect for the particularity of choice. To be a fully actualized individual is to grasp the universal significance of who one is in particular. As a self-realizing individual, I thus become reconciled to the knowledge that my particular choices may appear to others as arbitrary, even while I regard them as rationally determined. This reconciliation occurs when I take account of the meaning of my actions to them in making my choice, and when others acknowledge that arbitrary choice would be meaningless to someone who does not think he has reasons for choosing. In grasping the relation between the "particular" significance of my choices for others and their "universal" significance for me, I more fully realize both what I am doing and why.[6]

Having derived the Idea of the individual from the Concept of the will, Hegel devotes the remainder of the *Philosophy of Right* to deriving the Idea of freedom from the Concept of the individual. The main features of Hegel's mature method are summarized in figure 2, where all of the terms in a given column are mutually supporting; all of the terms in a given row are mutually contrasting.

[5] As we shall see, below, it is in this respect like a legitimate institution.

[6] We can rehearse Hegel's terminology as follows. The *universal* moment is the moment through which one understands one's freedom as a kind of a *negation*. I could be anything. (I could go out with anyone.) The significance of my desires is precisely that my desires can change. (For the moment you happen to be the one I love – a description which, under the universal, is the negation of who you happen to be in particular.) The *particular* moment, on the other hand, is the *negation of the negation*. (It is because I could love anyone – because anyone in the world could attract me – that it is significant that I love you.) Hegel suggests that both the universal and the particular must be understood as two moments of the same reality. Each can be exaggerated in a one-sided development. When they appear to be mutually necessary, then the Idea is realized (as we saw in chapter 2, above, when the Idea of free love was realised in the institution of marriage.)

Figure 2.   The Logic: Universal vs. Particular ("For Itself" vs. "In Itself")

The Concept (2 moments)		**The Idea**
(1) Universality	**(2) Particularity**	**(3) Individuality**
negativity	positivity (negation of negation)	self-related negativity
immediate	mediated	concrete
for itself	in itself	in and for itself
for us	for another	(institutional)
ideal	(empirical)	realized or actual

The Left-Hegelians

Bauer, Feuerbach, and Stirner all retained the basic structure of the Hegelian phenomenology of alienation and liberation that we saw in figure 1. In rejecting Hegel's apparent complacency, however, they saw alienation everywhere. To reflect this they implicitly revised his triad of "consciousness," "self-consciousness," and "alienation," replacing it with the triad of "conscious alienation," "the alienation of consciousness," and "the consciousness of alienation." Each of the three variants of Left-Hegelianism located the real problem of alienation as a relationship between two of these terms, and found the chance for liberation in the third. Essentially, however, all of them were running around the same Hegelian track – the self-alienation of the embodied mind.

In rejecting Hegel's hope of liberation through Absolute Knowledge, the Left-Hegelians differed mainly in their view of which form of alienation they would accept as liberating ($+$), and which forms they would regard as fundamentally oppressive ($-$). For Stirner, liberation would be the consciousness of alienation with the full sense of irony that this implies. The other two moments of consciousness, he thought, were merely unreflective forms of alienation, amounting to either role-absorption or role-withdrawal, respectively. Bauer and Feuerbach would have rotated the orientation of Hegel's schematism while preserving its form. As we have seen, Bauer celebrated conscious alienation as liberating, and attacked role-absorption (the alienation of consciousness) as oppressive once we become aware of it. In contrast, Feuerbach glorified the alienation of consciousness as a way of liberating ourselves from the conscious oppression of role-withdrawal (see figure 3).

Figure 3. Varieties of Left-Hegelianism
Key: (+) = *liberating*
     (−) = *oppressive*

Hegel

alienation −
Absolute Knowledge +

consciousness   self-consciousness

"The German Ideology"

consciousness of alienation
Stirner +
Bauer/Feuerbach−

alienated consciousness   alienation of consciousness
Bauer +   *Feuerbach +*
Stirner/Feuerbach−   *Stirner/Bauer−*

Marx

Marx began his critique of Hegel by reproducing in prose the schemata of
the phenomenological and logical approaches given in figures 1 and 2. We
can summarize Marx's composite analysis as follows.

In Hegel "consciousness" and "self-consciousness" do not automatically
correspond to "subjectivity" and "objectivity." What fills our minds when
we are not self-conscious is the world. So consciousness is also unself-
conscious objective knowledge. Consciousness only becomes our subjectivity when we distinguish ourselves from the world by having a point of
view. It is from the point of view of the objective self that we call our
consciousness "subjective." (The self is identified here as other than consciousness.) But this does not mean that self-consciousness is therefore
always objective. The self that is conscious is obviously also taken to be
the *subject* of the experience. (It is only by identifying with the other that
we can be aware of what it means to be a subject of experience.) Thus
interpreted, nothing in Hegel depends upon "subjectivity" and "objectivity"

as such. Everything depends, rather, upon the kind of object we identify ourselves as being in order to regard our consciousness as subjective, and the kind of subject we take ourselves to be in order to have those objects. In this reconstruction of Hegel's view, alienation and objectification appear in general not as the epistemological scandals they were for the Left-Hegelians, but as valuable properties of human nature.[7] Our real problems, then, lie in the specific contradictions between our alternative objectifications of the world and our alternative subjectifications of the self. Such problems, however, may not be purely philosophical, at least in Hegel's sense.

[7] "To *be* objective, natural and sensuous and to have object, nature and sense outside oneself, or to be object, nature and sense for a third person is one and the same thing. A being which does not have its nature outside itself is not a natural being ... a being which has no object outside itself is not an objective being. A being which is not itself an object for a third being ... has no objective relationships and its existence is not objective ... A non-objective being is a *non-being*." Marx, "Critique of Hegel's Dialectic and General Philosophy" (tr. Livingstone and Benton), p. 390. For further discussion of this passage see chapter 4, above.

Appendix 2   Democracy and Elections

This appendix restates the problems of democracy and deradicalization discussed in chapters 5 and 6 using the conceptual tools developed in part I.

Hegel

For many people there are two aspects to the experience of voting. On the one hand the vote is a form of political action – by voting we collectively exercise the sovereign power to transform society from within. On the other hand the vote is a form of co-optation – by participating in the election we help to legitimate the outcome. Since by voting we *both* express our views and contribute to the validity of the election, the two aspects of voting pose a problem for those who choose to vote expecting to be disappointed in the result.

Yet an individual cannot avoid this problem by simply choosing not to vote in an election that is actually taking place. For the political system the significance of my refusal to vote is that the state goes on as it was. The significance for me is that I feel free. But this is exactly the intended result of voting in the Hegelian state.

From a Hegelian standpoint this seeming paradox of democracy would reduce to the question of why it is necessary for the election to actually take place, whether or not people vote, in order for them to understand themselves to be free.[1] His answer would be that the ordinary man feels

---

[1] The following discussion extrapolates a Hegelian view of established electoral democracy. In the *Philosophy of Right* Hegel explicitly recognizes that popular suffrage can lead to voter apathy, and suggests that the establishment electoral democracy would be superfluous in a state that has successfully institutionalized political participation through the non-electoral mechanisms described in chapter 8, above. see *Hegel's Philosophy of Right* (tr. Knox), pp. 202–3.

free when he votes, and that some special individuals can feel free without even voting, just because the election is held. Holding the election is necessary for the state to accommodate both sorts of citizen. Elections are the medium through which citizens can understand their politics in terms of their freedom, and their freedom in terms of their politics.

Hegel could have explained the need for elections to actually be held in a democracy by invoking his logical method to describe our vote as having two "moments": the vote for us, and the vote in itself. For each of us the vote we cast opens potentially universal possibilities insofar as it allows us to think about our government as a whole. But voting in itself describes the way in which our particular vote appears to the person who counts it. Here it is simply part of the system.[2]

Both of these "moments" of voting would be necessary to the realization that the elections must actually occur.[3] A one-sided emphasis on either leads to disillusionment. It is disillusioning to think that democracy is real only if we can transform the system totally from the inside, but ultimately no less disillusioning to think that, because our vote doesn't make a difference, not voting does make a difference. By recognizing that he could feel free in an election by either voting or not voting, the Hegelian citizen would perceive the election as an opportunity to give yet another interpretation of himself in a political world in which this is all that is ultimately asked of him.

The Left-Hegelians

Whether or not we decide to vote, our present-day radical democrats typically give us three types of reason for being cynical about elections – for rejecting them in our minds. The main radical positions on this question implicitly track the Left-Hegelian views that we sketched in chapter 3.

1 A radical descendent of Bauer would decide whether or not to vote by determining whether the election offers him a way of realizing his deepest principles.[4] Whenever organized elections discourage us from

---

[2] From the state's point of view the aggregate vote may sometimes change the government, but our particular votes are really a ratification of the electoral process itself. As our votes are counted we become reconciled to the actuality of whatever is going to happen as a result.

[3] Consider the importance placed on elections actually taking place in US foreign policy toward Nicaragua and El Salvador in the 1980s.

articulating our collective ideals, the Bauerite democrat would dismiss the official political process as the behavior of the "mass."[5]

2   In contrast the radical descendent of Feuerbach would find it desirable for us to sincerely immerse ourselves in the mass. We would only be able to do so, however, on those rare occasions when we have a candidate who appears as the direct representative of our "species being." To the Feuerbachian democrat an election that lacks the element of spontaneous communion between the candidate and the masses would not provide the kind of immediate satisfaction that we should expect from political participation.

3   The radical descendent of Stirner would encourage us to vote in a way that preserves our authenticity.[6] This means avoiding immersion in mass behavior, but without necessarily holding out for our highest ideals. Since the point of voting is to make up one's own mind, Stirner's individual would insist that no one else must influence his vote. Such an individual would eventually become able to vote cynically — realizing how little his vote counts and not even liking the candidate for whom he is voting — provided that he is willing to accept responsibility for the outcome.

Marx

Following Hegel, Marx would have seen this series of moves as part of the situation within which they are made, and about which they are judgements. Each Left-Hegelian position would be an appropriate response to the problem of voting, only if that problem is how to understand oneself better. All are essentially the affectation of attitudes that would allow one to better accept oneself within a potentially unacceptable situation. None of the radical critiques of democratic participation described above would allow one to see what part of oneself one must reject in withdrawing from the situation, or what part of the situation one must internalize to become acceptable to oneself.

---

[4] He would thus reject participation in those elections where strategic compromises would preclude the possibility of achieving consensus upon a vision of a future society. Cf. the dilemmas posed in Przeworski, *Capitalism and Social Democracy.*

[5] Bauer himself distinguished between the "mass" and the "genus." See Bauer, "The Genus and the Crowd."

[6] Our paramount objective throughout an electoral campaign would be to preserve our sense of ourselves as unique.

To put the point politically, none of these responses has anything to do with determining how one should vote. They do not depend upon specific analyses of what kinds of vote might be regressive or progressive in the development of political struggles that go on within us, and that will continue without us. Each Left-Hegelian response is concerned rather with a single issue — one's view of the ideological significance of voting. For this reason each Left-Hegelian response is working in just the way that Hegel might have argued that unself-conscious participation in an election works for ordinary people. From a Marxian perspective the main ideological function of the Left-Hegelian would be to supply alternative attitudes for those people who have difficulty in identifying with their role as voters.

Unlike the Left-Hegelians, Marx would have characteristically responded to the inherent contradiction in the experience of *being* a voter by stressing the need for political analysis in an election. Such analysis might appear to be cynical to the likes of Bauer and Feuerbach, but it would lead a Marxist to care about the outcome. While a Left-Hegelian might take some satisfaction in the low voter turnout in the United States in 1980 and 1984, it would matter more to Marx that Reagan won those elections. To understand such phenomena Marx·undertook the sort of political analysis described in chapters 7 through 12.

Appendix 3　Marx's Critique of Political Economy

This appendix distinguishes and enumerates the various forms of Marxian critique of political economy that appear in chapters 3 and 10–12.

Phenomenological critique

In his earliest writings Marx uses Hegel's phenomenological method (as discussed in part I) to describe the subjective and objective contradictions in the experience of a person who is understood to be participating in a market such as that described by the classical political economists. Marx's 1844 critique of James Mill, for example, describes production for exchange in starkly phenomenological terms. In the following extended passage Marx expertly develops the critical implications for market theory of the Hegelian point that production for sale (alienation) gives one an alienated relation to one's product.

> Man ... *produces* only in order to *have* ... [S]urplus production ... is ... a form of *mediation* by means of which it becomes possible to satisfy a need which does not find its objectification directly in *one's own* production, but in the production of another.
> . . .
> [O]ur production is not man's production for man as man, i.e. it is not *social* production. As men none of us can claim to enjoy the product of another ... For our products are not united for each other by the bond of *human nature* ... Each of us sees in his product only his *own* objectified self-interest, hence in the product of others the objectification of a *different* ... self-interest ... Naturally, as a human being ... you have *need* of my product ... But your need, your desire and your will are impotent as far as my product is concerned ... Far from their being the *means* giving you *power* over my production, they are rather the *means* whereby I acquire power over you.
> When I produce *more* of a thing than I can use myself, then my surplus production is *calculated* and adapted to your *need*. I produce a surplus of the

object only in *appearance*. In reality I produce a *different* object ... [T]he labour I perform to satisfy your need ... is ... merely an *appearance* ... based on our mutual plundering of each other.

The thing that gives your need for my possessions a *value*, a *worth* and an *effect* in my eyes is simply and solely your *possession*, the *equivalent* of my possession ... Your *demand* and your equivalent possessions are synonymous, convertible terms for me, and your demand has an effective *meaning* only if it has ... an effect upon me. In the absence of this, you are merely a human being and your demand is no more than an ungratified desire ... [W]e each regard our own products as the *power* each has over the other and over himself.

The only comprehensible language we have is the language our possessions use together. We would not understand a human language and it would remain ineffectual. From the one side, such a language would be felt to be begging, imploring and hence *humiliating* ... From the other side, it would be received as *impertinence* or *insanity* and so rejected ... We are so estranged from our human essence that the direct language of man strikes us as an *offence against the dignity of man*, whereas the estranged language of objective values appears as the justified, self-confident and self-acknowledged dignity of man incarnate.
...
Let us suppose that we had produced as human beings ... (1) In my *production* ... I would ... have enjoyed the *expression* of my own individual life ... I would experience an individual pleasure. (2) In your use or enjoyment of my product I would have the *immediate* satisfaction and knowledge that in my labour I had gratified a *human* need ... (3) I would be acknowledged by you as the complement of your own being, as an essential part of yourself. I would thus know myself to be confirmed both in your thought and your love. (4) In the individual expression of my own life I would have brought about the immediate expression of your life, and so in my individual activity I would have directly *confirmed* ... my *human, communal* nature.

Our productions would be as many mirrors from which our natures would shine forth ... My labour would be the *free expression* and hence the *enjoyment of life*.[1]

The foregoing critique of production for exchange is not specific to the relationship between wage labor and capital. Everything that Marx says could equally apply to the relations between two artisans or two capitalists.[2]

In 1844 Marx focused his mastery of the phenomenological method on Adam Smith's description of wage labor. The first of Marx's "Economic

---

[1] Marx, "Excerpts from James Mill's *Elements of Political Economy*," pp. 274–8.
[2] See Gerald A. Cohen, "Bourgeois and Proletarians."

and Philosophical Manuscripts" is in reality an excerpting of descriptive insights from Adam Smith's "Of the Wages of Labour"[3] — restated as critique. In the well-known discussion of "Estranged Labour" that follows these excerpts, Marx applies Hegel's phenomenological method to Smith's frank admissions about the effect of wage labor on the worker.

> We shall start out from *present-day* economic fact.
>   The worker becomes poorer the more wealth he produces ... [He] becomes an ever cheaper commodity the more commodities he produces.
>   . . .
> So much does objectification appear as loss of the object that the worker is robbed of the objects he needs most not only for life but also for work ...
> So much does the appropriation of the object appear as an estrangement that the more objects the worker produces the fewer can he possess and the more he falls under the domination of his product, of capital.[4]

Marx never entirely abandoned the phenomenological approach to the critique of political economy. Some of the most powerful passages in *Capital*, volume I echo the passage above in describing what it would be like to *be* a worker who recognized himself in the picture painted by political economy.[5]

Historical critique

Throughout his life Marx inveighed against political economy for presupposing that in all historical periods economic man must inevitably behave like Defoe's Robinson Crusoe — a rational maximizer cast adrift in a world of limited resources with no preexisting social structure and a fortuitously available supply of human labor power. In opposition to this view Marx argued that capitalism is an *essentially* historical phenomenon that could not be understood by any theory that presupposed that all of the preconditions for the relationship between wage labor and capital have always existed.

Marx's historical critique of political economy appears (in an undeveloped form) even in his earliest writing.

[3] Adam Smith, *The Wealth of Nations*, ch. 8.
[4] Marx, "Economic and Philosophical Manuscripts," pp. 323–4. For discussions of the role of these writings in the development of Marx's thought, cf. Althusser, *For Marx*; Hyppolite, "On the Structure and Philosophical Presuppositions of Marx's *Capital*"; and McLellan, *Marx Before Marxism*, chs 7–8.
[5] See, e.g., *Capital*, vol. I, ch. 19, pp. 681–2.

Political economy proceeds from the fact of private property. It does not explain it ... For example when it defines the relation of wages to profit it takes the interests of capitalists as the basis of its analysis; i.e. it assumes what it is supposed to explain ... We must avoid repeating the mistake of the political economist who bases his explanations on some imaginary primordial condition. Such a primordial condition explains nothing ... It assumes as facts and events what it is supposed to deduce, namely the necessary relationship between two things, between for example, the division of labor and exchange.[6]

This theme is carried forward in Marx's mature work. In his introduction to *The Grundrisse* Marx directly attacks Smith and Ricardo for indulging in eighteenth-century "Robinsonades"[7] – an argument developed at some length in *Capital*, volume I.[8] Not until the end of that volume, however, does Marx actually describe the way in which the fundamental relation between wage labor and capital first emerged out of the historical conditions of feudalism. His classic discussion of the secret of the "So-Called Primitive Accumulation" in Adam Smith's theory reveals the historical violence required to separate feudal peasants from access to the means of subsistence, and hence to create the conditions under which the capitalist and the wage laborer could come face to face in the process of commodity production.[9]

Ricardian critique

Just as Marx devoted considerable attention to criticizing the philosophical views of the Left-Hegelians, so too he engaged in extensive critique of the economic views of the Ricardian socialists. These theorists concluded from Ricardo's labor theory of value that the capitalist's appropriation of profit is a form of theft and that all wealth should be distributed as wages paid in proportion to each worker's expenditure of labor time.[10] Against these

[6] Marx, "Economic and Philosophical Manuscripts," pp. 322–3. cf. *Capital*, vol. I, p. 274.
[7] Marx, *Economic Manuscripts of 1857–58* [*The Grundrisse*] (tr. Wangermann), p. 17.
[8] *Capital*, vol. I, pp. 169–172.
[9] Ibid., part 8.
[10] See, e.g., Bray, *Labour's Wrongs and Labour's Remedy*; Hodgskin, *Labour Defended against the Claims of Capital*; William Thompson, *Labour Rewarded: The Claims of Labour and Capital Conciliated* and *An Inquiry into the Principles of the Distribution of Wealth Most Conducive to Human Happiness*; and Torrens, *On Wages and Combination*.

left-wing appropriations of the labor theory of value, Marx consistently
upheld the integrity of Ricardo's own view by arguing that the appropriation
and accumulation of a surplus is essential to the continuing production of
commodities for the market — a point that Ricardo himself had not fully
theorized.[11]

Marx published his most extended attack on the Ricardian Left in the
form of a critique of Proudhon's *Philosophy of Misery*. Here Marx argued
against the illusion that negative features of capitalist production could be
eliminated while preserving its positive features.[12] Throughout *The Poverty
of Philosophy* we see a Marx who is committed to the rigorous holism of
classical political economy — a holism that would later enable him to
argue that the negative consequences of capitalism are in large part necessary
to its continuing development.

Logical critique

The main body of this book gives primary emphasis to what might crudely
be called a "logical critique" of classical political economy. Put more
precisely, this critique first imagines that the conceptual categories of
political economy actually function within the market in the manner
described by Hegel's logical method[13] and then criticizes both those categories and the economy itself using the general approach outlined in
chapter 4 above.

Marx's "logical critique" is based on the fact that classical political
economy implicitly proceeds by distinguishing conceptually between pairs
of concepts that it then shows to be theoretically equivalent through the
operation of the market. Among these pairs are production and consumption, distribution and production, exchange and circulation[14] — and, Marx
would later add, circulation and distribution, and realization and accumulation. In analyzing each of these analogous pairs Marx typically noted a
common pattern: in each pair the members reflected each other as a whole,
and yet each member also appeared within the other as a particular
"moment." (Exchange, for example, encompasses the entire circulation of

---

[11] See Marx, *The Poverty of Philosophy*, ch. 1, and *Theories of Surplus Value*, part
3, pp. 69–84 and 263–325.
[12] Marx, *The Poverty of Philosophy*, ch. 2. See also "Marx to P.V. Annenkov"
and "On Proudhon," which recast some of Marx's criticisms while presenting a
slightly more positive view of Proudhon's *What is Property?*
[13] See chapter 2 and appendix 1.
[14] See Marx, *Economic Manuscripts of 1857–58* [*The Grundrisse*] (tr.
Wangermann), introduction.

commodities and also appears as a specific act within the circulation of commodities.)

Marx's style of argument throughout *The Grundrisse, Capital,* and *Theories of Surplus Value* is to constantly suggest that each of the elements that the economist tries to connect as part of a single system already reflects the others as a part of itself. Where Hegel might have seen a system of structural analogies, however, Marx saw structural contradictions. In chapter 10 we saw, for example, that the economists describe exchange twice over, once as a moment within the division of labor, and once as a system of which the division of labor is only a part.[15] According to Marx these two descriptions, which are intended to be equivalent, are in fact contradictory in various ways. Parallel arguments might be made about the other pairs of terms that economists both distinguish and equate, such as production and consumption in Say's Law.[16]

By tracing the effects of these structural contradictions throughout economic theory, Marx believed that he could identify the points of material stress in the economy as it becomes conscious of itself through politics.[17] In almost every case Marx found that various contradictions among economic categories tend to surface in the description of wage labor – as a commodity, as capital, as a force of production. His paradigmatic critique of classical political economy is that the conceptual categories that it tries to equate continue to give essentially divergent pictures of the role of human labor power in the production of commodities.[18] According to Marx, the standpoint of wage labor thus provides the perspective from which the contradictions implicit in the system of analogies set up by the economists can be revealed.[19]

[15] Cf., above, chapter 4 (on wholes and parts) and chapter 9 (on state and civil society).

[16] Cf. Marx, *Economic Manuscripts of 1857–58* [*The Grundrisse*] (tr. Wagermann) pp. 26–32 and Samuelson, "Concerning Say's Law."

[17] Marx returns to this general method whenever he introduces a new topic in *Capital.* In volume III, for example, Marx relies heavily on a Hegelian manipulation of concepts to analyze the role of interest-bearing capital in the overall mode of production. (See *Capital,* vol III, chs 21–25, esp. ch. 21.)

[18] For example, labor power is purchased as a commodity in exchange for wages, which are also seen as a capital investment in the production of other commodities. We thus have a paradigm case of the contradiction between viewing commodities as capitals and capitals as commodities.

[19] Rosdolsky stresses Marx's use of Hegel's logical method in Rosdolsky, *The Making of Marx's 'Capital.'* For alternative views of how Marx's method in *Capital* is based on the *Grundrisse* see the editor's commentary in Marx, *Texts on Method,* and Fine and Harris, *Rereading 'Capital,'* ch. 1. For a provocative effort to integrate the range of issues touched upon in this appendix see Godelier, *Rationality and Irrationality in Economics,* sec. 2.

References

"Feuerbach, Marx, and the Left Hegelians." *Philosophical Forum Quarterly* 8:2–4 (1978): 1–324.

"Hegel and Legal Theory Symposium." *Cardozo Law Review* 10 (March–April 1989).

"The No-Growth Society." *Daedalus* 102:4 (Fall 1973).

"Poor Man's Burden: A Survey of the Third World." *The Economist* (September 23, 1989): 3–58.

"The Redstocking Manifesto." In *Sisterhood is Powerful: An Anthology of Writings from the Women's Liberation Movement*. Edited by Robin Morgan. New York, Vintage Books, 1970: 598–601.

"Responses to Fukuyama." *The National Interest* 16 (Summer 1989): 19–35.

"The SCUM Manifesto." In *Sisterhood is Powerful: An Anthology of Writings from the Women's Liberation Movement*. Edited by Robin Morgan. New York, Vintage Books, 1970: 577–83.

Aglietta, Michel. "World Capitalism in the Eighties." *New Left Review* 136 (November–December 1982): 5–41.

————— *A Theory of Capitalist Regulation*. London, New Left Books, 1979.

Alberoni, Francesco. *Movement and Institution*. New York, Columbia, 1984.

Alford, Robert, and Friedland, Roger. *The Powers of Theory*. Cambridge [Eng.], Cambridge University Press, 1985.

Althusser, Louis. "Ideology and Ideological State Apparatuses." In *Lenin and Philosophy and Other Essays*. Translated by Ben Brewster. London, New Left Books, 1971: 127–86.

————— "Lenin Before Hegel." In *Lenin and Philosophy and Other Essays*. Translated by Ben Brewster. London, New Left Books, 1971: 107–26.

————— "Marx's Relation to Hegel." In *Montesquieu, Rousseau, Hegel, and Marx*, Translated by Ben Brewster. London, New Left Books, 1972: 161–86.

————— *For Marx*. Translated by Ben Brewster. London, Allen Lane, 1969.

Althusser, Louis, and Balibar, Etienne. *Reading Capital*. Translated by Ben Brewster. London, New Left Books, 1970.

Amin, Samir. *Unequal Development*. New York, Monthly Review Press, 1973.

Anderson, Benedict R. *Imagined Communities: Reflections on the Origin and Spread of Nationalism*. London, Verso, 1983.

Anderson, Charles W. "Political Design and the Representation of Interests." *Comparative Political Studies* 10 (1977): 127–52.

Anderson, Perry. "The Antinomies of Antonio Gramsci." *New Left Review* 100 (November 1976–January 1977): 5–78.

——— "Origins of the Present Crisis." In *Towards Socialism*. Edited by Perry Anderson and Robin Blackburn with an introduction by Andrew Hacker. Ithaca, Cornell University Press, 1966: 11–52.

——— "Socialism and Pseudo-Empiricism." *New Left Review* 35 (January–February 1966): 2–42.

——— *Arguments Within English Marxism*. London, Verso, 1980.

——— *Considerations on Western Marxism*. London, New Left Books, 1976.

——— *In The Tracks of Historical Materialism*. London, Verso, 1983.

Aristotle. *Constitution of Athens and Related Texts*. Translated by Kurt von Fritz and Ernst Kapp. New York, Hafner Publishing Co., 1974.

——— *The Politics*. Translated by T.A. Sinclair. New York, Penguin Books, 1981.

Atkinson, Ti-Grace. *Amazon Odyssey*. New York, Links Books, 1974.

Augustine. *The City of God*. Garden City, N.Y., Image, 1968.

——— *On Christian Doctrine*. Translated by D.W. Robertson, Jr. Indianapolis, Liberal Arts Press, 1958.

Avineri, Shlomo. "Hegel and Nationalism." In *Hegel's Political Philosophy*. Edited by Walter Kaufmann. New York, Atherton Press, 1970: 109–36.

——— *Hegel's Theory of the Modern State*. London, Cambridge University Press, 1972.

——— *The Making of Modern Zionism*. New York, Basic Books, 1981.

——— "Moses Hess: Socialism and Nationalism as a Critique of Bourgeois Society." In *The Making of Modern Zionism*. New York, Basic Books, 1981: ch. 3.

——— *The Social and Political Thought of Karl Marx*. New York, Cambridge University Press, 1968.

Bahro, Rudolf. *The Alternative in Eastern Europe*. Translated by David Fernbach. London, New Left Books, 1978.

——— *From Red to Green: Interview with New Left Review*. Translated by Gus Fagan and Richard Hurst. London, New Left Books, 1984.

——— *Socialism and Survival*. Translated by David Fernbach. Introduced by E.P. Thompson. London, Heretic Books, 1982.

Balbo, Laura. "Family, Women, and the State: Notes Toward a Typology of Family Roles and Public Intervention." In *Changing Boundaries of the Political: Essays on the Evolving Balance Between State and Society, Public and Private in Europe*. Edited by Charles S. Maier. Cambridge [Eng.], Cambridge University Press, 1987: 201–19.

Balbus, Isaac. *Marxism and Domination: A Neo-Hegelian, Feminist, Psychoanalytic Theory of Sexual, Political and Technological Liberation*. Princeton, Princeton University Press, 1982.

Balibar, Etienne. "The Vacillation of Ideology." In *Marxism and the Interpretation of Cultures*. Edited by Gary Nelson and Lawrence Grossberg. Urbana, University of Illinois Press, 1988: 159–209.

————— The Dictatorship of the Proletariat. Translated by Grahame Lock. Introduction by Grahame Lock. Afterword by Louis Althusser. London, New Left
Books, 1977.

Baran, Paul. The Political Economy of Growth. New York, Monthly Review Press,
1957.

Baran, Paul, and Sweezy, Paul. Monopoly Capital. New York, Monthly Review
Press, 1966.

Barrett, Michele. Women's Oppression Today. London, New Left Books, 1980.

Barry, Brian M. "The Public Interest." In Political Philosophy. Edited by Anthony
Quinton. Oxford, Oxford University Press, 1967: 112–26.

————— Sociologists, Economists, and Democracy. London, Collier–Macmillan,
1970.

Bastiat, Frederic. Economic Harmonies. Translated by W. Hayden Boyers. Edited
by George B. de Huszar. Princeton, Van Nostrand, 1964.

————— Economic Sophisms. Translated by Arthur Goddard. Irvington-on-
Hudson, N.Y., The Foundation for Economic Education, 1964.

Baudrillard, Jean. The Mirror of Production. Translated by Mark Poster. St. Louis,
Telos Press, 1975.

Bauer, Bruno. "The Capacity of Present Day Jews and Christians to Become Free."
Translated by Michael P. Malloy. The Philosophical Forum 8:2–4 (1978):
135–49.

————— "The Genus and the Crowd." Translated by Michael P. Malloy. The
Philosophical Forum 8:2–4 (1978): 126–34.

————— "The Jewish Problem." In The Young Hegelians: An Anthology. Edited
by Lawrence S. Stepelevich. Cambridge [Eng.], Cambridge University Press,
1983: 187–97.

————— "The Trumpet of the Last Judgement over Hegel." In The Young Hegelians:
An Anthology. Edited by Lawrence S. Stepelevich. Cambridge [Eng.], Cambridge
University Press, 1983: 177–86.

Beauvoir, Simone de. The Second Sex. Translated and edited by H.M. Parshley.
New York, Vintage Books, 1974.

Beer, Samuel. British Politics in the Collectivist Age. New York, Alfred Knopf,
1965.

Belenky, Mary, Clichy, B., Goldberger, N., and Tarule, J. Women's Ways of
Knowing: The Development of Self, Voice, and Mind. New York, Basic Books,
1987.

Bell, Daniel. The Cultural Contradictions of Capitalism. New York, Basic Books,
1976.

Benhabib, Seyla, and Cornell, Drucilla (eds). Feminism as Critique. Minneapolis,
University of Minnesota Press, 1987.

Benjamin, Walter. "The Work of Art in the Age of Mechanical Reproduction." In
Illuminations. Edited and with an introduction by Hannah Arendt. Translated
by Harry Zohn. New York, Schocken Books, 1968: 217–51.

Berger, Suzanne (ed.). Organizing Interests in Western Europe: Pluralism, Corporatism, and the Transformation of Politics. Cambridge [Eng.], Cambridge
University Press, 1981.

Berger, Suzanne, and Piore, Michael. *Dualism and Discontinuity in Industrial Societies.* Cambridge [Eng.], Cambridge University Press, 1980.

Bergson, Abram. "A Note on Consumer's Surplus." *Journal of Economic Literature* 13:1 (March 1975): 38−44.

Berki, R.N. "Perspectives in the Marxian Critique of Hegel's Political Philosophy." In *Hegel's Political Philosophy: Problems and Perspectives.* Edited by Z.A. Pelczynski. Cambridge [Eng.], Cambridge University Press, 1971: 199−219.

Berlin, Isaiah. "Benjamin Disraeli, Karl Marx and the Search for Identity." In *Against the Current: Essays in the History of Ideas.* Edited by Henry Hardy. New York, Viking Press, 1980: 252−86.

─────── "'From Hope and Fear Set Free'." In *Concepts and Categories: Philosophical Essays.* Edited by Henry Hardy. New York, Viking Press, 1979: 173−98.

─────── "Historical Inevitability." In *Four Essays on Liberty.* New York, Oxford University Press, 1970: 41−117.

─────── "The Life and Opinions of Moses Hess." In *Against the Current: Essays in the History of Ideas.* Edited by Henry Hardy. New York, Viking Press, 1980: 213−51.

─────── "Two Concepts of Liberty." In *Four Essays on Liberty.* New York, Oxford University Press, 1970: 118−72.

─────── *Four Essays on Liberty.* New York, Oxford University Press, 1970.

Bernstein, Richard J. *The Restructuring of Social and Political Theory.* New York, Harcourt Brace Jovanovich, 1976.

Binder, Leonard. "The Crises of Political Development." In *Crises and Sequences in Political Development.* Edited by Leonard Binder et al. Princeton, Princeton University Press, 1971.

Blake, Judith. "Coercive Pronatalism and American Population Policy." In *Pronatalism: The Myth of Mom and Apple Pie.* Edited by Ellen Peck and J. Senderowitz. New York, Thomas Y. Crowell, 1974: 44−50.

Blau, Peter M. *Exchange and Power in Social Life.* New York, John Wiley, 1964.

Blauner, Robert. *Alienation and Freedom: The Factory Worker and His Industry.* Chicago, University of Chicago Press, 1964.

Bleaney, Michael F. *Underconsumption Theories.* London, Lawrence and Wishart, 1976.

Block, Fred. "Cooperation and Conflict in the Capitalist World Economy." In *Revising State Theory.* Philadelphia, Temple University Press, 1987: ch. 4.

─────── "Political Choice and the Multiple 'Logics' of Capital." In *Revising State Theory.* Philadelphia, Temple University Press, 1987: ch. 9.

─────── "Postindustrial Development and the Obsolescence of Economic Categories." In *Revising State Theory.* Philadelphia, Temple University Press, 1987: ch. 8.

─────── "The Ruling Class Does Not Rule." In *Revising State Theory.* Philadelphia, Temple University Press, 1987: ch. 3.

─────── *The Origins of International Economic Disorder: A Study of United States International Monetary Policy from World War II to the Present.* Berkeley, University of California Press, 1977.

———— *Revising State Theory.* Philadelphia, Temple University Press, 1987: ch. 8.

Bloom, Allan. "Responses to Fukuyama." *The National Interest* 16 (Summer 1989): 3–18.

Bloom, Harold. *The Anxiety of Influence: A Theory of Poetry.* New York, Oxford University Press, 1973.

Bluestone, Barry, and Harrison, Bennett. *The Deindustrialization of America: Plant Closings, Community Abandonment and the Dismantling of Basic Industry.* New York, Basic Books, 1982.

Bobbio, Norberto. "Civil Society." In *Democracy and Dictatorship: The Nature and Limits of State Power.* Translated by Peter Kennealy. Minneapolis, University of Minnesota Press, 1989.

———— "Gramsci and the Conception of Civil Society." In *Which Socialism?* Translated by Roger Griffin. Introduction by Richard Bellamy. Minneapolis, University of Minnesota Press, 1987: 139–61.

———— "Is There a Marxist Doctrine of the State?" In *Which Socialism?* Translated by Roger Griffin. Introduction by Richard Bellamy. Minneapolis, University of Minnesota Press, 1987: 47–64.

———— *Democracy and Dictatorship: The Nature and Limits of State Power.* Translated by Peter Kennealy. Minneapolis, University of Minnesota Press, 1989.

———— *Which Socialism?* Translated by Roger Griffin. Introduction by Richard Bellamy. Minneapolis, University of Minnesota Press, 1987.

Böhm-Bawerk, Eugen von. *Capital and Interest.* 3 vols in one. South Holland, Ill., Libertarian Press, 1959.

Bookchin, Murray. *Post-Scarcity Anarchism.* Berkeley, Ramparts Press, 1971.

Boulding, Kenneth. "The Shadow of the Stationary State." *Daedalus* 102:4 (Fall 1973): 89–102.

Bourdieu, Pierre. *Outline of a Theory of Practice.* Translated by Richard Nice. Cambridge [Eng.], Cambridge University Press, 1977.

Boyte, Harry. *The Backyard Revolution: Understanding the New Citizen Movement.* Philadelphia, Temple University Press, 1980.

Bradley, Francis Herbert. *Ethical Studies.* 2nd edn. Oxford, The Clarendon Press, 1959.

Bray, John Francis. *Labour's Wrongs and Labour's Remedy; or, the Age of Might and the Age of Right.* [reprint edn] New York, Augustus M. Kelley, 1965.

Brenner, Johanna, and Ramas, Maria. "Rethinking Women's Oppression." *New Left Review* 144 (March–April 1984), 33–71.

Brenner, Robert. "The Origins of Capitalist Development: A Critique of Neo-Smithian Marxism." *New Left Review* 104 (1977): 25–93.

———— "The Social Bases of Economic Development." *Analytical Marxism.* Edited by John Roemer. Cambridge [Eng.], Cambridge University Press, 1986: ch. 2.

Brewer, Anthony. *Marxist Theories of Imperialism: A Critical Survey.* London, Routledge and Kegan Paul, 1980.

Brown, Lester. "Rich Countries and Poor in a Finite, Interdependent World." *Daedalus* 102:4 (Fall, 1973): 153–64.

Brown, Norman O. "Revisioning Historical Identities." Unpublished Manuscript.

———— *Life Against Death*. Middletown, Wesleyan University Press, 1959.

———— *Love's Body*. New York, Vintage Books, 1966.

Buber, Martin. *Paths in Utopia*. Translated by R.F.C. Hull. Boston, Beacon Press, 1958.

Buchanan, Allen. *Marx and Justice: The Radical Critique of Liberalism*. Totowa, N.J., Rowan & Littlefield, 1982.

Buchanan, James M., and Tullock, Gordon. *The Calculus of Consent*. Ann Arbor, University of Michigan Press, 1962.

Bukharin, Nicolai. *Economic Theory of the Leisure Class*. Introduction by Donald J. Harris. New York, Monthly Review Press, 1972.

———— *Imperialism and the Accumulation of Capital*. In Rosa Luxemburg/ Nicolai Bukharin, *The Accumulation of Capital – An Anti-Critique/Imperialism and the Accumulation of Capital*. Translated by Rudolf Wichmann. Edited and with an introduction by Kenneth Tarbuck. New York, Monthly Review Press, 1972.

Burawoy, Michael. "Marxism without Micro-Foundations." *Socialist Review* 19:2 (April–June 1989): 53–86.

———— "Should We Give Up on Socialism?" *Socialist Review* 19:1 (January–March, 1989): 57–74.

Burke, Edmund. *Reflections on the Revolution in France*. Chicago, Gateway Editions, 1955.

Burke, Kenneth. *A Grammar of Motives and a Rhetoric of Motives*. Cleveland, Meridian Books, 1962.

Burnham, Walter Dean. *The Current Crisis in American Politics*. Oxford, Oxford University Press, 1982.

Butler, Judith. "Variations on Sex and Gender: Beauvoir, Wittig, and Foucault." In *Feminism as Critique*. Edited by Seyla Benhabib and Drucilla Cornell. Minneapolis, University of Minnesota Press, 1987.

Cabral, Amilcar. "Brief Analysis of the Social Structure in Guinea." In *Revolution in Guinea*. Translated and edited by Richard Handyside. New York, Monthly Review Press, 1969.

Cain, Glen. "The Challenge of Segmented Labor Market Theories to Orthodox Theory: A Survey." *Journal of Economic Literature* 14:4 (December 1976): 1215–57.

Capra, Fritjof, and Spretnak, Charlene. *Green Politics: The Global Promise*. New York, E.F. Dutton, 1984.

Carey, Henry Charles. *The Past, the Present and the Future*. [reprint edn] New York, Augustus M. Kelley, 1963.

———— *Principles of Political Economy*. [reprint edn] New York, Augustus M. Kelley, 1965.

Carver, Terrell. "Marx – and Hegel's *Logic*." *Political Studies* 24:1: 57–68.

———— "Marx's Commodity Fetishism." *Inquiry* 18: 39–63.

———— *Marx's Social Theory*. Oxford, Oxford University Press, 1982.

Chandler, Alfred. *The Visible Hand: The Managerial Revolution in American Business*. Cambridge, Mass., Harvard University Press, 1977.

Chayes, Abram. "The Modern Corporation and the Rule of Law." In *The Corporation in Modern Society*. Edited and with an introduction by Edward S. Mason. New York, Atheneum, 1966: 25–45.

Chodorow, Nancy. *The Reproduction of Mothering: Psychoanalysis and the Sociology of Gender*. Berkeley, University of California Press, 1978.

Cixous, Hélène. "The Laugh of the Medusa." Translated by Keith Cohen and Paula Cohen. In *The Signs Reader: Women, Gender, and Scholarship*. Edited by Elizabeth Abel and Emily K. Abel. Chicago, University of Chicago Press, 1983: 279–97.

Clark, Gordon L., and Dear, Michael. *State Apparatus: Structures and Language of Legitimacy*. London, Allen and Unwin, 1984.

Cohen, Gerald A. "Beliefs and Roles." *Proceedings of the Aristotelian Society*, New Series. 67 (1966–67): 17–34.

———— "Bourgeois and Proletarians." *Journal of the History of Ideas* 29 (April–June 1968): 211–30.

———— "Capitalism, Freedom and the Proletariat." In *The Idea of Freedom*. Edited by Alan Ryan. Oxford, Oxford University Press, 1979: 9–25.

———— "Forces and Relation of Production." In *Analytical Marxism*. Edited by John Roemer. Cambridge [Eng.], Cambridge University Press, 1986: ch. 1.

———— "Forces and Relations of Production." In *Marx: A Hundred Years On*. Edited by Betty Matthews. London, Lawrence and Wishart, 1983. 111–34.

———— "Functional Explanation, Consequence Explanation, and Marxism." *Inquiry* 25:1 (March 1982): 27–56.

———— "Karl Marx and the Withering Away of Social Science." *Philosophy and Public Affairs* 1 (1972): 182–203.

———— "The Labor Theory of Value and the Concept of Exploitation." *Philosophy and Public Affairs* 8:4 (1979): 338–60.

———— "Reconsidering Historical Materialism." In *Marxism (Nomos xxvi)*: 227–252.

———— "Robert Nozick and Wilt Chamberlain." In *Justice and Economic, Distribution*. Edited by John Arthur and William Shaw. Englewood Cliffs, N.J., Prentice–Hall, 1978: 246–62.

———— "The Structure of Proletarian Unfreedom." *Philosophy and Public Affairs* 12 (1983): 3–33.

———— "The Workers and the Word: Why Marx Had the Right to Think He Was Right." *Praxis* 4:3–4 (1968): 376–90.

———— *Karl Marx's Theory of History: A Defence*. Princeton, Princeton University Press, 1978.

Cohen, Marshall, Nagel, Thomas, and Scanlon, Thomas (eds). *Marx, Justice, and History*. Princeton, N.J., Princeton University Press, 1980.

Cohen, Morris Raphael. "Property and Sovereignty." *Cornell Law Quarterly* 13 (1927): 8–30.

Coleridge, Samuel Taylor. *On The Constitution of Church and State*. Princeton, Princeton University Press, 1976.

Colletti, Lucio. "Marxism and the Dialectic." *New Left Review* 93 (September–October 1975): 3–29.

——— "A Political and Philosophical Interview." *New Left Review* (July–August 1974): 3–28

——— *From Rousseau to Lenin*. Translated by John Merrington and Judith White. London, New Left Books, 1972.

——— *Marxism and Hegel*. Translated by Lawrence Garner. London, New Left Books, 1973.

Commons, John Roger. *Legal Foundations of Capitalism*. Madison, University of Wisconsin Press, 1957.

Connor, Walker. *The National Question in Marxist–Leninist Theory and Strategy*. Princeton, Princeton University Press, 1984.

Cott, Nancy F. *The Bonds of Womanhood: "Woman's Sphere" in New England, 1780–1835*. New Haven, Yale University Press, 1977.

Coward, Rosalind, and Ellis, John. *Language and Materialism*. London: Routledge and Kegan Paul, 1977.

Crozier, Michel, Huntington, Samuel P., and Watanuki, Joji. *The Crisis of Democracy*. New York, New York University Press, 1975.

Dahl, Robert Allan. *After the Revolution? Authority in a Good Society*. New Haven, Yale University Press, 1970.

——— *Dilemmas of Pluralist Democracy: Autonomy vs. Control*. New Haven, Yale University Press, 1982.

Dahl, Robert Allan and Lindblom, Charles E. *Politics, Economics, and Welfare*. New York, Harper, 1953.

Dalton, Russell, Flanagan, Scott C., and Beck, Paul Allen (eds). *Electoral Change in Advanced Industrial Democracies: Realignment or Dealignment?* Princeton, Princeton University Press, 1984.

Daly, Mary. *Gyn/Ecology: The Metaethics of Radical Feminism*. Boston, Beacon Press, 1978.

Davis, Natalie Zemon. "'Women's History' in Transition: The European Case." *Feminist Studies* 3:3–4 (1976): 82–103.

——— *Society and Culture in Early Modern France*. Stanford, Stanford University Press, 1975.

Defoe, Daniel. *Robinson Crusoe*. New York, Modern Library, 1948.

Deleuze, Gilles, and Guattari, Felix. *Anti-Oedipus: Capitalism and Schizophrenia*. New York, Viking, 1977.

——— *A Thousand Plateaus: Capitalism and Schizophrenia*. Minneapolis, University of Minnesota Press, 1983.

Delphy, Christine. *Close to Home: A Materialist Analysis of Women's Oppression*. Translated and edited by Diana Leonard. University of Massachussetts Press, 1984.

Deutscher, Isaac. *The Prophet Armed: Trotsky, 1879–1921*. New York, Oxford University Press, 1954.

——— *The Prophet Outcast: Trotsky, 1929–40*. New York, Oxford University Press, 1963.

——— *The Prophet Unarmed: Trotsky, 1921–1929*. New York, Oxford University Press, 1959.

Dicey, Albert Venn. *Lectures on the Relation Between Law and Public Opinion in England During the Nineteenth Century.* New Brunswick, N.J., Transaction Books, 1981.

Diderot, Denis. *The Paradox of Acting.* Translated by Walter Herries Pollock. New York, Hill and Wang, 1957.

Dinnerstein, Dorothy. *The Mermaid and the Minotaur: Sexual Arrangements and Human Malaise.* New York, Harper and Row, 1976. \

Doeringer, Peter B., and Piore, Michael J. *Internal Labor Markets and Manpower Analysis.* 2nd edn. Armonk, N.Y., M.E. Sharpe, 1985.

Douglas, Ann. *The Feminization of American Culture.* New York, Alfred Knopf, 1977.

Douglas, Mary. *How Institutions Think.* Syracuse, Syracuse University Press, 1986.

Downs, Anthony. *An Economic Theory of Democracy.* New York, Harper, 1957.

Dumont, Louis. *From Marx to Mandeville: The Genesis and Triumph of Economic Ideology.* Chicago, University of Chicago Press, 1977.

——— *Homo Hierarchicus: The Caste System and Its Implications.* Chicago, University of Chicago Press, 1970.

Dunn, John. *The Politics of Socialism: An Essay in Political Theory.* Cambridge [Eng.], Cambridge University Press, 1984.

Durkheim, Emile. *The Division of Labor in Society.* Translated by George Simpson. New York, Free Press, 1964.

Dworkin, Andrea. *Pornography: Men Possessing Women.* New York, Perigree, 1981.

Dworkin, Ronald. "'Spheres of Justice': An Exchange." *New York Review of Books* (July 21, 1983): 43–46.

——— "To Each His Own." *New York Review of Books* (April 14, 1983): 4–6.

——— "What is Equality?" Parts I and II. *Philosophy and Public Affairs* 10:3–4 (1981): 185–246, 283–345.

——— *Law's Empire.* Cambridge, Mass., Harvard University Press, 1986.

——— *A Matter of Principle.* Cambridge, Mass., Harvard University Press, 1985.

——— *Taking Rights Seriously.* Cambridge, Mass., Harvard University Press, 1978.

Echols, Alice. "The New Feminism of Yin and Yang." In *Powers of Desire: The Politics of Sexuality.* Edited by Ann Snitow, Christine Stansell, and Sharon Thompson. New York, Monthly Review Press, 1983: 439–58.

Edwards, Richard. *Contested Terrain: The Transformation of the Workplace in the Twentieth Century.* New York, Basic Books, 1979.

Eliot, T.S. *The Complete Poems and Plays, 1909–1950.* New York, Harcourt, Brace, and World, 1952.

Ellis, Adrian, and Kumar, Krishan (eds). *Dilemmas of Liberal Democracies.* New York, Tavistock Publications, 1983.

Elster, Jon. "Further Thoughts on Marxism, Functionalism, and Game Theory." In *Analytical Marxism.* Edited by John Roemer. Cambridge [Eng.], Cambridge

University Press, 1986: ch. 9.

———— "Three Challenges to Class." In *Analytical Marxism.* Edited by John Roemer. Cambridge [Eng.], Cambridge University Press, 1986: ch. 7.

———— *Making Sense of Marx.* Cambridge [Eng.], Cambridge University Press, 1985.

———— *Sour Grapes: Studies in the Subversion of Rationality.* Cambridge [Eng.], Cambridge University Press, 1983.

Ely, John Hart. *Democracy and Distrust: A Theory of Judicial Review.* Cambridge, Mass., Harvard University Press, 1980.

Emmanuel, Arghiri. *Unequal Exchange.* New York, Monthly Review Press, 1972.

Engels, Friedrich. *Anti-Dühring.* Moscow, Progress Publishers, 1947.

Enzensberger, Hans Magnus. "The Critique of Political Ecology." *New Left Review* 84 (March–April 1974): 3–31.

Erikson, Erik H. *Identity and the Life Cycle.* New York, Norton, 1980.

Evans, Peter B., Rueschemeyer, Dietrich, and Skocpol, Theda (eds). *Bringing the State Back In.* Cambridge [Eng.], Cambridge University Press, 1985.

Fanon, Frantz. *The Wretched of the Earth.* Preface by Jean-Paul Sartre. Translated by Constance Farrington. New York, Grove Press, 1963.

Feuerbach, Ludwig. *The Essence of Christianity.* Translated by George Eliot. Introduction by Karl Barth. Foreword by H. Richard Niebuhr. New York, Harper, 1957.

———— *The Fiery Brook: Selected Writings of Ludwig Feuerbach.* Translated by Zawar Hanfi. Garden City, New York, Anchor Books, 1972.

Fine, Ben, and Harris, Laurence. "State Expenditures in Advanced Capitalism: A Critique." *New Left Review* 98 (July–August 1976): 97–112.

———— *Rereading 'Capital.'* New York, Columbia University Press, 1979.

Firestone, Shulamith. *The Dialectic of Sex: The Case for a Feminist Revolution.* New York, Morrow, 1970.

Fiss, Owen. "Foreword: The Forms of Justice." *Harvard Law Review* 93 (1979): 1–58.

———— "Groups and the Equal Protection Clause." In *Equality and Preferential Treatment.* Edited by Marshall Cohen, Thomas Scanlon, and Thomas Nagel. Princeton, Princeton University Press, 1977: 84–154.

Flaubert, Gustave. *A Sentimental Education.* Translated by Perdita Burlingame. Afterword by F.W. Dupee. New York, New American Library, 1972.

Flax, Jane. "The Political Unconscious and the Patriarchal Unconscious." In *Discovering Reality: Feminist Perspectives on Epistemology, Metaphysics, Methodology, and Philosophy of Science.* Edited by Sandra Harding and Merrill Hintikka. The Netherlands, Reidel, 1983.

———— "Post-Modernism and Gender Relations in Feminist Theory." *Signs* 12 (Summer 1987).

Fleischmann, Eugene. "The Role of the Individual in Pre-Revolutionary Society: Stirner, Marx, and Hegel." In *Hegel's Political Philosophy: Problems and Perspectives.* Edited by Z.A. Pelczynski. Cambridge [Eng.], Cambridge University Press, 1971: 220–9.

Foley, Duncan. "The Value of Money, the Value of Labor Power, and the Marxian Transformation Problem." *Review of Radical Political Economics* 14:2 (1982): 37–47.

———— *Money, Accumulation, and Crisis*. Chur, Harwood Academic Publishers, 1986.

———— *Understanding 'Capital': Marx's Economic Theory*. Cambridge, Mass., Harvard University Press, 1986.

Forrester, Jay. *World Dynamics*. Cambridge, Mass., Wright Allen. 1971.

Foster, Michael B. *The Political Philosophies of Plato and Hegel*. Oxford, Clarendon Press, 1968.

Foucault, Michel. *The Birth of the Clinic*. Translated by A. Sheridan Smith. New York, Pantheon Books, 1973.

———— *Discipline and Punish: The Birth of the Prison*. Translated by Alan Sheridan. New York, Pantheon Books, 1977.

———— *Madness and Civilization*. Translated by Richard Howard. New York, Pantheon Books, 1965.

———— *Power/Knowledge: Selected Interviews and Other Writings, 1972–1977*. Translated and edited by Colin Gordon. New York, Pantheon Books, 1980.

French, Marilyn. *The Women's Room*. New York, Summit Books, 1977.

Freud, Sigmund. *Beyond the Pleasure Principle*. Translated by James Strachey. Introduction and notes by Dr. Gregory Zilborg. New York, Bantam, 1967.

Friedan, Betty. *The Feminine Mystique*. New York, Norton, 1963.

———— *The Second Stage*. New York, Summit Books, 1981.

Frug, Gerald. "The Ideology of Bureaucracy in American Law." *Harvard Law Review* 97:6 (1984): 1277–1388.

Fukuyama, Francis. "The End of History?" *The National Interest* 16 (Summer 1989): 3–18.

Furet, Francois, and Ozouf, Mona (eds). *The Critical Dictionary of the French Revolution*. Translated by Arthur Goldhammer. Cambridge, Mass., Harvard University Press, 1989.

Galbraith, John. *The New Industrial State*. Boston, Houghton Mifflin, 1967.

Geertz, Clifford. "After the Revolution: The Fate of Nationalism in the New States." In *The Interpretation of Cultures: Selected Essays*. New York, Basic Books, 1973: 234–54.

———— "Ideology as a Cultural System." In *The Interpretation of Cultures: Selected Essays*. New York, Basic Books, 1973: 193–233.

———— "The Integrative Revolution: Primordial Sentiments and Civil Politics in the New States." In *The Interpretation of Cultures: Selected Essays*. New York, Basic Books, 1973: 255–310.

———— "The Politics of Meaning." In *The Interpretation of Cultures: Selected Essays*. New York, Basic Books, 1973: 311–26.

———— "Politics Past and Present: Some Notes on the Uses of Anthropology in Understanding the New States." In *The Interpretation of Cultures: Selected Essays*. New York, Basic Books, 1973: 327–41.

———— *Agricultural Involution: The Processes of Ecological Change in Indonesia*. Berkeley, University of California Press, 1963.

————— *The Interpretation of Cultures: Selected Essays.* New York, Basic Books, 1973.

————— *Negara: The Theatre State in Nineteenth Century Bali.* Princeton, Princeton University Press, 1980.

Gendzier, Irene L. *Managing Political Change: Social Scientists and the Third World.* Boulder, Colo., Westview Press, 1985.

George, Henry. *Progress and Poverty.* New York, Modern Library, 1929.

Georgescu-Roegen, Nicholas. *The Entropy Law and the Economic Process.* Cambridge, Mass., Harvard University Press, 1971.

Giddens, Anthony. *The Class Structure of Advanced Societies.* New York, Harper Torchbooks, 1975.

Gilbert, Alan. *Marx's Politics: Communists and Citizens.* New Brunswick, N.J., Rutgers University Press, 1981.

Gilligan, Carol. *In a Different Voice: Psychological Theory and Women's Development.* Cambridge, Mass., Harvard University Press, 1982.

Gilpin, Robert. *The Political Economy of International Relations.* Princeton, Princeton University Press, 1987.

————— *U.S. Power and the Multinational Corporation: The Political Economy of Foreign Direct Investment.* New York, Basic Books, 1975.

Gimenez, Martha E. "Feminism, Pronatalism, and Motherhood." *International Journal of Women's Studies* 3:3 (1980): 215–40.

Glazer, Nathan. *Affirmative Discrimination: Ethric Inequality and Public Policy.* New York, Basic Books, 1975.

————— and Moynihan, Daniel P. *Beyond the Melting Pot.* Cambridge, Mass., M.I.T. Press 1963.

Glucksmann, André. *The Master Thinkers.* Translated by Brian Pearce. New York, Harper and Row, 1980.

Godelier, Maurice. "Infrastructures, Societies, and History." *New Left Review* 112 (November–December 1978): 84–96.

————— *Rationality and Irrationality in Economics.* New York, Monthly Review Press, 1972.

Goldthorpe, John, and Hirsch, Fred (eds). *The Political Economy of Inflation.* Cambridge, Mass., Harvard University Press, 1978.

Goldthorpe, John, Lockwood, David, Bechhofer, Frank, and Platt, Jennifer. *The Affluent Worker in the Class Structure.* Cambridge [Eng.], Cambridge University Press, 1969.

Gordon, David M., Edwards, Richard, and Reich, Michael. *Segmented Work, Divided Workers: The Historical Transformation of Labor in the United States.* Cambridge [Eng.], Cambridge University Press, 1982.

Gordon, Mary. *Final Payments.* New York, Random House, 1978.

Gordon, Robert W. "Critical Legal Histories." *Stanford Law Review* 36:1–2 (January 1984): 57–125.

Gorz, André. *Ecology as Politics.* Translated by Patsy Vigderman and Jonathan Cloud. Boston, South End Press, 1980.

Gough, Ian. "Productive and Unproductive Labour in Marx." *New Left Review* 76 (November–December 1972): 47–72.

———— *The Political Economy of the Welfare State.* London, Macmillan, 1979.

Gouldner, Alvin W. *The Two Marxisms: Contradictions and Anomalies in the Development of Theory.* New York, Oxford University Press, 1980.

Gramsci, Antonio. *Selections from the Prison Notebooks.* Translated and edited by Quinton Hoare and Geoffrey Nowell Smith. New York, International Publishers, 1971.

Greenstone, David. "Group Theories." In *Micropolitical Theory: Handbook of Political Science*, vol. 2. Edited by Fred Greenstein and Nelson Polsby. Reading, Mass., Addison-Wesley, 1975: ch. 4.

Greer, Germaine. *Sex and Destiny: The Politics of Human Fertility.* New York, Harper and Row, 1984.

Griffin, Keith, and Gurley, John. "Radical Analyses of Imperialism, the Third World, and the Transition to Socialism: A Survey Article." *Journal of Economic Literature* 23 (September 1985): 1089–1143.

Guha, Ranajit. "Dominance without Hegemony, and its Historiography." *Subaltern Studies*, vol. 6 (*Writings on South Asian History and Society*). Edited by Ranajit Guha. New Delhi, Oxford University Press, 1989: 211–309.

———— *Elementary Aspects of Peasant Insurgency in Colonial India.* Delhi, Oxford University Press, 1983.

Guha, Ranajit, and Spivak, Gayatri Chakravorty (eds). *Selected Subaltern Studies.* New York, Oxford University Press, 1988.

Habermas, Jürgen. "Between Philosophy and Science: Marxism as Critique." *Theory and Practice.* Translated by John Viertel. Boston, Beacon Press, 1973: 195–252.

———— "Hegel's Critique of the French Revolution." In *Theory and Practice.* Translated by John Viertel. Boston, Beacon Press, 1973: 121–41.

———— *Communication and the Evolution of Society.* Translated and with an introduction by Thomas McCarthy. Boston, Beacon Press, 1979.

———— *Legitimation Crisis.* Translated by Thomas McCarthy. Boston, Beacon Press, 1973.

———— *Theory and Practice.* Translated by John Viertel. Boston, Beacon Press, 1973.

Haight, Gordon S. *George Eliot: A Biography.* New York, Oxford University Press, 1968.

Hale, Robert Lee. "Bargaining, Duress, and Economic Liberty." *Columbia Law Review* 43 (1943): 85–97, 603–28.

———— "Coercion and Distribution in a Supposedly Non-Coercive State." *Political Science Quarterly* 38 (1923): 470–94.

———— "Force and the State: A Comparison of 'Political' and 'Economic' Compulsion." *Columbia Law Review* 35:2 (1935): 149–201.

Hampshire, Stuart. *Freedom of Mind, and Other Essays.* Princeton, Princeton University Press, 1971.

———— *Freedom of the Individual.* Princeton, Princeton University Press, 1975.

———— *Spinoza.* Baltimore, Penguin, 1965.

———— *Thought and Action.* New York, Viking Press, 1960.

Haraway, Donna. "A Manifesto for Cyborgs: Science, Technology, and Socialist

Feminism in the 1980s." *Socialist Review* 80 (March–April 1985): 65–107.

————— "Situated Knowledges: The Science Question in Feminism and the Privilege of Partial Perspective." *Feminist Studies* 14:3 (Fall 1988): 575–600.

Harcourt, Geoffrey C. *Some Cambridge Controversies in the Theory of Capital.* Cambridge [Eng.], Cambridge University Press, 1972.

Harding, Sandra, and Hintikka, Merrill (eds). *Discovering Reality: Feminist Perspectives on Epistemology, Metaphysics, Methodology, and Philosophy of Science.* The Netherlands, Reidel, 1983.

Hartmann, Heidi. "Capitalism, Patriarchy, and Job Segregation by Sex." In *The Signs Reader: Women, Gender, and Scholarship.* Edited by Elizabeth Abel and Emily K. Abel. Chicago, University of Chicago Press, 1983: 193–225.

Hartmann, Klaus. "Towards a New Systematic Reading of Hegel's *Philosophy of Right.*" In *The State and Civil Society: Studies in Hegel's Political Philosophy.* Edited by Z.A. Pelczynski. Cambridge [Eng.], Cambridge University Press, 1984: 114–36.

Hartsock, Nancy C.M. "The Feminist Standpoint: Developing the Ground for a Specifically Feminist Historical Materialism." In *Discovering Reality: Feminist Perspectives on Epistemology, Metaphysics, Methodology, and Philosophy of Science.* Edited by Sandra Harding and Merrill Hintikka. The Netherlands, Reidel, 1983.

————— *Money, Sex, and Power: Toward a Feminist Historical Materialism.* New York, Longman, 1983.

Hays, Samuel P. "Political Choice in Regulatory Administration." In *Regulation in Perspective.* Edited by Thomas McGraw. Cambridge, Mass., Harvard University Press, 1981: 124–54.

Hechter, Michael. "Group Formation and the Cultural Division of Labor." *American Journal of Sociology* 84:2 (1978): 293–318.

Hegel, Georg Wilhelm Friedrich. *Early Theological Writings.* Translated by T.M. Knox. Introduction by Richard Kroner. Philadelphia, University of Pennsylvania Press, 1948.

————— *Hegel's Aesthetics: Lectures on Fine Art.* 2 vols. Translated and with a preface by T.M. Knox. Oxford, Oxford University Press, 1975.

————— *Hegel's 'Logic': Being Part One of the Encyclopedia of the Philosophical Sciences (1830).* Translated by William Wallace. Foreword by J.N. Findlay. Oxford, The Clarendon Press, 1975.

————— *Hegel's 'Philosophy of Mind': Being Part Three of the Encyclopedia of the Philosophical Sciences (1830).* Translated by William Wallace and A.V. Miller. Foreword by J.N. Findlay. Oxford, The Clarendon Press, 1971.

————— *Hegel's 'Philosophy of Right.'* Translated with notes by T.M. Knox. Oxford, Oxford University Press, 1965.

————— *Hegel's Political Writings.* Translated by T.M. Knox. Introduction by Z.A. Pelczynski. Oxford, The Clarendon Press, 1969.

————— *Hegel's Science of Logic.* Translated by A.V. Miller. New York, Humanities Press, 1969.

————— *Lectures on the History of Philosophy.* 3 vols. Translated by E.S.

Haldane and Frances H. Simson. New York, Humanities, 1974.

——— *On Tragedy*. Edited and with an introduction by Anne and Henry Paolucci. New York, Harper, 1962.

——— *The Phenomenology of Spirit*. Translated by A.V. Miller. Oxford, Clarendon Press, 1977.

——— *The Philosophy of History*. Translated by J. Sibree. Introduction by C.J. Friedrich. New York, Dover, 1956.

Heiman, G. "The Sources and Significance of Hegel's Corporate Doctrine." In *Hegel's Political Philosophy: Problems and Perspectives*. Edited by Z.A. Pelczynski. Cambridge [Eng.], Cambridge University Press, 1971: 111–35.

Hess, Moses. "The Recent Philosophers." In *The Young Hegelians: An Anthology*. Edited by Lawrence S. Stepelevich. Cambridge [Eng.], Cambridge University Press, 1983: 359–75.

Hewlett, Sylvia Ann. *A Lesser Life: The Myth of Women's Liberation in America*. New York, W. Morrow, 1986.

Hibbs, Douglas. "On the Political Economy of Long-Run Trends in Strike Activity." *British Journal of Political Science* 8 (1978): 153–75.

Hinton, William. *Fanshen*. New York, Vintage Books, 1966.

Hirsch, Fred. *Social Limits to Growth*. Cambridge, Mass., Harvard University Press, 1976.

Hirsch, Fred, and Goldthorpe, John (eds). *The Political Economy of Inflation*. Cambridge, Mass., Harvard University Press, 1978.

Hirschman, Albert O. "On Hegel, Imperialism, and Structural Stagnation." In *Essays in Trespassing: Economics to Politics and Beyond*. Cambridge, Mass., Cambridge University Press, 1981: 167–176.

——— "Rival Interpretations of Market Society: Civilizing, Destructive, or Feeble?" *Journal of Economic Literature* 20 (December 1982): 1463–1484.

——— "The Social and Political Matrix of Inflation: Elaborations on the Latin American Experience." In *Essays in Trespassing: Economics to Politics and Beyond*. Cambridge, Mass., Cambridge University Press, 1981: 177–207.

——— *Essays in Trespassing: Economics to Politics and Beyond*. Cambridge, Mass., Cambridge University Press, 1981.

——— *Exit, Voice, and Loyalty*. Cambridge, Mass., Harvard University Press, 1970.

——— *The Passions and the Interests: Political Arguments for Capitalism Before its Triumph*. Princeton, Princeton University Press, 1977.

Hodgskin, Thomas. *Labour Defended against the Claims of Capital: or, the Unproductiveness of Capital Proved. With reference to the present combinations amongst journeymen*. [reprint edn]. Introduction by G.D.H. Cole. New York, Augustus M. Kelley, 1969.

Holmes, Stephen. "The Community Trap." *New Republic*. 199:22 (November 28, 1988): 24–8.

——— "On Reading Marx Apolitically." In *Marxism (Nomos xxvi)*. Edited by Roland Pennock and John Chapman. New York, New York University Press, 1983.

Hook, Sidney. *From Hegel to Marx: Studies in the Intellectual Development of*

Karl Marx. Ann Arbor, Mich., Ann Arbor Paperbacks, The University of Michigan Press, 1962.

Horwitz, Morton J. *The Transformation of American Law*. Cambridge, Mass., Harvard University Press, 1977.

Huntington, Samuel P. "The Democratic Distemper." *The Public Interest* 41 (Fall 1975): 9–38.

————— "Post Industrial Politics: How Benign Will it Be?" *Comparative Politics* (January 1974): 163–91.

————— "The United States." In *The Crisis of Democracy*. Edited by Michel Crozier, Samuel P. Huntington, and Joji Watanuki. New York, New York University Press, 1975: 59–118.

————— *American Politics: The Promise of Disharmony*. Cambridge, Mass., Harvard University Press, 1981.

————— *Political Order in Changing Societies*. New Haven, Yale University Press, 1968.

Huntington, Samuel P., and Moore, Clement H. (eds). *Authoritarian Politics in Modern Society*. New York, Basic Books, 1970.

Hurst, James Willard. *Law and the Conditions of Freedom in the Nineteenth-Century United States*. Madison, University of Wisconsin Press, 1956.

————— *Law and Markets in the United States History: Different Modes of Bargaining Among Interests*. Madison, University of Wisconsin Press, 1982.

Hypppolite, Jean. "Alienation and Objectification: Commentary on G. Lukács's *The Young Hegel*." In *Studies on Marx and Hegel*. Translated and edited by John O'Neill. New York, Basic Books, 1969: 70–90.

————— "Marx and Philosophy." In *Studies on Marx and Hegel*. Translated and edited by John O'Neill. New York, Basic Books, 1969: 93–105.

————— "Marx's Critique of the Hegelian Concept of the State." In *Studies on Marx and Hegel*. Translated and edited by John O'Neill. New York, Basic Books, 1969: 106–25.

————— "On the *Logic* of Hegel." In *Studies on Marx and Hegel*. Translated and edited by John O'Neill. New York, Basic Books, 1969: 169–84.

————— "On the Structure and Philosophical Presuppositions of Marx's *Capital*." In *Studies on Marx and Hegel*. Translated and edited by John O'Neill. New York, Basic Books, 1969: 126–49.

————— "The Significance of the French Revolution in Hegel's *Phenomenology*." In *Studies on Marx and Hegel*. Translated and edited by John O'Neill. New York, Basic Books, 1969: 35–69.

————— *Genesis and Structure of Hegel's 'Phenomenology of Spirit.'* Evanston, Northwestern University Press, 1974.

————— *Studies on Marx and Hegel*. Translated and edited by John O'Neill. New York, Basic Books, 1969.

Ilting, K.-H. "The Dialectic of Civil Society." In *The State and Civil Society: Studies in Hegel's Political Philosophy*. Edited by Z.A. Pelczynski. Cambridge [Eng.], Cambridge University Press, 1984: 211–26.

————— "Hegel's Concept of the State and Marx's Early Critique." In *The State and Civil Society: Studies in Hegel's Political Philosophy*. Edited by Z.A.

Pelczynski. Cambridge [Eng.], Cambridge University Press, 1984: 93–113.

———— "The Structure of Hegel's *Philosophy of Right*." In *Hegel's Political Philosophy: Problems and Perspectives*. Edited by Z.A. Pelczynski. Cambridge [Eng.], Cambridge University Press, 1971: 90–110.

Inwood, M.J. "Hegel, Plato, and Greek 'Sittlichkeit.'" In *The State and Civil Society: Studies in Hegel's Political Philosophy*. Edited by Z.A. Pelczynski. Cambridge [Eng.], Cambridge University Press, 1984: 40–54.

Irigaray, Luce. "And the One Doesn't Stir Without the Other." Translated by Hélène Vivienne Wenzel. *Signs* 7:1 (Autumn 1981): 60–7.

Isaacs, Harold R. *India's Ex-Untouchables*. New York, John Day Co., 1965.

Jacoby, Russell. "The Politics of Subjectivity." *New Left Review* 79 (May–June 1973): 37–49.

Jaffe, Louis Leventhal. *Judicial Control of Administrative Action*. Abridged student edn. Boston, Little, Brown, 1965.

Jameson, Fredric. "Marxism and Postmodernism." *New Left Review* 176 (July–August 1989): 31–45.

———— "Postmodernism, or the Cultural Logic of Late Capitalism." 146 (July–August 1984): 53–92.

———— "Symbolic Inference; or, Kenneth Burke and Ideological Analysis." In *The Ideologies of Theory: Essays, 1971–86*, vol. 1. Foreword by Neil Larson. Minneapolis, University of Minnesota Press, 1988: 139–57.

———— *The Ideologies of Theory: Essays, 1971–86*. 2 vols. Foreword by Neil Larson. Minneapolis, University of Minnesota Press, 1988.

———— *The Political Unconscious: Narrative as a Socially Symbolic Act*. Ithaca, Cornell University Press, 1981.

Jay, Martin. *Marxism and Totality: The Adventures of a Concept from Lukacs to Habermas*. Berkeley, University of California Press, 1984.

Jessop, Bob. *The Capitalist State*. New York, New York University Press, 1982.

Johnson v. Transportation Agency, Santa Clara County, 480 U.S. 616.

Kalecki, Michal. "Class Struggle and the Distribution of National Income." In *Selected Essays on the Dynamics of the Capitalist Economy, 1933–1970*. Cambridge [Eng.], Cambridge University Press, 1971: 156–64.

———— "Political Aspects of Full Employment." In *Selected Essays on the Dynamics of the Capitalist Economy, 1933–1970*. Cambridge [Eng.], Cambridge University Press, 1971: 138–45.

———— "The Problem of Effective Demand with Tugan-Baranovski and Rosa Luxemburg." In *Selected Essays on the Dynamics of the Capitalist Economy, 1933–1970*. Cambridge [Eng.], Cambridge University Press, 1971: 146–55.

Kamenka, Eugene. *Marxism and Ethics*. London, Macmillan, 1969.

Kant, Immanuel. *Critique of Pure Reason*. Translated by Norman Kemp Smith. New York, Macmillan, 1964.

———— *Fundamental Principles of the Metaphysics of Morals*. Translated by Thomas Abbott. Indianapolis, Bobbs-Merrill, 1949.

Kautsky, Karl. *The Dictatorship of the Proletariat*. Ann Arbor, Mich., The University of Michigan Press, 1964.

Kaysen, Carl. "The Corporation: How Much Power? What Scope?" In *The Cor-*

poration in Modern Society. Edited and with an introduction by Edward S. Mason. New York, Atheneum, 1966: 85–105.

Keane, John. *Democracy and Civil Society*. London, New Left Books, 1988.

Keane, John (ed.). *Civil Society and the State: New European Perspectives*. London, New Left Books, 1988.

Kelly, George Armstrong. "Hegel's America." *Philosophy and Public Affairs* 2:1 (Fall 1972): 3–36.

———— *Hegel's Retreat From Eleusis: Studies in Political Thought*. Princeton, Princeton University Press, 1978.

———— *Idealism, Politics, and History: Sources of Hegelian Thought*. Cambridge [Eng.], Cambridge University Press, 1969.

Kelly-Gadol, Joan. "Did Women Have a Renaissance?" In *Becoming Visible: Women in European History*. 2nd edn. Edited by Renate Bridenthal and Claudia Koonz. New York, Houghton and Mifflin, 1987: 175–201.

———— "The Social Relations of the Sexes: Methodological Implications of Women's History." *Signs* 1 (1975–6): 809–24.

Kennedy, Duncan. "The Stages of the Decline of the Public/Private Distinction." *University of Pennsylvania Law Review* 130 (1982): 1349–57.

Kennedy, Paul. *The Rise and Fall of the Great Powers*. New York, Random House, 1987.

Keohane, Robert O., and Nye, Joseph. "Understanding Interdependence." In *Power and Interdependence: World Politics in Transition*. Boston, Little, Brown, and Co., 1977: 3–60.

Keynes, John Maynard. *The End of Laissez-Faire*. 2nd Impression. London, Leonard and Virginia Woolf, 1926.

———— *Essays in Persuasion*. London, Macmillan, 1931.

———— *The General Theory of Employment, Interest, and Money*. London, Macmillan, 1967.

———— *Laissez-Faire and Communism*. New York, New Republic, 1926.

Kojève, Alexandre. *Introduction to the Reading of Hegel*. Translated by James H. Nichols, Jr. Edited by Allan Bloom. New York, Basic Books, 1969.

Kolakowski, Leszek. *Main Currents of Marxism*. 3 vols. Oxford, Oxford University Press, 1978.

Kortian, Garbis. "Subjectivity and Civil Society." In *The State and Civil Society: Studies in Hegel's Political Philosophy*. Edited by Z.A. Pelczynski. Cambridge [Eng.], Cambridge University Press, 1984: 197–210.

Krasner, Steven. *Structural Conflict: The Third World Case Against Global Liberalism*. Berkeley, University of California Press, 1985.

Kristeva, Julia. "Women's Time." Translated by Alice Jardine and Harry Blake. In *Feminist Theory: A Critique of Ideology*. Edited by Barbara Gelpi, Nannerl Keohane, and Michelle Rosaldo. Chicago, University of Chicago Press, 1982: 31–53.

Kuhn, Thomas. *The Structure of Scientific Revolutions*. Chicago, University of Chicago Press, 1970.

Kundsin, Ruth B. (ed.). *Women and Success: Anatomy of Achievement*. New York, Morrow, 1974.

Kung, Hans. *The Incarnation of God*. Translated by J.R. Stephenson. New York, Crossroad, 1987.

Kurth, James. "Political Consequences of the Product Cycle: Industrial History and Political Outcomes." *International Organization* 33:1 (Winter 1979): 1–34.

Kuznets, Simon. *Modern Economic Growth*. New Haven, Yale University Press, 1966.

Laclau, Ernesto. "Feudalism and Capitalism in Latin America." In *Politics and Ideology in Marxist Theory*. London, New Left Books, 1977.

Laclau, Ernesto, and Mouffe, Chantal. *Hegemony and Socialist Strategy: Towards a Radical Democratic Politics*. Translated by Winston Moore and Paul Cammack. London, Verso, 1985.

Landes, Joan B. "Hegel's Conception of the Family." In *The Family in Political Thought*. Edited by Jean Bethke Elshtain. Amherst, Mass., The University of Massachussetts Press, 1982: 125–44.

Lehmbruch, Gerhard, and Schmitter, Philippe (eds). *Patterns of Corporatist Policy-Making*. Beverly Hills, California, Sage Publications, 1982.

Lenin, Vladimir Ilich. "Conspectus of Hegel's Science of Logic." In *Collected Works*, vol. 38. Moscow, Foreign Languages Publishing House, 1963.

———— "The Socialist Revolution and the Rights of Nations to Self-Determination." In *Selected Works*. London, Lawrence and Wishart, 1969: 159–68.

———— *Imperialism: The Highest Stage of Capitalism*. In *Selected Works*. London, Lawrence and Wishart, 1969: 169–263.

———— *Left-Wing Communism – An Infantile Disorder*. In *Selected Works*. London, Lawrence and Wishart, 1969: 506–91.

———— *The State and Revolution*. In *Selected Works*. London, Lawrence and Wishart, 1969: 264–351.

———— *Selected Works*. London, Lawrence and Wishart, 1969.

Leontief, Wassily, W. "The Significance of Marxian Economics for Present-day Economic Theory." In *Essays in Economics*. Vol. 1. Oxford, Basil Blackwell, 1966: 72–83.

Lerner, Gerda. "Placing Women in History: Definitions and Challenges." *Feminist Studies* 3:1–2 (Fall 1975): 5–14.

Levine, Andrew. *The End of the State*. London, Verso, 1987.

Levine, Andrew and Sober, Elliott. "What's Historical About Historical Materialism?" *Journal of Philosophy* 82:6 (June 1985): 304–26.

Levine, Andrew and Wright, Erik Olin. "Rationality and Class Struggle." *New Left Review* 123 (September–October 1980): 47–68.

Liebich, André. *The Selected Writings of August Cieszkowski*. Cambridge [Eng.], Cambridge University Press, 1979.

Lijphart, Arend. *Democracies*. New Haven, Yale University Press, 1984.

———— *Democracy in Plural Societies*. New Haven, Yale University Press, 1977.

Lindberg, Leon N. and Maier, Charles S. (eds). *The Politics of Inflation and Economic Stagnation*. Washington, The Brookings Institution, 1985.

Lindberg, Leon N. et al. (eds). *Stress and Contradiction in Modern Capitalism*. Lexington, Mass., Lexington Books, 1975.

Lindblom, Charles E. "Another State of Mind: Presidential Address, American

Political Science Association." *American Political Science Review* 76 (1982): 9–21.

————— *Politics and Markets: The World's Political Economic Systems*. New York, Basic Books, 1977.

Lipietz, Alain. *The Enchanted World*. London, New Left Books, 1985.

Lobkowicz, Nikolaus. *Theory and Practice: A History of a Concept from Aristotle to Marx*. Notre Dame, Ind., University of Notre Dame Press, 1967.

Lowenthal, Leo. *Literature and Mass Culture*. New Brunswick, Transaction Books, 1984.

Lowi, Theodore J. "American Business, Public Policy, Case Studies, and Political Theory." *World Politics* 16 (1964): 677–715.

————— "Party, Policy, and Constitution in America." In *The American Party Systems*. Edited by William Nisbet Chambers and Walter Dean Burnham. New York, Oxford University Press, 1967: 238–76.

————— *American Government: The Incomplete Conquest*. Hinsdale, Ill., The Dryden Press, 1976.

————— *The End of Liberalism*. 2nd edn. New York, Norton, 1979.

————— *The Politics of Disorder*. New York, Basic Books, 1971.

Lubasz, Heinz. "Marx's Initial Problematic: The Problem of Poverty." *Political Studies* 24:1 (1976): 24–42.

Luhmann, Niklas. *The Differentiation of Society*. Translated by Stephen Holmes and Charles Larmore. New York, Columbia University Press, 1982.

Lukács, Georg. *History and Class Consciousness: Studies in Marxist Dialectics*. Translated by Rodney Livingstone. Cambridge, Mass., M.I.T. Press, 1971.

————— *The Young Hegel*. Translated by Rodney Livingstone. London, Merlin, 1975.

Luker, Kristin. *Abortion and the Politics of Motherhood*. Berkeley, University of California Press, 1984.

Luther, Martin. "The Freedom of a Christian." In *Martin Luther: Selections from His Writings*. Edited and with an introduction by John Dillenberger. Garden City, N.Y., Anchor Books, 1961.

Luxemburg, Rosa. *The Accumulation of Capital*. Translated by Agnes Schwarzchild. Introduction by Joan Robinson. New York, Monthly Review Press, 1968.

————— *The National Question: Selected Writings by Rosa Luxemburg*. Edited and with an introduction by Horace B. Davis. New York, Monthly Review Press, 1976.

————— *The Accumulation of Capital – An Anti-Critique*. In Rosa Luxemburg/ Nicolai Bukharin, *The Accumulation of Capital – An Anti-Critique/Imperialism and the Accumulation of Capital*. Translated by Rudolf Wichmann. Edited and with an introduction by Kenneth Tarbuck. New York, Monthly Review Press, 1972.

McClelland, David Clarence. *The Achieving Society*. New York, The Free Press, 1967.

McConnell, Grant. *Private Power and American Democracy*. New York, Knopf, 1967.

MacKinnon, Catherine. "Feminism, Marxism, Method, and the State: An Agenda for Theory." In *Ferminist Theory: A Critique of Ideology.* Edited By Barbara Gelpi, Nannerl Keohane, and Michelle Rosaldo. Chicago, University of Chicago Press, 1982: 1–31.

McLellan, David. *Marx Before Marxism.* New York, Harper and Row, 1970.

——— *The Young Hegelians and Karl Marx.* New York, Praeger, 1969.

Magleby, David. *Direct Legislation: Voting on Ballot Propositions in the United States.* Baltimore, Johns Hopkins University Press, 1984.

Maier, Charles S. "'Fictitious Bonds of Wealth and Law': On the Theory and Practice of Interest Representation." In *Organizing Interests in Western Europe.* Edited By Suzanne Berger. Cambridge [Eng.], Cambridge University Press, 1981: 27–61.

——— *Recasting Bourgeois Europe.* Princeton, Princeton University Press, 1975.

Maier, Charles S. (ed.). *Changing Boundaries of the Political: Essays on the Evolving Balance Between State and Society, Public and Private in Europe.* Cambridge [Eng.], Cambridge University Press, 1987.

Mandel, Ernest. "Introduction" to Karl Marx, *Capital, A Critique of Political Economy.* Vol. ii. New York, Vintage Books, 1981.

——— *The Formation of the Economic Thought of Karl Marx.* Translated by Brian Pearce. New York, Monthly Review Press, 1971.

——— *Late Capitalism.* Translated by Joris de Bres. London, New Left Books, 1975.

——— *Marxist Economic Theory.* 2 vols. Translated by Brian Pearce. New York, Monthly Review Press, 1969.

Mao Tse Tung. "On Contradiction." In *Selected Readings from the Works of Mao Tse-Tung.* Peking, Foreign Languages Press, 1976: 70–108.

——— "On the Correct Handling of Contradictions Among the People." In *Selected Readings from the Works of Mao Tse-Tung.* Peking, Foreign Languages Press, 1976: 350–87.

——— *Selected Readings from the Works of Mao Tse-Tung.* Peking, Foreign Languages Press, 1976.

Marglin, Stephen W. "What Do Bosses Do? The Origins and Functions of Hierarchy in Capitalist Production." Part 1. *Review of Radical Political Economics* 6 (1974): 60–112. Part 2. *Review of Radical Political Economics* 7 (1975): 20–37.

——— *Growth, Distribution and Prices.* Cambridge, Mass., Harvard University Press, 1984.

Markus, Maria. "Women, Success and Civil Society: Submission to, or Subversion of, the Achievement Principle." In *Feminism as Critique.* Edited by Seyla Benhabib and Drucilla Cornell. Minneapolis, University of Minnesota Press, 1987: 96–109.

Marx, Karl. "The Civil War in France." In *The First International and After: Political Writings Volume iii.* Edited and introduced by David Fernbach. New York, Vintage Books, 1974: 187–268.

——— "Class Struggles in France: 1848 to 1850." In *Surveys From Exile: Political Writings Volume ii.* Translated by Paul Jackson. Edited and introduced by David Fernbach. New York, Vintage Books, 1974: 35–142.

——— "Concerning Feuerbach." In *Early Writings*. Translated by Rodney Livingstone and Gregor Benton. Edited by Quintin Hoare. Introduction by Lucio Colletti. New York, Vintage Books, 1975: 421–3.

——— "A Contribution to the Critique of Hegel's *Philosophy of Right*: Introduction." In *Early Writings*. Translated by Rodney Livingstone and Gregor Benton. Edited by Quintin Hoare. Introduction by Lucio Colletti. New York, Vintage Books, 1975: 243–57.

——— "A Contribution to the Critique of Hegel's *Philosophy of Right*: Introduction." In *Critique of Hegel's 'Philosophy of Right.'* Edited by Joseph O'Malley. Translated by Joseph O'Malley and Annette Jolin. Cambridge [Eng.], Cambridge University Press, 1970: 129–142.

——— "The Critique of the Gotha Program." In *The First International and After: Political Writings Volume III*. Translated by Joris de Bres. Edited and introduced by David Fernbach. New York, Vintage Book, 1974: 339–59.

——— "Critique of Hegel's Dialectic and General Philosophy." In *Early Writings*. Translated by Rodney Livingstone and Gregor Benton. Edited by Quintin Hoare. Introduction by Lucio Colletti. New York, Vintage Books, 1975: 379–400.

——— "Critique of Hegel's Dialectic and General Philosophy." In *Early Writings*. Translated and edited by T.B. Bottomore. Foreword by Erich Fromm. New York, McGraw-Hill, 1964: 195–219.

——— "The Difference Between the Democritean and Epicurean Philosophy of Nature" [the Doctoral Dissertation]. *Karl Marx and Friedrich Engels: Collected Works*. Vol. 1. Translated by Richard Dixon. New York, International Publishers, 1975: 25–108.

——— "Economic and Philosophical Manuscripts." In *Early Writings*. Translated by Rodney Livingstone and Gregor Benton. Edited by Quintin Hoare. Introduction by Lucio Colletti. New York, Vintage Books, 1975: 279–400.

——— "The Eighteenth Brumaire of Louis Bonaparte." In *Surveys From Exile: Political Writings Volume II*. Translated by Ben Fowkes. Edited and introduced by David Fernbach. New York, Vintage Books, 1974: 143–249.

——— "Excerpts from James Mill's *Elements of Political Economy*." In *Early Writings*. Translated by Rodney Livingstone and Gregor Benton. Edited by Quintin Hoare. Introduction by Lucio Colletti. New York, Vintage Books, 1975: 259–78.

——— "Inaugural Address of the Working Men's International Association." In *Karl Marx and Frederick Engels: Selected Works in Two Volumes*. Vol. 1. Moscow, Foreign Languages Publishing House, 1962: 377–85.

——— "Marx to Engels in Manchester, January 28, 1863." In *Karl Marx and Frederick Engels: Selected Correspondence*. Translated by I. Lasker. Edited by S. Ryazanskaya. Moscow, Progress Publishers, 1965: 137–9.

——— "Marx to P.V. Annenkov in Paris, December 28, 1846." In *Karl Marx and Frederick Engels: Selected Correspondence*. Translated by I. Lasker. Edited by S. Ryazanskaya. Moscow, Progress Publishers, 1965: 34–44.

———— "On the Jewish Question." In *Early Writings*. Translated by Rodney Livingstone and Gregor Benton. Edited by Quintin Hoare. Introduction by Lucio Colletti. New York, Vintage Books, 1975: 211–41.

———— "On Proudhon." In *Karl Marx and Friedrich Engels: Collected Works*. Vol. 20. New York, International Publishers, 1985: 26–33.

———— "Theses on Feuerbach." In *Karl Marx and Frederick Engels: Selected Works in Two Volumes*. Vol. 1. Moscow, Foreign Languages Publishing House,

———— "Wage Labor and Capital." In *Karl Marx and Frederick Engels: Selected Works in Two Volumes*. Vol. 1. Moscow, Foreign Languages Publishing House, 1962: 79–105.

———— *Capital: A Critique of Political Economy*. Vol. I. Introduced by Ernest Mandel. Translated by Ben Fowkes. New York, Vintage Books, 1977.

———— *Capital: A Critique of Political Economy*. Vol. II. Introduced by Ernest Mandel. Translated by David Fernbach. New York, Vintage Books, 1981.

———— *Capital: A Critique of Political Economy*. Vol. III. Introduced by Ernest Mandel. Translated by David Fernbach. New York, Vintage Books, 1981.

———— *A Contribution to the Critique of Political Economy*. Translated by S.W. Ryazanskaya. Edited and with an introduction by Maurice Dobb. New York, International Publishers, 1970.

———— *Critique of Hegel's 'Philosophy of Right.'* Edited by Joseph O'Malley. Translated by Joseph O'Malley and Annette Jolin. Cambridge [Eng], Cambridge University Press, 1970.

———— *Early Writings*. Translated by Rodney Livingstone and Gregor Benton. Edited by Quintin Hoare. Introduction by Lucio Colletti. New York, Vintage Books, 1975.

———— *Economic Manuscripts of 1857–58* [The *Grundrisse*]. In *Karl Marx and Friedrich Engels: Collected Works*. Vols 28–29. Translated by Ernst Wangermann with Victor Schnittke and Yuri Sdobnikov. New York, International Publishers, 1986–7.

———— *The First International and After: Political Writings Volume III*. Edited and introduced by David Fernbach. New York, Vintage Books, 1974.

———— *The Grundrisse*. Translated and with a foreword by Martin Nicolaus. New York, Vintage Books, 1973.

———— *The Poverty of Philosophy*. New York, International Publishers. 1975.

———— *The Revolutions of 1848: Political Writings Volume I*. Edited and introduced by David Fernbach. New York, Vintage Books, 1974.

———— *Surveys From Exile: Political Writings Volume II*. Edited and introduced by David Fernbach. New York, Vintage Books, 1974.

———— *Texts on Method*. Translated and edited by Terrell Carver. New York, Barnes and Noble, 1975.

———— *Theories of Surplus Value*. Part 1. Translated by Emile Burns. London, Lawrence and Wishart, 1969.

———— *Theories of Surplus Value*. Part 2. Translated by Renate Simpson. London, Lawrence and Wishart, 1969.

———— *Theories of Surplus Value*. Part 3. Translated by Jack Cohen and S.W. Ryazanskaya. London, Lawrence and Wishart, 1969.

Marx, Karl, and Engels, Frederick. "The Manifesto of the Communist Party." In *The Revolutions of 1848: Political Writings Volume 1*: Edited and introduced by David Fernbach. New York, Vintage Book, 1974: 62–98.

Marx, Karl, and Engels, Friedrich. "A Reply to Bruno Bauer's Anti-Critique." In *Karl Marx and Friedrich Engels: Collected Works*. Vol. 5. Translated by Clemens Dutt. New York, International Publishers, 1976: 15–18.

Marx, Karl, and Engels, Friedrich. *The German Ideology*. In *Karl Marx and Friedrich Engels: Collected Works*. Vol. 5. Translated by Clemens Dutt, W. Dough, and C.P. McGill. New York, International Publishers, 1976: 19–549.

Marx, Karl, and Engels, Friedrich. *The Holy Family or Critique of Critical Criticism*. In *Karl Marx and Friedrich Engels: Collected Works*. Vol. 4. Translated by Richard Dixon and Clemens Dutt. New York, International Publishers, 1975: 5–211.

Matthews, Betty (ed.). *Marx: A Hundred Years On*. London, Lawrence and Wishart, 1983.

Mattick, Paul. *Marx and Keynes: The Limits of the Mixed Economy*. London, Merlin Press, 1969.

Mauss, Marcel. *The Gift: Forms and Functions of Exchange in Archaic Societies*. Translated by Ian Cunnison. Introduction by E.E. Evans-Pritchard. New York, Norton, 1967.

Meadows, Donella, et al. *The Limits to Growth: A Report of the Club of Rome's Project on the Predicament of Mankind*. London, Pan Books, 1974.

Meek, Ronald. "The Marginal Revolution and its Aftermath." In *Studies in the Labour Theory of Value*. London, Lawrence and Wishart, 1956.

Meister, Robert. "Discrimination Law Through the Looking Glass." *Wisconsin Law Review* 4 (1985): 937–88.

————— "Journalistic Silence and Governmental Speech: Can Institutions Have Rights?" *Harvard Civil Rights – Civil Liberties Law Review* 16:2 (Fall 1981): 319–76.

————— "The Logic and Legacy of *Dred Scott*: Marshall, Taney, and the Sublimation of Republican Thought." *Studies on American Political Development*. Vol. 3. New Haven, Yale University Press, 1989: 199–260.

Merton, Robert. *Social Theory and Social Structure*. New York, Free Press, 1968.

Mészáros, Istvan. *Marx's Theory of Alienation*. London, Merlin, 1970.

Miliband, Ralph. *Capitalist Democracy in Britain*. Oxford, Oxford University Press, 1982.

————— *Marxism and Politics*. Oxford, Oxford University Press, 1977.

————— *Parliamentary Socialism*. London, Merlin, 1973.

————— *The State in Capitalist Society*. New York, Basic Books, 1969.

Mill, John Stuart. *Principles of Political Economy*. London, Longman's Green, 1936.

Mills, C. Wright. *The Power Elite*. New York, Oxford University Press, 1956.

Milton, John. *Paradise Lost*. Edited by Scott Elledge. New York, Norton, 1975.

Mishan, E.J. "Ills, Bads, and Disamenities: The Wages of Growth." *Daedalus* 102: 4 (Fall 1973): 63–88.

Moore, Barrington Jr. *Injustice: The Social Bases of Obedience and Revolt*. White

Plains, N.Y., M.E. Sharpe, 1978.

———— *Political Power and Social Theory.* Cambridge [Eng.], Cambridge University Press, 1958.

———— *Social Origins of Dictatorship and Democracy.* Harmondsworth, Penguin, 1967.

Morgan, Marabel. *The Total Woman.* Old Tappan, N.J., F.H. Revell, 1973.

Morgan, Robin (ed.). *Sisterhood is Powerful: An Anthology of Writings from the Women's Liberation Movement.* New York, Vintage Books, 1970.

Morishima, Michio. *Marx's Economics.* Cambridge [Eng.], Cambridge University Press, 1974.

Moynihan, Daniel Patrick. *Maximum Feasible Misunderstanding: Community Action in the War on Poverty.* New York, Free Press, 1969.

Musgrave, Richard A. "Theories of Fiscal Crises: An Essay in Fiscal Sociology." In *The Economics of Taxation.* Edited by Henry J. Aaron and Michael Boskin. Washington, Brookings Institution, 1980: 361–90.

Nagel, Thomas. *The View from Nowhere.* New York, Oxford University Press, 1986.

Nairn, Tom. "The Nature of the Labor Party." In *Towards Socialism.* Edited by Perry Anderson and Robin Blackburn. Introduction by Andrew Hacker. Ithaca, New York, Cornell University Press, 1966: 159–217.

———— *The Break-Up of Britain: Crisis and Neo-Nationalism.* London, New Left Books, 1977.

Negri, Antonio. "Is There a Marxist Doctrine of the State: a Reply." In Norberto Bobbio, *Which Socialism?* Translated by Roger Griffin. Introduction by Richard Bellamy. Minneapolis, University of Minnesota Press, 1987: 121–38.

Nelson, Cary, and Grossberg, Lawrence (eds). *Marxism and the Interpretation of Culture.* Urbana, University of Illinois Press, 1988.

Nietzsche, Friedrich. "The Genealogy of Morals." In *The Birth of Tragedy and the Genealogy of Morals.* Translated by Francis Golfing. Garden City, N.Y., Doubleday Anchor Books, 1956.

———— *Beyond Good and Evil: Prelude to a Philosophy of the Future.* Translated and with commentary by Walter Kaufmann. New York, Vintage Books, 1966.

Nisbet, Robert. *The Twilight of Authority.* New York, Oxford University Press, 1975.

Nove, Alec. *The Economics of Feasible Socialism.* London, George Allen and Unwin, 1983.

Nozick, Robert. *Anarchy, State and Utopia.* New York, Basic Books, 1974.

———— *Philosophical Explanations.* Cambridge, Mass., Harvard University Press, 1981.

Nygren, Anders. *Agape and Eros.* Translated by Philip S. Watson. Philadelphia, Westminster Press, 1953.

O'Connor, James. "The Meaning of Crisis." *International Journal of Urban and Regional Research* 5:3 (1981): 302–27.

———— "Scientific and Ideological Elements in the Economic Theory of Government Policy." *Science and Society* 33 (1969): 385–414.

———— *Accumulation Crisis.* Oxford, Basil Blackwell, 1984.

————— *The Fiscal Crisis of the State*. New York, St. Martin's Press, 1974.

O'Malley, Joseph, "Marx's 'Economics' and Hegel's *Philosophy of Right:* An Essay on Marx's Hegelianism." *Political Studies* 24:1 (1976): 43–56.

Offe, Claus. "Alternative Strategies in Consumer Policy." In *Contradictions of the Welfare State*. Edited by John Keane. Cambridge, Mass., M.I.T. Press, 1984: ch. 10.

————— "The Attribution of Public Status to Interest Groups: Observations on the West German Case." In *Organizing Interests in Western Europe*. Edited by Suzanne Berger. Cambridge [Eng.], Cambridge University Press, 1981: 23–158.

————— "Challenging the Boundaries of Institutional Politics: Social Movements Since the 1960s." In *Changing Boundaries of the Political: Essays on the Evolving Balance Between State and Society, Public and Private in Europe*. Edited by Charles S. Maier. Cambridge [Eng.], Cambridge University Press, 1987: 63–105.

————— "Competitive Party Democracy and the Keynesian Welfare State." In *Contradictions of the Welfare State*. Edited by John Keane. Cambridge, Mass., M.I.T. Press, 1984: ch. 8.

————— "'Crises of Crisis Management': Elements of a Political Crisis Theory." In *Contradictions of the Welfare State*. Edited by John Keane. Cambridge, Mass., M.I.T. Press, 1984: ch. 7.

————— "Democracy Against the Welfare State? Structural Foundations of Neo-conservative Political Opportunities." *Political Theory* 15:4 (November 1987): 501–37.

————— "The Growth of the Service Sector." In *Disorganized Capitalism: Contemporary Transformations of Work and Politics*. Edited by John Keane. Cambridge, Mass., M.I.T. Press, 1985: ch. 4.

————— "Legitimation Through Majority Rule?" In *Disorganized Capitalism: Contemporary Transformations of Work and Politics*. Edited by John Keane. Cambridge, Mass., M.I.T. Press, 1985: ch. 9.

————— "The New Social Movements: Challenging the Boundaries of Institutional Politics." *Social Research* 52:4 (Winter 1985): 817–68.

————— "The Political Economy of the Labor Market." In *Disorganized Capitalism: Contemporary Transformations of Work and Politics*. Edited by John Keane. Cambridge, Mass., M.I.T. Press, 1985: ch. 1.

————— "Political Legitimation Through Majority Rule." *Social Research* 50 (Winter 1983): 709–56.

————— "Reflections on the Welfare State and the Future of Socialism." In *Contradictions of the Welfare State*. Edited by John Keane. Cambridge, Mass., M.I.T. Press, 1984: ch. 12.

————— "The Separation of Form and Content in Liberal Democracy." In *Contradictions of the Welfare State*. Edited by John Keane. Cambridge, Mass., M.I.T. Press, 1984: ch. 7.

————— "Social Policy and the Theory of the State." In *Contradictions of the Welfare State*. Edited by John Keane. Cambridge, Mass., M.I.T. Press, 1984: ch. 3.

————— "The Theory of Capitalist State and the Problem of Policy Formation." In *Stress and Contradiction in Modern Capitalism.* Edited by L. Lindberg et al. Lexington, Mass., Lexington Books, 1975: 125–44.

————— "Theses on the Theory of the State." In *Contradictions of the Welfare State.* Edited by John Keane. Cambridge, Mass., M.I.T. Press, 1984: ch. 4.

————— "Two Logics of Collective Action." In *Disorganized Capitalism: Contemporary Transformations of Work and Politics.* Edited by John Keane. Cambridge, Mass., M.I.T. Press, 1985: ch. 7.

————— "'Ungovernability': The Renaissance of Conservative Theories of Crisis." In *Contradictions of the Welfare State.* Edited by John Keane. Cambridge, Mass., M.I.T. Press, 1984: ch. 2.

————— "Work: The Key Sociological Category?" In *Disorganized Capitalism: Contemporary Transformations of Work and Politics.* Edited by John Keane. Cambridge, Mass., M.I.T. Press, 1985: ch. 5.

————— *Contradictions of the Welfare State.* Edited by John Keane. Cambridge, Mass., M.I.T. Press, 1984.

————— *Disorganized Capitalism: Contemporary Transformations of Work and Politics.* Edited by John Keane. Cambridge, Mass., M.I.T. Press, 1985.

Offe, Claus, and Wiesenthal, Helmut. "Two Logics of Collective Action: Theoretical Notes on Social Class and Organizational Form." *Political Power and Social Theory* 1 (1980): 67–115.

Okun, Arthur. *Prices and Quantities.* Washington: The Brookings Institution, 1981.

Ollman, Bertell. *Alienation: Marx's Conception of Man in Capitalist Society.* Cambridge [Eng.], Cambridge University Press, 1971.

Olsen, Frances. "The Family and the Market: A Study in the Ideology of Legal Reform." *Harvard Law Review* 96 (1983): 1497–1578.

Olson, Mancur. *The Rise and Decline of Nations: Economic Growth, Stagflation, and Social Rigidities.* New Haven, Yale University Press, 1982.

Ossowski, Stanislaw. *Class Structure in the Social Consciousness.* Translated by Sheila Patterson. London, Routledge and Kegan Paul, 1963.

Owen, Roger, and Sutcliffe, Bob (eds). *Studies in the Theory of Imperialism.* London, Longman, 1975.

Page, Benjamin. *Who Gets What from Government.* Berkeley, University of California Press, 1983.

Paine, Thomas. *The Rights of Man.* Garden City, New York, Dolphin-Double Day, 1961.

Palmer, Robert R. *The Age of Democratic Revolution.* 2 vols. Princeton, Princeton University Press, 1959, 1964.

Panitch, Leo. "Recent Theorizations of Corporatism: Reflections on a Growth Industry." *British Journal of Sociology* 31 (1980): 159–87.

Parekh, Bhikhu. *Marx's Theory of Ideology.* London, Croom Helm, 1982.

Parkin, Frank. *Class, Inequality, and Political Order.* London, Granada (Paladin), 1981.

————— *Marxism and Class Theory: A Bourgeois Critique.* London, Tavistock, 1979.

Parkinson, G.H.R. (ed.). *Marx and Marxisms*. Cambridge [Eng.], Cambridge University Press, 1982.

Peattie, Lisa, and Rein Martin. *Women's Claims: A Study in Political Economy*. Oxford, Oxford University Press, 1983.

Pelczynski, Z.A. "The Hegelian Conception of the State." In *Hegel's Political Philosophy: Problems and Perspectives*. Edited by Z.A. Pelczynski. Cambridge [Eng.], Cambridge University Press, 1971: 1–29.

———— "Hegel's Political Philosophy: Some Thoughts on its Contemporary Relevance." In *Hegel's Political Philosophy: Problems and Perspectives*. Edited by Z.A. Pelczynski. Cambridge [Eng.], Cambridge University Press, 1971: 230–43.

———— "Introduction: The Significance of Hegel's Separation of the State and Civil Society." In *The State and Civil Society: Studies in Hegel's Political Philosophy*. Cambridge [Eng.], Edited by Z.A. Pelczynski. Cambridge University Press, 1984: 1–13.

———— "Nation, Civil Society, State: Hegelian Sources of the Marxian Nontheory of Nationality." In *The State and Civil Society: Studies in Hegel's Political Philosophy*. Edited by Z.A. Pelczynski. Cambridge [Eng.], Cambridge University Press, 1984: 262–78.

———— "Political Community and Individual Freedom in Hegel's Philosophy of the State." In *The State and Civil Society: Studies in Hegel's Political Philosophy*. Edited by Z.A. Pelczynski. Cambridge [Eng.], Cambridge University Press, 1984: 55–76.

Pelczynski, Z.A. (ed.). *Hegel's Political Philosophy: Problems and Perspectives*. Cambridge [Eng.], Cambridge University Press, 1971.

———— *The State and Civil Society: Studies in Hegel's Political Philosophy*. Cambridge [Eng.], Cambridge University Press, 1984.

Pepper, Stephen C. *World Hypotheses*. Berkeley, University of California Press, 1942.

Peterson, Paul. "Federalism, Economic Development, and Redistribution." In *Public Values and Private Powers in American Politics*. Edited by J. David Greenstone. Chicago, University of Chicago Press, 1981: 246–75.

Piercy, Marge. *Going Down Fast*. New York, Trident Press, 1969.

Piore, Michael J., and Sabel, Charles F. *The Second Industrial Divide*. Basic Books, New York, 1984.

Piven, Francis Fox, and Cloward, Richard A. "American Road to Democratic Socialism." *Democracy* 3:3 (Summer 1983): 58–69.

———— *The New Class War: Reagan's Attack on the Welfare State and Its Consequences*. New York, Pantheon Books, 1982.

———— *Poor People's Movements: Why They Succeed, How They Fail*. New York, Pantheon Books, 1977.

———— *Regulating the Poor: The Functions of Public Welfare*. New York, Pantheon Books, 1971.

Pizzorno, Allessandro. "Interests and Parties in Pluralism." In *Organizing Interests in Western Europe*. Edited by Suzanne Berger. Cambridge [Eng.], Cambridge University Press, 1981: 249–84.

———— "Politics Unbound." In *Changing Boundaries of the Political: Essays on the Evolving Balance Between State and Society, Public and Private in Europe*. Edited by Charles S. Maier. Cambridge [Eng.], Cambridge University Press, 1987: 27–62.

Plant, Raymond. "Hegel on Identity and Legitimation." In *The State and Civil Society: Studies in Hegel's Political Philosophy*. Edited by Z.A. Pelczynski. Cambridge [Eng.], Cambridge University Press, 1984: 227–43.

———— "Hegel and Political Economy." Part 1. *New Left Review* 103 (May–June 1977): 79–92. Part 2. *New Left Review* 104 (July–August 1977): 103–13.

Plato. *Gorgias*. Translated by Terence Irwin. New York, Oxford University Press, 1979.

———— *The Republic*. Translated by Francis MacDonald Cornford. New York, Oxford University Press, 1945.

Poggi, Gianfranco. *The Development of the Modern State: A Sociological Introduction*. Stanford, Stanford University Press, 1978.

Popper, Karl Raimund. *The Logic of Scientific Discovery*. New York, Harper & Row, 1968.

———— *The Open Society and Its Enemies*. 5th edn. Princeton, Princeton University Press, 1966.

Posner, Richard A. *The Economics of Justice*. Cambridge, Mass., Harvard University Press, 1981.

Poulantzas, Nicos. *Classes in Contemporary Capitalism*. London, New Left Books, 1975.

———— *Political Power and Social Classes*. London, New Left Books, 1973.

Proudhon, Pierre-Joseph. *System of Economical Contradiction; or The Philosophy of Misery*. Translated by Benjamin Tucker. [reprint edn] New York, Arno Press, 1972.

———— *What is Property? An Inquiry into the Principle of Right and Government*. Translated by Benjamin Tucker. Introduction by George Woodcock. [reprint edn] New York, Dover, 1970.

Przeworski, Adam. "Class, Production, and Politics: A Reply to Burawoy." *Socialist Review* 19:2 (April–June 1989): 87–111.

———— "Democratic Capitalism at the Crossroads." In *Capitalism and Social Democracy*. Cambridge [Eng.], Cambridge University Press, 1985: ch. 6.

———— "The Ethical Materialism of John Roemer." *Politics and Society* 11 (1982): 289–313.

———— "Exploitation, Class Conflict, and Socialism: The Ethical Materialism of John Roemer." In *Capitalism and Social Democracy*. Cambridge [Eng.], Cambridge University Press, 1985: ch. 7.

———— "Material Bases of Consent." In *Capitalism and Social Democracy*. Cambridge [Eng.], Cambridge University Press, 1985: ch. 4.

———— "Material Bases of Consent: Politics and Economics in a Hegemonic System." *Political Power and Social Theory* 1 (1980): 23–68.

———— "Material Interests, Class Compromise, and the Transition to Socialism." *Politics and Society* 10 (1980): 125–53.

———— "Party Strategy, Class Organization, and Individual Voting." In *Capitalism and Social Democracy.* Cambridge [Eng.], Cambridge University Press, 1985: ch. 3.

———— "Postscript: Social Democracy and Socialism." In *Capitalism and Social Democracy.* Cambridge [Eng.], Cambridge University Press, 1985: 239–48

———— "Proletariat Into a Class: The Process of Class Formation." In *Capitalism and Social Democracy.* Cambridge [Eng.], Cambridge University Press, 1985: ch. 2.

———— "Social Democracy as an Historical Phenomenon." *New Left Review* 122 (July–August 1980): 27–58.

———— "Social Democracy as an Historical Phenomenon." In *Capitalism and Social Democracy.* Cambridge [Eng.], Cambridge University Press, 1985: ch. 1.

———— *Capitalism and Social Democracy.* Cambridge [Eng.], Cambridge University Press, 1985.

Przeworski, Adam, and Wallerstein, Michael. "The Structure of Class Conflict in Capitalist Societies." *American Political Science Review* 76 (1982): 215–38.

Quine, Willard van Orman. *Word and Object.* Cambridge, Mass, M.I.T. Press, 1960.

Quinton, Anthony (ed.). *Political Philosophy.* Oxford, Oxford University Press, 1967.

Rae, Douglas, et al. *Equalities.* Cambridge, Mass., Harvard University Press, 1981.

Rawls, John. "Justice as Fairness: Political Not Metaphysical." *Philosophy and Public Affairs* 14:3 (Summer 1985): 223–51.

———— *A Theory of Justice.* Cambridge, Mass., Harvard University Press, 1971.

Reich, Robert. *The Next American Frontier.* New York, Times Books, 1983.

———— *Tales of a New America.* New York, Times Books, 1987.

Reichenbach, Hans. *Experience and Prediction.* Chicago, University of Chicago Press, 1938.

Revel, Jean François. *The Totalitarian Temptation.* Translated by David Hapgood. Garden City, N.Y., Doubleday, 1977.

———— *Without Marx or Jesus: The New American Revolution Has Begun.* Translated by S.F. Bernard. Afterword by Mary McCarthy. Garden City, N.Y., Doubleday, 1971.

Ricardo, David. *On the Principles of Political Economy and Taxation.* In *The Works and Correspondence of David Ricardo.* Vol. 1. Edited by Piero Sraffa with the collaboration of M.H. Dobb. Cambridge [Eng.], Cambridge University Press, 1962.

Rich, Adrienne. *Of Woman Born: Motherhood as Experience and Institution.* New York, Norton, 1976.

———— *On Lies, Secrets, and Silence.* New York, Norton, 1979.

Riedel, Manfred. "Nature and Freedom in Hegel's *Philosophy of Right.*" In *Hegel's Political Philosophy: Problems and Perspectives.* Edited by Z.A. Pelczynski. Cambridge [Eng.], Cambridge University Press, 1971: 136–50.

Roberts, Marc. "On Reforming Economic Growth." *Daedalus* 102:4 (Fall 1973): 119–138.

Robinson, Joan. *The Accumulation of Capital.* London, Macmillan, 1969.

———— *Economic Philosophy.* Harmondsworth, Pelican, 1964.

—————— *An Essay on Marxian Economics*. London, Macmillan, 1960.

Roemer, John. "The Mismarriage of Bargaining Theory and Distributive Justice." *Ethics* 97:1 (1986): 88–110.

—————— "New Directions in the Marxian Theory of Exploitation and Class." *Politics and Society* 11 (1982): 253–88.

—————— "Should Marxists Be Interested in Exploitation." *Philosophy and Public Affairs* 14 (1985): 30–65.

—————— *Analytical Foundations of Marxian Economic Theory*. Cambridge [Eng.], Cambridge University Press, 1981.

—————— *Free to Lose: An Introduction to Marxist Economic Philosophy*. Cambridge [Eng.], Cambridge University Press, 1988.

—————— *A General Theory of Exploitation and Class*. Cambridge, Mass., Harvard University Press, 1982.

Roemer, John (ed.). *Analytical Marxism*. Cambridge [Eng.], Cambridge, University Press, 1986.

Rokkan, Stein. "Dimensions of State Formation and Nation-Building: A Possible Paradigm for Research on Variations within Europe." In *The Formation of National States in Western Europe*. Edited by Charles Tilly. Princeton, Princeton University Press, 1975: 562–600.

—————— "Norway: Numerical Democracy and Corporate Pluralism." In *Political Oppositions in Western Democracies*. Edited by Robert A. Dahl. New Haven, Yale University Press, 1966: 70–115.

—————— *Citizens, Elections, Parties*. New York, McKay, 1970.

Rosdolsky, Roman. *The Making of Marx's 'Capital.'* London, The Pluto Press, 1977.

Rose, Hilary. "Women's Work, Women's Knowledge." In *What is Feminism?* Edited by Juliet Mitchell and Ann Oakley. New York, Pantheon Books, 1986: 161–83.

Rotenstreich, Nathan. "On the Ecstatic Sources of the Concept of Alienation." *The Review of Metaphysics*. 16:3 (March 1963): 550–5.

—————— *Basic Problems of Marx's Philosophy*. New York, Bobbs-Merrill, 1965.

Rousseau, Jean-Jacques. *Discourse on the Origins of Inequality*. Translated and with an introduction by G.D.H. Cole. New York, Dutton, 1950.

—————— *The Social Contract*. Translated and with an introduction by G.D.H. Cole. New York, Dutton, 1950.

Rowthorn, Bob. "Conflict, Inflation, and Money." In *Capitalism, Conflict, and Inflation*. London, Lawrence and Wishart, 1980: 148–81.

Rubin, Isaak Illich. "Marx's Labour Theory of Value." In *Essays on Marx's Theory of Value*. Montreal, Black and Red Books, 1973: 51–275.

—————— *Essays on Marx's Theory of Value*. Montreal, Red and Black Books, 1973.

Ruddick, Sara. "Maternal Thinking". *Feminist Studies* 6:2 (Summer 1980): 342–67.

Rudolph, Lloyd, and Rudolph, Suzanne Hoeber. *The Modernity of Tradition: Political Development in India*. Chicago, University of Chicago Press, 1967.

Ruge, Arnold. "Hegel's 'Philosophy of Right' and the Politics of our Times." In

The Young Hegelians: An Anthology. Edited by Lawrence S. Stepelevich. Cambridge [Eng.], Cambridge, University Press, 1983: 211–36.

———— "A Self-Critique of Liberalism." In *The Young Hegelians: An Anthology.* Edited by Lawrence S. Stepelevich. Cambridge [Eng.], Cambridge University Press, 1983: 237–59.

Sabel, Charles. "The Internal Politics of Trade Unions." In *Organizing Interests in Western Europe.* Edited by Suzanne Berger. Cambridge [Eng.], Cambridge University Press, 1981: 209–44.

———— *Work and Politics: The Division of Labor in Industry.* Cambridge [Eng.], Cambridge University Press, 1982.

Sachs, Jeffrey D. (ed.). *Developing Country Debt and the World Economy.* Chicago, University of Chicago Press, 1989.

Samuelson, Paul. "1983: Marx, Keynes and Schumpeter." In *The Collected Scientific Papers of Paul A. Samuelson.* Vol. 5. Edited by Kate Crowley. Cambridge, Mass., M.I.T. Press, 1986: 261–74.

———— "Alvin Hansen as a Creative Economic Theorist." In *The Collected Scientific Papers of Paul A. Samuelson.* Vol. 4. Edited by Hiraoki Nagatani and Kate Crowley. Cambridge, Mass., M.I.T. Press, 1977: 921–28.

———— "A Brief Survey of Post-Keynesian Developments." In *The Collected Scientific Papers of Paul A. Samuelson.* Vol. 2. Edited by Joseph E. Stiglitz. Cambridge, Mass., M.I.T. Press, 1966: 1557–87.

———— "Concerning Say's Law." In *The Collected Scientific Papers of Paul A. Samuelson.* Vol. 2. Edited by Joseph E. Stiglitz. Cambridge, Mass., M.I.T. Press, 1966: 1182.

———— "The Economics of Marx: An Ecumenical Reply." In *The Collected Scientific Papers of Paul A. Samuelson.* Vol. 4. Edited by Hiraoki Nagatani and Kate Crowley. Cambridge, Mass., M.I.T. Press, 1977: 277–83.

———— "Economic Theory and Wages." In *The Collected Scientific Papers of Paul A. Samuelson.* Vol. 2. Edited by Joseph E. Stiglitz. Cambridge, Mass., M.I.T. Press, 1966: 1557–87.

———— "Economists and the History of Ideas." In *The Collected Scientific Papers of Paul A. Samuelson.* Vol. 2. Edited by Joseph E. Stiglitz. Cambridge, Mass., M.I.T. Press, 1966: 1499–1516.

———— "The General Theory." In *The Collected Scientific Papers of Paul A. Samuelson.* Vol. 2. Edited by Joseph E. Stiglitz. Cambridge, Mass., M.I.T. Press, 1966: 1517–33.

———— "Marxian Economics as Economics." In *The Collected Scientific Papers of Paul A. Samuelson.* Vol. 3. Edited by Robert C. Merton. Cambridge, Mass., M.I.T. Press, 1972: 268–75.

———— "Marx Without Matrices: Understanding the Rate of Profit." In *The Collected Scientific Papers of Paul A. Samuelson.* Vol. 5. Edited by Kate Crowley. Cambridge, Mass., M.I.T. Press, 1986: 359–74.

———— "A Modern Theorist's Vindication of Adam Smith." In *The Collected Scientific Papers of Paul A. Samuelson.* Vol. 5. Edited by Kate Crowley. Cambridge, Mass., M.I.T. Press, 1986: 622–9.

———— "Quesnay's 'Tableau Economique' as a Theorist Would Formulate it

Today." In *The Collected Scientific Papers of Paul A. Samuelson*. Vol. 5. Edited by Kate Crowley. Cambridge, Mass., M.I.T. Press, 1986: 630–63.

————— "Rigorous Observational Positivism: Klein's Envelope Aggregation; Thermodynamics and Economic Isomorphisms." In *The Collected Scientific Papers of Paul A. Samuelson*. Vol. 5. Edited by Kate Crowley. Cambridge, Mass., M.I.T. Press, 1986: 220–57.

————— "The Theory of Pump-Priming Reexamined." In *The Collected Scientific Papers of Paul A. Samuelson*. Vol. 2. Edited by Joseph E. Stiglitz. Cambridge, Mass., M.I.T. Press, 1966: 1125–39.

————— "Understanding the Marxian Notion of Exploitation: A Summary of the So-Called Transformation Problem Between Marxian Values and Competitive Prices." In *The Collected Scientific Papers of Paul A. Samuelson*. Vol. 3. Edited by Robert C. Merton. Cambridge, Mass., M.I.T. Press, 1972: 276–308.

————— "Wages and Interest: A Modern Dissection of Marxian Economic Models." In *The Collected Scientific Papers of Paul A. Samuelson*. Vol. 1. Edited by Joseph E. Stiglitz. Cambridge, Mass., M.I.T. Press, 1965: 341–72.

————— *The Collected Scientific Papers of Paul A. Samuelson*. Vol. 3. Edited by Robert C. Merton. Cambridge, Mass., M.I.T. Press, 1972.

————— *Economics*. 10th edn. New York, McGraw-Hill, 1976.

Santomero, Anthony M., and Seater, John J. "The Inflation–Unemployment Trade-off: A Critique of the Literature." *Journal of Economic Literature* 16:2 (June 1978): 499–544.

Sartre, Jean-Paul. "Merleau Ponty." In *Situations*. Translated by Benita Eisler. Greenwich, Conn. Fawcett World Library, 1965: 156–226.

————— *Being and Nothingness: An Essay in Phenomenological Ontology*. Translated by Hazel E. Barnes. New York, Citadel Press, 1968.

Say, Jean-Baptiste. *A Treatise on Political Economy: On the Production, Distribution, and Consumption of Wealth*. [reprint edn] New York, Augustus M. Kelley, 1964.

Schama, Simon. *Citizens: A Chronicle of the French Revolution*. New York, Alfred Knopf, 1989.

Schattschneider, E.E. *Party Government*. New York, Farrar and Rinehart, 1942.

————— *The Semi-Sovereign People*. Hinsdale, Ill., The Dryden Press, 1960.

Schmidt, Alfred. *The Concept of Nature in Marx*. London, New Left Books, 1971.

Schmitter, Philippe. "Democratic Theory and Neo-Corporatist Practice." *Social Research* 50 (1983): 885–928.

————— "Interest Intermediation and Regime Governability in Contemporary Western Europe and North America." In *Organizing Interests in Western Europe*. Edited by Suzanne Berger. Cambridge [Eng.], Cambridge University Press, 1981: 287–327.

————— "Modes of Interest Intermediation and Models of Societal Change in Western Europe." *Comparative Political Studies* (April 1977): 7–38.

————— "Reflection on Where the Theory of Neo-Corporatism Has Gone and Where the Praxis of Neo-Corporatism May Be Going." In *Trends in Corporatist Intermediation*. Edited by Gerhard Lembruch and Philippe Schmitter. Beverly Hills, Sage Publications, 1979: 259–79.

———— "Still the Century of Corporatism?" *Review of Politics* 36 (1974): 85–131.

Schneidau, Herbert. *Sacred Discontent: The Bible and Western Tradition.* Berkeley, University of California Press, 1977.

Schumpeter, Joseph A. *Capitalism, Socialism, and Democracy.* London, Unwin University Books, 1970.

———— *History of Economic Analysis.* New York, Oxford University Press, 1954.

Schweitzer, Albert. *The Quest of the Historical Jesus: A Critical Study of its Progress from Reimarus to Wrede.* New York, Macmillan, 1960.

Sen, Amartya. "On Some Debates in Capital Theory." In *Resources, Values, and Development.* Cambridge, Mass., Harvard University Press, 1984.

———— "Utilitarianism and Welfarism." *Journal of Philosophy* 76 (1979): 463–89.

———— *On Economic Inequality.* Oxford, Oxford University Press, 1973.

———— *Resources, Values, and Development.* Cambridge, Mass., Harvard University Press, 1984.

Sennett, Richard. *The Uses of Disorder: Personal Identity and City Life.* New York, Knopf, 1970.

Sensat, Julius, Jr., and Constantine, George. "A Critique of the Foundations of Utility Theory." *Science and Society* 39:2 (Summer 1975): 157–79.

Shklar, Judith N. "Hegel's *Phenomenology*: An Elegy for Hellas." In *Hegel's Political Philosophy: Problems and Perspectives.* Edited by Z.A. Pelczynski. Cambridge [Eng.], Cambridge University Press, 1971: 73–89.

———— *Freedom and Independence: A Study of the Political Ideas of Hegel's 'Phenomenology of Mind.'* Cambridge [Eng.], Cambridge University Press, 1976.

Sieyes, Emmanuel Joseph. *What is the Third Estate?* Translated by M. Blondel. Edited by S.E. Finer. New York, Praeger, 1964.

Simmel, Georg. *The Philosophy of Money.* Translated by Tom Bottomore and David Frisby. Boston, Routledge and Kegan Paul, 1978.

Sismondi, Jean-Claude-Leonarde Simonde de. *Political Economy and the Philosophy of Government: Selections.* [reprint edn] New York, Augustus M. Kelley, 1966.

Sklar, Kathryn Kish. *Catherine Beecher: A Study in American Domesticity.* New Haven, Yale University Press, 1973.

Skocpol, Theda. "Wallerstein's World Capitalist System: A Theoretical and Historical Critique." *American Journal of Sociology* 82 (1977): 1075–90.

Smith, Adam. *The Wealth of Nations.* Edited by Edwin Cannan. New York, Modern Library, 1937.

Smith, Dorothy. "Women's Perspective as a Radical Critique of Sociology." *Sociological Enquiry* 44:1 (1974): 7–14.

Smith, Steven B. *Hegel's Critique of Liberalism: Rights in Context.* Chicago, University of Chicago Press, 1989.

Smith-Rosenberg, Carroll. "The Female World of Love and Ritual." In *The Signs Reader: Women, Gender, and Scholarship.* Edited by Elizabeth Abel and Emily K. Abel. Chicago, University of Chicago Press, 1983: 27–55.

Snitow, Ann. "Pages from a Gender Diary: Basic Divisions in Feminism." *Dissent*

36:2 (Spring 1989): 205—24.

Sombart, Werner. *Why Is There No Socialism in the United States?* Foreword by Michael Harrington. White Plains, N.Y., M.E. Sharpe, 1976.

Spinoza, Benedictus. *Ethics: Preceded by The Improvement of the Understanding.* Edited and with an introduction by James Gutmann. New York, Hafner Library of the Classics, 1955.

Spitz, Elaine. *Majority Rule.* Chatham, N.J., Chatham House, 1984.

Sraffa, Piero. *Production of Commodities by Means of Commodities.* Cambridge [Eng.], Cambridge University Press, 1973.

Steedman, Ian. *Marx After Sraffa.* London, New Left Books, 1973.

Steedman, Ian, et al. *The Value Controversy.* London, New Left Books, 1981.

Stepelevich, Lawrence S. (ed.). *The Young Hegelians: An Anthology.* Cambridge [Eng.], Cambridge University Press, 1983.

Stewart, Richard. "The Reformation of American Administrative Law." *Harvard Law Review* 88:8 (1975): 1667—813.

Stirner, Max. *The Ego and His Own: The Case of the Individual Against Authority.* Translated by Steven T. Byington. New York, Dover, 1973.

Stokes, Eric. *The English Utilitarians and India.* Oxford, Clarendon Press, 1959.

Strauss, Leo. *Natural Right and History.* Charles R. Walgreen Foundation Lectures. Chicago, University of Chicago Press, 1953.

Strawson, P.F. *The Bounds of Sense.* Methuen, London, 1966.

Suter, J.-F. "Burke, Hegel, and the French Revolution." In *Hegel's Political Philosophy: Problems and Perspectives.* Edited by Z.A. Pelczynski. Cambridge [Eng.], Cambridge University Press, 1971: 52—72.

Sweezy, Paul. *The Theory of Capitalist Development.* New York, Monthly Review Press, 1968.

Talmon, Jacob L. *The Myth of the Nation and the Vision of Revolution.* London, Secker and Warberg, 1981.

———— *The Origins of Totalitarian Democracy.* London, Paladin, 1970.

———— *Political Messianism: The Romantic Phase.* New York, Praeger, 1968.

Tarbuck, Kenneth. "Editor's Introduction" to Rosa Luxemburg, *The Accumulation of Capital — An Anti-Critique.* New York, Monthly Review Press, 1976.

Taylor, Arthur J. *Laissez-Faire and State Intervention in Nineteenth-Century Britain.* London, Macmillan, 1972.

Taylor, Charles. "Legitimation Crisis?" In *Philosophy and the Human Sciences: Philosophical Papers.* Vol. 2. Cambridge [Eng.], Cambridge University Press, 1982: 248—88.

———— "On the Opening Arguments of the *Phenomenology.*" In *Hegel: A Collection of Critical Essays.* Edited by Alasdair MacIntyre. Garden City, N.Y., Anchor Books, 1972: 151—87.

———— *Hegel.* Cambridge [Eng.], Cambridge University Press, 1975.

———— *Hegel and Modern Society.* Cambridge [Eng.], Cambridge University Press, 1979.

Therborn, Goran. "The Dictatorship of the Proletariat and the Class Character of the State Apparatus." In *What Does the Ruling Class Do When it Rules?* London, New Left Books, 1978: 23—125.

————— "State Power – On the Dialectics of Class Rule." In *What Does the Ruling Class Do When it Rules?* London, New Left Books, 1978: 129–244.

————— "The Theorists of Capitalism." *New Left Review* 87–88 (September–December 1974): 125–44.

————— "Why Some Classes are More Successful than Others." *New Left Review* 138 (March–April 1983): 37–55.

————— *The Ideology of Power and the Power of Ideology.* London, Verso, 1980.

————— *What Does the Ruling Class Do When it Rules?* London, New Left Books, 1978.

Thom, René. *Structural Stability and Morphogenesis: An Outline of a General Theory of Models.* Translated by D.H. Fowler. Foreword by C.H. Waddington. Reading, Mass., W.A. Benjamin, 1975.

Thompson, Edward P. "The Moral Economy of the English Crowd in the Eighteenth Century" in *Past and Present* 50 (1971): 76–113.

————— "The Peculiarities of the English." In *The Poverty of Theory and Other Essays.* New York, Monthly Review Press, 1978: 245–301.

————— *The Making of the English Working Class.* New York, Pantheon Books, 1964.

Thompson, William. *An Inquiry into the Principles of the Distribution of Wealth Most Conducive to Human Happiness; applied to the newly proposed system of voluntary equality of wealth.* [reprint edn] New York, Augustus M. Kelley, 1969.

————— *Labour Rewarded: The Claims of Labour and Capital Conciliated: Or How to Secure to Labour the Whole Product of its Exertion, by one of the idle classes.* [reprint edn] New York, Augustus M. Kelley, 1969.

Thurow, Lester. "A Surge in Inequality." *Scientific American* 256:7 (May 1987): 30–7.

————— *Generating Inequality: Mechanisms of Distribution in the U.S. Economy.* New York, Basic Books, 1975.

————— *The Zero-Sum Society.* New York, Basic Books, 1980.

Tillich, Paul. *The Protestant Era.* Translated by James Luther Adams. Chicago, University of Chicago Press, 1957.

Timpanaro, Sebastiano. "Considerations on Materialism." *New Left Reviews* 85 (May–June 1974): 3–22.

————— *On Materialism.* London, New Left Books, 1976.

Tocqueville, Alexis de. *Democracy in America.* 2 vols. Translated by Henry Reeve. Edited by Phillips Bradley. New York, Random House, 1945.

————— *The Old Regime and the French Revolution.* Translated by Stuart Gilbert. Garden City, N.Y., Doubleday, 1955.

————— *Recollections.* Translated by George Lawrence. Edited by J.P. Mayer and A.P. Kerr. Introduction by J.P. Mayer. Garden City, N.Y., Doubleday Anchor Books, 1971.

Torrance, John. *Estrangement, Alienation, and Exploitation: A Sociological Approach to Historical Materialism.* London, Macmillan, 1977.

Torrens, Robert. *An Essay on the External Corn Trade. With an Appendix on the*

Means of Improving the Conditions of the Labouring Classes. [reprint edn] Clifton, N.J., Augustus M. Kelley, 1972.

———— *On Wages and Combination.* [reprint edn] New York, Augustus M. Kelley, 1969.

Tribe, Laurence H. *American Constitutional Law.* 2nd edn. New York, The Foundation Press, 1988.

Trilling, Lionel. *Sincerity and Authenticity.* Cambridge, Mass., Harvard University Press, 1973.

Truman, David B. *The Governmental Process.* Borzoi Books in Political Science. New York, Alfred Knopf, 1951.

Tucker, Robert W. *The Inequality of Nations.* New York, Basic Books, 1977.

Tucker, Robert. *Philosophy and Myth in Karl Marx.* Cambridge [Eng.], Cambridge University Press, 1961.

Tufte, Edward. *Political Control of the Economy.* Princeton, Princeton University Press, 1978.

Unger, Roberto Mangabeira. *The Critical Legal Studies Movement.* Cambridge, Mass., Harvard University Press, 1986.

———— *Politics.* 3 vols. Cambridge [Eng.], Cambridge University Press, 1987.

Venable, Vernon. *Human Nature: The Marxian View.* Cleveland, Meridian, 1966.

Vilar, Pierre. "Marxist History, A History in the Making: Dialogue with Althusser." *New Left Review* 80 (July–August 1973): 65–106.

Vining, Joseph. *Legal Identity: The Coming of Age of Public Law.* New Haven, Yale University Press, 1978.

Walker, Pat (ed.). *Between Labor and Capital: The Professional Managerial Class.* Boston, South End Press, 1979.

Wallerstein, Immanuel. *The Capitalist World Economy.* Cambridge [Eng.], Cambridge University Press, 1979.

———— *The Modern World System.* 2 vols. New York, Academic Press, 1974, 1980.

———— *The Politics of the World Economy.* Cambridge [Eng.], Cambridge University Press, 1984.

Walton, A.S. "Economy, Utility, and Community in Hegel's Theory of Civil Society." In *The State and Civil Society: Studies in Hegel's Political Philosophy.* Edited by Z.A. Pelczynski. Cambridge [Eng.], Cambridge University Press, 1984: 244–61.

Walzer, Michael. "Dissatisfaction in the Welfare State." In *Radical Principles: Reflections of an Unreconstructed Democrat.* New York, Basic Books, 1980: 23–53.

———— "Liberalism and the Art of Separation." *Political Theory.* 12:3 (August, 1984): 315–330.

———— "Pluralism in Political Perspective." In *The Politics of Ethnicity.* Edited by M. Walzer et al. Cambridge, Mass., Harvard University Press, 1982: 18–28.

———— "Radical Politics in the Welfare State." *Dissent* (January–February 1968): 26–40.

———— "A Theory of Revolution." *Marxist Perspectives* 2 (Spring 1979): 30–45.

————— *Radical Principles: Reflections of an Unreconstructed Democrat.* New York, Basic Books, 1980.

————— *Spheres of Justice: A Defence of Pluralism and Equality.* New York, Basic Books, 1983.

Walzer, Michael, et al. *The Politics of Ethnicity.* Cambridge, Mass., Harvard University Press, 1982.

Warren, Bill. *Imperialism: Pioneer of Capitalism.* Edited by John Sender. London, New Left Books, 1980.

Weber, Max. *Economy and Society.* 2 vols. Edited by Guenther Roth and Claus Wittich. Translated by Ephraim Fischoff and others. Berkeley, University of California Press, 1968.

Weiner, Myron. *Party Building in a New Nation; The Indian National Congress.* Chicago, University of Chicago Press, 1967.

Weitzman, Lenore. *The Divorce Revolution: Unexpected Social and Economic Consequences for Women and Children in America.* New York, The Free Press, 1985.

Westphal, Merold. "Hegel's Radical Idealism: Family and State as Ethical Communities." In *The State and Civil Society: Studies in Hegel's Political Philosophy.* Edited by Z.A. Pelczynski. Cambridge [Eng.], Cambridge University Press, 1984: 77–92.

White, Hayden. *Metahistory: The Historical Imagination in Nineteenth-Century Europe.* Baltimore, The Johns Hopkins University Press, 1973.

————— *Tropics of Discourse: Essays in Cultural Criticism.* Baltimore, The Johns Hopkins University Press, 1978.

Williams, Bernard Arthur Owen. *Ethics and the Limits of Philosophy.* Cambridge, Mass., Harvard University Press, 1985.

Williams, Raymond. "Base and Superstructure in Marxist Cultural Theory." *New Left Review* 82 (November–December 1973): 3–16.

————— "Problems of the Coming Period." *New Left Review* 140 (July–August 1983): 7–18.

————— *Culture and Society: 1780–1850.* Harmondsworth, Penguin Books, 1963.

————— *The Long Revolution.* Harmondsworth, Penguin Books, 1965.

Williamson, Oliver. *Markets and Hierarchies, Analysis and Antitrust Implications (A Study in the Economics of Internal Organization).* New York, The Free Press, 1975.

Wilson, Graham K. "Why Is There No Corporatism in the United States?" In *Patterns of Corporatist Policy-Making.* Edited by Gerhard Lehmbruch and Philippe Schmitter. Beverly Hills, Sage Publications, 1982: 219–36.

Wittig, Monique. "The Category of Sex." *Feminist Issues* 2:2 (Fall 1982): 62–8.

————— "One is Not Born a Woman." *Feminist Issues* 1:2 (Winter 1981): 47–54.

————— "The Straight Mind." *Feminist Issues* 1:1 (Fall 80): 103–12.

Wolf, Eric. *Europe and the People Without History.* Berkeley, University of California Press, 1982.

Wolff, Robert Paul. *Understanding Marx: A Reconstruction and Critique of*

Capital. Princeton, Princeton University Press, 1984.

Wolin, Sheldon. "Democracy and the Welfare State: The Political and Theoretical Connections Between Staatsräson and Wolfahrtsstaatsräson." *Political Theory* 15:4 (November 1987): 467–500.

———— *The Presence of the Past: Essays on the State and the Constitution.* Baltimore, Johns Hopkins University Press, 1989.

Woloch, Isser. *The Jacobin Legacy*. Princeton, Princeton University Press, 1970.

Wood, Ellen Meiksins. "Rational Choice Marxism: Is the Game Worth the Candle?" *New Left Review* 177 (September–October 1989): 41–88.

Wright, Erik Olin. "Bureaucracy and the State." In *Class, Crisis and the State.* London, New Left Books, 1978: ch. 4.

———— "The Class Structure of Advanced Capitalist Societies." In *Class, Crisis and the State.* London, New Left Books, 1978: ch. 2.

———— "Historical Transformation of Capitalist Crisis Tendencies." In *Class, Crisis and the State.* London, New Left Books, 1978: ch. 3.

———— "The Status of the Political in the Concept of Class Struggle." *Politics and Society* 2:3 (1982): 321–42.

———— *Class, Crisis and the State.* London, New Left Books, 1978.

———— *Classes*. London, Verso, 1985.

Yack, Bernard. *The Longing for Total Revolution: Philosophic Sources of Social Discontent.* Princeton, Princeton University Press, 1986.

Zeckhauser, Richard. "The Risks of Growth." *Daedalus* 102:4 (Fall 1973): 103–18.

Index

56/. 38

on the differentiation of society, 166, 174
on liberalism, 148n
on pluralism, 166, 174
on welfare state, 200n
war, 109, 202n
War on Poverty, 141
Warren, Bill, 339n
Weber, Max, 151n, 155n, 190n, 247n
Weiner, Myron, 182n
Weitzman, Lenore, 272n
welfare, 26n
and groups, 213
in Hegelian state, 116–19, 184n
and reform, 189, 229
and utility, 117–19
welfare state, 71n, 142–3, 213
and Hegel, 144
and Keynes, 322
and planning, 197m
and rights, 175n
see also social democracy
Western Marxism, 15–22
Westphal, Merold, 64n, 164n
White, Hayden, 342n
Wiesenthal, Helmut, 198n
Williams, Bernard, 91n, 92
Williams, Raymond, 262n, 324n
Williamson, Oliver, 263n, 268n
Wilson, Graham, 199n
Witting, Monique, 65n, 68n

Wolf, Eric, 155n
Wolff, Robert Paul, 5n, 283n, 295n, 297n, 305n, 313n
Wolin, Sheldon, 143n, 189n, 344n
Woloch, Isser, 113n
women, see feminism
Wood, Ellen, 251n
working class, 2, 24, 27, 130–2, 153
and class analysis, 107–8, 127–8, 203–5
and labor unions, 204
and Marxist intellectuals, 15–19
and pensions, 320n
and savings, 320–1
and social democracy, 106, 130–5
world markets, 8, 11, 291n, 308, 311–12, 332n
and commodity prices, 334–40
and division of labor, 8, 304n
and economic rents, 261
and flow of capital, 315n, 334–40
and immigration, 321n, 338
and mode of production, 8, 336–8
and Smith and Ricardo, 8, 260–1, 334–5
Wright, Erik O., 5n, 247n, 253n, 280n

Yack, Bernard, 110n, 120n

Zeckhauser, Richard, 262n